# Fine
# WoodWorking
# TECHNIQUES 9

# Fine WoodWorking
# TECHNIQUES 9

The Taunton Press

Cover photo by Alex Thigpen

Photo, p. 1, by Erik Borg

Photo, p. 39, by Bill Stankus

Photo, p. 73, by John Barkin

Photo, p. 119, by Elizabeth Jean Shaw

Photo, p. 151, by Fritz Haddick

Drawing, p. 163, by Lee Hov

Typeface: Garamond and Univers
Paper: Warrenflo, 70 lb., neutral pH

The Taunton Press, Inc.
63 South Main Street
Box 355
Newtown, Connecticut 06470

A FINE WOODWORKING Book

FINE WOODWORKING® is a trademark of
The Taunton Press, Inc., registered in the
U.S. Patent and Trademark Office.

International Standard Book Number 0-918804-84-1
Library of Congress Catalog Card Number 78-58221
Printed in the United States of America

# CONTENTS

# INTRODUCTION

When we began publishing *Fine Woodworking* magazine in 1975, part of our editorial charter was to record the resurgent interest in woodworking techniques then underway. We were surprised and pleased to find that contemporary craftsmen had rediscovered many traditional techniques, even as they invented new ones to solve the peculiar problems of building artisan furniture in the 1970s and 1980s.

This book, the ninth in our series of *Fine Woodworking Techniques* books, continues and extends this documentation. It is based upon articles first published in *Fine Woodworking* during 1985, issues #50 through #55. Where necessary, the original text has been corrected, but sources of supply and prices are current as of 1985.

# JOINERY

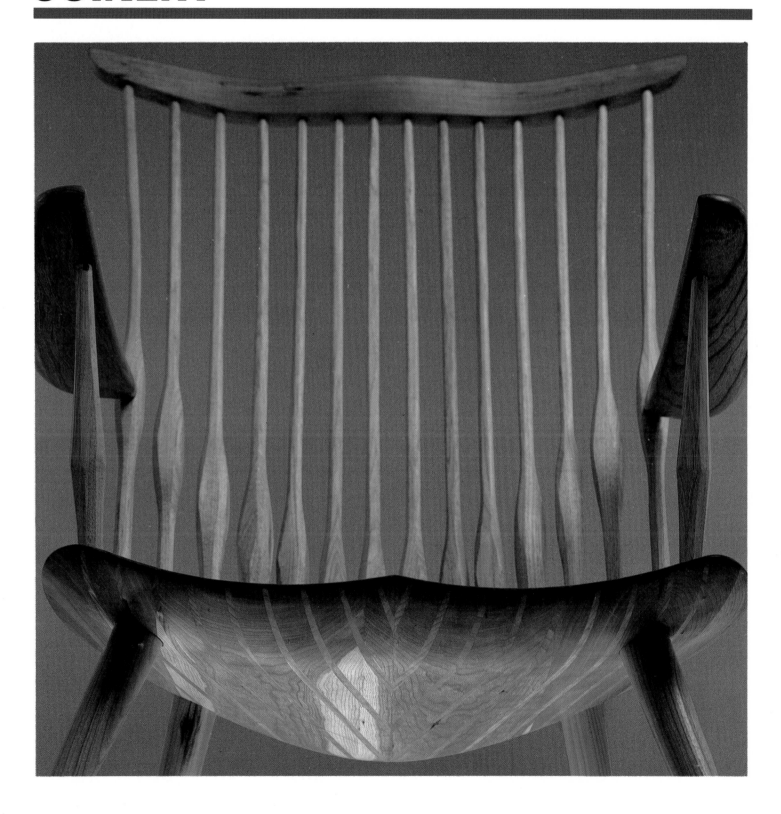

# Form Laminating Curved Carcases

*Glued-up layers look like solid wood*

by Anthony Giachetti

*Each curved side of Giachetti's French walnut butterfly cabinet was made by gluing up resawn plies in a curved, two-part form then edge-gluing four 5-in.-wide curved sections into a panel. Lamello plates join the carcase components.*

I started making curvilinear furniture because I was no longer excited with my straight-line casework. Curved elements now form the basis for almost all of my furniture designs. I like the dynamic springlike energy that curved sides impart to my sideboards, desks and blanket chests. The sides appear to be bent from single, wide pieces of solid wood, but they're actually made up of several narrow sections, each form-laminated to the desired curve, then edge-glued to form a panel. Form laminating is a process of gluing up thin strips of wood by clamping them into or around a curved form. When the laminates are resawn from one board and reassembled in the same order, glue lines are barely visible.

Form laminating may not be for everybody. Resawing and surfacing the laminates is time consuming and wastes a lot of wood. Working up curved side panels can take the better part of a week. But it has its advantages, as I discovered the hard way. For my first attempt at curved sides—a jewelry case—I simply bandsawed the curve from thick rosewood, planning to edge-glue two 6-in.-wide pieces to make a 12-in.-wide panel. It wasn't long after sawing that the pieces began to cup badly, the result of a rapid change in moisture content in the now exposed interior of each board. Weak short grain, another problem with bandsawn curves, is also solved by form laminating because the grain follows the curve.

Form laminating also has several advantages over steam bending. Species that are almost impossible to steam bend, such as teak, rosewood and mahogany, can be bent by laminating. Even a fairly small radius can be achieved by using thin laminates. Springback, the tendency of bent wood to return to its original shape when removed from the mold, is both less severe and more predictable with form laminating than it is with steam-bent solid wood.

**My designs often start as a sketch** scribbled on the back of an envelope or a scrap of wood. Once the idea is firmly established, I make scale drawings and finally, full-size drawings on heavy tracing paper, working out all the joinery details and the relationships between curved and straight parts (see box, p. 6). Full-size drawings force the designer to confront aesthetic and technical problems that may not be apparent in a sketch. Is the curve graceful or comical? Are good joints possible at the angles that the curved members join the other wood elements? Such problems should be solved on paper.

I start the full-scale drawing with the curved side. I draw uniform-radius curves with trammel points mounted on a long stick, adding the thickness of the lamination to the radius to draw the outside line of the curve. For more complex curves, I draw one line by bending a length of thin, straight-grained wood or a flexible plastic spline. Next, I mark off the parallel line with a compass and the arc method shown in figure 1.

Once the curvature of the cabinet side and its position in a vertical plane have been established, I add the remaining structural elements. If the cabinet is symmetrical I draw only to the center line. Approximate dimensions for the top, side and bottom panels can be taken from this drawing but, because the actual curve of the panel may differ, you'll need to trace the panel on the drawing then redraw the angles and joints based on the new shape.

Almost any wood can be form bent if the laminations are thin enough. I design curves and select wood for the best appearance, then worry about the bending afterward, although the gluing ability of the wood is an important consideration. A beginner

*Curved door slats (top and facing page) are tongue-and-grooved without glue and pinned through sliding-dovetail battens. Blanket chest (above) has form-bent sides, veneered-plywood front and back. Carcase details are shown on pp. 6-7.*

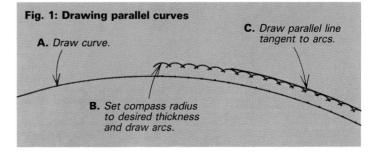

**Fig. 1: Drawing parallel curves**

A. Draw curve.

C. Draw parallel line tangent to arcs.

B. Set compass radius to desired thickness and draw arcs.

would do well to start with straight-grained walnut rather than oily woods, like teak or rosewood, that are often difficult to glue. (Thickness planing or sanding oily wood immediately before gluing helps overcome these problems.)

In general, light-colored woods more readily show glue lines; highly-figured woods are difficult to resaw accurately and impossible to thickness without an abrasive surfacer. I prefer to reserve showy figure for the tops of my furniture.

To determine the number of laminates you'll need you must consider wood species, the degree of curvature and the amount of springback deemed acceptable. To minimize springback, I don't recommend using fewer than four plies. For a 30-in.-long, ¾-in.-thick panel that deflects 2 in. or 3 in., I'll typically use five plies. Tight curves and hard-to-bend woods require thinner laminates, but overestimating the number of laminates is costly in both wood and time. Test-bending a few assemblies will save time in the long run.

Springback is a direct function of the number of laminates. With two plies, springback will be approximately 33% of the initial radius of the form. With five plies, springback drops to

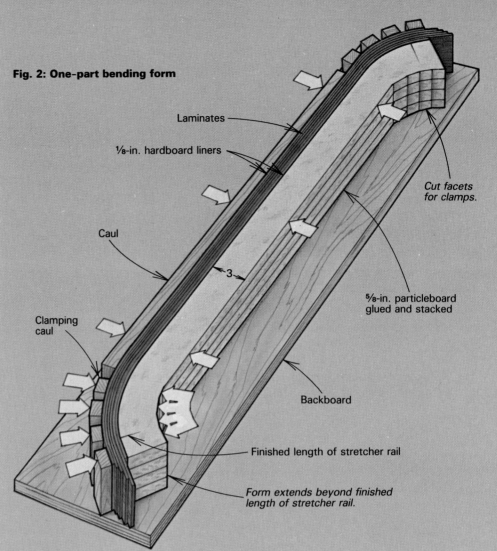

**Fig. 2: One-part bending form**

Laminates

1/8-in. hardboard liners

Cut facets for clamps.

Caul

3

5/8-in. particleboard glued and stacked

Clamping caul

Backboard

Finished length of stretcher rail

Form extends beyond finished length of stretcher rail.

*A pivot-block fence (top) permits feed-angle changes to correct bandsaw-blade drift. A face vise is convenient for initial clamping of two-part forms (center). Pipe clamps are applied once the vise is closed and the clamped form is removed from the vise to dry. The edges are squared up on the tablesaw (bottom).*

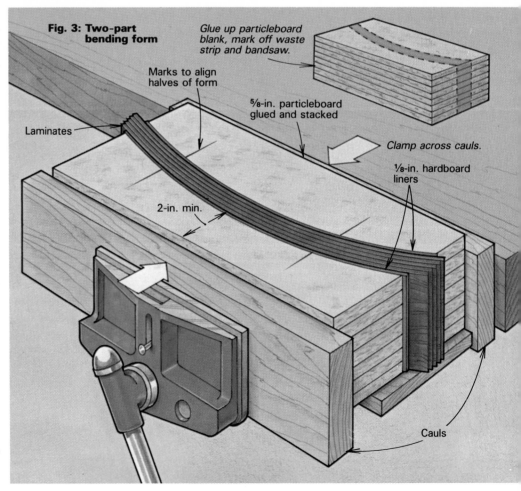

**Fig. 3: Two-part bending form**

Glue up particleboard blank, mark off waste strip and bandsaw.

Marks to align halves of form

5/8-in. particleboard glued and stacked

Laminates

Clamp across cauls.

1/8-in. hardboard liners

2-in. min.

Cauls

4

4%. The formula for determining springback is $100(1/n^2-1)$, where n equals the number of laminates.

I resaw all the laminates in each assembly from one board then reassemble the plies in the same order. This looks good and minimizes cupping and twisting in the glued-up piece. The only exception is when I bookmatch adjacent sections in the glued-up panel, and even then I keep most of the plies in the same sequence.

For a five-ply, ¾-in.-thick assembly, I start with a dressed board at least 1½ in. thick to allow for saw kerfs, thicknessing the laminates, and an extra ply or two as insurance against mistakes. The board should be 3 in. longer than the finished length, measured along the curve, to allow for the planer sniping the ends of the laminates and to ensure a smooth curve through the ends of the piece. To avoid problems with warping, I rarely resaw boards wider than 7 in.

Resawing can be done on any properly tuned bandsaw as long as the blade is sharp and the guides set to close tolerances (see pp. 81-83). I use a ½-in., 4 tooth-per-inch skip-tooth blade and a pivot block fence which allows any drift in the blade to be quickly corrected by adjusting the angle of the feed (top photo, facing page). Joint the board before each cut and scribe a guideline along the entire length of the top edge, ⅟₁₆ in. over the finished laminate thickness.

When thickness planing pieces ¼ in. or thinner, run the stock through on a piece of ¾-in. hardwood plywood, a little longer and wider than the stock to be planed. To minimize tearout, reduce the planer feed rate, if possible, or angle the workpiece into the cutterhead to obtain a skew cut. Even a superbly tuned planer may completely destroy thin pieces of wavy-grained wood, so you may want to surface them on an abrasive surfacer. Many millwork shops rent time on their abrasive surfacers at reasonable rates. A finished grit of 60 or 80 will be fine for gluing.

**When designing a bending form,** the most important consideration is even distribution of clamping pressure. Pressure should be as nearly perpendicular to the curves as possible. I make both one-part and two-part forms, and each type has certain advantages.

For curved cabinet sides I usually make a two-part form as shown in figure 2, facing page. This type of form distributes pressure evenly across wide laminates, 4 in. or more, that are bent into relatively shallow curves. For narrow laminations or complex bends, I make a simple one-part form, also shown in figure 2, that allows me to get clamps all around a complex curve while maintaining clamping pressure at right angles to the curve. On the other hand, clamping pressure isn't as evenly distributed and it's possible to end up with dents in the finished lamination.

I make my forms of ⅝-in. particleboard and yellow glue. These solid forms work well for laminations up to 7 in. wide. Wider laminations usually require ribbed forms (see pp. 8-10).

For a two-part form, I glue up a particleboard blank then bandsaw it into two pieces. While gluing the blank, keep the layers in line with cauls, then trim the two long clamping edges parallel and square to the faces using either the bandsaw or the tablesaw. Transfer the curve from the full-scale drawing to tracing paper, allowing for the ⅛-in.-thick hardboard liners that flank the laminates. To compensate for springback, modify the curve on the tracing paper by flexing a plastic spline into a tighter curve and tracing around it. Transfer the modified curve directly onto the form blank. Position the curve so that the clamping pressure will be as nearly perpendicular to as much of the curve as possible. To make two or more identical forms, I make a thin, flexible template from ⅛-in. hardboard. By pulling the template into a tighter curve before tracing onto the form, I can compensate for springback.

Before cutting out the waste strip, where the laminations will go, I mark the form so that the two sections can be lined up accurately during glue-up. I bandsaw the waste with a sharp blade, just enough to negotiate the curve. This ensures the straightest possible tracking through the thickness of the form. I cut to the waste side of the line, leaving no margin for cleanup— the hardboard liners will even out minor irregularities.

One-part forms are much simpler to make. I just bandsaw the male curve from a particleboard blank, relieve the back side for the clamps, then screw the form to a backboard for support. Faceting the back side of a curve prevents the clamps from sliding around.

Before gluing-up, I lay out all the laminate bundles and arrange them to get the best possible grain match in the finished panel. I mark the outside laminates in each section with "out" and "up" to ensure that the bundle goes into the form in the correct way.

Glue for laminating must be strong enough to withstand the tendency of each lamination to return to it's original shape. White glues (polyvinyl acetate) are flexible when dry and particularly susceptible to cold creep. Yellow glues (aliphatic resin) are somewhat more resistant, but resorcinol and urea formaldehyde (plastic resin) glues are most resistant to creep. These types also set slowly enough to allow time for glue application and clamping. Urac 185, a modified urea formaldehyde (available from Nelson Paints, P.O. Box 907, Iron Mountain, Mich. 49801) has given me good results and has the added advantage of having medium-brown color. Resorcinol's dark color makes it unsuitable for light-colored woods. With either of these adhesives, a shop temperature of 65°F must be maintained during the entire eight- to ten-hour curing period.

During glue-up, it's important to work quickly, but in an orderly way. Clamps and forms should be ready for use. To make glue cleanup easier, wax the forms and the hardboard liners with paste wax. I find it convenient to use my face vise, as shown in the center photo on the facing page, to hold the two-part forms while putting on the clamps.

I apply the glue to all surfaces with a 3-in.-wide hard rubber roller, available from photographic supply houses. Small drops of squeeze-out should be expected. Large rivers of squeeze-out indicate too much glue and result in a nightmarish cleanup job.

Once the glue is applied, I slip the assembled laminates into the form, align them, close the vise, then apply one or two bar clamps to each side of the form near the center point. When applying clamps, always start at the center and work toward the ends. Once the clamps are on I remove the form from the vise and let the glue cure overnight.

After removing the assembly from the form I clean up one edge with a scraper then joint it with the convex curve against the jointer fence. I'm after a straight edge, not necessarily a square edge—I rely on the tablesaw to produce square edges for gluing. I use a 60-tooth carbide rip blade with collars on either side to reduce blade wobble. With the convex side down and the jointed edge against the fence, I trim the glue off the other edge. Then I trim the jointed edge to achieve squareness. The stock must contact the table right next to the saw blade. A slow but constant rate of feed yields best results.

With only one form, it takes four days to glue up four sections

# Joinery on a curve

Making curved panels takes a long time, so to keep the project economically viable I need an efficient way to join the carcase. Plate joinery is fast, strong and well suited for curved casework. Plate joinery requires a hand-held plunge-cutting machine that cuts a slot in each of the pieces to be joined. An eye-shaped, compressed-beech plate slips into the slots, expands when glue is applied, and locks tight in about 15 minutes. During this time, the joints can be adjusted about ⅛ in. for proper fit (see *FWW #34*, pp. 95-97).

As an alternative, I'd suggest a loose spline joint, but I don't recommend dowels for attaching curved sides. Dowel holes must match up exactly and this kind of accuracy isn't feasible when working with curves. The spline would allow some leeway to adjust parts during assembly.

My Lamello machine has an adjustable fence that makes slotting the angled ends of the top and bottom panels easy. To cut the corresponding slots in the case sides, all I need to guide the Lamello is a straightedge clamped against the inside face of the panel. Both sets of slots are cut perpendicular to the line of the joint, not parallel to the top of the case.

I build two basic types of carcases. The first type has structural top and bottom panels joined to the curved sides. The ½-in. to ⅝-in.-thick vertical interior panels are plate jointed to the top and bottom panels. On these verticals, I hang drawers, shelves or whatever the design calls for.

To assemble the case, first I glue the verticals to the bottom panel, with the top panel dry-clamped to the verticals, to ensure squareness. When these joints have dried, I glue the top to the verticals at the same time that I attach the curved sides. Because of the angles involved, the joints between the top, bottom and curved sides won't slip together unless the top can be lifted up slightly.

Attaching the curved sides is a hectic

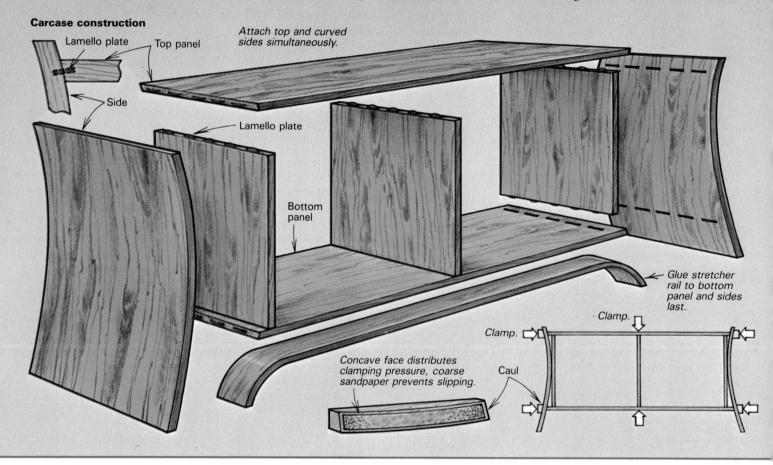

**Carcase construction**

Lamello plate — Top panel

Attach top and curved sides simultaneously.

Side

Lamello plate

Bottom panel

Glue stretcher rail to bottom panel and sides last.

Clamp.

Clamp.

Concave face distributes clamping pressure, coarse sandpaper prevents slipping.

Caul

*Edge gluing curved sections into a panel is best done on two sawhorses. Waxed cauls clamped across the panel ensure proper section alignment and keep the panel from bowing.*

for one curved panel: I make four forms, reducing laminating time to two days. If I use the forms a second or third time, the investment in form-making is well worth it. An expensive alternative is to use a radio-frequency or dielectric gluing machine (see *FWW #38*, p. 26). This electronic machine cures water-based glues in a few seconds.

The bent sections are now ready to be glued into panels. I set them in order on two sawhorses, convex side down. This arrangement provides room for clamping cauls, critical for proper joint alignment—it's too easy to sand through a laminate trying to correct misaligned surfaces. These waxed cauls run across the width of the panel and help keep the panel from bowing under the pressure of the bar clamps.

I make a dry trial-assembly to check the joints and wax the surfaces adjacent to them. Waxing eliminates the possibility of part of the assembly process that requires planning and an extra pair of hands. I use four cauls to distribute clamping pressure across the width of the side panels. One face of each caul is ripped at an angle and planed slightly convex from end to end so that pressure will be distributed from the center of the panel to the edges. Coarse sandpaper glued to the cauls keeps them from slipping.

Once the cabinet has been assembled, I glue the stretcher rail to the underside of the bottom.

I use a different construction for my blanket chests. The front and back panels are ½-in. Baltic birch plywood veneered on both sides. I bandsaw the panels about ½ in. oversize in length and width, and

trim them to final shape with a straight bit in my pin router. A portable router with a straight bit and rub collar would do as well. Guide it against a ¼-in. hardboard template made by tracing the curved sides and stretcher profile on the hardboard then bandsawing to shape. I set the router bit to cut about ⅓ of the panel thickness from each side, which leaves a tongue in the middle. The tongue fits in grooves in the curved sides and stretcher rails.

To assemble, glue the stretcher rails to the front and back panels. Plate join the bottom panel to the front and back and glue the bottom panel to the stretcher rails. Plate join the bottom to the curved sides and glue the front and back panels to the sides. —A.G.

*Blanket-chest bottom panel and stretcher rail detail shows Lamello plate slots.*

**Blanket-chest construction**

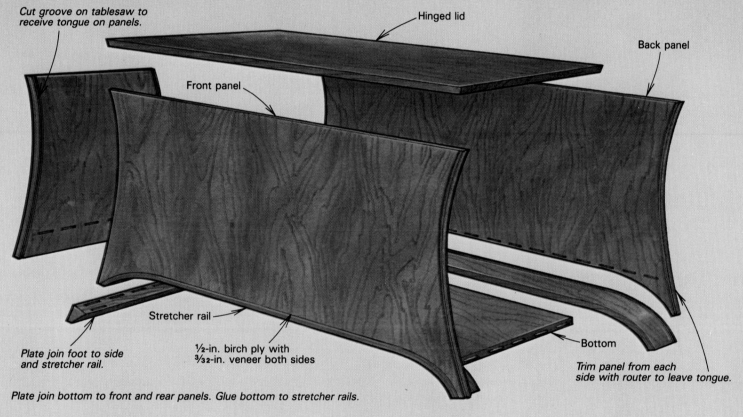

Cut groove on tablesaw to receive tongue on panels.

Hinged lid

Back panel

Front panel

Plate join foot to side and stretcher rail.

Stretcher rail

½-in. birch ply with ³⁄₃₂-in. veneer both sides

Bottom

Trim panel from each side with router to leave tongue.

Plate join bottom to front and rear panels. Glue bottom to stretcher rails.

tearing out wood while scraping off glue. Yellow glue would work fine for edge gluing, but I use urea formaldehyde glue here as well, for no better reason than consistency.

When the glue is dry, I trim the joints flush with a compass plane or a scraper. The convex surface must be perfectly straight where the horizontal members join it—I lay a straightedge across the width of the panel to check. Make any corrections with a low-angle block plane by planing across the grain.

I rip the panel to just over finished dimension then compare it to the curve on the full-scale drawing. If, as is often the case, the panel curve differs from the drawing, I redraw the curve to match the panel before going any further.

I've made a sliding cutoff jig for crosscutting curved panels on the tablesaw. It is simply a large piece of veneer-core plywood with two hardwood strips on the bottom that ride in the

sawtable's miter-gauge grooves. A wooden fence across the front edge of the plywood keeps the stock square to the blade. I place the panel convex side down on the jig, with one end blocked up so that the end I'm going to crosscut rests on the jig next to the line of cut. To determine the blade angle, I represent the saw table on the full-scale drawing by drawing a tangent line at the cut-off point, another line to represent the cut, then measure the angle between the lines with a protractor. For a smooth cut, a panel hold-down helps. For panels that are wider than the 26-in. capacity of my sliding table, I resort to cross cutting with a Skilsaw guided along a fence clamped to the work. □

*Anthony Giachetti is a furniture designer/maker in East Boothbay, Maine.*

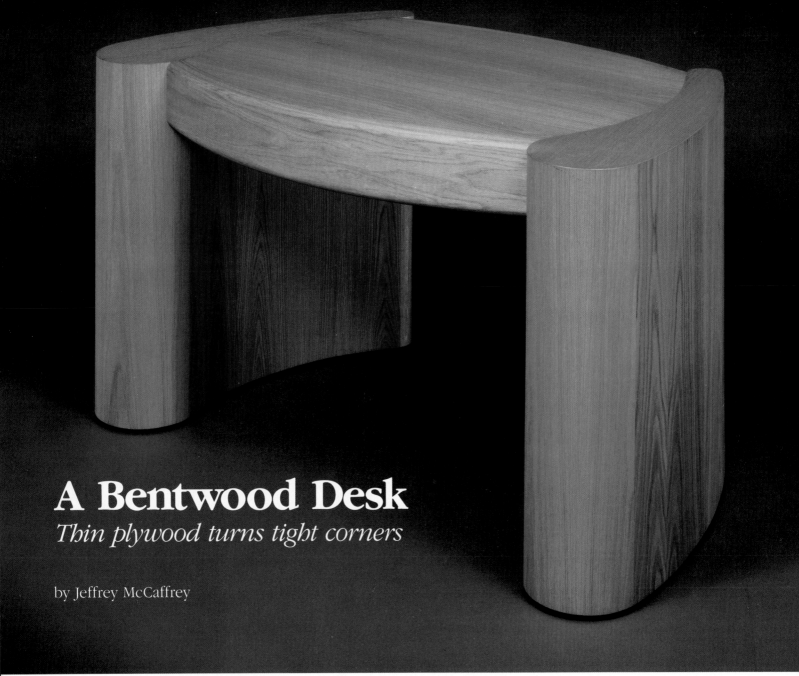

# A Bentwood Desk
## Thin plywood turns tight corners

by Jeffrey McCaffrey

*Author's writing desk suggests solid wood, but it's actually constructed of lightweight, bentwood panels joined by a framework. Each of the desk's two columns consists of three separately bent panels.*

I've been working with bentwood since I was a student. For me, it presents an opportunity to create unusual furniture while tackling processes not yet learned—a combination of careful planning and blind ignorance that I find both stimulating and humorous. Like most woodworkers, I learned to bend wood by gluing up thin strips of it around a form. Shaped and joined, these glued-up curves became components of larger structures, perhaps a chair or a curvilinear casepiece.

It was a natural progression for me to widen the strips until it was no longer practical to use solid wood. At this point, I began using ⅛-in.-thick plywoods and my bends became curved planes instead of curved lines. This expanded my design vocabulary to include furniture like the desk shown above. It consists of hollow, monolithic volumes joined together to make a form impossible or impractical to achieve in solid wood. The desk's upright columns are hollow volumes, each made up of several, separately bent panels. They are extraordinarily rigid yet light enough to be easily moved.

In principle, bending plywood panels is a lot like bending solid strips using conventional form lamination. Plywood has some

important advantages over solid wood laminae, however. First of all, it's available in sheets at thicknesses suitable for bending so you can skip the tedious, dusty job of resawing thick boards into thin ones. For most applications, plywood will bend to a tighter curve than will an equivalent thickness of solid wood. The columns of my desk, for example, are bent to a radius as small as 4-in. To get away with that in solid wood, the strips would need to be ¹⁄₁₆ in. thick, which is asking a lot of your resawing technique, not to mention requiring twice as many laminae.

Though they aren't sold in a wide variety of species, ⅛-in.-thick plywoods are usually available from local lumberyards or plywood suppliers in oak, ash, walnut and cherry. One supplier here in Portland sells a two-ply ³⁄₁₆-in.-thick lauan plywood capable of bending around a 3-in. radius. Some suppliers sell three-ply bending plywood which consists of a core of soft, bendable basswood faced with another species. Probably the best bargain in bending plywood is the ⅛-in. lauan plywood sold by lumberyards as doorskins for hollow-core doors. If you need a thick bent panel, lay up a core of cheap lauan faced with an outer veneer of nicer wood.

So plywood sheets won't warp, manufacturers generally lay up

Photo: Jim Piper

odd numbers of plies. It's probably good practice to follow this rule where possible, but sometimes an odd number of plywood sheets won't add up to the final panel thickness desired, while an even number will. In this case, I go ahead and use an even number. In laminating multiple sheets, two face plies glued to each other with the grain running in the same direction become, in effect, one ply. Thus, for purposes of stability, two three-ply sheets behave as one five-ply.

Forms for bending panels are more demanding to build than those for bending solid strips. Because they are larger, there's more chance of introducing errors that could produce a twisted panel, so it's important to draw and measure carefully. Your project may require more than one simple curve, in which case you'll have to make a series of bends and then join the parts. Segment the curves wherever it seems logical to do so. I try to divide the curves so the forms and panels will be of manageable size, and so I can clamp with downward pressure only. Lateral clamping makes things too complicated. However divided, you will need a form for each separate curve.

As the photo at right shows, my two-part forms consist of a series of particleboard ribs sawn to the desired curve then mounted on a backing board which keeps them in correct alignment. For accuracy, I make up two templates for each series of ribs—one for one half of the form and the other for the nesting or mating half. I begin with a full-scale drawing of my piece on paper or poster board. I transfer the curves to ¼-in. hardboard, from which I bandsaw out the first template, smoothing lumps or quick turns with a file.

To generate the mating template, set a compass to the desired panel thickness, allowing room for a liner between the form and each side of the bundle of plies. I use a piece of ⅛-in. lauan for a liner. Place the first template on a fresh piece of hardboard and trace the outline for your second template with the compass. Bandsaw, then file the profile fair. For form ribs, I use 1-in. particleboard. It's harder to find than ¾ in., but the extra thickness reduces the number of ribs needed and distributes pressure more evenly. Use the templates to mark out the ribs, then bandsaw close to the line. To finish, screw or tack the template to the rib blank and trim to the line with a flush-trimmer bit in your router or router table.

To assemble the form, place the ribs on a flat surface, curved-side up. Slip a ¾-in. scrapwood spacer between each rib, align the ribs and clamp-up the assembly. Flip the whole thing over and screw a squared piece of particleboard or plywood to the rib backs. This will keep the form from shifting into a parallelogram under clamping pressure.

Now comes the fun part: gluing and clamping. After spending several days planning and building forms, it's thrilling to see if it all works. A dry clamp-up is advisable. This will turn up any problems and you'll find out if you have enough clamps and cauls. For a typical 24-in.-wide panel, you'll need six 4x6 battens the length of the form, three on top and three on the bottom.

If everything checks out, spread glue on the plies (I use plastic resin glue) with a small paint roller. Before laying up the bundle, put a piece of paper between the liners and the bundle so there's no chance of smeared glue sticking them together. As you build the stack, align the long edge of each ply with the edge of the form. This will give you a straight reference edge for ripping the panel to width later. Also, make sure to put the good ply or veneer on the correct side of the bundle. I have an extra panel in my shop because I glued the good face to the wrong side of the bend. Apply clamping pressure first to the center of

*Each bent panel requires its own form constructed of 1-in. particleboard ribs spaced ¾ in. apart and fastened together with battens and/or backing boards to keep them aligned. Stout cauls and heavy bar clamps distribute pressure evenly at glue up.*

*For fair, twist-free panels, ribs must be of consistent size and shape. McCaffrey marks out a template for the mating half of a form (above middle). Tacked to a particleboard blank, the template guides on the pilot bearing of a flush trimming bit, cutting the blank to final size (bottom).*

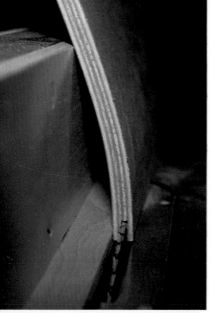

*Plywood splines in tablesawn or routed grooves join bent panels together. Blocks temporarily tacked to the panel near the joint with hot-melt glue provide bite for handscrews. Scrap ⅛-in. plywood makes good spline stock. A framework of solid oak joins the desk's two columns, providing support for the top and a hanging surface for a drawer. Bent panels proved too thin for conventional joinery so McCaffrey fitted glue blocks around each frame member—in effect building a mortise around a tenon.*

the form, then work outward. Check for inconsistent glue squeeze out, a tell-tale of uneven pressure.

After the glue has cured for 24 hours, I remove and clean up the panels. If one panel edge was held flush to the form, it should be no problem to scrape the glue and hand plane or joint the edge true. With that done, the opposite edge can be tablesawn parallel. Squaring the other edges is trickier. With a T-square, I mark a line along the rough edge then bandsaw to it, supporting the panel so the edge is as square to the table as I can get it. Hand planing checked with a square finishes the job. Actually, it's not as important that these edges be perfectly square as that they be true enough to join cleanly with another panel.

For joining bent panels together, splines seem to work best. If done carefully, a spline accurately aligns the surfaces of two adjacent panels, and it is more than strong enough for most applications. I have three methods to cut grooves for splines. The simplest is to pass the panel edge over the tablesaw, guided freehand against the fence. This is only practical for shallow bends and/or small panels, however. For larger panels, I clamp scraps to both sides of the edge being grooved. This provides a flat surface wide enough for a router and a fence to run against. If the panel is flat enough near the joint, run the router right on it, using a slotting cutter with a pilot bearing. Whichever method you choose to use, make sure that the groove is perpendicular to the edge being joined. Scrap ⅛-in. plywood makes excellent spline stock.

Clamping curved panels is always a challenge and some improvising will be necessary. If the panel assembly is a closed volume, such as the columns of my desk, band clamps might work perfectly. However, clamping blocks temporarily glued to the panels where the joints come together give more control. Cut scrapwood blocks about 1 in. square and 3 in. long. Attach them to both sides of the panels on either side of the joint with hot-melt glue, as shown in the photo above. Insert the glue-coated spline, then draw the joint together with wooden handscrews, which can pinch close to the surface without the handles getting in the way. Inspect the joint carefully. If you find any gaps, reposition the clamps to close them up.

Be careful when you remove the clamping blocks once the glue has cured. Hot-melt glue is stubborn stuff—if you try to knock off the blocks with a sharp hammer blow, chunks of the panel may come with them. A safer way is to split the block close to the surface with a chisel, then clean up the remainder with a plane and scraper, being careful not to plane through the show veneer, however.

Assembling bent assemblies into finished furniture calls for unorthodox joinery. The columns of my desk, for instance, are joined by a framework that supports the top and provides a place to hang a drawer. The columns are structurally strong but their walls aren't thick enough for proper mortise and tenons. One solution is to build up the wall thickness in the area of the joint, but I found it more practical (and fun) to mortise through one wall and extend the framework to butt against the opposite wall. It was then a simple matter to glue blocks around the framework, in effect building the mortise around the tenon.

Finishing the desk required some adroit router work. I capped the columns with Baltic birch plywood panels, cut with the aid of a template similar to that used for the form ribs. These caps were then veneered with white oak and another piece of oak-veneered birch plywood was fit between them to serve as the desk top. A shallow pencil drawer fitted beneath the top finished the project. ◻

*Jeffery McCaffrey is head of the wood department at the Oregon School of Arts and Crafts in Portland. Photos, except where noted, by the author.*

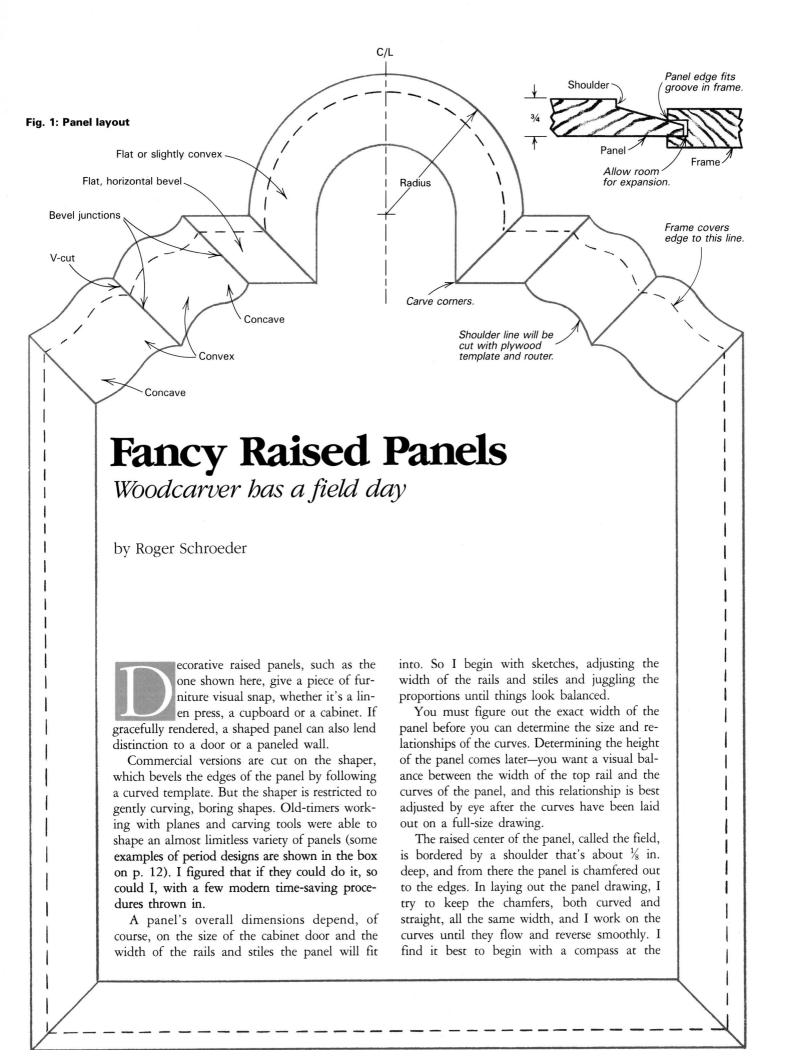

**Fig. 1: Panel layout**

Flat or slightly convex

Flat, horizontal bevel

Bevel junctions

V-cut

Concave

Convex

Concave

C/L

Radius

Shoulder

Panel edge fits groove in frame.

¾

Panel

Frame

Allow room for expansion.

Frame covers edge to this line.

Carve corners.

Shoulder line will be cut with plywood template and router.

# Fancy Raised Panels
## *Woodcarver has a field day*

by Roger Schroeder

Decorative raised panels, such as the one shown here, give a piece of furniture visual snap, whether it's a linen press, a cupboard or a cabinet. If gracefully rendered, a shaped panel can also lend distinction to a door or a paneled wall.

Commercial versions are cut on the shaper, which bevels the edges of the panel by following a curved template. But the shaper is restricted to gently curving, boring shapes. Old-timers working with planes and carving tools were able to shape an almost limitless variety of panels (some examples of period designs are shown in the box on p. 12). I figured that if they could do it, so could I, with a few modern time-saving procedures thrown in.

A panel's overall dimensions depend, of course, on the size of the cabinet door and the width of the rails and stiles the panel will fit into. So I begin with sketches, adjusting the width of the rails and stiles and juggling the proportions until things look balanced.

You must figure out the exact width of the panel before you can determine the size and relationships of the curves. Determining the height of the panel comes later—you want a visual balance between the width of the top rail and the curves of the panel, and this relationship is best adjusted by eye after the curves have been laid out on a full-size drawing.

The raised center of the panel, called the field, is bordered by a shoulder that's about ⅛ in. deep, and from there the panel is chamfered out to the edges. In laying out the panel drawing, I try to keep the chamfers, both curved and straight, all the same width, and I work on the curves until they flow and reverse smoothly. I find it best to begin with a compass at the

11

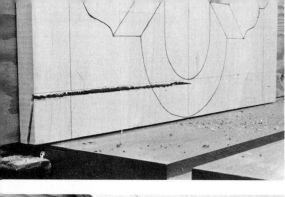

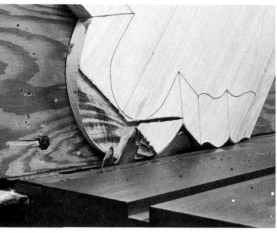

*First saw away the waste at the very top of the panel (top left), then chamfer the straight sides and bottom edge. Next bandsaw the top profile, and tablesaw some additional waste (left). A piece of Formica, slid under the rip fence, keeps the panel from slipping down between the fence and the blade. A router (above) with straight bit and pilot bushing cuts the top shoulder by guiding against a template derived from the layout drawing on p. 11. Square up the straight shoulders by routing along a straight fence.*

centerline, to determine the central arch, then work out from there to the sides.

The frame will cover about ⅜ in. of the panel when it's in the door, so I plot the rail line on the panel drawing at this stage—this lets me visualize what the panel will actually look like in place.

When the drawing looks right, I use machines to remove as much waste as I can, as shown in the photos above, and then rely on basic carving tools to shape the hollows and rounds. When I'm carving, I clamp the panel over a piece of plywood on my benchtop, with the plywood projecting beyond the edge of the panel to protect the bench from errant chisels. I like to keep the clamps well out of the way, which is easy on a long panel. I usually hot-glue smaller panels to a larger backing piece and then clamp the backing to the bench.

The rails and stiles of the frame are mortised and tenoned as usual, and a router—with a horizontal slotting cutter and a pilot bearing—makes the grooves for the panel. The router can cut most of the groove in the bandsawn top rail; there's just a little cleanup with a chisel necessary at the sharp inner corners.

The panel shown in this article, incidentally, wasn't just an idle exercise—by the time you read this, it will be a door to a corner cabinet in my kitchen. □

*Roger Schroeder, of Amityville, N.Y., is a woodworker and author of* How to Carve Wildfowl *(Stackpole Books, 1984). He wrote about wooden locks in* FWW #42. *Black-and-white photos by the author.*

## Variations on a panel

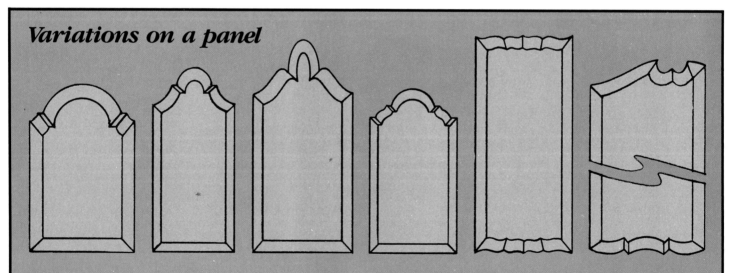

Panel types are named after things they resemble. There's the basic "tombstone" shape, such as the one on Carlyle Lynch's corner cabinet on p. 182. Variations are called ogee, arched, half-moon, quarter-moon, serpentine, cyma, linenfold-fan or whatever. Curiously, there doesn't seem to be a name for the entire class of raised panels with shaped edges.

The first four panels shown here are from various period pieces, most of them from Connecticut, where shaped-edge panels were particularly popular. The last two designs are my own, one for a curly-maple sideboard, the other for a pair of doors on a tall mahogany cabinet. There's virtually no limit to the ways a cabinetmaker can change the proportions of the curves and chamfers in a panel design to suit the mood and flavor of a project.
—R.S.

Drawings: Cynthia Lee Nyitray

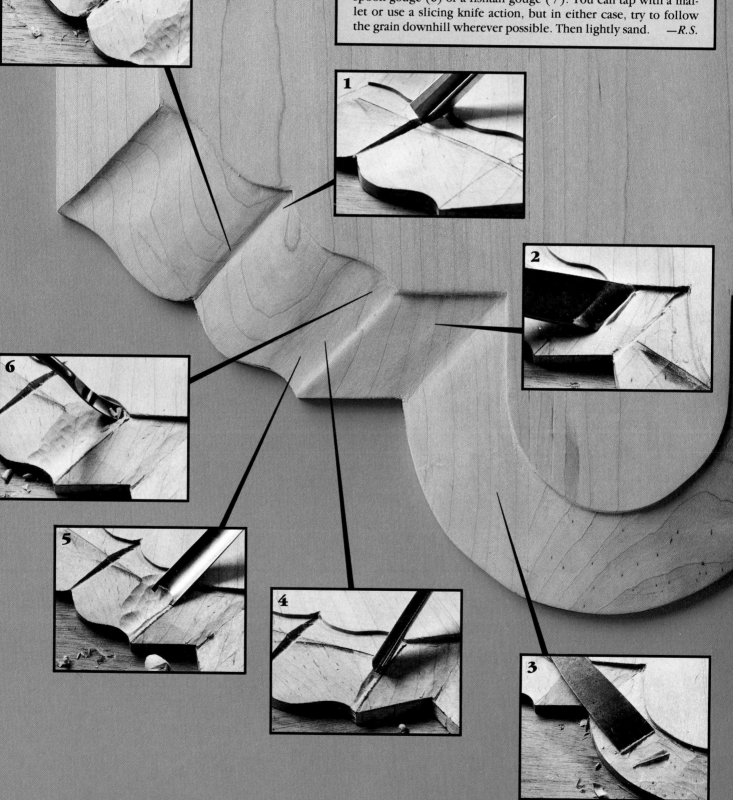

# *Carving the curves*

This basic set of carving tools defines the shapes. First draw a gauge line on the edge of the panel to show the thickness where it will fit into the frame, then carve down to it smoothly from the shoulder line. Step **1** shows a V-parting tool, which cuts a sharp-bottomed groove that allows the other tools room to work. Broad, relatively flat or convex areas are shaped with a skew chisel (**2**) or a square-nose chisel (**3**). A narrow, deep gouge (**4**) scoops away wood next to high profile lines, while a broad gouge (**5**) makes the more gentle hollows. Cleanup cuts are made with a small spoon gouge (**6**) or a fishtail gouge (**7**). You can tap with a mallet or use a slicing knife action, but in either case, try to follow the grain downhill wherever possible. Then lightly sand.  —*R.S.*

*Wedges forced into kerfs bend a flat blank into a seat that is pleasing in both comfort and looks. This Windbow rocking-chair seat was formed by bending the seat halves individually, then joining the shaped pieces.*

# Kerf-Bent Seats

*A tablesawn alternative to scooping*

by Jeremy Singley

Progress is often a matter of new inventions finding uses. When some unknown genius (from Windsor?) started building chairs with that new-fangled machine—the first practical lathe—the result was a happy event for every generation since. Though his fellow craftsmen may have branded him a heretic, it's certain he wasn't a purist. That's comforting, because it leads me to believe that he wouldn't mind me using even newer inventions to improve his designs. In fact, if he'd had a tablesaw and modern glues, I suspect he would have come up with innovations as interesting as my method for shaping hardwood seats.

I stumbled on the idea of bending seats by driving wedges into sawkerfs about six years ago when I found that a conventionally scooped seat felt better if its rear ridge was eliminated, so that the seat curved east to west but not north to south. This reduced the curve to two series of straight, parallel lines, and kerfing seemed an obvious possibility.

Obvious, but not easy. In the weeks of experimenting that followed, I grew wiser about wood, the laws of nature, and man's ability to endure disappointment. The first thing I learned was why woodworkers avoid wedge-bending. When you kerf wood across its grain, you cut away its strength, and it usually breaks. When you kerf wood along its grain, you exacerbate its weakness, and it usually splits. I finally resolved the dilemma when I found that wedges glued into kerfs cut at a slight bias to the grain strengthen the wood, not weaken it. The resulting bend, wider at the seat's front than at its back, turned out to be perfect for comfort.

After a lot of fooling around, I settled on a kerf angle of 77°, with the cuts spaced on 1-in. centers as shown in figure 1A. I found that eight kerfs, four in each direction, create a scoop deep enough to please both the bottom and the eye. I also discovered that I could make a center ridge by kerfing two half-blanks (figure 1B) and then joining the halves together.

Eventually these revelations evolved into a production system that's well suited to the small shop. The required jigs and fixtures can be made in a day or two, and no exotic tools or machines are needed. The single-blank method, because it is simple and cheap, became my preference for dining chairs. The double-blank method, whose effect is sinfully elegant, though costly, found its way into my top-of-the-line Windbow rocker, shown on the facing page. This rocker style, which sells for about $2,000, uses 18 wedges. If you use more than 12 on a single-bent seat, though, the scoop will be too deep to be comfortable.

I begin with the same edge-glued seat blank you'd normally hack at to carve out a conventional Windsor seat. I use 1⅜-in. stock for most of my single-bent dining chairs and 1½-in. for my double-bent Windbow rocker. All woods seem to wedge-bend equally well. Uniformly dense woods like maple and rosewood, which are too hard to be compressed slightly, don't make good wedges, however. I usually make the seat and the wedges from the same wood, but for maple seats I use oak or ash wedges.

When I'm making seats, I edge-glue two sets of blanks and have them surfaced to the same thickness at a local mill shop. One set is for the seats; the second, glued up from the wood with the straightest grain, is for wedge stock. I glue the wedge stock into blanks about 21 in. long and at least 14 in. wide to minimize waste—it's risky to run narrow wedge stock through the tablesaw, so the outside inch or so of every board gets thrown away. I make the seat blanks wide enough to fit the pattern for the particular chair I intend to build.

I work on the seat blanks as soon as I get them back from the

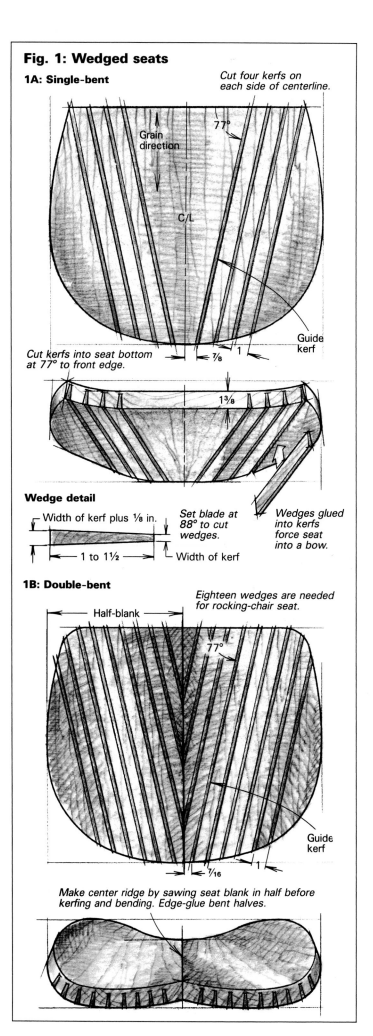

**Fig. 1: Wedged seats**

**1A: Single-bent**

Cut four kerfs on each side of centerline.

Grain direction

77°

C/L

Cut kerfs into seat bottom at 77° to front edge.

⅞

1

Guide kerf

1⅜

**Wedge detail**

Width of kerf plus ⅛ in.

1 to 1½

Width of kerf

Set blade at 88° to cut wedges.

Wedges glued into kerfs force seat into a bow.

**1B: Double-bent**

Eighteen wedges are needed for rocking-chair seat.

Half-blank

77°

Guide kerf

7/16

1

Make center ridge by sawing seat blank in half before kerfing and bending. Edge-glue bent halves.

Photos, except where noted: Erik Borg; drawings: David Dann

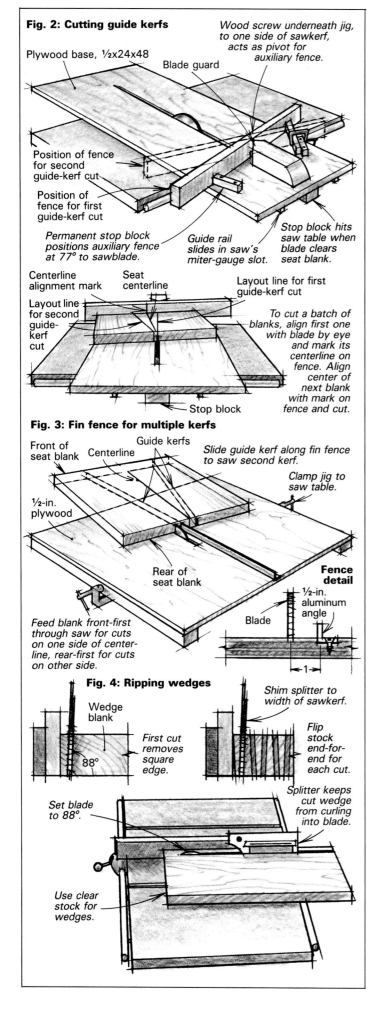

**Fig. 2: Cutting guide kerfs**

**Fig. 3: Fin fence for multiple kerfs**

**Fig. 4: Ripping wedges**

mill shop, before they can warp. The edges of these glued-up blanks are usually rough and irregular, so I first cut their fronts square and straight: I place my paper pattern on each seat blank, mark the center of the front edge, and use the front of the pattern as a straightedge to draw a line on the blank. I extend this line across the full width of the blank, bandsaw just shy of the line freehand, then nibble to it with a jointer. To prevent the jointer from sniping off the trailing end of the blank, I chamfer that corner slightly before running the blank over the jointer.

For a single-bent seat, I place a framing square perpendicular to the front of the blank and draw a line down the blank from the center point I previously marked. Then I align the centerline of the seat pattern and the blank's centerline, and transfer the position marks for the guide kerfs. I don't worry about the seat outline just yet—it will be traced onto the blank after bending. For most designs, the position marks should be $7/8$ in. on either side of the centerline at the back of the seat. Using a homemade bevel gauge set at 77°, I lay out the two guide kerfs (figure 1), and to make it easier to see the lines when setting up the saw, I extend these lines down the back edge of the blank. I mount the blank on the carriage shown in figure 2 and rotate the blank until the sawblade is centered on the guide-kerf line. Then I push the carriage and blank through the saw, which I set to cut to within $5/32$ in. of the blank's top surface. To obtain a good gluing surface, I use a sharp carbide blade with at least 40 teeth for cutting both the kerfs and the wedges.

After I've cut the first guide kerf on one side, left or right, of all the blanks, I switch the carriage fence over to the opposite angle and repeat the procedure. Then I change to the fin fence shown in figure 3. The guide kerf drops over the fin fence—a piece of aluminum angle stock let into a plywood saw base—and guides the blank while the next kerf is cut an inch from the previous one, then that kerf lines up the next, and so on. The trick is to always bear to the left side of the fence, keep the blank firmly aligned, and push it through at a slow, even rate. The blank is fed tail-first into the blade to cut the kerfs on one side of the centerline, and front-first to cut those on the other side. This step usually isn't any trouble, but I have been known to lose count and cut one too many kerfs. It's also important to handle the blanks carefully—they're stiff enough to require gentle persuasion when the wedges are inserted, but if you snap them, they may break. Once all the blanks are kerfed, I usually cut the bottom front chamfers on a tablesaw or a bandsaw, using a fine-cut blade to keep from tearing out the walls of the kerfs. I don't cut the back seat chamfers until later.

Because setting up to cut wedges is so tedious, I always cut plenty of extras once I have the saw adjusted. The wedges won't be accurate unless the blanks are dead flat, so I hand-plane off any irregularities left by the surfacer. Before trying to cut the wedges, I shim the tablesaw's splitter, which on my Rockwell is part of the blade guard, with veneer and paper until it is exactly the width of a sawkerf (figure 4). I also replace the saw's metal throatplate with a plywood one that fits tightly against the blade, to eliminate the danger of the wedge hanging up on the throatplate slot. For ease of adjustment, I then crank the blade to maximum height and set the splitter behind and parallel to it.

I tilt the blade to 88°, lower it so it just protrudes from the wedge stock, and adjust the fence by trial and error. I initially set the fence so that the wedge point will equal the width of the sawkerf in the seat. I joint one edge of the blank and saw the first wedge, which, being tapered on only one side, is dis-

*When inserting wedges, it helps to have an assistant (above). One person holds the blank with the glued kerf over the edge of the bench and pushes down on the overhanging section to fold the kerf open. The helper inserts the glue-covered wedge and forces its ends down while the first person forces the middle section down. The blank is then upended in a vise (right) and C-clamped just enough to squeeze out excess glue and to seat the wedges. When all the wedges are secure, the blank is placed on the floor and bar-clamped across its width (see next page).*

carded. Then I flip the stock end-for-end and feed it far enough to cut a trial kerf about ⅛ in. long. I measure the width of this wedge tip with calipers and fine-tune the fence accordingly.

The setup tolerance for cutting workable wedges is a hundredth of an inch, more or less. Back in the old days, when I owned a used Sears saw that in a former life must have been a corn chopper, I achieved this accuracy by attrition: every third wedge or so went into the recycling box. My Rockwell does much better, but even so I'm never short of paint-stirring sticks.

Feeding the wedge stock past the blade is, unfortunately, not a science or even an art—the subtleties that can't be taught come with practice, however. So with a level head and a winning outlook, ease the stock forward at a steady rate, applying firm pressure downward and light pressure into the saw's fence. About halfway through I transfer to very light but steady pressure toward the splitter, which acts as a fence as the end of the blank approaches the sawteeth. As the blade completes the cut, I finish up with a clean follow-through to prevent the back sawteeth from scarring the blank, and lift the wedge clear of the blade with a push stick in the same motion. Do it right, and the wedge will be as smooth as a seamless stocking. Do it wrong, and you've won another paint stirrer for your collection.

Before going any further, I make sure that the wedge fits the kerfed seat blank. Gently folding the blank open over the edge of the workbench with the fingertips of one hand, I ease the wedge into the open kerf with my other hand. Once I'm assured that everything fits, I continue cutting wedges, flipping the stock end-for-end between each pass. After about ten passes, sometimes the sawn edge of the stock no longer rests against the fence without rocking, so I joint it again. I also discard any wedges that end up with glue joints down their spines.

The actual bending operation is the fun part—unless something goes wrong. Then it's a nightmare, but if you have your clamps and materials ready before you begin, your bending par-

ties should be pleasant. The wedging process is the same for both single- and double-bent seats, but the methods of clamping—as I'll explain—differ slightly. I begin by laying the blank kerf-side-up on the bench, then inserting glue-covered wedges. Yellow glue is best for wedging, and to get it on the kerf walls, I squeeze it in the kerf from the glue bottle and spread it with a flat stick, getting both sides good and gushy.

While I'm painting up the first kerf, my assistant, Jane Miller, spreads glue down both sides of a wedge with a 3-in. paint roller. Then I position the blank so that the glued kerf is directly over the edge of the workbench. Holding the center of the blank down against the bench with the fingertips of my right hand, I grasp the overhanging portion with my left hand and gently fold the blank open. Jane then inserts the wedge and pushes the ends of the piece home with her thumbs, grasping the underside of the blank with her fingertips for leverage. At the same moment, I force down the middle part of the wedge with my thumbs. As the wedge settles in, the seat makes a quiet cracking sound to tell us everything is all right. If everything isn't right (sometimes an improperly cut wedge turns up in the pile), we throw the wedge away and try another. Don't risk disaster by hammering the wedge in.

When all the wedges are in, I upend the blank in a vise and clamp the wedges home at one end of the seat while Jane does the same at the other end, using 4-in. C-clamps set in as far as their throats will allow. We snug up the clamps just enough to squeeze out the excess glue and to seat the wedges. Excess pressure may crack the seat. (If it does, a little back-and-forth action on the clamp screw will work glue into the crack, so it will be glued shut when the clamp is backed off and the pressure released slightly.)

With the C-clamps in place, I lay the single-bent blank bottom-up on the floor and apply the clamp dogs that I developed to counter the bar clamps' tendency to open rather than close the kerfs (figure 5). The dogs put the clamping pressure high enough over the seat bend to close the kerfs. In areas where the bend will be great, I sometimes have to notch the waste slightly so the dogs will fit. Once the bar clamps are tight, I remove the C-clamps.

When the glue is dry and the bar clamps are removed, I mount the blank bottom-up between the dogs on my bench. I hog off the projecting wedges with a large fishtail gouge, followed by a short plane with its iron ground slightly convex. The last $\frac{1}{32}$ in. or so of wedges, along with the glue beads, is removed with a smooth plane. I also plane any flat areas on the seat bottom, then belt-sand with 120-grit. After sanding the bottom, I flip the seat over and spokeshave away the flats that appear between the bends on the blank's top surface. To smooth contours, I tape a foam-rubber cushion, covered with a paper pad, on the platen of a belt sander and "bag sand" the surfaces to a sweet curve with 120-grit.

Once the top and bottom of the bent blank are cleaned up, I trace the seat-pattern outline onto the blank and cut it out on a bandsaw fitted with a plywood table extension. The curved blank is unstable on the bandsaw table, so to steady it I usually wedge my fist between the edge of the seat bottom and the table, in front of or behind (and well away from) the blade. Otherwise the drag of the blade would slam the seat down onto

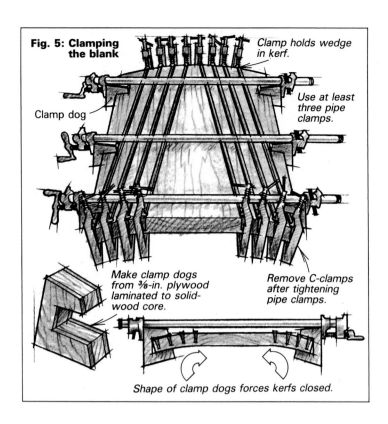

Fig. 5: Clamping the blank

Clamp holds wedge in kerf.

Clamp dog

Use at least three pipe clamps.

Make clamp dogs from ⅜-in. plywood laminated to solid-wood core.

Remove C-clamps after tightening pipe clamps.

Shape of clamp dogs forces kerfs closed.

*With a large gouge, Singley chops off projecting wedges (left) before hand-planing the seat bottom. Steadying it with his fist, he then bandsaws the seat to shape (above). Steel-strap clamping fixtures (below) and tabs along the back edge allow a double-bent blank's unwieldy shapes to be glued with pipe and C-clamps.*

the table, with unfortunate consequences for saw, seat and self-composure. Sometimes, if things aren't going well, I clamp a wooden block between the seat bottom and the saw table, stopping to move the block from in front of to behind the blade at about the midpoint of the cut.

If you want to try making double-bent seats, you begin with the same-size seat blanks as for single-bent ones, but this time saw each blank up the middle. Mark each set, so you can match up the pairs later. Next joint the sawn edge on each half and cut the front edges square on the tablesaw. Here the centerline will be the jointed edge. The guide kerf is the first full-length kerf nearest the centerline (figure 1B), and should be 7/16 in. from it at the back. Use the carriage to cut a guide kerf in each half-blank. Then with the fin fence, add three or more kerfs to *both* sides of each guide kerf. Run the blank front-first over the blade for the kerfs on one side of the guide kerf, tail-first for the opposite side. Regardless of the blank's orientation, however, always run the wall of the guide kerf against the left side of the fence.

Bend each seat half individually, using the method described for single-bent seats—you won't need clamping dogs for these small halves, though. After bending, clean off the wedge splines, then belt-sand each half's bottom to a smooth, continuous curve before gluing the two parts together. The jointed edges twist when the blank is bent, so they must be trued up again. Set the blank on an extended bandsaw table and use a try square to position the rear of the twisted edge so it's vertical to the table. Clamp a steady block under the blank to hold it in position, resaw the edge square, then run the edge freehand over the jointer (do this back-edge-first, or the wedges will tear out).

The seat halves must make an airtight fit, so you may have to touch up the edge with a hand plane. When I'm satisfied with the joint, I stand one half-seat, joint up, in the vise and hold the mating half against it. The two chamfers never match exactly, so I use a knife to trace the outline of the shallower one onto the edge of the overlapping fatter one, then I spokeshave the fat chamfer to the traced line. When both halves are matched, I use the homemade clamping brackets shown in the bottom photo on the facing page to glue up.

After the seat has been cut out and edge-sanded, all that remains is to make it into a chair. I explained how I do this in *FWW* #46, pp. 72-77. How you do it is up to your creativity, but be forewarned: whether double- or single-bent, the seat can be hard to handle, because it doesn't have any flat surfaces.

The biggest problem is that the underside of a bent seat curves upward and shows its underbelly for all the world to see. Instead of trying to hide my seat bottoms as traditional chairmakers do, I make them part of the design. Sometimes I round the bottom edges into an upward sweep, giving the seat a bowl-like effect. Other times I try for an undulating clamshell edge, with both the bottom and top saddled up to a thin line. I rough out much of this shaping work for the front edge on a tablesaw or a bandsaw before bending the seat, then finish with plane, spokeshave or sander shortly before assembling the chair. I also shape the back chamfers at this stage.

Designing chairs with bent seats is a challenge. Even though I've been doing it for years, the technique still excites me—there are so many things yet to try. In my wildest dreams I see chairs that wrap clear around the sitter, chairs that reach for the sky, chairs that ebb and flow, chairs tied in a bow. There are more possibilities than one person can explore in a lifetime.   □

*Jeremy Singley is a full-time woodworker in E. Middlebury, Vt.*

# A simply elegant chair

After I had developed a machine method to produce shaped hardwood chair seats, a customer asked me if I could design a chair that could be built in a day. Coincidentally, I had already been asking myself the same question, and decided to try to come up with a simple yet comfortably elegant chair.

I eventually settled on the flowing A-shaped form shown in the photo below. It's strong yet light, and with only six parts to keep clean, it's easy to care for. It's also the simplest chair I can think of—there are no turned or bent parts, no complex joints.

Begin by making full-size patterns for the seat and other shaped parts shown in the drawing on the next page. Edge-glue 1½-in. thick clear cherry to make a seat blank and kerf-bend it as already described.

Bandsaw the legs from 1¼-in. thick boards and taper their ends. I do this freehand on my jointer, but a taper jig on the tablesaw would also work. To cut the top leg notches, use the pattern to set up a tablesaw jig to hold each pair of legs while you cut a ⅛-in. wide, 2⁵⁄₁₆-in. deep notch in each one. I find it easiest to cut all the left-side pieces first, then all the right-side pieces.

The back rail is a three-step operation. First bandsaw the rail's front profile from 1⅞-in. thick stock, then cut the tenons. Screw a board as long as the rail to your miter gauge to steady the concave top edge of the face-down blank while you cut the tenon shoulders. Make another pass with the rail upright against a high fence to cut each cheek.

After cutting the tenons, trace the elevation-view curve on the top edge of the back, and bandsaw the contour. To hold the back vertical, make a cradle, or tape on the scrap that was sawn from the blank's bottom. Set the blade at 90° for the front curve and at 82° for the back curve. This produces a slight belly for shaping the bottom edge, as shown in the cross section on p. 20. Don't worry that the sawblade runs off the stock at the bottom

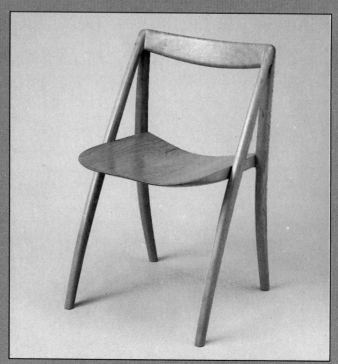

*Screws and glue replace complex joinery in simple chair.*

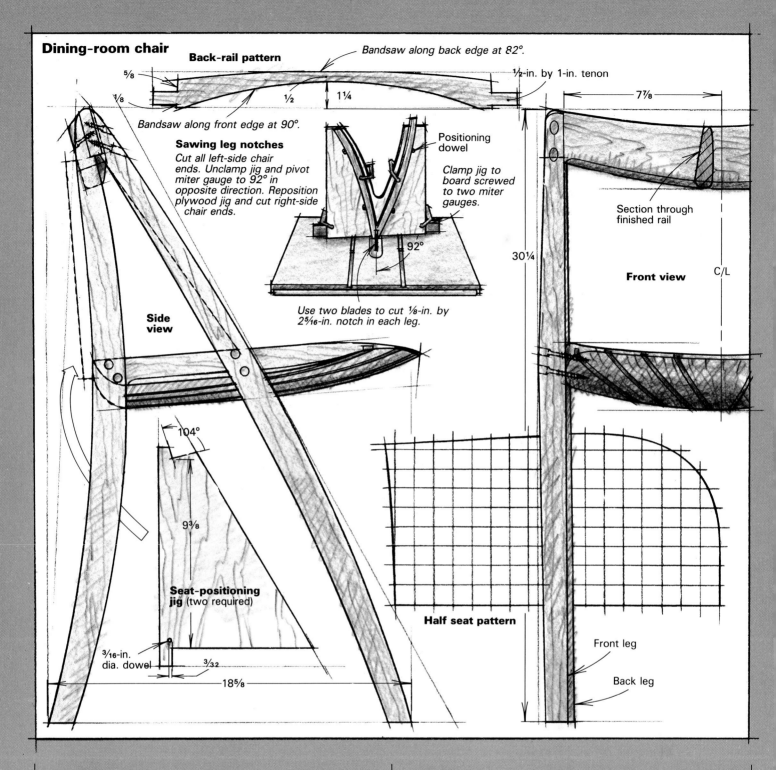

**Dining-room chair**

Back-rail pattern

Bandsaw along back edge at 82°.

⅝

⅛

Bandsaw along front edge at 90°.

½

1¼

½-in. by 1-in. tenon

7⅞

**Sawing leg notches**
Cut all left-side chair ends. Unclamp jig and pivot miter gauge to 92° in opposite direction. Reposition plywood jig and cut right-side chair ends.

Positioning dowel

Clamp jig to board screwed to two miter gauges.

92°

30¼

Section through finished rail

Front view

C/L

**Side view**

Use two blades to cut ⅛-in. by 2⁵⁄₁₆-in. notch in each leg.

104°

9⅜

**Seat-positioning jig** (two required)

Half seat pattern

³⁄₁₆-in. dia. dowel

³⁄₃₂

18⅝

Front leg

Back leg

edge—you can blend the curve when you sand the pieces.

Next rout the legs and back with a ½-in. piloted quarter-round bit, and finish-sand the flat surfaces of the legs. Shaping is matter of personal preference—I shape all the edges of the front legs, but stop the quarter-rounds on the back legs about 4 in. from the bottom of the seat. Centerbore the legs ⅜ in. deep with a ½-in. Forstner bit.

To assemble the frames, glue and screw the front leg to the back's tenon with a countersunk #8x1-in. wood screw in the top hole, and a #8x1¼-in. screw in the bottom hole. Angle the screws up and toward the center of the back to pull the shoulders tight. Then glue and screw on the back legs in the same way with #8x1½-in. screws.

Once the two frames are joined to the back, spoke-shave and sand the back to match the contour of the leg tops, blend in all quarter-rounds, and finish-sand the back. Clamp the two spacers to the legs to align the seat. If

necessary, rejoint the seat edges for a good fit, realign the seat in the frame and drill the legs for the bottom screws. I use shanked #10x2-in. screws here to pull the joint tight, then add #8x1¾-in. shankless drywall screws (which are threaded along their entire length) on the top to hold the joint tight against shrinkage. Drill for the top screws with a ⅛-in. twist bit (no shank hole). When you're satisfied with the way the seat fits, remove it from the frame, glue the joints and reassemble. If you prefinish the chair parts, except in areas where the legs meet the seat, excess glue will be easier to remove. Although I've found that this glue-and-screw joint is very strong, you might prefer to notch the legs to fit over the seat for additional strength.

Finally, plug the screw holes with wooden plugs or dowels, then sand. I apply two coats of gel polyurethane for protection, then a coat of polymerized tung oil to give the cherry a richer tone. —*J.S.*

# Tapered Legs on a Jointer

by Eric Schramm

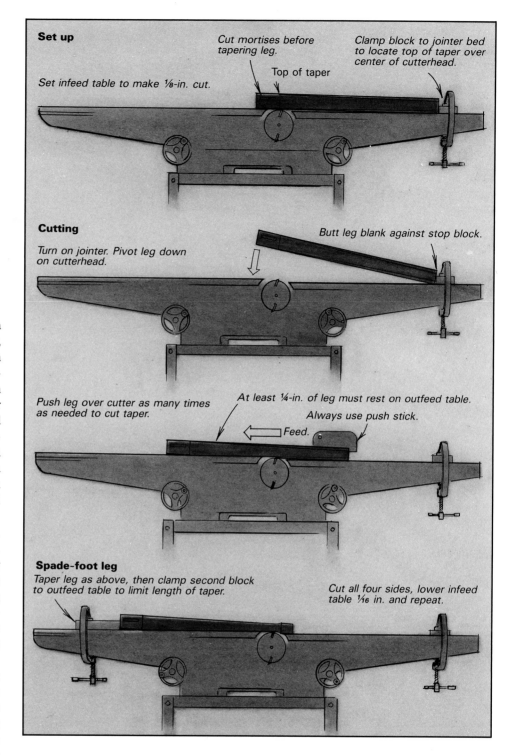

**Set up**

Cut mortises before tapering leg.

Clamp block to jointer bed to locate top of taper over center of cutterhead.

Top of taper

Set infeed table to make ⅛-in. cut.

**Cutting**

Butt leg blank against stop block.

Turn on jointer. Pivot leg down on cutterhead.

Push leg over cutter as many times as needed to cut taper.

At least ¼-in. of leg must rest on outfeed table.

Always use push stick.

Feed.

**Spade-foot leg**

Taper leg as above, then clamp second block to outfeed table to limit length of taper.

Cut all four sides, lower infeed table 1/16 in. and repeat.

If the turned legs on the pine table shown in *FWW* #54, p. 52 don't suit your fancy, you might want to build the piece with elegant tapered legs. I cut them with several passes on my jointer, which I fit with stop blocks to set the length of the taper and regulate the slope of cut. This method is fast, accurate and produces smooth surfaces. You could also taper the legs with a bandsaw or tablesaw, then finish with a smoothing plane, which is what I do with very short tapers rather than trying to pull small pieces over the cutterhead.

For a table like this I begin with 1¾-in. stock and taper it on all four sides to ⅞ in. Before you begin cutting, draw the taper on all four faces of the leg and carry the guidelines onto the bottom end of the leg so they remain visible after you start cutting. It's also easier to cut the leg mortises above the taper in the square stock before you begin shaping.

If you're tapering stock that's shorter than the length of the infeed table, set up the jointer as shown *before* starting the machine. Lower the infeed table to make a ⅛-in. cut. Place the stock on top of the infeed table and against the fence with its top section resting on the edge of the outfeed table. Butt a stop block against the end of the leg and clamp the block to the infeed table.

Now, remove the leg and start the jointer. Place the bottom end of the leg against the stop block, carefully open the blade guard wide enough for the leg to slide by and lower the leg until the top end rests on the outfeed table. Setting the top of the leg on the outfeed table like this will hold the end high, so that the cut will be tapered toward the other end of the stock as you push the leg through the jointer with the push stick. *Be very careful.* Don't use

the jointer without a push stick. Mine is a 6-in. by 4-in. block of wood notched on one long edge to fit over the leg. Continue cutting each side in turn, until the end is tapered to the guidelines you've laid out. Then plane or sand to smooth the transition from the square stock to the taper.

If the leg is to be tapered from end to end, you must leave extra length at the top of the leg and adjust the stop block to prevent the leg from missing the edge of the outfeed table. At least ¼ in. of the leg must be on the outfeed table to prevent the leg from dropping onto the cutterhead and kicking back. If the stock is longer than

the infeed table, you can use the same procedure outlined above, if you attach a movable extension that can be moved along with the infeed table.

If you want to make a spade-foot leg or another form requiring a stopped taper, taper leg as above, then attach a second stop block to the outfeed table. Repeat the procedure using the second block to stop the cut. After tapering each side, lower the infeed table about 1/16 in. and cut each side again. Repeat until the foot is formed. □

*Eric Schramm designs and builds custom furniture in Los Gatos, Calif.*

# Hexagonal Table From Buckled Burl

## A new approach to an old pressing problem

by Preston Wakeland

When I was approached by a customer to build a hexagonal table with an elm burl center and walnut trim, I decided on a pattern of triangles whose points would all meet in the center, as shown in the photo below.

Carpathian elm burl veneer is tricky to handle because the sheets are almost always badly buckled and puckered. This makes it impossible to lay out a pattern on the sheets and cut them to exact size. The traditional way of using such veneer is to flatten the slices first, as described in the box on p. 24, then cut the required triangles and tape them all together before veneering. Because burl veneer has grain running in all directions, it is very flaky. The prospect of flattening, cutting and taping 12 matched triangles without losing at least one crucial chip seemed very remote to me.

I decided to try an experiment which, I've since found out, is not entirely my own invention, although it isn't common knowledge either. I laminated the buckled veneer directly onto a ¼-in. fiberboard substrate, then cut the laminated pieces to the necessary shape with a router. I found that the technique makes the traditional flattening step unnecessary, provided that the veneers are not too dried out and brittle and that grain direction is random. Most burl can be laminated down quite well without pre-flattening, but some feather-figure veneer would probably crack up the middle. You can test pieces by trying to flatten them by hand. If they resist too much, dampen and flatten them first.

Once mounted, the backed-up veneers not only resist cracking and chipping, but the router's high-speed action makes cutting a breeze. The process is a little more complicated than conventional methods, but more than one book I have on veneering warns that making several pieces of veneer come together at a point is a difficult task, if not impossible. With this system it's relatively simple.

I began by selecting a grain pattern on the flitch that I thought would look good matched up, then I cut 12 consecutive pieces. It is not important at this stage what shape and size these pieces are, as long as they are big enough to cover the design. Mine, in fact, were rectangular. I arranged the slices as six sets of bookmatched pairs and numbered the sheets in the order they came from the flitch.

After selecting the pieces for the face, I cut an equal number for the back of the substrate, using a less attractive area of the same flitch. If both faces of the substrate are not laminated, the work will begin to warp almost instantly when removed from the press. I chose Fibercore (a 48-lb.-density fiberboard made by Plumb Creek, of Columbia Falls, Mont.) for the substrate instead of particleboard or plywood because I couldn't afford any chipping, no matter how small—any chip might take some of the surface veneer away with it. Fibercore has the texture of hardboard, a uniform thickness throughout the sheet and comes flat, not warped.

I use plastic resin glue for veneering, and I bend one cardinal

The finished surface of this burl-top table shows no evidence of its multi-layer construction.

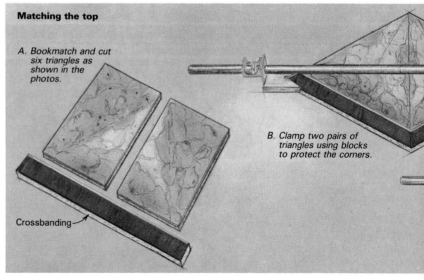

Matching the top

A. Bookmatch and cut six triangles as shown in the photos.

B. Clamp two pairs of triangles using blocks to protect the corners.

Crossbanding

*At top left, unflattened veneer sheets are laminated onto ¼-in. substrate in a small press made from a solid-core door. Particleboard spacers separate the layers. To rout the first seam, left, clamp the pieces and cut both sides of the seam in one pass, guiding the router against one of the clamp strips. Above, cut the sides of the triangles in two passes, the first with a guide bushing to rough-cut about ⅛ in. from the line, the second by running the flush-trim bit directly along the guide board.*

rule because I always apply a very thin coat of glue to the veneer itself, as well as a heavier coat to the substrate. I first apply glue to the substrate with a short-nap roller, then as the roller starts to dry out, I give the veneer a pass—it flattens enough under the pressure to be evenly covered. I take great pains not to get the veneer too wet, because too much moisture would cause it to expand in the press, then shrink and crack after the job was finished. If I don't have enough glue on the roller to get even coverage, I pick up some from the thin layer on the substrate, not from the pan. Using this method I have never had trouble with bubbles or loose edges, and my veneer has never yet cracked from excessive shrinkage.

Instead of my veneer press, which would have been cumbersome to load with so many small pieces at once, I made a press from two halves of a solid-core door and some particleboard spacers. It is imperative that waxed paper be placed between the veneer and the parts of the press, because elm burl is so porous and so full of small checks and cracks that some glue certainly will seep through (the defects are eventually filled with colored wood putty and sanded level). I glued the pieces up in a pair of stacks in the press: first waxed paper, then the bottom veneer with the substrate and the face veneer, then waxed paper and a particleboard spacer. And so on. I then applied pressure with bar clamps and let the whole works sit for 24 hours.

When I removed the pieces, I set them on edge for a day or so

to dry thoroughly. They must not be allowed to lie flat during this time, or moisture will escape faster from one face than the other, causing the pieces to warp.

The first step in bookmatching the tabletop was to make six pairs of matched panels to be cut into equilateral triangles. To cut the first seam, which would end up along the altitude of each triangle, I rough-sawed the joint about ⅛-in. oversize on the tablesaw, then set up to make the final cuts with a new carbide flush-trim router bit. To guide the router, I clamped the two panels as shown above in the lower-left photo. One of the clamp strips is a straight fence located so that the router bit runs down the middle of the seam, cutting about ⅛ in. from each side. With this system, any irregularities are cut into both pieces at once, and the seam closes up with very little pressure during gluing.

When the glue dried, I had six irregularly shaped rectangles with a nifty bookmatched seam up the middle. I used the tablesaw to square the pieces at a right angle to the seam, and glued on my 2-in. walnut crossband trim, which I had laminated to Fibercore in the same manner as the burl.

When these joints were dry, I laid out the other two sides of each triangle so that the baseline would be a tiny bit longer than the sides. This was to ensure that the two halves of the tabletop could be trimmed with the router without removing any of the triangles' points (see step D in the drawing below). I cut the sides of the triangles by laying a straightedge directly on

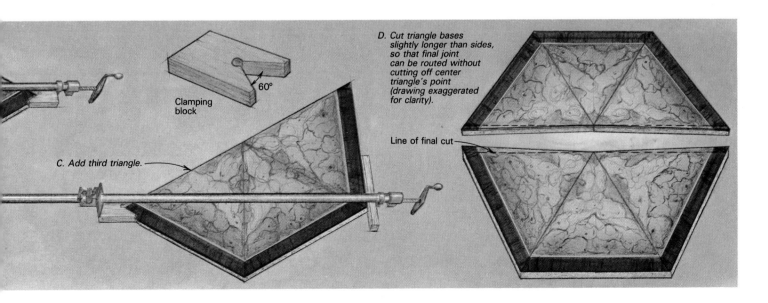

D. Cut triangle bases slightly longer than sides, so that final joint can be routed without cutting off center triangle's point (drawing exaggerated for clarity).

Clamping block

60°

C. Add third triangle.

Line of final cut

# Rejuvenating veneers

by Ian Kirby

Spectacular crotch, burl or wild-grain veneers are sometimes so badly buckled, cracked or brittle that they seem practically useless. But such veneers are too beautiful to pass up, especially if you can buy them at bargain prices. Veneer suppliers are often eager to get rid of small parcels of abused-looking veneers and cut-offs from much longer, flatter slices. If you can flatten this stuff, you can create spectacular effects by joining the pieces together end-to-end or with some type of multi-match method.

Veneers become brittle and buckled because of drying out, poor storage conditions and age, but you can rejuvenate them. The usual way is to introduce moisture into the veneer at a very slow rate, in order to increase its flexibility, then to flatten it and allow it to dry under pressure.

You'll need a clean, flat, moisture-resistant work surface—plastic laminate is fine, but you can use a table or floor covered with a plastic sheet. You'll also need a pad of newsprint paper, an inch or so larger than the veneer, and a spray bottle full of clean water. Be sure to use clean newsprint, not your daily newspaper, or you'll get ink all over everything. Dampen the newsprint and the veneer with a very light spray. Then stack the veneer sheets with two or three sheets of newsprint between each slice. Enclose the entire stack in a plastic sheet, then allow two or three days for the moisture to be absorbed by the veneer.

To test the veneer, lay a piece onto a flat surface and carefully try to flatten it by hand. In some cases, the veneer may resist being pressed or make cracking sounds, it which case it is not yet ready. If necessary, repeat the moisture treatment. Don't try to hurry the process. Raising the moisture content of the material without getting it too wet is a slow process. It's a fine line between sufficient and too much. The result of too much is mildew, which may permanently discolor the veneer.

When the veneer is sufficiently flexible to be pressed, the excess moisture is removed. Stack the veneer with three or four sheets of dry newsprint between each leaf and apply sufficient weight or pressure to flatten the stack. The newsprint will gradually wick the moisture from the veneer. Check the stack's progress after two days, and replace the newsprint with fresh, dry sheets if it seems necessary.

You might have to repeat the treatment a third time, but eventually, the veneer will be dry enough to use.

Now that you have workable sheets of veneer, don't leave them out in the open where they will quickly buckle again. Put a sheet of newsprint between each slice, wrap the whole package in plastic and store it on a flat surface under weight.

An old technique for handling buckled veneer was to size it with a dilute glue solution and glycerine before flattening. This method is messy and has never seemed to me to be worth the trouble.

It has long been the practice with fragile veneers to glue them onto a sturdier backing veneer such as African mahogany or poplar. Even after the pieces of veneer are glued together, store them under pressure on a flat surface.

This whole process isn't as long-winded as it may sound—it's a little work over a long period—and the net result is that you end up with some beautiful and usable material. □

*Ian Kirby is a designer, educator and cabinetmaker who operates Kirby Studios in Cumming, Ga. One of his articles on veneering is on pp. 209-213.*

*A little water, patience and pressure can transform bumpy veneers (bottom three sheets) into workable material (top sheets).*

---

the marks, then first routing a rough cut using a bushing. To make the final cut to the line, I simply removed the bushing and allowed the bit's shank to bear directly against the straightedge. After gluing the triangles together using 60° corner blocks as shown in the drawing, I matched the two halves of the top the same way.

The glued top at this stage was about ⁵⁄₁₆ in. thick, and I was prepared to treat it like a pane of glass. Yet when I tested some of the scrap-wood glue joints they turned out to be very strong. I sanded the back so that all surfaces were flush, then laminated the top to a piece of ¾-in. particleboard. The rest of the table was made in a conventional manner using particleboard and walnut veneer fastened with plastic resin glue.

I have used this system several times now, and have come away with the following conclusions: Bumpy veneers require no flattening, thus eliminating the addition of extra moisture into the veneer. Splitting and cracking from cutting are eliminated even when cutting to a sharp point. Differences in veneer thickness can be dealt with by simply putting the faces flush when gluing up the seams. Laminating small pieces first reduces the need for a large veneer press.

I don't pretend that all veneering should be done this way. Certainly, conventional methods are faster and easier most of the time, but for me it provided a very slick way out of what could have been a very sticky situation. □

*Preston Wakeland is a full-time cabinetmaker in Lockport, Ill. Photos by the author.*

# Inlaid Tambours
## *Floral patterns on a flexible door*

by David Convissor

John Seymour and his son Thomas were among the finest of the Boston cabinetmakers at the turn of the 19th century. Although they produced an amazing variety of furniture, they are best known for their Federal tambour desks and secretaries. The tambour doors on some of their fancier pieces were decorated with a delicate, draped cornflower design inlaid into the tambour slats. I reproduced this design on the doors of my Seymour-style desk shown at right. Inlaid tambours certainly look impressive, but they aren't nearly as difficult as they appear.

Inlaid tambour doors are basically the same as conventional tambours: thin wooden slats glued to a flexible canvas backing. The inlays appear to have been worked into each slat individually, but this isn't the case. The flowers are inlaid into a sheet of veneer. Wood strips are then clamped edge-to-edge and glued to the back of this marquetry sheet. The veneer is then cut apart along the strip lines with a knife. This technique can be used to add parquetry patterns, marquetry designs or just some beautiful grain pattern to contemporary-style tambours. I molded each slat on my desk doors but, if you leave the slats flat, the surface will look solid when the tambours are closed.

The tambours on my desk are mahogany inlaid with holly. Both woods cut easily and are available in nice, straight grain. Instead of being sawn out with a scroll saw, the inlays and the corresponding holes in the veneer are punched out with gouges. Since the desk-door slats will be molded, to allow enough thickness, start with veneer that is at least 1⁄16 in. thick. Most veneer suppliers sell 1⁄16-in. mahogany. However, you might have to plane down the holly from a thicker piece or resort to gluing together two pieces of 1⁄28-in.-thick veneer.

Start by drawing the pattern full size on paper. As you can see from the photo of the desk, the flower pattern repeats and reverses itself four times across each door. You need to draw only one section, not the entire pattern. The pattern has only two shapes, a football-shaped flower petal and a round dot. To draw the flower petals accurately you'll need a template and to make the template you'll need three gouges—one for each size flower. I made the design shown with three #6 sweep straight gouges: 1 in., 3⁄4 in. and 1⁄2 in. Make the template from 3- to 5-mil drafting film (available from any large art-supply store) by cutting out one petal shape with each chisel. Two chisel cuts punch out one petal, as shown in the drawing. Trace around the inside of the template cutouts to draw the flower petals on your full-scale drawing. Draw parallel lines 3⁄8 in. apart to represent the slats. Transfer the finished drawing to tracing paper and fasten the tracing with rubber cement to your mahogany veneer. Art stores also sell transparent pressure-sensitive vinyl which is more con-

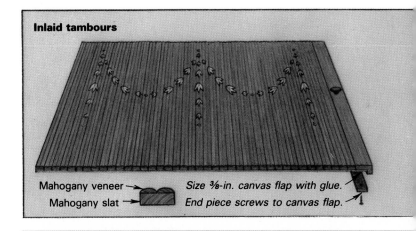

**Inlaid tambours**

Mahogany veneer →
Mahogany slat →

Size 3⁄8-in. canvas flap with glue.
End piece screws to canvas flap.

*Inlaid tambour doors decorate author's version of a Federal-style desk. Not a reproduction of any particular piece, it combines features of desks built by early Boston cabinetmakers John and Thomas Seymour.*

With full-size drawing on clear vinyl stuck to the veneer, Convissor punches out the center inlay recess with a #6 sweep straight gouge (top). The same gouge cuts the holly inlays. The hole for the side inlay cuts into center inlay piece to create a three-dimensional effect (bottom). The third side inlay hole cuts through the first two inlays. Cellophane tape holds inlays in place.

**Inlaying the veneer**

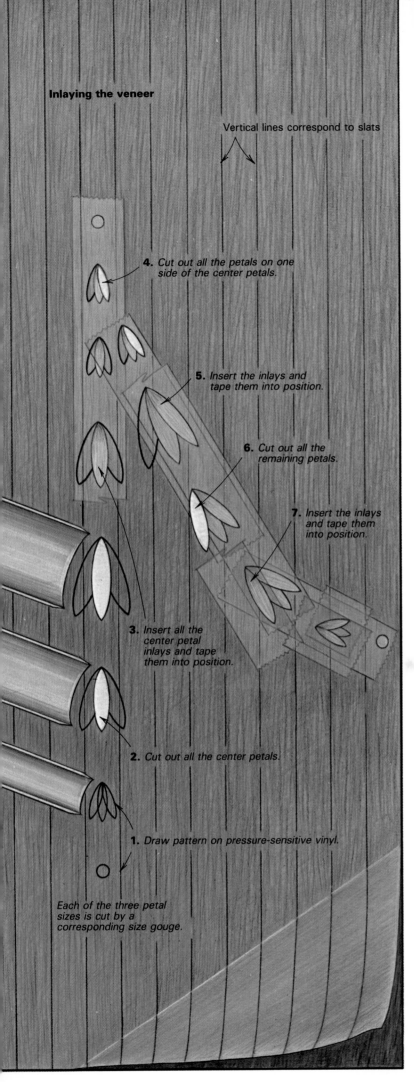

Vertical lines correspond to slats

4. Cut out all the petals on one side of the center petals.

5. Insert the inlays and tape them into position.

6. Cut out all the remaining petals.

7. Insert the inlays and tape them into position.

3. Insert all the center petal inlays and tape them into position.

2. Cut out all the center petals.

1. Draw pattern on pressure-sensitive vinyl.

Each of the three petal sizes is cut by a corresponding size gouge.

venient than tracing paper because it sticks without cement.

I suggest that you do the entire marquetry and veneering process with one section at a time. After you've finished four sections and cut apart the slats, you can glue canvas across the back of all four sections to complete one door. With the same gouges you used to make your template, cut out the center petal of each flower. Don't worry if the two cuts overlap at the ends of the opening because the overcuts won't show after the slats are molded. Cut the matching center petal inlays from the holly veneer with the same gouges. After working for a few minutes your eyes will become accustomed to the sizes and shapes and you'll be surprised how neatly the holly petals fit into the mahogany.

I shaded the inlays by charring one end slightly in hot sand. This shading adds depth to the flower design. Fill a cast-iron skillet with about 1-in. of fine builders' sand. Hold one end of each inlay in the hot sand for a few seconds so that the tip is shaded. Experiment to find the proper amount of time. Too long and you'll char the wood. With my electric hot plate on high, I find a 5-second count just right. After shading, insert the inlay into the veneer and hold it there with cellophane tape.

When all the center petals are installed, cut out all the petals on one side. To give the flower a three-dimensional appearance, cut right into the center petal so that the side petal appears to overlap it. Shade just the tip of the side petal in the sand and tape it in place. Now make the cuts for the third petal through both the center and side petals. Cut the dots at the end of the strings with a punch or a #9 gouge slowly twisted in a circle. Don't shade the inlays for the third petal or the dots.

When all the pieces are taped in place, turn the veneer over and brush a mixture of watered-down yellow glue and mahogany sawdust into the cracks. I force the mixture into the gaps with a

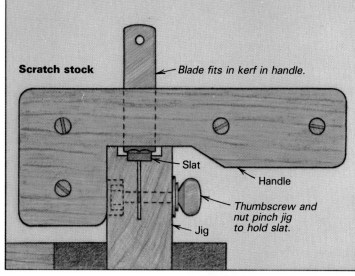

Scratch stock — Blade fits in kerf in handle.

Slat

Handle

Thumbscrew and nut pinch jig to hold slat.

Jig

*For veneering, the slats are locked up in a rigid frame. A wood strip tacked across the slat ends prevents movement when clamps are applied (top left). Edges of marquetry sheet must be trimmed so the lines on the drawing line up with the cracks between the slats underneath (left). The frame is large enough to hold the entire door for canvassing, but when working on one section of the pattern, plywood spacers take up the remaining space. After cutting the veneered slats apart, Convissor molds the slats with a scratch stock (right). A wooden fixture secures the strip.*

flat scrap of metal. When the glue has dried, level the back side with a cabinet scraper.

To make the slats, I cut mahogany strips ¾₁₆ in. thick and ⅜ in. wide and ½ in. longer than the finished door height. When the marquetry sheet is finished, it's ready to be glued to these slats. To keep the slats from moving around I've built a rectangular frame much like a printers' chase—the iron frame that holds hand-set metal type in place. Lock up the correct number of slats for one section of the pattern, as shown in the photo above. Tack a strip of wood over the bottom ends of the slats to secure them, and place the veneer face up over the clamped-up slats. Trim the ends and sides of the veneer so that the slat lines drawn on the tracing line up with the cracks between the strips underneath. Remember, the other sections of the pattern will later butt up against this one, so the end of the section must line up with a crack.

I cover the veneer with a heavy layer of newspaper or a piece of ¹⁄₁₆-in. sheet foam to take up any unevenness while clamping. A piece of ¾-in. plywood distributes pressure over the surface. When the alignment is right, clamp up a dry run to make sure that everything is ready and that no one has taken your clamps. Remove the veneer and brush a coat of white glue on the slats. Position the veneer and drive a few veneer pins or brads in the corners to keep the veneer from shifting when you apply the clamps. Cut the pins off ¹⁄₁₆ in. above the surface. Cover the veneer with the newspaper or foam, lay on the plywood and clamp it in place. A veneer press is nice if you have one.

Let the glue set for no more than 15 minutes. Remove the panel and flex it to be sure no glue has seeped between the slats. I flex the panel over a piece of half-round stock and run a razor knife blade between any slats that feel tacky. Now number the slats and draw some diagonal registration lines across the back

so that you can line up the slats and later reassemble them in the correct order. The slats are now ready to be cut apart. With a straightedge, score the veneer face along the slat lines with a sharp razor knife to prevent the cuts from following the grain, then turn the panel over. Rest it on a curved surface to spread the slats. Cut through the veneer with the razor knife using the edge of the slat as a guide.

When all the slats are cut apart they can be molded. I've made a simple fixture that holds one slat in place while I cut the molding with a scratch stock. A scratch stock, shown in the drawing above, is a simple, shop-made tool for making moldings, beadings and grooves for string inlays. A broken hacksaw blade makes a good cutter and you can grind or file any profile you want. To use the tool, set the blade to the depth you want to cut and pull the tool back and forth along the stock until the handle stops the cutting action. No, the inlays won't pop out. Sand the molded slats with 120-grit sandpaper, followed by 150-grit.

When you've completed the above process four times you'll have all the slats for one door and you'll be ready to glue on the canvas. Lock the slats for the entire door face down in the chase. Make sure that you have them in the correct order and that the diagonal lines are lined up. Apply white or yellow glue to the canvas and clamp it in place under a plywood batten for no more than 15 minutes. Remove the clamps and flex the tambour. Remove any glue from between the slats with a razor knife. I trim the door to width on the tablesaw with a hollow-ground planer blade after first scoring the back of the canvas with a knife. □

*David Convissor is a professional furnituremaker in Littleton, Mass. For more on tambour doors and their installation see* Fine Woodworking *#48. pp. 54-58.*

# Fox Wedging

## A sly joint for a 17th-century stool

by Alasdair G.B. Wallace

A request to copy a pair of 17th-century joynt stools in brown oak offered a welcome change and challenge for me. My customer had admired a pair of 19th-century reproduction stools in an antique shop, but found the price beyond her means and equally beyond the realm of reason. Though English brown oak costs three to four times as much as domestic red oak, a quick calculation suggested that I could produce two stools for less than the price of a single 100-year-old reproduction.

Joynt stools date from the late 16th century and the advent of the technique of framing and the pegged mortise-and-tenon joint. (The term joynt comes from joined.) In addition to plain, totally unadorned joynt stools, some exhibited simple moldings and carving, while others for churches and manor houses were elaborately carved and molded. I was asked to copy the most basic stool, the product of the country carpenter.

Construction of the stool is straightforward. When preparing the stock, make the leg blanks 1 in. longer than the finished dimension to allow for trimming. You can mortise the legs before or after turning them. I prefer to turn them first so that I can fine-tune the location of the mortises relative to the turnings.

The mortises and tenons should be laid out so that the outer faces of the apron rails and stretchers will finish flush with the outer faces of the legs. For maximum strength, the tenons should be offset as shown in the drawing on the facing page, and mortises for adjacent rails or stretchers shouldn't intersect in the leg. The legs are splayed 5° from perpendicular when the stool is viewed from the ends, so those mortises and tenons must be laid out accordingly. The Jacobeans didn't glue the mortise and tenons, relying instead on pegs and the shrinkage of slightly green legs around the tenons for strength. My brown oak was bone dry, so I chose to fox-wedge the tenons to help secure the joints.

Though little-used today, the fox-wedged tenon provides an exceptionally strong joint where a through-wedged tenon would be inappropriate or impossible. A fox-wedged tenon expands the tenon within its mortise, as does a through-wedged tenon, and both require tapered mortises to accommodate the tenon's expansion. The difference between the joints is that the fox-wedged mortise is blind and the wedges must be driven into the tenon by the bottom of the mortise. A great many things can go wrong if the joint isn't laid out and cut carefully. If, for example, the tenon or wedges are too long or the mortise insufficiently tapered, the joint won't pull tight; if the mortise is too wide or the wedges too slim, the joint will be loose. Regardless of whether you glue the joints (I preferred not to), they can be further secured by pegging.

*Wallace's brown oak copy of a 17th-century joynt stool, left, is held together by fox-wedged tenons. The top is attached to the apron rails with square wooden pegs. A fox-wedged tenon and mortise, above, is ready for assembly. Since the faces of the pieces are to be flush, the tenon is offset for greater strength. The mortise, right, has been too heavily undercut, causing the tenon to fracture at the end of the top kerf. The wedges and kerfs, however, are perfect.*

Lay out and cut the joint as you would a standard blind mortise-and-tenon. Then taper the mortise, kerf the tenons and make the wedges following these basic guidelines:

The depth of the mortise should be about $\frac{1}{16}$ in. to $\frac{1}{8}$ in. greater than the length of the tenon.

The taper of the mortise should equal the difference between the width of the sawkerfs and the thickness of the wedges.

Begin the mortise taper at a distance of about one-fifth the depth of the mortise beneath the shoulder. (Start tapering a 1$\frac{1}{4}$-in.-deep mortise about $\frac{1}{4}$ in. beneath the shoulder.) This ensures that the wedges will be driven into the tenon equally and that the tenon will be centered in the mortise.

Position the kerfs about one-fifth the tenon's width in from each of its edges (about $\frac{1}{4}$ in. on a 1$\frac{1}{4}$-in. wide tenon), and cut them to a depth of about four-fifths the tenon length.

Make hardwood wedges as long as or a bit less than the length of the kerf. At its thickest, a wedge should be about twice the width of the kerf, thinner if the wood is likely to split.

I assemble the sides of the stool first, then add the end rails and stretchers. When you assemble the fox-wedged joints, make sure that the wedges are firmly in place in the kerfs, and take care not to dislodge the wedges as you insert each tenon into its mortise. To avoid jarring the wedges loose, draw the joints together with a clamp rather than driving them together with a mallet. The original

stool's joints were pegged. I drove square pegs into slightly smaller round holes, then flushed them off with a chisel. To attach the top, I used the Jacobean method of driving square pegs through it into the apron rails. Nails, pocket screws or buttons can do the job, too.

Everyone in the business of reproduction has his or her own secret recipe for stain. These range from unlikely concoctions of manure, ashes and soot to commercial stains. Don't be afraid to experiment. I used a manure/ash/soot combination, painting it on liberally, filling cracks and hollows and leaving it for three or four months. Brushing the mixture off revealed a deep brown surface. Thorough wiping in areas of high wear and some judicious sanding achieved the antique effect my client desired. A beeswax, turpentine and lampblack mixture completes the finish. Apply it over five wiped-on coats of 1-1 white shellac/methylhydrate which seals the wood and gives it life and depth.

My customer's wish that the stool look old presented me with an ethical dilemma. Judging by the wealth of "authentic" joynt stools I saw on a recent trip to England, the Jacobean carpenter was much more prolific than we realize or current high prices have tempted their modern counterparts to augment the Jacobean output. I was able to satisfy the customer's desire for a piece that looked authentic by staining and distressing. By carving my name and the date on the back face of an apron rail I ensured that no one would ever be duped by my deception. □

---

*Alasdair G.B. Wallace makes furniture in Lakefield, Ontario.*

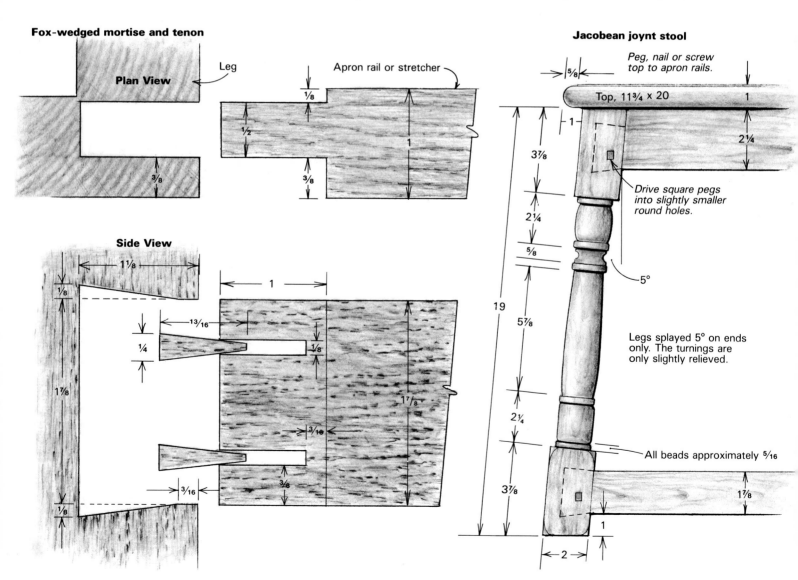

**Fox-wedged mortise and tenon**

Plan View

Leg

Apron rail or stretcher

$\frac{1}{8}$  $\frac{1}{2}$  $\frac{3}{8}$  1  $\frac{3}{8}$

Side View

1$\frac{1}{8}$  $\frac{1}{8}$  1  $\frac{13}{16}$  $\frac{1}{4}$  $\frac{1}{8}$  1$\frac{7}{8}$  $\frac{3}{16}$  $\frac{3}{8}$  $\frac{3}{16}$  $\frac{1}{8}$  1$\frac{7}{8}$

**Jacobean joynt stool**

Peg, nail or screw top to apron rails.

$\frac{5}{8}$  Top, 11$\frac{3}{4}$ x 20  1  2$\frac{1}{4}$  1

3$\frac{7}{8}$  2$\frac{1}{4}$  $\frac{5}{8}$  5°

Drive square pegs into slightly smaller round holes.

19  5$\frac{7}{8}$

Legs splayed 5° on ends only. The turnings are only slightly relieved.

2$\frac{1}{4}$  3$\frac{7}{8}$

All beads approximately $\frac{5}{16}$

1$\frac{7}{8}$  1  2

# Leather and Wood
## *Three clever combinations*

by Seth Stem

*Leather cemented onto a plywood panel can be an attractive alternative to a solid-wood panel in furniture. After applying contact cement to both leather and plywood, Stem positions the leather carefully and smooths it down onto the plywood.*

There are unlimited opportunities to use leather in furniture. Leather's color, texture, and surface character greatly complement the grain pattern and natural warmth of wood. Because its appearance can range from a natural look to slick surfaces or bizarre colors, leather works in almost any context, from utilitarian to purely decorative. I've covered flat surfaces, such as a desk top or panel, with leather, upholstered with it and formed it into three-dimensional shapes that function as containers or ornament on furniture. I'll discuss techniques for doing each of these, but first a little background.

Leather is a durable and strong yet flexible material, made up of fibers interwoven in all directions. Once removed from the animal, the hide is given baths in various chemicals, scraped of its hair and fat then submerged in tanning agents. Tanning keeps leather from putrifying and, depending on the tanning agent, increases its resistance to heat, water and chemicals. Chromium salts and vegetable matter containing tannin—oak bark for example—are the most commonly used tanning agents. (Chrome-tanned leather shows a bluish-gray color in cross section.)

Most retailers sell leather by the square foot in half hides, the hide being divided along the animal's backbone. Half cowhides are usually 20 to 25 sq. ft., and the measurement is stamped on the back side of the hide. It's most economical to buy a half hide, and many retailers won't cut a hide into smaller lots.

Leather is also classified by weight in ounces per square foot, and weight correlates directly to thickness—1 oz. equals 1/64 in. Garment leather is generally 2 oz. to 3 oz./sq. ft., belt leather is 7 oz. to 9 oz./sq. ft., and furniture sling leather is 8 oz. to 14 oz./sq. ft. Quite an amazing range of leather is available—cowhide, deerskin, lizard, pigskin, horsehide, and goatskin are common. Suede is a hide with the skin side removed.

Because there is such a variety of leather available, it's best to visit a leather retailer rather than rely on mail order. If you can't, here is a mail-order source I've used: Berman Leathercraft, 145 South St., Boston, Mass., 02111.

**Leather panels in a wood frame** are an attractive alternative to all-wood panels. I glue leather to plywood with contact cement, then I fix the panels in the frames using one of the methods shown in figure 1 on the facing page. Use at least 3-oz. leather for panels because surface irregularities in the plywood will telegraph through thinner leather. I also glue leather to both sides of the plywood so there is no chance of the plywood warping, just as it would if you applied wood veneer to only one side. Leather on only one side will probably do if the panel is held firmly in a frame.

The procedure for cementing the leather to the panel is the same for the methods shown in figure 1A, B and C. Cut the plywood panel to size and lay it over an area of leather that is free of defects. Mark and cut the leather about 1/2 in. to 1 in. away from each edge of the panel. I use a razor knife or single-edge razor for cutting and trimming leather. Apply contact cement to both the backside of the leather and to the plywood. Make sure that the gluing surfaces are free from dirt and cement lumps, which will telegraph through the surface. When the contact cement has dried (20 minutes or so), position the leather carefully and, starting from one edge, press it down smoothly on the plywood with the flat of your hand. Trim the excess, then glue and trim the other side.

A panel in a rabbet can be glued or screwed into place (figure 1A) or held by a molding strip (figure 1B). If a screwed or glued panel is to be seen from the inside, I first trim the leather on the inside surface so it overhangs the plywood slightly, then trim it accurately with a razor knife after the panel is in place.

A grooved frame and leather-covered panel can be assembled

permanently, but I prefer to be able to remove a damaged panel. Figure 1C shows a method for the side panel of a desk or cabinet. The panel slides into grooves in the stiles and bottom rail, and is held in place by a two-piece top rail. The outer half of the top rail is mortised to the stiles, the inner half is loose. Chamfer the edges of the panel with a razor knife so they can slide easily into the grooves without peeling the leather off the plywood.

The method shown in figure 1D raises the leather slightly above the frame. I used this method for the top panels on the desk shown at right. The effect of this raised panel is crisp and professional, whereas a flush panel made using the same method will show a crevice between the leather and the frame due to the curvature of the leather as it wraps around the plywood. The depth of the frame rabbet should be half the frame's thickness. Cut a plywood panel to fit snugly in the frame, then rabbet the panel to create a lip that's as thick as the frame rabbet is deep. (The plywood need not be the same thickness as the frame.) I do this on the tablesaw, placing the panel on end, top surface toward the fence for the first cut, then placing it flat on the table, top surface up, for the second. The thickness of plywood varies slightly throughout a single sheet, and this method ensures that the lip will be a uniform thickness.

Next, trim the panel to allow for the thickness of the leather. Place two pieces of leather scrap in the rabbet on each member of the frame, toward the corners, then try the panel in the frame. Saw or plane the edges until the panel fits the opening snugly. It may take several tries, but a good fit here is very important.

Cut the leather for the panel large enough to wrap over the edges of the plywood lip and allow for waste. Contact cement the leather to the face of the panel, then cut small squares out of the overlapping leather at each corner of the panel. The corner of a square should come to within ⅛ in. to 3/16 in. of the plywood corner. Cement the overlap to the edges of the lip, stretching the leather over the apex of each corner and smoothing out any puckering. Trim and chamfer the leather all around the panel; no leather should adhere to the underside of the lip. Finally, glue or screw the panel into place. Single-edge razor blades slipped between the leather and the frame work like shoehorns and help slide the panel in. Remember the leather will compress slightly, so a real tight fit is possible.

**Simple leather upholstery** can be done using the same frame-and-panel system and 1-in. to 2-in. thick foam-rubber padding. The round stool shown on p. 32 has a leather upholstered seat

*Stem's desk has raised-leather-panel writing surfaces; the side panels of desk and credenza are flat.*

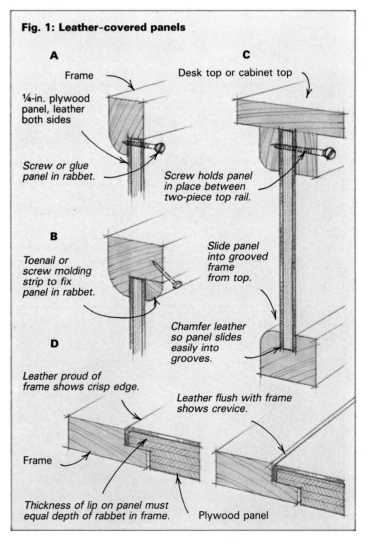

**Fig. 1: Leather-covered panels**

A

Frame

¼-in. plywood panel, leather both sides

Screw or glue panel in rabbet.

C

Desk top or cabinet top

Screw holds panel in place between two-piece top rail.

B

Toenail or screw molding strip to fix panel in rabbet.

Slide panel into grooved frame from top.

Chamfer leather so panel slides easily into grooves.

D

Leather proud of frame shows crisp edge.

Leather flush with frame shows crevice.

Frame

Thickness of lip on panel must equal depth of rabbet in frame.

Plywood panel

*Single-edge razor blades help ease a tight-fitting panel into place in a rabbeted frame.*

°Gary Gilbert

*By sandwiching foam between the leather and panel, you can adapt the frame-and-panel leatherworking method to upholster a seat, as in this stool made by Matthew Burke.*

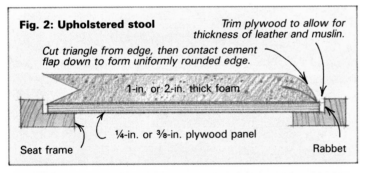

**Fig. 2: Upholstered stool**    *Trim plywood to allow for thickness of leather and muslin.*

*Cut triangle from edge, then contact cement flap down to form uniformly rounded edge.*

1-in. or 2-in. thick foam

¼-in. or ⅜-in. plywood panel

Seat frame          Rabbet

*Flat-nosed pliers give added pull when tacking the leather to the seat panel.*

fixed in a round frame, but the method will work for seats of any shape. Construct the frame, cut the plywood to fit, then glue the foam to the plywood with contact cement and trim it flush with the edges of the plywood (see figure 2). Left square, the edge of the foam would compress irregularly as the leather was stretched over it. Using a sharp razor blade, I cut a triangular section out of the edge and glue the foam flap down with contact cement so the edge will retain its shape.

Next, stretch muslin over the foam, tack or staple it to the plywood and trim off the excess. First tack the muslin in four places, 90° apart, so it won't gather too much during stretching. The muslin helps make the rounded foam edge uniform, and allows the leather to shift slightly over this surface when the stool is being used, without the leather wearing or pulling directly on the foam. Stretch 3-oz. to 4-oz. leather over the muslin and tack it in the same sequence, using flat-nosed pliers to stretch it if necessary. If the leather puckers or gathers at seat corners or around curves, wet it with a sponge and stretch it smooth. Trim off excess leather with a razor and screw the plywood backing to the seat frame from underneath.

**Wet leather can be molded** over a form and when dry, it will retain the form's shape. One-layer shells of 8-oz. to 10-oz. vegetable-tanned leather will be extremely stiff and hold their shape well. (Lighter-weight vegetable-tanned leather will also form, but won't be as stiff.) By gluing together two lightweight layers of chrome- or vegetable-tanned leather over a form, you can make a rigid leather shell with finished surfaces inside and out, like the one on the wall-hung basket on the facing page. Leather can be specially tanned to keep stretch at a minimum, so it is best to discuss the intended use of the leather with your retailer.

Single-layer and double-layer shells can be made on the same form. Try slightly rounded or bullnose shapes first, avoiding shapes that cause the leather to bunch or gather. Forms can be lathe-turned or hand-shaped of any material that will hold nails and that won't deteriorate when wet. The final surface must be smooth, as any imperfection will telegraph through the leather. I made the form for the wall basket of fiberboard, with a top layer of plywood to take the nails.

After you've made the form, collect a plastic bucket, regular flat-nosed pliers, a tack hammer and a razor knife or single-edge razor blade. Cut a piece of leather slightly oversize to go over the form. An easy way to measure the piece is to place the form on the leather and roll it to the form's edge, then mark 2 in. or 3 in. from the edge. Roll it to the opposite edge and so on. Soak the leather in a bucket of very hot water for approximately 20 minutes, then tack it along one edge of the form with 1¼-in. brads. Put the smooth side out if you're making a single-layer shell, smooth side in for a double-layer shell. Pull and stretch the leather over the form using flat-nosed pliers, and tack it down. To remove puckering, pull the brads out one at a time and stretch the leather further. Replace the brads with #6 upholstery tacks during the last round of stretching. The leather is dry when it returns to its original color. With a razor knife, remove a one-layer shell from the form now by cutting just inside the tacked area.

For a two-layer shell, stretch the first layer, finished side in, then brush on a very generous layer of yellow glue, such as Titebond, then wet-form a second layer of leather over the first, finish side out. The degree of stiffness can be controlled by the amount of glue applied. For a very hard shell, three or more layers of leather can be glued together.

Formed leather can be attached to a wood frame in a groove,

Leather shells or containers can be made by stretching wet leather over a form. When dry, the leather will retain the shape of the form, and can then be mounted in a wooden frame.

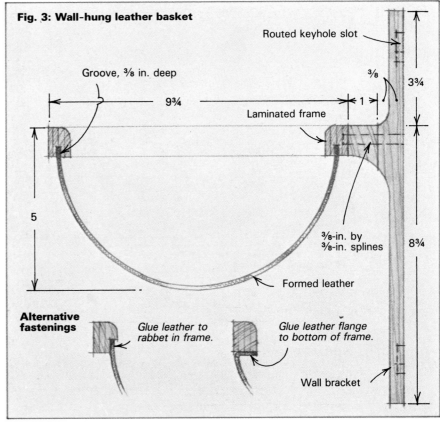

**Fig. 3: Wall-hung leather basket**

Routed keyhole slot

Groove, ⅜ in. deep

9¾

⅜

3¾

Laminated frame

1

5

⅜-in. by ⅜-in. splines

8¾

Formed leather

**Alternative fastenings**

Glue leather to rabbet in frame.

Glue leather flange to bottom of frame.

Wall bracket

Stretch the wet leather in stages, holding it temporarily in place with brads. Fix it with upholstery tacks during the last round of stretching. Glue two (or more) layers of leather together on a one-piece form for a very stiff shell. Wet, stretch and tack the first layer to the form. Spread yellow glue on this layer, then stretch and tack the next layer.

in a rabbet or by a flange, as shown in figure 3. The wall basket is glued into a groove routed in the form-laminated hickory rim; the groove must match the shell's perimeter exactly. The groove is as wide as the thickness of the leather and about ¼ in. to ⅜ in. deep. I usually chamfer the edge of the leather with a razor blade first, to allow for easier entry into the groove.

Leather glued to a rabbet can be stretched slightly to meet the rabbet, then it must be tacked or clamped in place while the glue dries. You'll also need to trim the shell's edge precisely to butt against the rabbet, unless the inside is hidden from view.

If when you cut the leather free of the form you retain the flange (the area of leather tacked to the form), you can glue this to a wood structure. Trim the puckered areas of the flange with a razor knife and pound them flat on the form with a hammer. Then trim the flange ½ in. to ¾ in. wide. If you're gluing the flange down with yellow glue, the frame must allow access for the clamps. If this is impossible, use contact cement.     □

*Seth Stem teaches at the Rhode Island School of Design and designs and makes furniture in Marblehead, Mass.*

## Edging plywood drawer fronts

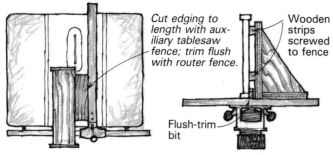

Cut edging to length with auxiliary tablesaw fence; trim flush with router fence.

Wooden strips screwed to fence

Flush-trim bit

Here are a couple of tricks I use to apply solid-wood edging to plywood drawer fronts. The first is a simple auxiliary tablesaw fence to trim the edging to length. I glue the edging to the ends of the drawer, leaving a ¼-in. overhang. Then, with the auxiliary fence adjusted for a perfect flush cut, I simply push each corner through the saw.

To trim the edging flush with the face of the drawer front, I use the router table and screw a couple of wooden strips to it. Chuck a ball-bearing flush-trim bit in the router and adjust the fence so the bearing is flush with the surface of the strips. When you run the panels through, the edging rides under the bottom strip and the tall fence makes it easy to keep the panel perpendicular.

—*Rick Turner, Petaluma, Calif.*

## All-wood adjustable shelf bracket

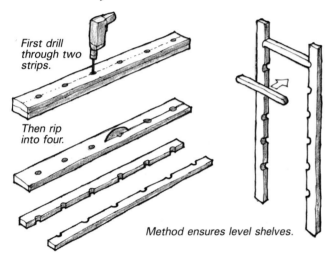

First drill through two strips.

Then rip into four.

Method ensures level shelves.

This easy-to-make shelf bracket ensures accuracy because both pairs of shelf-height notches are established with one hole. To make the bracket, clamp two 1x2 strips together and drill a series of holes down the centerline through both strips. The holes will set the spacing between shelf locations. Now rip each 1x2 on its centerline to produce two matching brackets for each end of the shelf unit. Install the brackets in the carcase and cut several ¾-in. square shelf supports to fit in the notches. Round the ends of the shelf supports to match the half-round notches in the brackets.

—*Rollie Johnson, Sauk Rapids, Minn.*

## Clamping round tabletops revisited

Here's an alternative to Jim Small's clamp-perch idea (*FWW* #47) for gluing circular tabletops. First place the tabletop on the bench and clamp three stops as shown in the sketch. Place a free-floating 2x4 against the workpiece and drive paired wedges between the clamped and floating 2x4s to apply pressure to the glue joint. Here are some additional tips: Place newspaper on the bench to catch the glue that will squeeze out, and dowel the edge joint to keep the pieces from shifting.

It's best to raise the tabletop up with a few thin scraps of wood—this centers the clamping pressure and allows glue to drip out without smearing. I put weights on top of the work if necessary to keep it flat while the glue sets. And as with any glue-up, it's a good idea to make a dry run first.

—*Ken Jones, Lisle, Ill.*

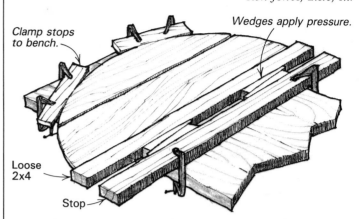

Wedges apply pressure.

Clamp stops to bench.

Loose 2x4

Stop

## Routing V-grooves in tongue-and-groove

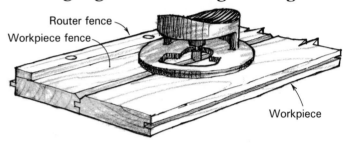

Router fence

Workpiece fence

Workpiece

To produce identical chamfers on matching edges of tongue-and-groove stock, I use an extra piece of stock with a nailed-on router fence, as shown in the sketch. Both the tongued and the grooved edges can be pushed flush to the jig, ensuring a balanced V-groove in the finished work and eliminating the extra setup that would be required with a shaper or a tablesaw. You could adapt the idea to a router table just as easily.

—*W.A. Ward, Underhill, Vt.*

## Frame joint for a job-site table

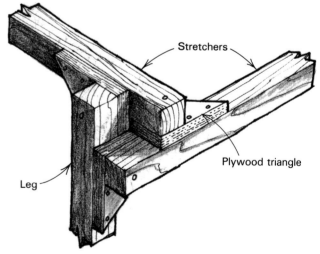

Stretchers

Plywood triangle

Leg

It's often useful to be able to quickly construct a solid table or bench frame at the job site. I simply cut legs and stretchers to length from scrap, then join with three 45° triangles of ⅜-in. plywood at each corner, glued and nailed. Variations of this joint—with a little mathematical figuring and diamond-section ribs—can be used for quick geodesic domes and other timber structures.

—*Chris Yonge, Edinburgh, Scotland*

# Adventure in Chair Design

*In which a student discovers some limits*

by David Veleta

by David Veleta

S traight, flat and square had been the staple diet of my first year as a student of furniture design and construction, so I was anxious to try curves when I began my second year with my first chair design. I started out wanting an upright chair suitable for reading and conversation. I had in mind an upholstered tall-back and curves and tapers that would give the chair a light and elegant look.

These initial ideas reined-in my imagination somewhat, but the constraint was helpful. It seems that the more indefinite the design parameters, the more difficult it is to focus the design process; the diversity of possibilities becomes a distraction. Within these still roomy boundaries, my design evolved in a "see-saw" manner. The "see" mostly involved looking at classic chairs, but it also meant taking a fresh, close look at the lines and shapes of anything else that caught my attention. The "saw" was sketching side and front elevations: drawing by drawing upon what I had seen.

Eventually I came up with a freehand perspective drawing (which, as it turned out, proved to be pretty close to the final form). I attribute its curved rear legs and parallel arms to an adjustable armchair adapted by Phillip Webb from a traditional design for Morris and Co. (c. 1865). The extra-tall back and the piercing crest rail were inspired by a Charles Rennie Mackintosh chair. In general, I feel that the design reflects my attraction to Japanese forms, but the association here is more vague. In fact, although you can attribute certain aspects of a design to historical precedents, original designs invariably incorporate some unpredictable and unidentifiable leap of imagination on the part of the designer.

To bring this idea for a chair down to earth, I had to make a working drawing. In addition to satisfying structural integrity, I wanted to make sure that the chair would be comfortable. Trying to figure this out on paper before anything was constructed proved to be baffling. I consulted the textbooks, but found a vast tangle of heights, depths and angles. These floating figures brought home the fact that because of the endlessly varied shapes, sizes and proportions of people, no non-adjustable chair can be really comfortable for everyone. So, using myself as a model and with tape measure in hand, I sat in a lot of chairs and discovered what I liked about how they felt and then measured them. These clues were enough to make a full-scale side-elevation working drawing, though the only way to confirm or reject my guesses was to build a mock-up.

Working from my drawings, I quickly bandsawed the parts in poplar, then half-lapped and screwed them together. Quarter-inch Masonite screwed to the seat and back and topped by an

*Veleta's first chair taught him that designing doesn't end on the drawing board. The finished chair is walnut with velvet upholstered over foam and webbing on maple frames.*

inch of foam completed the mock-up. I sat down. Naturally, something was not right. I cut some scrap strips of plywood into a slightly different back curve, screwed these pieces directly to the existing frame, and reattached the Masonite. This felt better. Next, I adjusted the tilt of the back by blocking up the front legs. Finally, I was satisfied.

Unfortunately, the motley looking mock-up I now had was not true to my working drawings. The abundance of curves in my three-dimensional design provided no ready reference point, so the dilemma was how to transfer the changes I had made on the mock-up to a final side-elevation working drawing. The solution, provided by a teacher, was to drop a plumb line from various points on the chair (upright and laid on its back) to a grid drawn on the floor. When connected, the points on the grid defined the curves and their relationships. Measurements up from the floor helped too, filling in any missing details.

After completing the working drawing, I began construction by form-laminating the rear legs. If excessive springback occured it would be possible to alter the other parts to fit. I tapered the laminates for strength and appearance following Jere Osgood's method (*FWW #14*, pp. 48-51). Twin mortise and tenons (side by side) connect front and rear legs, and I found the full-scale drawing indispensable for laying out the shoulder lines accurately. By laying the rear leg on the drawing I could tick-off two points of the shoulder and then scribe around at the appropriate angle. I cut the shoulders shy of the line, then trimmed them to fit with a Record 073 shoulder plane.

The inside taper of the front legs begins just below the front rail so joining the rail and legs was straightforward. Joining the rear stretcher to the rear legs, however, was an entirely different matter. First, I made a simple jig for mortising the rear legs. I laid a leg on a scrap of 8/4 poplar, aligning the long layout lines of the mortises parallel with the jointed edge of the poplar. I then traced the inside curve of the leg on the poplar. Bandsawn to the line and clamped to the leg, as shown in the drawing, the jointed edge of the poplar provided a true guide for the fence on a plunge router.

So far so good. Looking at my drawing, I assumed that the shoulder angles of the rear stretcher were the same as those for the rear legs, so I proceeded to cut them with confidence. When I dry-assembled the lower frame, however, everything fit closely except the rear-stretcher shoulders. After a little head scratching, I realized that because the stretcher is canted to be flush with the curve of the leg, its shoulder angles are different than the drawing led me to believe. The only solution was to take the correct angles directly off the clamped-up frame and make a new piece. Orthographic drawings are immensely helpful, but they can sometimes obscure what is really happening in three dimensions. No matter how long and hard you look for trouble spots in a complex drawing, making the piece is the only way to work everything out. Only then can you truly finish the rest of the plans.

Now that the base frame was together I could start building up. This work was straightforward enough, until I came to the arms. These were a three-strip, straight lamination, and I used the male inner half of the rear-leg laminating form to repeat the curve. A single finger joint attaches the arm to the front leg; the full thickness of the arm is mortised into the side of the back stile and screwed from inside. Laying out these joints was a Catch-22 situation. In order to know where the final lines would be, the joints had to be home, but the joints would have to be cut already in order get them home. Caution, trial and error, and one veneer

shim yielded success. It had been so easy to draw!

Now I made the upholstery frame. I chose maple for strength and joined the pieces with bridle joints. Using the existing seat and back curves as templates I bandsawed the frame pieces so that they would sit ½ in. back from the front edge of the chair frame, as shown in the drawings. I also left a gap of ⅛ in. between the chair frame and the upholstery frames to allow for webbing and fabric. (It is better to be a little generous here since it is less trouble to pack the upholstery than to remove more wood from the frames). With the frames glued up, I beveled their faces toward the middle with a spokeshave so that someone sitting in the chair would not "bottom-out" and feel the frame through the upholstery. The seat frames are screwed in place, as shown on the drawing. Finally, since no structural cross-member supports the back of the seat frame, I mortised and screwed metal L-brackets into the rear legs beneath the frame.

Many of the techniques, procedures and pitfalls that I encountered building this chair were new to me, but they were all still woodworking, so at least somewhat familiar. However, when it came to upholstery I felt completely naive. Exploring fabric samples was overwhelming. The choice of color, texture, material and pattern was vast. I finally chose conservatively, picking a traditional burgundy velvet. Before upholstering, it was necessary to finish the chair completely to eliminate the risk of getting finishing materials on the fabric. I chose a rubbed oil-varnish mix. It was a lot of work, but the results were worth the effort.

Now it was finally time to go to the upholsterer. Not being fond of over-stuffed furniture, I had designed the chair for a minimum of padding, just enough to be comfortable. I explained this to the upholsterer and he agreed to do as I bid. But I was shocked by the completed job, which was overly stuffed compared with my expectation. My disappointment wounded the upholster's professional pride. He explained that he had tried less stuffing but the fabric did not "lay right;" it looked "flat," so he adjusted things as he saw fit. In retrospect, I believe he was probably correct, and I am pleased with the firm feel of the upholstery. Viewed from the side, however, the thin back uprights look imbalanced next to the generous stuffing. Fortunately, this imbalance is not noticeable from any other view. The main point is this, before going to an upholsterer be sure that you know what you want and can explain it clearly, and be sure that you are consulted if the upholsterer decides that what you want won't work.

Now that I have some distance from this project, I feel capable of criticizing it. As far as comfort and fidelity to my design are concerned, I feel the chair is a success. However, the design process itself had some drawbacks. Working with side-elevation drawings is useful, but you can end up with a "cookie-cutter" design: two side-elevation outlines held together with rails. Using parts that are rectilinear in section reinforces this feeling, and side elevations alone don't suggest how various members might be otherwise shaped.

The other thing that I learned is the importance of simplifying construction. The amount of time it takes to hand-fit joints through trial and error adds up quickly. This can also be seen as a fault in the design. On the other hand, most pieces of fine furniture require some careful hand work, and I am happy for that. I hope my next chair can be made a little more efficiently, now that I have plowed through the first one. ☐

---

*David Veleta, a graduate of Leeds Design Workshop, makes furniture in Northampton, Mass.*

# Armchair

### Detail: Leg-mortising jig

*Bandsaw scrap to conform to inside curve of leg. Position straight edge of scrap parallel to mortises to guide plunge-router fence.*

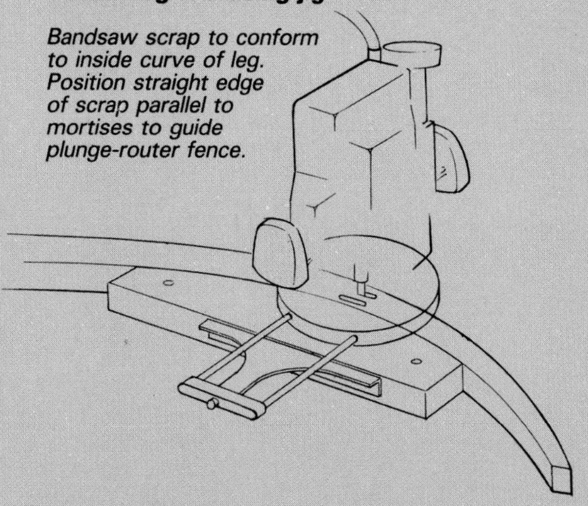

### Plan view

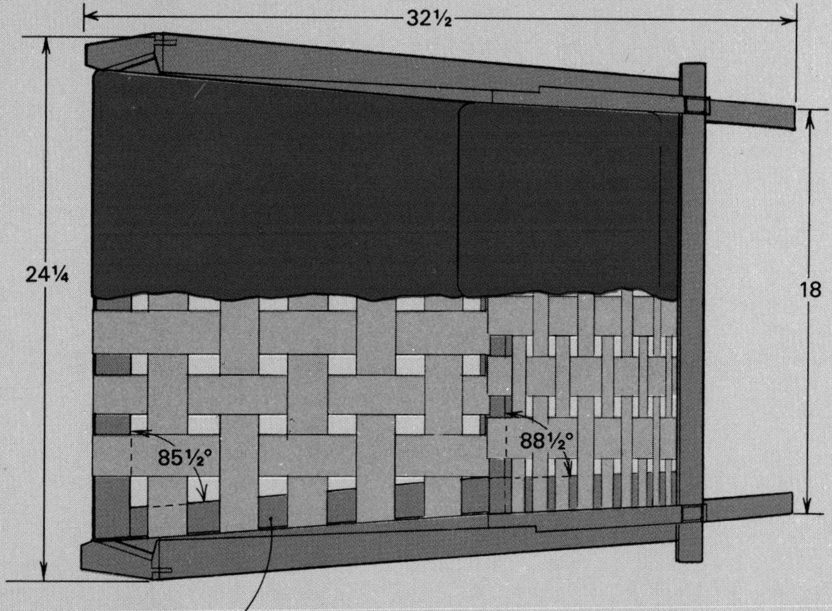

32½
24¼
18
85½°
88½°
Seat frame, 1½-in. wide


### Front elevation

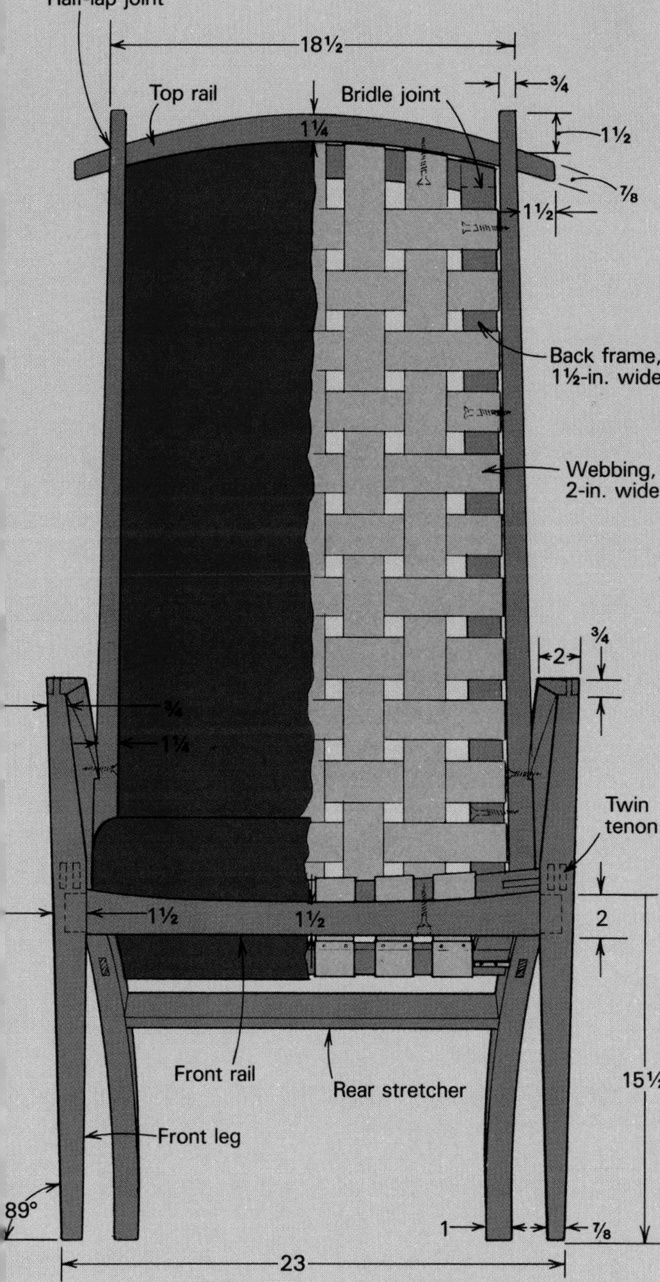

Half-lap joint
18½
Top rail
Bridle joint
1¼
¾
1½
⅞
1½
Back frame, 1½-in. wide
Webbing, 2-in. wide
2
¾
¾
1⅛
Twin tenon
1½
1½
2
Front rail
Rear stretcher
15½
Front leg
89°
1
⅞
23


*Screw upholstered back and seat frames to chair frame. Handsew fabric to back frame after frame is installed.*

### Side elevation

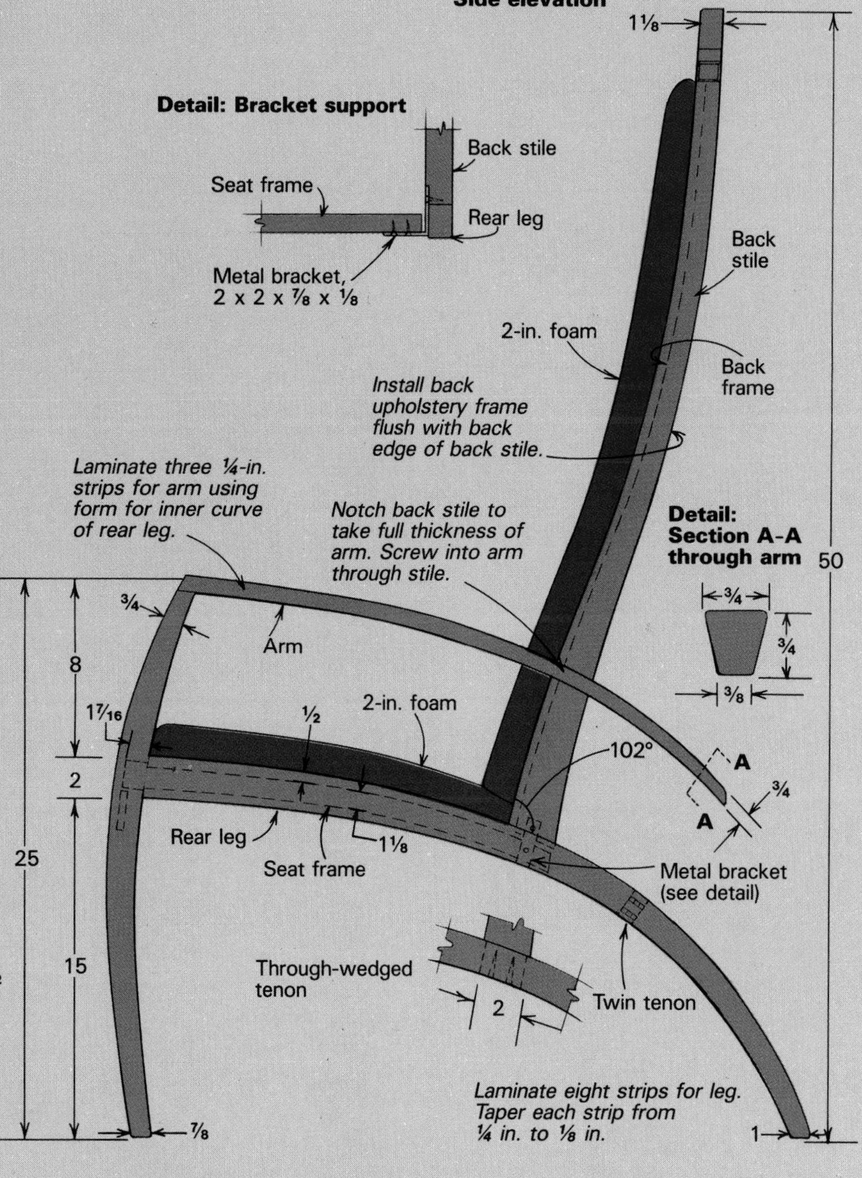

1⅛
Detail: Bracket support
Back stile
Seat frame
Rear leg
Metal bracket, 2 x 2 x ⅞ x ⅛
Back stile
2-in. foam
Back frame
Install back upholstery frame flush with back edge of back stile.
Laminate three ¼-in. strips for arm using form for inner curve of rear leg.
Notch back stile to take full thickness of arm. Screw into arm through stile.
Detail: Section A-A through arm
50
¾
¾
⅜
¾
Arm
8
1⁷⁄₁₆
½
2-in. foam
102°
A
A
¾
2
25
Rear leg
Seat frame
1⅛
Metal bracket (see detail)
15
Through-wedged tenon
2
Twin tenon
Laminate eight strips for leg. Taper each strip from ¼ in. to ⅛ in.
⅞
1

# HAND TOOLS

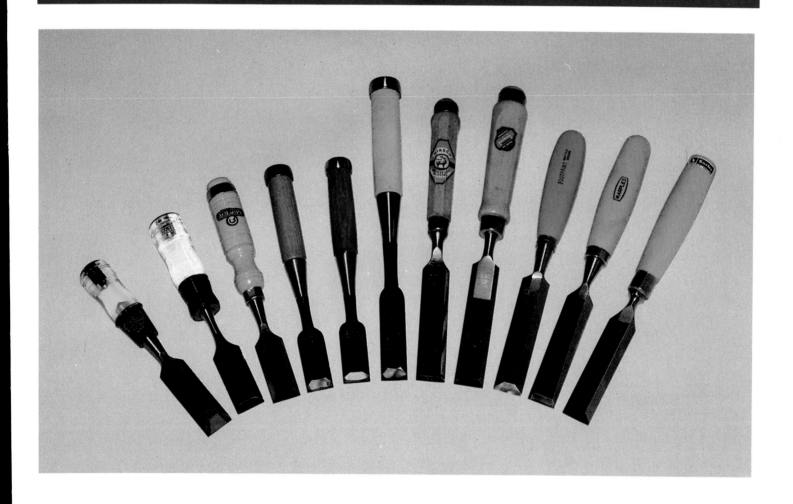

# Making a Panel Plane
## A tool for the consummate cabinetmaker

by Charles Dolan

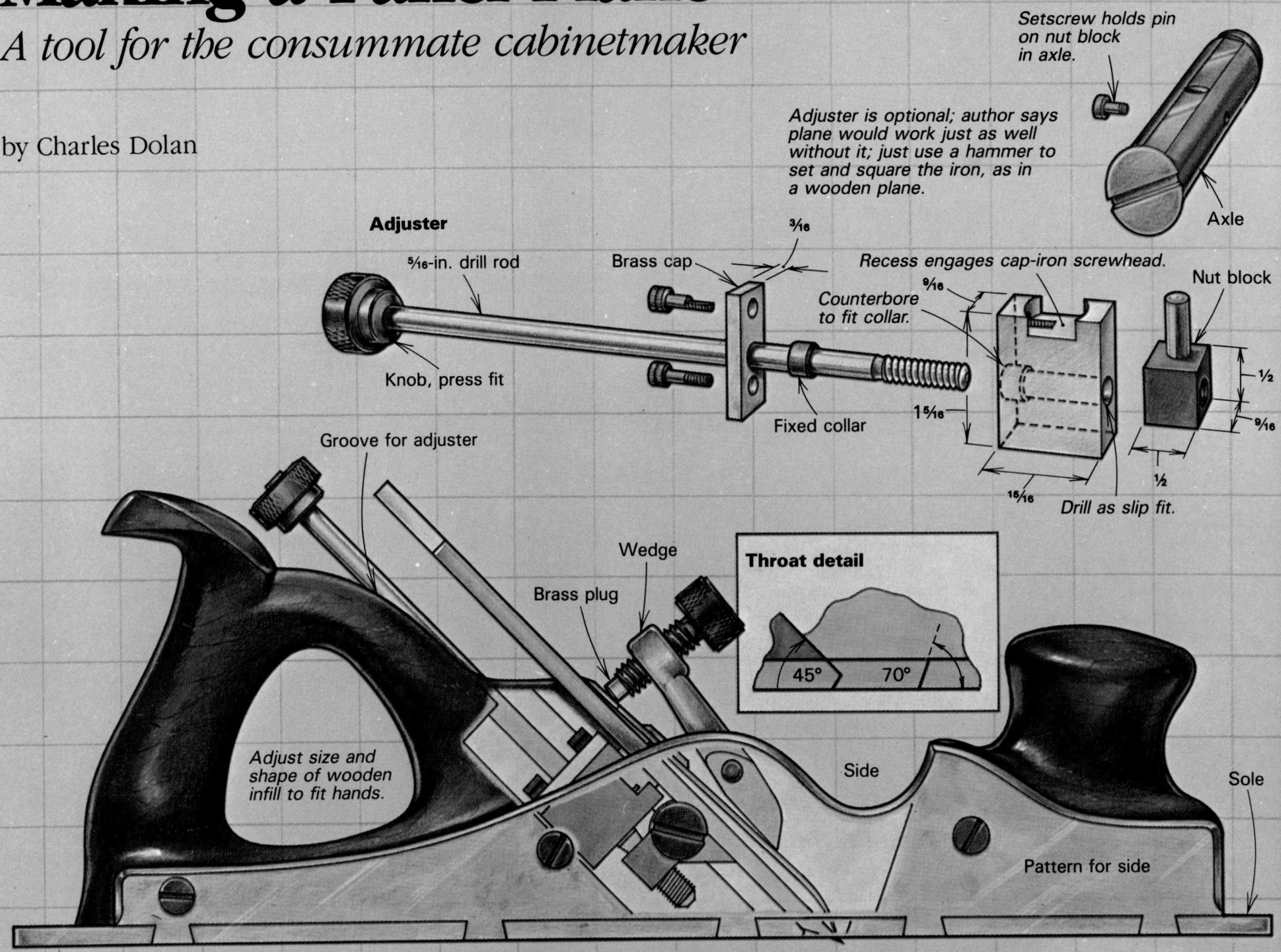

**Setscrew holds pin on nut block in axle.**

**Adjuster**

**Adjuster is optional; author says plane would work just as well without it; just use a hammer to set and square the iron, as in a wooden plane.**

Axle

⁵⁄₁₆-in. drill rod

Brass cap

³⁄₁₆

**Recess engages cap-iron screwhead.**

Nut block

Knob, press fit

⁹⁄₁₆

**Counterbore to fit collar.**

Groove for adjuster

Fixed collar

1⁵⁄₁₆

½

⁹⁄₁₆

½

¹⁵⁄₁₆

**Drill as slip fit.**

Wedge

Brass plug

**Throat detail**

45°  70°

Adjust size and shape of wooden infill to fit hands.

Side

Sole

Pattern for side

---

Some years ago I was fortunate enough to acquire an old cast gun-metal smoothing plane made by J. Rodgers of Minshull Street, Manchester, England and bearing the date 1886. The plane, however, lacked its original iron, and after much searching in vain, I finally decided to try making one for it myself. The resurrected plane performed so well that I thought I'd attempt to make a companion for it—a 16-in. panel plane of similar design—from scratch. A panel plane is the cabinetmakers' refined equivalent of the jack plane used by carpenters and joiners.

At first glance, making a tool such as this might seem too daunting, yet I found the task pleasant on the whole, and ultimately very rewarding. I use the plane almost daily in my work as a specialty contractor and restorer, and I continue to be amazed at the way this hefty tool seems to sit down on the wood, leaving me free to push and control it rather than having to force the iron into the work.

It is very unlikely that a tool such as this could ever be made commercially today and few of the old ones ever find their way to the marketplace. When new, this grade of plane cost several times the price of the Stanley/Bailey tools, which were, in turn, much more expensive than the wooden planes in general use. Planes like this were the prerogative of the most conscientious craftsmen executing consummate work to the highest standards.

The first step is to make the iron, a process described on p. 43. Those who have already made steel tools will be quite familiar with how it is done. This article, however, is more concerned with cutting and soldering the body and flattening the plane's sole. Even if you never make a plane, flattening is a process that you can use to bring any plane sole to very close tolerances, something the factories can no longer afford to do.

**Cutting the body**—My first inclination was to have a casting made, as the idea of making a wooden pattern and having someone else translate it into shiny gun-metal was particularly appealing. However, none of the foundries that I approached would cast fewer than five pieces (at substantial cost). Plane makers at the turn of the century often made plane bodies by joining the sides to the sole with through dovetails in the metal. I decided to do the same, soldering the joints together. This proved to be a first-class way to fabricate a body in brass and I am sure that it will do just as well in steel for those who prefer it.

I bought one bar of rolled brass 3 in. by ¼ in. by 16 in. and two of 2⅝ in. by ³⁄₁₆ in. by 14 in. The two smaller pieces had been cut from sheet and accordingly required some flattening with a ham-

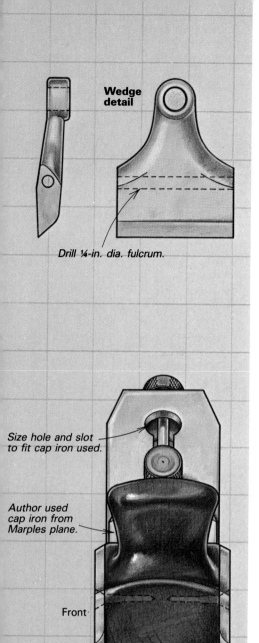

**Wedge detail**

Drill ¼-in. dia. fulcrum.

Size hole and slot to fit cap iron used.

Author used cap iron from Marples plane.

Front

1 square = 1 inch

*A plane like this is comparable to the highest grade commercial tools at the turn of the century. Such tools are scarce, and rarely reach the marketplace, but you can make one from dovetailed brass plate. The author spent many hours working on the screw-type adjuster (right), but realized at the end that he seldom changed the set of the iron. He recommends that readers omit the adjuster and simply set the iron's depth and lateral adjustment by tapping with a hammer, as in a wooden plane, with the wedge screw snug but not fully tight.*

mer. [Conklin Brass, 345 Hudson St., N.Y.C., N.Y. 10014 sells brass by mail order. The bars should cost about $70, postpaid.]

Using blue layout paint (a colored shellac that cuts down glare and allows you to see fine scribed lines), I marked out the sides very much as I would a drawer joint. I cut the narrow tails in the sides first and used these to mark out the broad pins in the sole.

A number of methods will work to remove the waste—jigsaw, hacksaw, jewelers' piercing saw, metal-cutting bandsaw, whatever is most convenient. Various files serve to work down to the layout lines. Files that have been used on steel don't work too well on nonferrous metals, and it is worthwhile having a set for each. The most difficult part of the job is to produce flat square lands between the tails on the side plates. I ground one edge of a 10-in. second-cut file (a medium-cutting file) to an angle that allowed me to clean out right into the corners (photo, p.42).

When the tails are finished, use them to mark the sole. Rough cut first, then clean up with a four-square file with one of its sides ground smooth to act as a safe bearing surface. When the joints are as near perfect as you can make them, you can drill a line of holes across the sole to begin the mouth slot. Clean up the edges by filing, but leave the throat undersize for the time being, because final shaping will be done after the iron is fitted.

**Soldering**—Ordinary 50/50 solder is not in any way difficult to work with provided three requirements are met: there must be adequate heat, a good flux, and surgically clean surfaces, as shiny and clean as a guardsman's buttons. Wire the parts securely together and use some pieces of hardwood to spread everything square and true. You can provide sufficient heat by placing the work on one of the rings of an electric cooking stove at medium heat for half an hour. Bring the work to a heat where the solder will just go pasty but not run freely and then heat locally with a propane torch, flowing the solder into the joints all around. Use plenty of solder or it may not completely fill the joints (I had to reheat some spots with the torch and refill them). It is safe to ignore any runs or drips—they won't stick to the stove rings, and the excess can be filed away from the plane when it has cooled.

When all is run in, stand back, turn off the stove and leave well enough alone until cold. Moving the work too soon will cause frosted joints that will have to be heated all over again. Then remove all the excess solder and file the work flat.

**Making the infill**—I chose walnut for the infill as it is both strong and easy to work. I recommend a bed angle of 45° for the general work to be expected of this plane. This can be cut on the

*Brass can be bandsawn with an 18-TPI blade (top left). The metal has been sprayed with layout dye, a colored shellac that cuts glare and shows fine scribe lines clearly. With both sides clamped in the vise (top center), bandsaw marks can be filed away. To reach into tight corners (top right), grind the edge of a file to an angle that will fit. For soldering, pre-heat the brass on a stove (left) until it reaches a temperature where the solder almost flows. Use a propane torch to bring each successive joint up to full heat.*

*To flatten the sole, test it on a reference plate of heavy glass spread with blue oil paint (left). The thin paint transfers only to high spots on the sole. File and scrape these areas down, then test again on the glass, repeating until the critical areas at toe, heel and throat are fully covered by blue (for the rest of the sole an even spread of about 70% is adequate). A metal scraper (above) is used something like a paring chisel, working in a crosshatched pattern. The tool takes a series of fine, powdery shavings about ⅛ in. wide.*

tablesaw using the miter gauge. I next cut the grooves for the adjuster. I put a lot of time into making the adjuster, but have decided it was more trouble than it is worth. I'd advise you not to bother with one, but simply to adjust the iron by tapping it with a hammer when necessary. The set of the iron in this sort of plane is not changed very often anyway.

For the actual shaping of the handle and knob, I simply drilled through the block to define the important radii inside and out, then I gradually shaped the wood with rasps and files, checking the fit and feel often. There are much faster ways to shape a handle, of course, and anyone in a hurry will doubtless use his own methods. But the handle and knob, to me, are critical parts of the plane, and I wanted to get mine right.

**Making the wedge**—The wedge is cut from a solid slab of ½-in. brass by drilling adjacent holes around its perimeter (line drilling). I began the shaping with a big rat-tail file, then moved on to a half-round, a small flat file, and a smooth file for the finishing cuts. I then evened out the surface with 200-grit wet/dry paper.

It remains to tap the wedge for the screw, and drill a hole clear through it for its pivot pin, which is a length of ¼-in. drill rod with one end peened slightly so it is a friction fit in one side of the plane body.

The wedge screw is best made on a metalworkers' lathe but an alternative would be to epoxy a hardwood knob onto the head of a ½-in. socket-head screw.

**Finishing up and flattening**—Mount the iron in the plane and start to refine the size of the mouth slot. I feel that there has been a recent tendency to overstate the advantages of a very narrow mouth and would personally never have one thinner than ³⁄₆₄ in. for a plane such as this, which will occasionally be required to "shift some stuff." Make sure that the mouth is square across the body and have the top of the front edge sloping away from the iron by a few degrees, as shown in the drawing on p. 40.

The last job is to flatten the sole. The heating of the body during soldering will inevitably have left some distortion, which will now have to be removed. The most suitable low cost way to flatten the sole of a plane is by filing and scraping, using a surface plate as a reference.

Flattening to a plate is a technique well worth learning as it allows precision flats to be put on any machine pieces or tools with just hand work and patience. You will need some good files and also a scraper, which can be bought quite cheaply or can even be made from an old file for nothing. You will also need a tube of artists' thalo blue or Prussian blue oil paint, some light oil and of course a surface plate.

If you do not expect to be doing much of this work, buy an 18-in. by 12-in. rectangle of plate glass, ¾-in. thick. To avoid twist, house the glass in a strong plywood box supported by only three feet. Plate glass is ground and lapped to quite fine limits of flatness to achieve optical truth and if treated carefully is more than adequate for this purpose—you should be able to flatten to tolerances well under a thousandth. If you intend to do more serious fitting than that, I would advise you to buy a granite bench plate of the same size. Avoid all used cast-iron plates like the plague. These are very sensitive to abuse and there is no easy way of diagnosing or correcting faults. A piece of new glass is infinitely preferable to an old iron plate that may have been used as an anvil.

Fit the iron in the plane and tighten the wedge screw to stress the tool to working conditions. Apply a thin glaze of paint and oil over the surface of the plate and lightly rub the sole of the plane on it. The blue will adhere only to the high spots.

Carefully file these blue areas away. For control and precision, press the front of the file down with your left thumb, and file in short strokes right on the mark. When the first set of spots has been filed off, repeat the marking and remove the new ones. The high spots will increase in number and gradually spread all over the surface of the sole.

When the file begins to do as much harm as good, change to the scraper, which can remove fine, precise shavings. The scraper should be kept sharp and is used rather like a paring chisel being pushed into the work. By repeated marking and scraping, the spots will progressively become more numerous until they cover the whole of the surface. Work slowly and deliberately and crosshatch the cuts frequently. There is no denying that this is a tedious business, but it is, in fact, very reliable.

You can now strip everything down and finish file the metal parts. A good rub with 120-grit wet/dry paper will give a very smart finish to the brass. All the steel parts can be blued with cold gun-bluing solution if such meets your fancy.

You now have a tool that will last several lifetimes and which will constantly delight you with its performance. I hope that the use of the plane as well as the elementary fitter's skills that you have learned in making it will provide you with greater scope and more satisfaction in your trade.  □

*Charles Dolan lives in Montreal West, Quebec, Canada.*

## Making the iron

I feel that the principal reason old irons (and modern Japanese ones, for that matter) are held in such high regard is that they have great weight and thickness, and not that the steel is superior to modern alloy steel. For my iron I chose an alloy of carbon, manganese, chromium, tungsten and vanadium, a steel made in Sheffield by Sanderson Kayser Ltd., and sold as Precision Ground Flat Stock Oil Hardening Non-Distorting Pitho Alloy Tool Steel. Similar tool steels are available from any industrial hardware supplier and should work as well, as long as they contain tungsten and vanadium for toughness.

Blanks are available in a great size range—mine (18 in. by 2½ in. by ¼ in.) cost $18. There is still enough of it left for two more irons. The steel is sold in the annealed, soft state—22 on the Rockwell hardness scale. With a little patience, a good hacksaw, some sharp files and a drill press, an afternoon is all you need to make as good an iron as can be had at any price.

Much has already been said about making tools in past issues of this magazine, so I will concentrate on some fine points. I decided to hacksaw the iron to length at a 25° bevel angle, in order to save a lot of filing afterwards. Not much has been written about hacksawing. A rigid frame and a good high-speed-steel blade make a lot of difference. Saw with long full strokes without forcing the blade. Some 3-in-1 oil in the kerf will ease friction. If the blade begins to lead off the line, lightly dress the teeth on that side with a whetstone to get the blade going

straight again. If it continues to run out, put in a new blade and saw from the other edge until the cuts meet.

To file the bevel, position the iron with the bevel uppermost and horizontal in a vise. I'd recommend a clean, sharp 14-in. mill-bastard file for this job. It helps a good deal to rub chalk over the faces of the file and use it only until it starts to slide. Then clean the file with a file card and remove any "pins" with the point of a soft iron nail. Then chalk the faces again and continue.

You will by now have seen how much effort is needed to work this stuff, but there should be some light at the end of the tunnel. You must next mark out the size and position of the hole and slot for the cap-iron screw. I used the cap iron from a Marples plane.

Drill a hole the width of the slot at the bottom and one big enough to clear the head of the screw at the top. Back the iron with a piece of mild steel to prevent the drill from grabbing when it breaks through. Then drill carefully with the drill running slowly, and use enough pressure on the quill to make the drill really cut. It is essential to clamp the work firmly. Trying to hold the work free-hand would be very dangerous. The swarf will be coming off the drill at a very high temperature and will certainly burn skin. Lastly, be sure to wear good eye protection.

The slot is cleared by drilling a row of adjacent ⅛-in. holes around the perimeter of the piece to be removed. When the row is complete the cutout will fall free, looking something like a metal centipede. If any of the holes don't quite touch each other the waste can be cleared by sawing or chiseling. The edges of the slot are cleaned up by "drawfiling" smooth, a technique in which the file is used crossways along

the work, as explained in *FWW #46.* Next file the top corners of the iron at your chosen angle and finish-file all the edges smooth. Do all the filing now as the next step is to harden the steel after which it can be shaped only by grinding.

The article on pp. 87-90 of this book explains basic heat treating, but this plane iron is rather heftier than most of the tools the author discusses. I found I needed a charcoal barbecue force-drafted by a hair dryer to generate enough heat. Also, I tested the temperature of the steel by using a magnet, because it is very difficult to discern color changes in the midst of the fire. I attached the magnet to a longish wire, and gradually fanned the flame hotter, testing from time to time until the magnet was no longer attracted to the steel. Then I quenched the iron in 2½ gallons of old motor oil in a 3-gallon metal bucket. Quenching produces all sorts of spectacular fulminations—have the bucket's lid handy in case the oil catches fire, and on no account use a plastic bucket.

If you have used the magnet correctly and not overheated the steel, no scale will have formed—the iron will come out of the oil clean and smooth, apart from some minor surface staining. I cleaned the surface with 200-grit wet/dry paper and tempered the iron in a kitchen oven at 200°F for two hours. This brings it to a hardness of about 60 RC, tough enough to be driven through a nail without chipping and capable of taking an edge you could shave with. Despite the myths about laminated irons, Victorian blacksmiths, magic swords and hobbits and dragons, I am certain that properly heat-treated modern alloy steel is in every way superior to the old stuff.  —*C.D.*

# Tips From a London Carving Shop
## A sharp pencil cuts through the problems

by Ben Bacon

Carving is one of the most difficult woodworking skills to acquire, so it's not surprising that many craftspeople find it frustrating to try to carve scrolls, foliage and other ornaments on furniture. Lack of experience is part of the problem, but the major factor is that most woodworkers go about carving in the wrong way: they start at the end, carving fine details first, instead of at the beginning of every carving job—drawing.

While there's no magic way to make carving easy, you can simplify the process by dividing it into five steps, with each step laying the foundation for the next. The most basic step is to do a good detailed drawing, as shown in figure 1. Drawing makes you think concretely about the carving and decide what it should be, then the next four steps—making a model in clay or plasticine, basic construction, rough carving, and final carving or "improving"—can reduce to manageable tasks the complexities of bringing your ideas alive in wood.

Many inexperienced carvers avoid drawing, saying "it stifles creativity" or "I'd rather do real work." Actually the reverse is true. If you skip the drawing, you'll always have the "what exactly is it that I wanted to make?" feeling, which leads to mistakes, confusion and wasted time. Remember the old axiom that carving is 75% drawing, 15% sharp tools and 10% manual dexterity—learn to draw, either by attending classes or by sketching furniture. For most people, carving without drawing is like sawing without measuring.

To illustrate this five-step approach to carving, I'll describe how I carved an ornate wall mirror in a style popular in early 18th-century England, but the process can be applied to any carving. I picked this piece because I like 18th-century carvings and had never done a mirror in this style. I don't make exact copies, however. Here in England, one-of-a-kind antiques are treasures because they are unique, and making exact copies is considered unethical. So for this project, I combined elements from several mirrors to develop a new design. You can also study a particular period until you know enough about its fashions and techniques to think like a craftsman of that period, and design a new piece in an old style. Knowledge is important here—otherwise you might design something that never would have been made in the period you've selected. I found most of the information I needed on mirror construction and style of carving in furniture books and museums. I also consulted my sketchbooks, which contain drawings I've made of some of the period pieces we've restored in the London carving and gilding shop where I work.

Once I've completed my research, I usually do a detailed line drawing. Unless I'm working in a style that's new to me, I make one drawing and modify it until it's right, rather than develop a whole series of intermediate sketches. First I study the old pieces until I understand how the original makers handled problems of design, composition and construction, then I build on these ideas when I do my drawing. I prefer full-size drawings, unless the piece is 8 ft. to 10 ft. high, in which case I reduce it to $\frac{1}{10}$ or $\frac{1}{12}$ scale, with some full-size detail drawings where necessary.

For the mirror, I drew a rectangle the size of the frame and divided it into three areas, corresponding to the carved pediment on top, the bottom plinth, and the mirror glass and pilasters in between. Then I roughly sketched the ornaments to get an idea of the feel of the piece. You often have to move the ornaments around or make them larger or smaller so they work well together. A good way to do this is to draw the ornaments on separate pieces of tracing paper. When I was satisfied with the rough sketch of the mirror, I refined it by drawing in all the fine details.

Before you go any further, step back and make sure all the components fit together well. Is the piece in proportion? Is there enough detail? Are the curves regular and flowing? Does the whole have unity? It's easier and cheaper to resolve these questions on paper now rather than in wood later.

Even when you're finished drawing, you still may be confused about how to begin carving. This is where step two, modeling in clay or plasticine, comes in. Drawings, even with full front and side elevations and a plan view, are still two-dimensional. You can't draw undercutting or all the subtleties of texture and depth that are essential to a good carving. If you can't visualize these three-dimensional characteristics exactly in your mind, you should model. Usually, you have to model only the areas that confuse you, but you can do the whole thing. Modeling is easy—just put the clay on a board and shape it with your fingers or the modeling tools available at most art supply stores. You could also make an extra copy of your drawing and work the clay right on it to establish the initial outline. If you need only a rough guide for elevations, model roughly; if you need to work out all the details, model finely. The object of drawing and modeling is to remove doubt, so do whatever is necessary to establish the shape of the carving in your mind so that you can tackle the wood with confidence. Once you've done that, it's time to work in wood.

If you're making something small such as a statue from a single piece of wood, you can begin carving right now. If you're doing a large sculpture or a piece of furniture, you'll probably have to do some construction work or cabinetmaking first. Most

Photos, except where noted: Robert Aberman

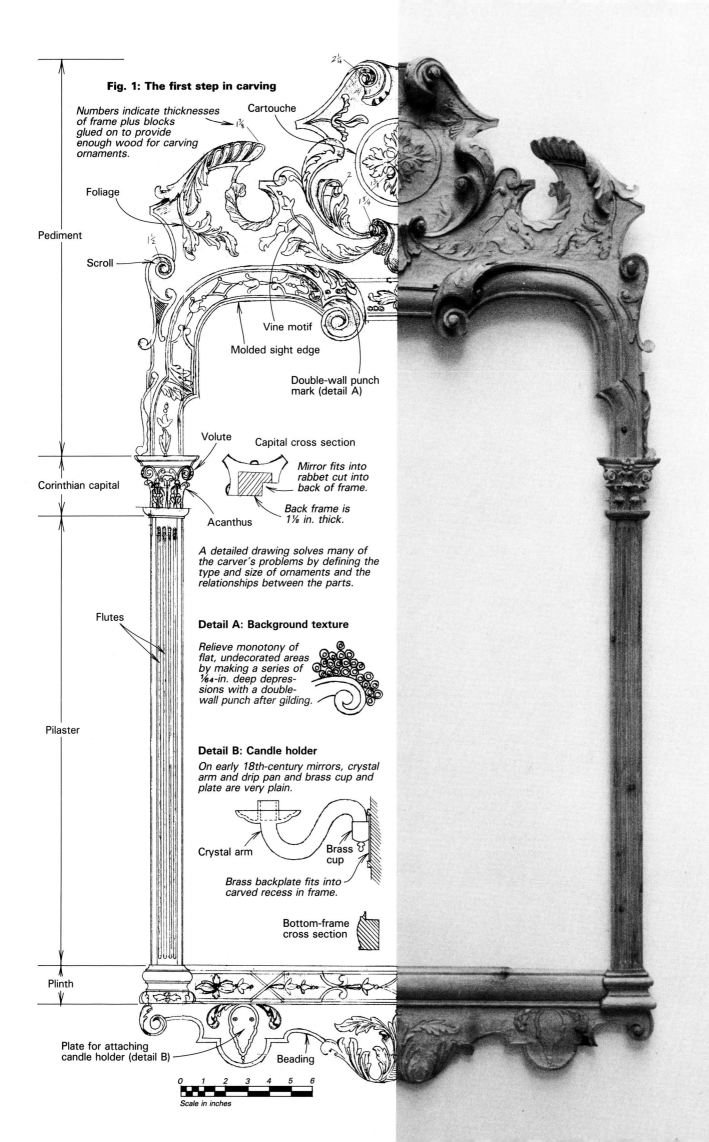

**Fig. 1: The first step in carving**

Numbers indicate thicknesses of frame plus blocks glued on to provide enough wood for carving ornaments.

Cartouche

1⅛

2¼

Foliage

2

1¾

Pediment

Scroll

1½

Vine motif

Molded sight edge

Double-wall punch mark (detail A)

Volute

Capital cross section

Corinthian capital

Mirror fits into rabbet cut into back of frame.

Acanthus

Back frame is 1⅛ in. thick.

A detailed drawing solves many of the carver's problems by defining the type and size of ornaments and the relationships between the parts.

**Detail A: Background texture**

Flutes

Relieve monotony of flat, undecorated areas by making a series of ¹⁄₆₄-in. deep depressions with a double-wall punch after gilding.

Pilaster

**Detail B: Candle holder**

On early 18th-century mirrors, crystal arm and drip pan and brass cup and plate are very plain.

Crystal arm

Brass cup

Brass backplate fits into carved recess in frame.

Bottom-frame cross section

Plinth

Plate for attaching candle holder (detail B)

Beading

0 1 2 3 4 5 6

Scale in inches

45

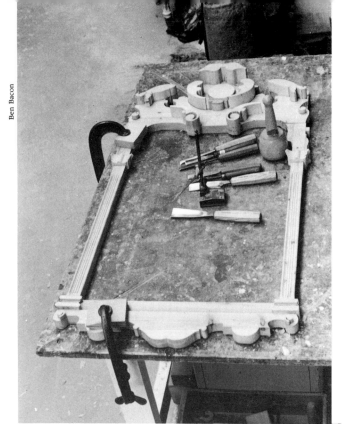

Ben Bacon

*Shaped wooden blocks (above left) make the basic frame thicker in areas where ornamentation will be carved. When the frame is nearly finished, Bacon uses a small veining tool to recut the fine fluting into the gesso (above right).*

traditional mirror frames are simple constructions. For a gilded or painted frame, clear pine is fine; if the frame is to be waxed or treated with some other clear finish, walnut, oak or mahogany will look better. For the mirror shown here, I first made a 1⅛-in. thick, half-lapped frame and assembled it dry. Then I transferred the outline of the drawing, bandsawed the frame to shape, and cut the rabbet for the glass before gluing up the basic frame. Since this frame is flattish with projecting ornaments, you can glue on ½-in. to 1½-in. shaped blocks where you need more wood for carving scrolls, capitals, or column tops and foliage. The frame will be gilded, so the gluelines won't show.

Now you're ready to start the rough carving. Next to making the initial drawing, this is probably the most daunting moment—there's something intimidating about taking the first cut. But forge on. And don't be discouraged at the amount of time it has taken to get to this point—your preliminary work will soon bear fruit in speed and ease of carving. As you begin, remember that there are two carving steps, rough carving and final carving. Don't ever try to combine the two and plunge right into the final details. That would be similar to dovetailing a drawer before cutting the sides to length. Beginners carving a leaf often carve the stem first, or if they're carving a head, they carve the nostrils first—only to find that they have to recarve the piece because the stem is in the wrong place or the nose is too long.

Rough carving deals with *big* shapes. I generally use #2 through #6 gouges, 20mm to 35mm wide, and form the shapes quickly. You should carve big areas, thinking exclusively about elevations, dominant forms, relationships of planes, and overall appearance and feel. Carve as if you were looking at the piece from five to ten feet away. This is somewhat difficult to explain in terms of foliage and ornaments, so you might be able to visualize the process better if you think in terms of more human shapes. If you were carving a head, for example, at this stage you'd do the general shape of the skull and hair first; you'd carve the details into these bold forms later. On the mirror, I started at the top and worked down, first knocking the corners off the bandsawn shapes and establishing all the impor-

tant heights, such as the slightly domed cartouche and other ornamentation at the center of the top, and the overall shape of the two capitals on the pilasters. Then I roughed in the molding that surrounds the glass and all the scrolls. Measuring carefully with dividers and calipers, I checked the positions of the ornaments against the drawing, and I used a depth gauge to ensure that paired ornaments were the same height.

Still thinking in terms of rough carving and big shapes, refine your forms slightly. If you were carving a head, at this stage you'd rough in the eye sockets but not the eyelids or eyebrows. You're still looking for an overall feel, not minute detail. On my mirror, this involved lowering and shaping the background behind the ornaments, more clearly defining the molding and scrolls, and giving overall shape and flow to the leaves.

Now stand back from the piece and ask yourself if you like the proportions and balance. Do the overall shapes and directions of the various parts work well individually and as a group? Remember that the immediate impact of a piece most often sells it visually and financially. This impact is not achieved through fineness and detail of carving, but by overall harmony and cohesiveness. This is the whole point of rough carving, and why traditionally it was considered the most difficult part of any job and was assigned to the most experienced workers with imagination and foresight. If you're not satisfied with the general look, carve a little more. Since you haven't carved any details yet, you'll be refining and adapting, not ruining any good work.

Don't be afraid to experiment at this stage, either. Often you can improve your drawing by exploiting the grain, color and other characteristics of the wood to give your work more direction, liveliness and flair. If you encounter major problems, though, you've probably skimped on the initial steps.

Once you're pleased with the overall form, you're ready to start the last stage, final carving or "improving." Here carving irregularities are smoothed out and the final detail carved, at last. Concentrate on the finish of the piece: remove all tool marks, clean each surface, and make sure that the curves and lines are sweetly flowing. In a sculpture of a head, you would now carve the eyelids and eyebrows and do the final modeling of the mouth. In furniture carving, you'd give the leaves and ornaments their final shape and do the fine modeling, fluting and undercutting.

For this style of gilded mirror, this final detail-carving isn't done in the wood, but in a thick layer of gesso (a liquid made from powdered chalk and animal sizing, which is the consistency of cream when wet and like plaster when dry). The gesso is brushed on the unfinished wood before gold leaf is applied. This is what I did for the mirror, but the carving steps would be the same if you wanted to do all the carving in wood.

Most of the fine detail on the mirror involves flat foliage work, such as the carved molding around the sight edge or the foliage around the large ornaments on the top. To be effective, this shallow, ⅛-in. deep foliage must be fine and delicate. After drawing on the foliage, use a fluter or a V-tool to carve around the outside of the pencil line to a depth of about ⅛ in., thereby separating the foliage from the background. Then recess the background area about ⅛ in. so the foliage is proud. This is a tedious process, especially in this style where the background must be smooth and regular so that the foliage appears to float on top.

After the background is lowered, you can "set in" or redefine the pattern outline with a variety of shaped carving tools. Take a tool with a shape similar to the section of the outline you're shaping, and press the tool straight into the surface at about a 90° angle to create a crisp, vertical wall between the outline and the background. The trick to setting in details is to match the curves and transitions of one tool shape to the next to create a smoothly flowing, harmonious shape. If marks left by the carving tools show, each detail will seem awkward and asymmetric. Once the outline is set in, model the top surfaces by carving in the flows, swells and dips that give the leaves life and movement. This setting-in and modeling procedure is always followed in flattish foliage work, be it on frames or furniture, and is also used in low-relief work, such as the carving on drawer fronts in 18th-century American lowboys and highboys.

*Tool marks spoil leaf.*

*Well-cut leaf flows smoothly.*

When the final carving is completed, set up the work again and have another look before you do any finishing. Is the detail harmonious throughout? Do the forms and detail read well? Are there any unsightly walls or areas of excess wood, especially around the edges? This is your last chance to tidy up the piece before you or someone else has to live with it for a long time. If you're happy with it, carry on.

Most traditional work is gilded or covered with a clear finish, but finishes for carving are pretty much a matter of personal choice. A word of caution, though: Most high-gloss or thick finishes such as polyurethane, varnish and lacquer make carving look harsh and brassy. It's much better to bring out carving's soft look with thin shellac, wax or oil. I water-gilded the mirror shown here in the traditional way (*FWW #46*, pp. 82-85). After applying and burnishing a 23½-karat gold leaf, I punched the background areas with a ¼-in. double-wall punch (available from Wood Carvers Supply Co., 3056 Excelsior Blvd., Minneapolis, Minn. 55416) to visually relieve the monotony of the large, undecorated surfaces behind the carving. This background

*Author's gilded 18th-century-style mirror frame is a new design based on careful study of original pieces in museums and furniture anthologies.*

texturing is done after gilding so the gold will be forced down into the ring impressions. I then toned the mirror (photo, above) to simulate aging, and fitted the brass and crystal swan-neck candle holders and the beveled glass.

The steps I've outlined won't solve every problem you encounter—carving is too vast and subtle a craft to be bound by a few rules. But they do work in most cases; in fact, they're still taught to apprentices in traditional carving shops, where planning and foresight are considered as important as hand skills and tools. Approaching work systematically will always reduce problems, or at least present them in such a way that they can be tackled more effectively and with a minimum of heartache. It's the difference between having a street map in an unfamiliar town and relying on strangers for directions. □

*Ben Bacon is an American carver now working in London, where he completed a five-year apprenticeship in carving, gilding and framing. Drawings by the author.*

# Shopmade Bowsaw

## Tailor its size to suit the job

by Simon Watts

Although an ancient tool—they've been used at least since Roman times—bowsaws still have some distinct advantages over either powered bandsaws or saber saws. They need no electric power, are light and portable, and take up little space when dismantled. Also, they can be fitted with different-width blades—narrow ones for sawing tight curves, wider ones for more general work. Bowsaws are especially useful when you have to saw a curve with a changing bevel. I find my saw an excellent tool for cutting the curved transoms and sculling notches in the lapstrake boats I build.

You can tailor the bowsaw described here to your specific needs. For example, you might want a deeper throat, more or less blade length, a handle at each end or no handle at all. You could also make different-size stretchers to accommodate several lengths of blade. I've found the saw shown here to be a convenient size, well-balanced and not too heavy. The blade is 20¼ in. from pin to pin, one of several standard sizes available. Blades can be bought, or you can make them from broken bandsaw blades, just as long as they're sharp and still have some set. To cut the blade, just touch it to the corner of a grinder and snap it

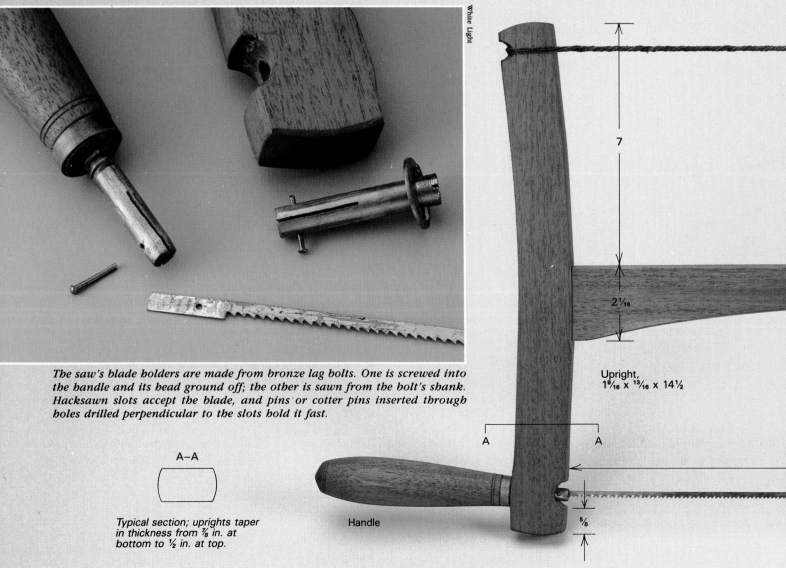

White Light

*The saw's blade holders are made from bronze lag bolts. One is screwed into the handle and its head ground off; the other is sawn from the bolt's shank. Hacksawn slots accept the blade, and pins or cotter pins inserted through holes drilled perpendicular to the slots hold it fast.*

A–A

*Typical section; uprights taper in thickness from ⅞ in. at bottom to ½ in. at top.*

Handle

Upright, 1⁹⁄₁₆ x ¹³⁄₁₆ x 14½

7

2¹⁄₁₆

A          A

⅝

off. Drill ³⁄₃₂-in. holes at each end, but as a kindness to your twist bits, soften the spring steel first—heat the ends red-hot with a torch, then let them cool slowly.

Use any strong, straight-grained hardwood for the frame. Mahogany is my first choice because it looks good with copper and bronze, and I like the way the color gets richer as the wood matures. First make patterns in cardboard for the curved uprights and stretcher, then cut out rectangular blanks for these parts. Mark out and cut the mortises before doing any shaping. To form the notches for the blade holders and tensioning cord, clamp the uprights together edge-to-edge and drill a ⅞-in. dia. hole with a sharp Powerbore or machine spur bit centered on the crack. Inevitably, half the hole will be in each upright, neatly forming the notch. Drill ⅜-in. holes for the blade holders, shape the uprights, and cut the tenons on the stretcher, which should fit without forcing. For looks and lightness, I tapered the uprights in thickness from ⅞ in. at the bottom to about ½ in. at the top.

I turned the handle on a lathe, but you could equally well carve it by hand—an octagonal section might give a better grip than the more usual round. Without a metal collar, called a ferrule, the handle would eventually split, so I made a ferrule by cutting a ½-in. long section off a piece of ¾-in. thin-walled copper pipe. I tapped the ferrule into the end grain of the handle's rough blank, then used a heavy vise to press it into the end grain, flush with the surface. I then turned the blank to the shape shown. If you have a chuck center for the tailstock, drill the handle for the blade holder while it's still in the lathe; if not, you would do best to drill it before turning.

For the hardware, you'll need two ⅜-in. by 4-in. bronze lag screws and a ⅜-in. bronze washer. I use bronze only for the looks and because it doesn't rust. You can get bronze hardware from Jamestown Distributors, 22 Narragansett Ave., Jamestown, R.I. 02825. You could perfectly well use cheaper and more easily obtainable steel lags, however. For this saw, I pinned the blade in the holder with brass escutcheon pins I happened to have around, but they bent when I tensioned the frame. Stainless-steel cotter pins would do better. Make the blade holders as shown in the photo on the facing page. Mount the blade and tension it by looping nylon cord—¹⁄₁₆-in. to ⅛-in. dia.—loosely three or four times around the notches in the upper end of the uprights and then twisting it with a tapered piece of hardwood. You'll find that thinner blades need more tension than thicker ones.

Bowsaws can be used with the teeth pointing either way—you can cut on the push stroke or the pull. There's no need to reverse the blade—just turn the saw around and grasp it by the upright. I usually use bowsaws two-handed, especially when cutting tight curves with a thin blade. Speed and assurance come only with practice, but it's well worth persevering. □

*Simon Watts is an* FWW *contributing editor who spends his summers in Nova Scotia and his winters in California teaching boatbuilding.*

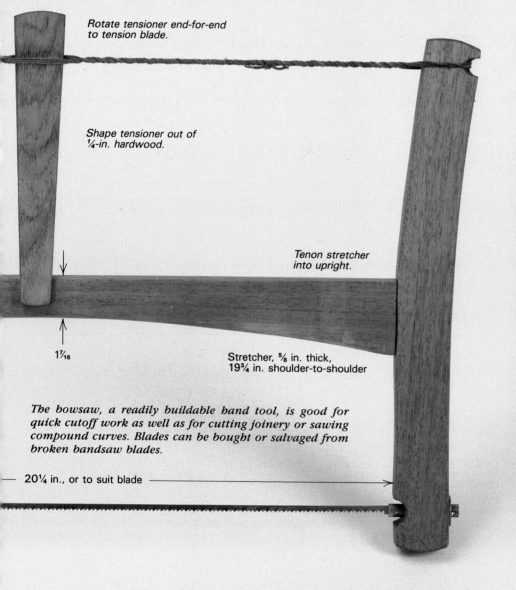

Rotate tensioner end-for-end to tension blade.

Shape tensioner out of ¼-in. hardwood.

Tenon stretcher into upright.

1⁷⁄₁₆

Stretcher, ⅝ in. thick, 19¾ in. shoulder-to-shoulder

**The bowsaw, a readily buildable hand tool, is good for quick cutoff work as well as for cutting joinery or sawing compound curves. Blades can be bought or salvaged from broken bandsaw blades.**

20¼ in., or to suit blade

*To bore notches for the blade holders and tensioning cord, clamp the uprights together and center the bit line between the parts.*

*Frank Klausz created his ideal work area in a small space by pairing a hefty workbench with a utility table. The bench provides lots of clamping power and the table contains storage bins and drawers.*

# A Classic Bench
*Workstation's center is worth building right*

by Frank Klausz

I f you are a serious woodworker who prefers handtools, one of your first investments should be a hefty, well-designed workbench. My joiner's workbench, shown in the photo above, is the heart of the ideal workstation. Based on a traditional design, my bench is outfitted with shoulder and tail vises and steel dogs that can clamp a workpiece in a variety of positions. And it's built solidly enough to be stable under any kind of sawing, planing, scraping, or pounding.

Near my workbench is a wooden chest with my chisels and other handtools, all sharpened and ready to use. To make it easier to use the chest I built a small platform that raises the box

10 in. to 15 in. off the floor. If your bench is near a wall, you might prefer a wall-hung cabinet, as workmen in Europe often do. A 27-in.-high utility or helping table with a 40-in. by 60-in. work surface is located about 4 ft. behind the bench. This table, shown in figure 1 on the facing page, houses 12 plastic drawers (available from W.W. Grainger, Inc., 5959 W. Howard St., Chicago, Ill. 60648): small ones for dowel pins or screws, larger ones for chisels and other tools. Larger planes and portable power tools fit on its bottom shelf. Don't try to save steps by putting the drawers in your main workbench—if you clamp a large piece in the shoulder vise, you can't open the drawers. You could build drawers

Frank Klausz

*Assemble the 27-in. high utility table with mortise-and-tenon joints. Locate shelves to fit standard plastic drawers for small tools and odds and ends. Larger tools go on the bottom shelf. Make the 40-in. by 60-in. top from particleboard and 1/4-in. maple plywood. To plane long boards, right, Klausz uses a bench slave with the shoulder vise.*

that open from both sides of the bench, but putting them in the utility table is much handier.

By arranging my workspace like this, I have plenty of room to work comfortably and can easily step over to get a chisel or a handful of screws. Everything is at my fingertips. The workbench and table also work well together. I do all of my planing, sawing and joint cutting on the bench, then assemble the pieces on the table. The table, being several inches lower than the bench, is perfect for holding a chair or a chest of drawers at a comfortable work height. When I'm assembling on the table, I still have a clear workbench for trimming joints and other last minute touches.

Apart from the knots in the base, my workbench looks pretty much like any other traditional cabinetmaker's bench. Our ancestors invested more than 1,000 years in developing its design and they left very little for us to change. When I worked in Europe, I visited many different shops and the workbenches were always the same design and about the same size—7 ft. by 3 ft.—although the bench height was tailored to the height of the cabinetmaker who used it. Apart from little touches like the stops and oil dish shown in figure 2, the only difference I found was that some craftsmen treat their benches with loving care and some don't.

All the European cabinetmakers I visited used similar shoulder and tail vises to hold their work. The bench screw (available from Garrett Wade Co. in New York City and Woodcraft Supply Inc., Woburn, Mass.) on my shoulder vise gives it about a 7-in. capacity. It can hold a short piece by itself or, working with a bench slave (see figure 2), hold a long piece in an efficient work position. The slave is a notched 1½-in. by 2-in. piece of hardwood tenoned into a cross-lapped base. A wooden block hanging from two wooden ears connected with a dowel supports the work.

The tail vise can hold wood in the same manner as the shoulder vise, but it's most often used with the bench dogs to lock pieces down flat on the benchtop. I use traditional square metal dogs (I ordered mine from Garrett Wade). It's crazy to try to use dowels for bench dogs. They might work if the dogs just kept the wood from sliding on the benchtop, but they must also clamp the work tightly against the top. Square dogs have slightly angled faces so you can pinch the board between the jaws, then drive the dogs down to snug the piece against the top. A workpiece suspended in midair between the dogs will chatter when you work on it.

A good bench should be built of hardwood, heavy enough so that you can't move the bench with a stroke of your handplane. Hardwood is expensive, so I cut costs by buying green wood and drying it myself or scavenging rejects at local sawmills. The bench legs and base are cut from second- or third-class chunks of red oak, white ash and beech—any hardwood will do. It's not scrap, but it's not good enough for furniture.

Though each workbench is a little different, depending on the material you have to work with, don't drastically alter the basic dimensions shown on the drawings. You could go a little wider or longer without creating a monster, but scaling the bench down and using much thinner stock eliminates the weight essential to a good bench. The correct height of the bench is easy to determine. Stand up, put your hands next to your pockets and your palms parallel to the floor. The distance between your

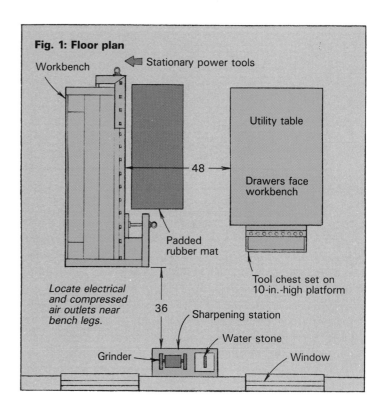

**Fig. 1: Floor plan**

Workbench

Stationary power tools

Utility table

48

Drawers face workbench

Padded rubber mat

Tool chest set on 10-in.-high platform

*Locate electrical and compressed air outlets near bench legs.*

36

Sharpening station

Water stone

Grinder

Window

palms and the floor equals the bench's height. If you make the bench higher, you can't take advantage of your body weight when handplaning. Using your body weight, not just your arm muscles, will give you hours of easy planing while the other guy is pushing and shoving.

**Construction of the base**—My bench is supported by a sturdy base: two heavy uprights joined by a pair of wide stretchers. The pieces for the uprights are mortise and tenoned; the leg-to-top-brace joints are through-wedged; the others blind. So the bench can be broken down to be moved, the stretchers are fastened to the legs with bolts and captured nuts. To position the top, bullet-shaped dowel pins in the top braces of the uprights fit into holes

bored in heavy bearers screwed to the underside of the bench top. The weight of the top holds it on the base.

Begin base construction by determining the height of your bench, as discussed above. I'm 6-ft. tall and my bench is 33-in. high. Adjust the leg length, up or down, in the area between the stretchers and feet, then cut all the parts as shown in the plan. I cut the mortises with a hollow-chisel mortiser, but you could chop them by hand or mill them with a router. Drill a bolt hole through each stretcher mortise from the inside of the mortise. Insert the stretcher tenon and use the hole in the leg as a guide to bore into the end of the stretcher. Remove the stretcher and deepen the hole to accept a 6-in. hex-head bolt. I rout a slot at the end of the bolt hole to house the captured nut.

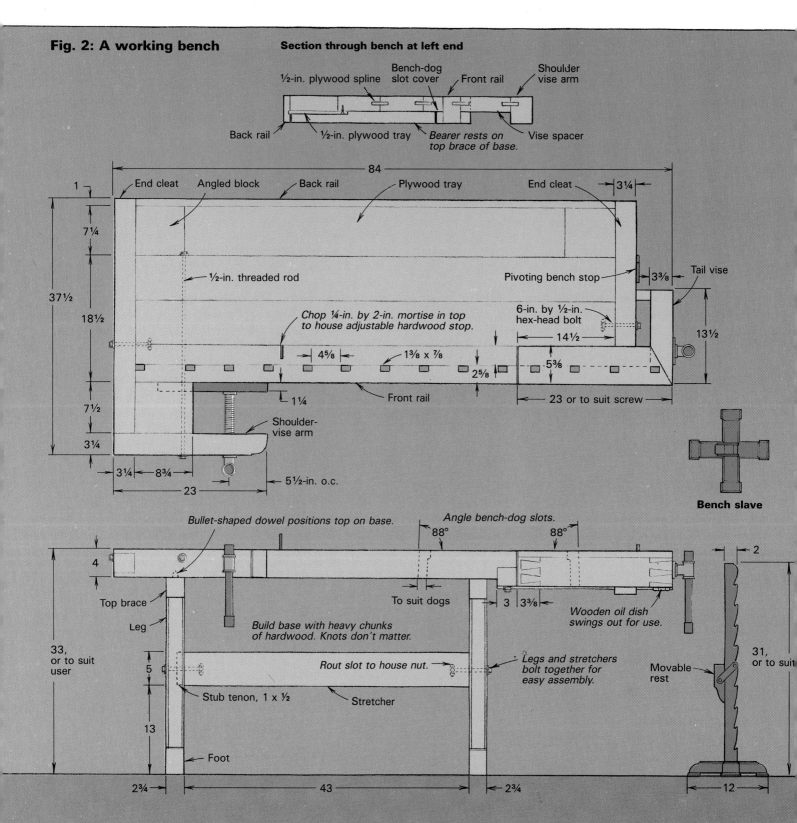

**Fig. 2: A working bench**

**Assembling the top**—The benchtop, with its tool tray and two vises, is the most complicated part of the bench so you must measure very carefully when making the parts. It consists of 2½-in. thick boards sandwiched between a thick front rail, which is mortised for the dog slots, and the tray and back rail assembly in back. Both ends are capped by heavy cleats. All pieces are splined and glued. The vises themselves are constructed separately and then fitted to the top.

For the 2½-in. stock, I used quartersawn maple, but you might want to jazz up your top by using several different woods. That's OK if the different species are about the same density and will move with the seasons and wear at similar rates. Lay out the glue joints so that the notch for the tail vise is created in gluing up—

this avoids a lot of sawing and awkward cleaning up later. Since you want to reinforce the shoulder vise with a threaded rod through the top, as shown in the drawing, remember to bore a ½-in. diameter hole through each component before assembly. You can take care of the splines and minor alignment problems when you attach the vise. Glue the 2½-in. pieces together with 1½-in. by ½-in. plywood splines, trim the assembly to size, then cut the grooves for the end cleats, as shown in the drawings. Although the glued-up top is big and heavy, you can cut the grooves by standing the top on end and passing it over your tablesaw's dado head. If this sounds too nerve-racking, use a router. Always reference the top surfaces of the benchtop and cleats against the fence or router base so the grooves will line up. Next,

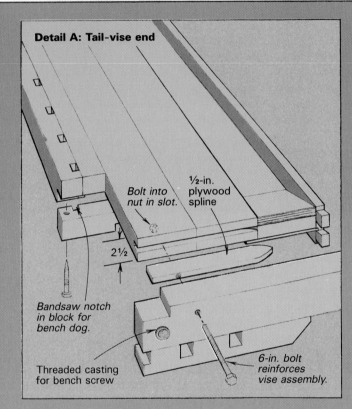

**Detail A: Tail-vise end**

Bolt into nut in slot.

½-in. plywood spline

2½

Bandsaw notch in block for bench dog.

Threaded casting for bench screw

6-in. bolt reinforces vise assembly.

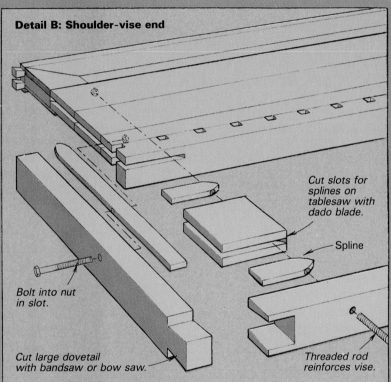

**Detail B: Shoulder-vise end**

Cut slots for splines on tablesaw with dado blade.

Spline

Bolt into nut in slot.

Cut large dovetail with bandsaw or bow saw.

Threaded rod reinforces vise.

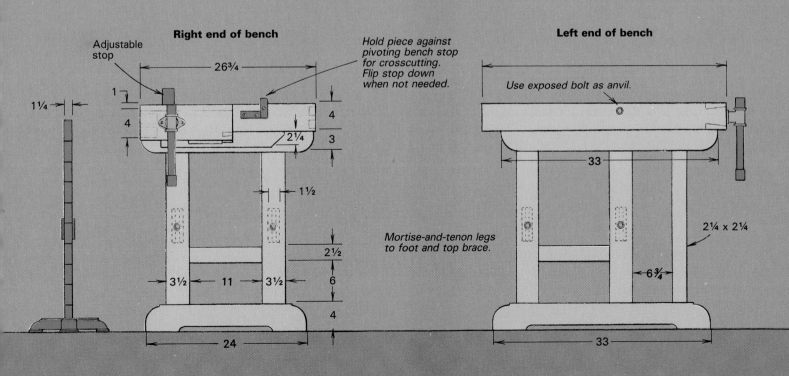

**Right end of bench**

Adjustable stop

Hold piece against pivoting bench stop for crosscutting. Flip stop down when not needed.

26¾

1¼

1

4

4

2¼

3

1½

2½

3½    11    3½    6

24

4

**Left end of bench**

Use exposed bolt as anvil.

33

Mortise-and-tenon legs to foot and top brace.

2¼ x 2¼

6¾

33

*Benchtop is positioned on the base by bullet-shaped dowels, left. The base itself is low-grade hardwood. Before assembling the top, above, chisel out dadoed slots so L-shaped dogs fit flush with top.*

mill the front rail and the bench-dog slots in it. Note that the front rail and tail-vise face must be the same thickness so the bench-dog slots line up. I cut the slots with a dado head on my radial-arm saw, then chisel the L-shaped notch for the dog's head by hand. After assembly, I glue a backing piece to the front rail to enclose the notches. Test the fit of each dog before you glue up. If they are too tight, it will be hard to trim the slots after the rail is glued to the top. I set the dogs into the bench at an 88° angle, nearly perpendicular to the surface. A greater angle might increase the dog's down-clamping pressure, but you'd lose the ability to reverse the dogs and use them to pull something apart—the dogs would slide out of the angled slots. I use the dog's pulling ability in my restoration work. If I have to disassemble a chair that's too fragile to withstand much hammering, for example, I reverse the dogs, fit the chair parts between the padded dogs, then crank the tail vise out until the joints separate. This technique also works on other kinds of furniture.

The tool tray is a piece of ½-in. plywood screwed to the underside of the 2½-in. top and housed in a groove in the back rail, which is in turn dovetailed to the end cleats. I glued two angled blocks in each end of the tray to make it easier to clean.

The end cleats support the two vises. Six-inch by ½-in. hex-head bolts and captured nuts reinforce the splined glue joints. The holes are not too long to bore with standard hand or power auger bits. Chisel or rout the blind notches for the nuts in the underside of the top. I leave the bolt heads exposed. That good-looking hex head makes a handy little anvil for blunting nails so they won't split wood, or for tapping out hinges or other hardware. Before you glue on the cleats, however, make the vise parts and assemble everything dry to make sure it works okay.

**Design of vises**—I prefer 2-in. dia. wooden bench screws for vises, but they are so rare that most people use metal screws, even though they don't have as nice an action. Tailor your vise to fit the length of the screws you have. The shoulder-vise screw in

the drawing is 1¼ in. in diameter by 13 in. long. The tail-vise screw is 1¼ in. by 17 in. Be sure to have the screw (and all other hardware) before you build the vise.

The tail vise has two parts—a jaw assembly and guides fixed to the benchtop. The jaw assembly consists of a heavy jaw and face piece dovetailed together. The jaw houses the screw, the face piece is the same thickness as the front benchtop rail and is likewise slotted for bench dogs. A guide rail, parallel to the jaw, is dovetailed to the face piece and a runner connects it and the jaw. This assembly is further held together by two top caps, whose top surfaces will be flush with the benchtop. Two guide blocks bolted under the bench are notched for the runners that guide the jaw assembly. The vise-screw nut is housed in the end cleat.

I cut the large dovetails on the bandsaw or with a bowsaw. The dovetails are very strong, beautiful and show craftsmanship. Finger joints would work, too. You can cut these on the tablesaw. The dog slots are cut using the same method as on the front rails. Close off the open side of the slots by gluing on a piece of ¼-in. plywood after the jaw assembly is glued up.

To ensure proper alignment, bore the holes for both vise screws on a drill press before assembly. I first bored a 1⅞-in. dia. hole for the depth of the embedded nut, then, using the same center point, bored a 1¼-in. dia. hole through the piece for the screw. After boring the end cleat, I clamp the tail vise to the bench and use the drill bit to mark the center of the screw hole. Unclamp, transfer the center point to the outside of the piece and bore a 1¼-in. dia. hole. Make fine adjustments with a rasp.

After assembling the tail vise on the bench, I close it and, to make sure its faces are parallel, saw through where the end of the vise meets the bench with a sharp, fine-point backsaw, being careful to keep the saw between the two pieces. Then I glue top-grain cowhide to each face.

The shoulder vise is much more straightforward, but you may have a little trouble with the treaded rod running through the top to reinforce the dovetail joining the end cleat and vise arm.

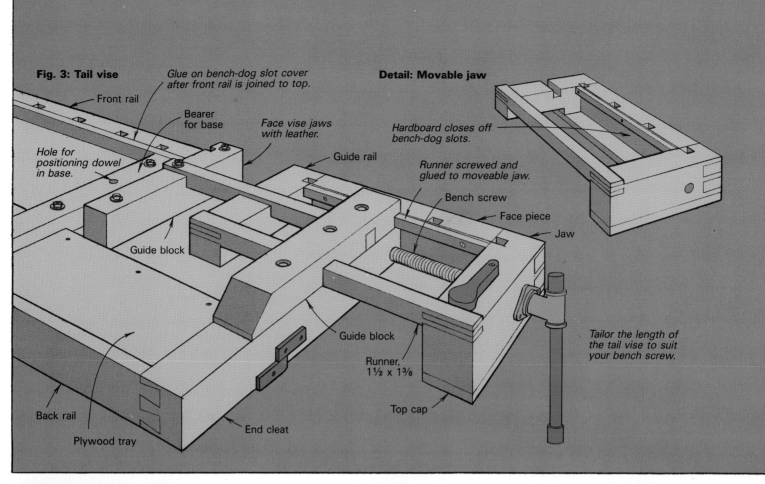

**Fig. 3: Tail vise**

Glue on bench-dog slot cover after front rail is joined to top.

Front rail

Bearer for base

Face vise jaws with leather.

Hole for positioning dowel in base.

Guide rail

Guide block

Guide block

Runner, 1½ x 1⅜

Back rail

Plywood tray

End cleat

Top cap

**Detail: Movable jaw**

Hardboard closes off bench-dog slots.

Runner screwed and glued to moveable jaw.

Bench screw

Face piece

Jaw

Tailor the length of the tail vise to suit your bench screw.

*Flip-up bench stop is handy for crosscutting near tail vise, top left. Carved oil cup under vise swings out when you need to lubricate plane sole or saw, left. Underside of bench near shoulder vise, above, shows hardwood bench stop and the track that guides vise jaw.*

Since you drilled the top pieces before assembly, you should be able to clear the splines and any misalignments by running a bit on a 12-in. extension in from the front and back. Then bore the vise block and arm separately before attaching the unit to the top.

To finish the bench, level the top with a sharp jointer plane, checking by eye, straightedge or winding sticks, then sand with a large vibrator-type finish sander. I put two coats of Waterlox (available at large building supply houses) on every wood surface, then add several more coats to the top. Next rub on paste wax for a beautiful shine that will protect the top from glue or stain. Wax your bench regularly and resurface it every year. I believe lots of people, including customers, look at your bench as an indication of your craftsmanship. Besides, I am spending about 10 hours a day looking at and working at the thing, and it should be beautiful. □

*Frank Klausz makes furniture and restores antiques in Plucke-min, N.J. Klausz's two videotape workshops,* Dovetail a Drawer *and* Wood Finishing, *are available from The Taunton Press. For more on building workbenches, see FWW #4.*

# Testing Wood Chisels
## *Lab finds no secrets in the steel*

by Bill Stankus

A wood chisel is a very simple tool, but there are so many brands to choose from, and such a wide range of prices, that deciding which one to buy is anything but simple. It helps if you can examine a chisel, try the edge with your thumb, and heft the tool to feel how well the handle fits your hand. It's important that a chisel *feel* right. But what about the most important part—the steel? Are the more expensive chisels made of better steel? Just by looking, there's no way to tell how a chisel will sharpen or hold an edge. Advertising copy isn't any help either. Some tool-sellers' claims notwithstanding, there hasn't been a magic blade forged since Excalibur.

As a tool consultant and woodworker I've used many chisels over the years, and I've noticed that they don't all perform in the same way. Determined to find out why, I enlisted the help of Paul Horgan, a metals quality-control manager and amateur woodworker. We decided to run a series of metallurgical tests on chisel blades to see if steel quality differs between brands and, if so, what effect this has on sharpening and edge-holding properties. *Fine Woodworking* agreed to pay for the tests, which were conducted by Anderson Laboratories, Inc. in Greendale, Wisconsin, and confirmed by another Wisconsin lab. We don't claim our tests to be the last scientific word on tool-steel metallurgy, but the results do shed some light on a confusing subject.

We couldn't test every chisel on the market, so we chose 11 popular brands: Craftsman and Stanley (United States); Footprint, Marples and Sorby (England); Hirsch and Spannsage (West Germany); Iyoroi, Oiichi and Sentora (Japan); and Mifer (Spain). So we wouldn't base our findings on a chance bad chisel, we tested two of each brand bought from mail-order and retail outlets around the country. To correlate the lab analysis with performance, I sharpened the chisels on waterstones (800-, 1200-, 4,000- and 8,000-grits) and worked with them at the bench.

Interestingly, despite the wide range in price ($7.60 for the Footprint to $31.95 for the Oiichi), the tests showed that 8 of the 11 chisels tested are made of very similar water-hardening tool steels. The lab tests did show some variations in carbon content and alloys, but no significant differences except for the Sorby, which was a different type of tool steel, and the Sears Craftsman, which was a plain carbon steel with a low carbon content. The other U.S.-made chisel, the Stanley, was made of a plain high-carbon steel. Differences that directly affect how the tool sharpens and holds an edge—hardness and grain size—were more pronounced and quite noticeable during sharpening and use, suggesting that the type of steel probably has less to do with how well a chisel works than does how carefully the factory forges, grinds, and, most importantly, hardens and tempers the tool.

To make sense of the lab tests, it's helpful to understand a little about tool metallurgy. To cut well, a wood chisel needs steel hard enough to hold an edge for a reasonable time but soft enough to be sharpened on benchstones. It also has to be tough enough to resist chipping when hammered through dense wood such as maple. Mild steel, the stuff found in angle iron and I-beams, won't do the job because there's no practical way to make it hard enough.

Adding carbon to steel—anywhere from 0.45% to 1.40%—makes steel hardenable. Plunged red-hot into water, brine or oil, carbon steel's crystalline structure changes to a brittle, harder form. A cutting edge made from this brittle steel would fracture, so the hardness is reduced slightly by reheating the steel to a lower temperature. This is called tempering and makes the steel much tougher. Tool steels, which were actually developed not for hand tools but for industrial applications such as stamping dies and metal cutters, are a type of high-carbon steel that has been alloyed with metals such as chromium, manganese and vanadium to improve hardenability and wear resistance. The main difference between plain high-carbon steels and the tool steels commonly used for chisels is in the quality control. Tool steel is manufactured to a more rigorous set of quality standards than is ordinary high-carbon steel. Its chemical makeup is constantly tested, and each batch is routinely inspected for microstructure, cleanness, hardenability, and surface and internal flaws. This consistency means that the consumer is less likely to get a bum tool, but it also makes things easier for the manufacturer since, theoretically, each batch of steel will react about the same way when it's forged and hardened, thus producing tools of identical quality.

We had the labs perform three basic kinds of tests on the chisels: chemical analysis, hardness testing and inspection of the steel's microstructure. First, they mounted the $300 worth of new chisels on an abrasive cut-off wheel and sawed them up into small chunks in order to get at the steel inside. A spectrographic analysis of the pieces revealed their chemical makeup to be very similar. It's worth noting that steel standards vary from country to country, but all of the foreign-made chisels closely matched the U.S. definition of a family of tool steels called W-type water-hardening, except for the Sorby, which is a shock-resistant S-type tool steel. Both U.S. chisels were non-tool-steel grades of carbon steel. Carbon content of the 11 tools varied widely, from a barely hardenable 0.50% in the Sears to 1.24% in the Footprint.

Hardness, the quality most discernible at the bench and that which most governs a tool's edge-taking and edge-holding properties, was measured with a tool called a Tukon tester. Here's

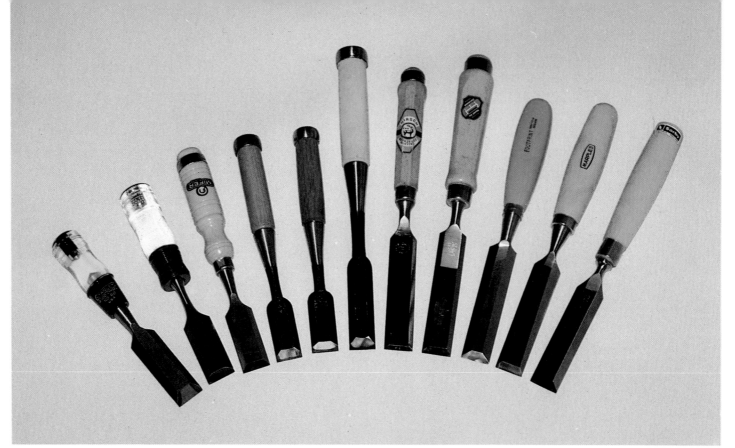

*The test chisels had a wide range of handle styles and blade lengths—both important factors to consider when selecting a chisel. From left: Stanley, Craftsman, Mifer, Sentora, Oiichi, Iyoroi, Hirsch, Spannsage, Footprint, Marples and Sorby.*

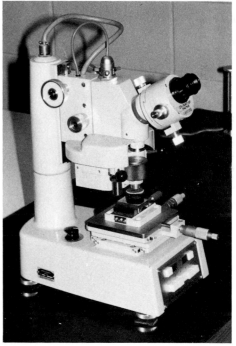

*To measure hardness, two slices from each chisel were cast in plastic and polished, then they were mounted on the Tukon tester (above right), which calculates hardness by measuring the penetration of a diamond stylus.*

how the test works: One longitudinal and one transverse slice of each chisel's blade are cast into a small disc of thermosetting plastic. The sample is polished and mounted under the tester's microscope. A tool with a tiny, diamond-tipped stylus called a Knoop indenter is next placed on the steel. Weighed down by a 500-gram weight, the indenter penetrates minutely into the steel; the deeper it goes, the softer the steel. The depth of the nick is measured and converted to a hardness number on the Rockwell C scale. The microscope allows the technician to place the indenter away from soft spots or contaminants that might give a false reading. For our tests, three separate readings were taken near the cutting edge on each sample and the results averaged.

As the chart on p. 58 shows, the chisels varied in hardness by as much as 7 points on the Rockwell C scale (RC), which ranges from 20 to 70. At 52 RC, the Sears Craftsman was the softest of the test chisels—too soft to hold an edge. The three Japanese chisels were the hardest at more than 60 RC.

**Hardness tells only part** of a tool's metallurgical story. Peering through a microscope, a metallurgist can learn a lot about a steel's properties just by looking at it, reading its texture just as a wood technologist might study pores to identify a wood sam-

## Chisel Characteristics

| | Brand name | Price (1-in. chisel) | Steel | Average hardness at cutting edge* | Carbon content | Grain size | Blade thickness at top of bevel | Handle | Edge-retention rating |
|---|---|---|---|---|---|---|---|---|---|
| **United States** | Stanley | $10.25 | High-carbon (AISI 1095), trace of carbides | 59.5 RC | 0.94% | #11 | 9/64 in. | Plastic, round | Very good |
| | Sears Craftsman | $ 7.99 | Plain-carbon (AISI 1050), no carbides | 56.0 RC | 0.50% | # 9 | 5/32 in. | Plastic, round | Poor |
| **England** | Footprint | $ 7.60 | W-type tool steel | 59.0 RC | 1.24% | ** | 9/64 in. | Beech, oval | Very good |
| | Marples | $13.15 | W-type tool steel | 60.0 RC | 1.18% | # 6 | 1/8 in. | Boxwood, round | Fair (edge breaks down when dull) |
| | Sorby | $11.75 | S-type tool steel, no carbides | 57.5 RC | 0.57% | #10 | 11/64 in. | Boxwood, round | Very good |
| **West Germany** | Hirsch | $14.95 | W-type tool steel, no carbides | 58.5 RC | 0.80% | #11 | 3/32 in. | Ash, octagonal | Very good |
| | Spannsage | $ 9.25 | W-type tool steel, no carbides | 59.5 RC 62.0 RC | 0.81% | #11 | 9/64 in. | Ash, round-flats | Very good |
| **Japan** | Iyoroi | $27.95 | W-type tool steel, mild steel back | 61.5 RC | 1.04% | # 8 | 7/32 in. | Boxwood, round | Excellent |
| | Oiichi | $31.95 | W-type tool steel, mild steel back | 63.5 RC | 1.09% | # 9 | 11/64 in. | Red oak, round | Excellent |
| | Sentora | $ 9.95 | W-type tool steel, mild steel back | 60.5 RC | 0.81% | #10 | 3/16 in. | Red oak, round | Excellent |
| **Spain** | Mifer | $ 8.10 | W-type tool steel | 59.5 RC | 1.10% | # 8 | 9/64 in. | Boxwood, round | Fair (edge breaks down when dull) |

*Knoop indenter, 500-gram load. Average of three readings.
**Not determined.*

*The chart above lists significant chisel characteristics. The prices given are the retail prices paid for the test chisels; current prices may vary. The edge-retention rating is based on the results of the bench test. The micrograph at right (magnified 100X) of a section of the Marples chisel shows the steel's microstructure. The small white particles are primary carbides, a hard-wearing combination of carbon and iron that improves edge retention. The large dark island is an oxide inclusion.*

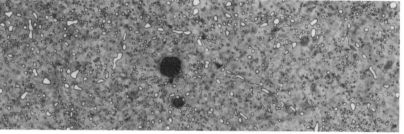

Anderson Labs

ple. The lab tests sought two important microstructures in our chisels: carbides and grain. Carbides are a compound of carbon and iron present in the steel as it comes from the mill. Ideally, when the chisel is heated and quenched, some of these very hard carbide particles will disperse throughout the crystalline structure of the steel. The higher the initial carbon content of the steel, the more likely it is that the heat-treated chisel will contain carbides. Carbides are desirable because they greatly increase the wear resistance of the steel. In theory, a blade with fine and evenly distributed carbides will hold an edge longer than will a blade of the same hardness with no carbides.

Grain refers to the crystalline particles that make up the steel. The size of the grain is a measure of the "fineness" of the steel. A fine grain is important for edge retention and, in combination with evenly distributed carbides, will give the longest edge life. Grain is measured on a numerical scale: #1 is extremely coarse, #10 or above is extremely fine. Any steel with a grain size of 8 or higher can be considered a fine-grain steel.

Again, the results of the laboratory tests more or less agreed with my findings at the bench. But the really interesting thing that the microstructure analysis showed is that hardness alone doesn't necessarily mean the best edge retention. After sharpening each chisel, I pared away at a variety of hardwoods and pine until the edge dulled, then I resharpened. I noticed a considerable difference in edge retention between brands. The six chisels that contained carbides (Footprint, Marples, Mifer, Oiichi, Iyoroi and Sentora) seemed to take an excellent edge from the waterstones. With their hard edge and evenly distributed carbides, the Japanese chisels held keen edges longer than any of the Western chisels. The Hirsch, Spannsage, Sorby and Stanley—all fine-grained but slightly softer than the Japanese chisels—took and held very good edges. The Mifer and Marples are almost as hard as the Japanese chisels, yet when dull their edges seemed to fragment and become ragged. It took longer to get them sharp again because more steel had to be removed during the sharpening process. This is due, I suspect, to their relatively coarse grain. The Sears Craftsman chisel fragmented badly as it dulled.

A common complaint about Japanese chisels is that they're brittle, and tend to chip. I experienced this once when I cut a mortise with a new Japanese chisel without first sharpening it. Perhaps because I removed a fair amount of steel at the initial sharpening, however, chipping wasn't a problem with any of the Japanese chisels in the test.

The lab examined each steel sample for impurities such as slag. These are called inclusions (photo, above). From a metal-

# A visit to a chisel factory

by David Sloan

Buck Bros. has been making woodworking tools in Millbury, Mass., since 1853, when Charles and Richard Buck picked out a spot with good water power. Water and steam turned the wheels at Buck Bros. until the 1940s, but today wood chisels are produced on modern machines. The factory also makes carving and turning tools, screwdrivers, scrapers, crowbars, spade bits, hatchets, and pitching horseshoes.

Last summer I visited the firm to see how wood chisels are made. According to the company manager, J.C. Cort, Buck Bros. manufactures all their chisels from plain high-carbon steel (AISI 1095) with manganese added to improve hardenability. They specify carbon and manganese content (each about 1%), and rely on their steel supplier for quality control. Buck Bros. does not test the steel.

Chisels are rough-formed by forging, but any romantic notions I might have had about wheezing bellows and ringing anvils were soon put to rest by what I saw. Hand-forging—at least for production tools made in the United States—is a thing of the past. Today, chisels are drop-forged in two-part dies.

The blacksmith's modern counterpart is the hammerman. He works in semidarkness as his predecessor did, but instead of a hammer and anvil, he presides over a hulking drop hammer that packs a 1600-lb. punch. Judging the temperature of the steel by the color, the hammerman seizes one of the long steel rods from the gas furnace at his side. With the timing and speed of a juggler, he brushes off scale on a wire wheel, then places the glowing end of the rod in the bottom half of a two-part die. Quick as thought, the hammer slams down, rises and slams down again, bringing the die halves together. The first blow rough-forms the blank, the second finishes it. A good hammerman handles two rods at once and can forge as many as 2400 chisels in an eight-hour shift.

Turning to a press, the hammerman separates the chisel from the rod and flash, the excess steel that squeezed out of the die. The still-glowing chisel travels down a conveyor and drops into a wheelbarrow.

When cool, the chisel is ready for heat-treating. First, the front, back and edges are ground by machine to remove surface imperfections. The chisels are heated in a device called a high-frequency induction heater coil. Twelve chisels are placed on end in a fixture. In a few seconds they're heated to a temperature of 1800°F. After 24 seconds at this temperature, the chisels automatically drop into a tank of quenching oil. A circular conveyor lifts out the hardened chisels and drops them into a soda wash to remove the oil. At this point, the steel has a hardness of about 64 to 65 RC. The clean, hardened chisels are then loaded into gas-fired air draw furnaces for tempering at 440°F. When the chisels come out, they have a hardness of 59 to 60 RC throughout.

Before 1950, one highly skilled man ground the entire chisel by hand. Today, it's done by machine in five separate steps: edges, front and back, side bevels, barrel, and cutting bevel. There's a separate automatic watercooled grinding machine for each operation. The loading and unloading of the machines was the only handwork I saw.

The machine that grinds the front and back holds forty-five 1-in. chisels in a circular fixture called a spider. The spider spins horizontally under an abrasive wheel. When one chisel face is finished, the chisels are manually turned over and ground on the other face.

After grinding, each finished blade is inspected by eye, and any rejects are cast aside. The ones that pass inspection are hand-wiped with oil to prevent rust. Then the blades are ready for handles.

Most of the chisels get plastic handles. These plastic-handled tools are intended for mass-market sales, so the blades get dipped in lacquer to prevent rust. Many of these chisels are packaged on cardboard cards, others go as sets in plastic pouches. A small percentage of the blades get wooden handles, but none were being fitted the day I visited.

I was surprised to learn that only about 15% of the total chisel production carries the Buck Bros. trademark. Some of the remaining 85% might carry the Great Neck brand (Buck Bros.' parent company). Others will carry the brand of the hardware or discount-store chain that ordered them (not Sears, however—Craftsman-brand chisels are made by Western Forge in Colorado Springs, Colo.). There's no difference in steel, manufacturing process or quality control—just a different name on the plastic handle and, most likely, a different price, too. Funny, before my visit I equated the name Buck Bros. with high quality, but who ever heard of Great Neck? I would have turned up my nose at the discount-store chisel, thinking that it was inferior.

I've never owned a Buck Bros. chisel, so I don't know how the blade stacks up to the German and Japanese chisels I use for fine work, or the 15-year-old Sears chisels

At Buck Bros., chisels are drop-forged in two-part dies. The monstrous drop hammer above slams the die halves together with a force of 1600 lb., squeezing the hot plastic steel between them. Two quick blows forge a chisel.

I carry in my carpenters' toolbox. From what I saw, Buck Bros. makes a chisel carefully and efficiently. The manager is well versed in metallurgy and knows what a woodworker expects from a tool. His dilemma is to try to satisfy the skilled user and at the same time avoid injuring the chap who grabs a chisel to pry open a paint can. This dichotomy dictates the tool he makes. When asked how his chisels would be different if serious woodworkers were his only customers, Cort replied, "We'd increase the hardness. The edge would be brittler, but much keener." ☐

*David Sloan is an assistant editor at Fine Woodworking.*

lurgical viewpoint, inclusions are a red flag because they often indicate sloppy quality control in the steel-making. The Sears Craftsman was the only chisel we tested that had a metallurgically unacceptable level of inclusions. The tests turned up some slag in the Iyoroi and Sentora chisels, but in the welds, not in the steel itself. Adhering to tradition, the Japanese make their chisels by forge-welding (often by hand, with a power hammer substituting for a sledge-wielding apprentice) a hardenable tool-steel blank to a mild-steel billet that forms the tool's front face. Chemical segregation was another steelmaking quality-control problem that turned up in the Mifer, Spannsage, Sentora and Iyoroi chisels. This means that elements in the steel that should be thoroughly mixed weren't.

Apart from the metal quality and hardness, we noticed some other things about the chisels that shed some light on how carefully they are manufactured. The Japanese chisels were carefully prepared at the factory. They came accurately ground to the 30° bevel recommended by the manufacturers. Setting the steel ring on the handle was the only "tune-up" that these chisels required. The Western chisels, however, were less carefully prepared. Some were ground to a bevel that was way off the 25° most woodworkers aim for, and this required quite a few minutes at the benchstone to correct. The Stanley had a double-bevel knife-edge grind, so the back had to be ground down to remove the extra bevel. I found the Hirsch to be buffed so heavily that the edges were rounded, making it difficult to see if the cutting edge was square to the body or shank.

**I always hand-sharpen chisels,** and to me it's important for a chisel to have a perfectly flat back, especially in the area immediately behind the cutting edge. Stoning the bevel leaves a wire edge that must be removed by lapping the back of the chisel. If the back isn't flat, part of the wire edge won't contact the stone and may not be completely removed. A flat back rests solidly on the benchstone and eliminates the possibility that you might unintentionally lift the handle and stone a slight second bevel on the back of the chisel. A flat back also provides a bearing surface when you're using a chisel for paring. Except for the Sorby and the Japanese chisels, which came from the factory with flat backs, all of the chisels failed the flatness test—some miserably. The backs of the Craftsman and Stanley chisels were so wavy that it was very difficult to remove enough steel by hand to get them flat. In contrast, the Japanese chisels all have hollow-ground backs, which makes deburring easy.

Having read the lab reports after actually using the tools, I came away with some very definite ideas about chisel buying. The main thing to consider, I think, is your attitude toward sharpening. With one exception, the Sears Craftsman, any of these chisels properly tuned and sharpened will work adequately. If you're satisfied with your sharpening skills but aren't really fussy about getting the best possible edge, any of the Western chisels, except the Craftsman, should do fine. The steel is so similar in five of the eight Western chisels that only a very skilled sharpener could consistently tell the difference between them. That said, you might just as well let tactile factors such as the tool's weight and balance, blade length and handle shape govern your decision. Or the price.

If you're adept at sharpening and strive for the keenest edge, the Japanese chisels may be for you. As the tests showed, they are harder and made of fine-grained steel with evenly distributed carbides. But as with all Japanese blades, they require careful hand-sharpening and they won't tolerate being bashed around loose inside a toolbox.

So which would I buy? My favorite Western chisels were the Footprint and the Hirsch. Both had very comfortable handles and good edge retention, and at $7.60, the Footprint is an excellent value. For the very sharpest edge and the best retention, my favorite was the Oiichi, although at $31.95 it was the most expensive of our test chisels. □

---

*Bill Stankus is a tool consultant, lecturer and woodworker in Bayside, Wis. John Boyzych of Kelsey Hayes Labs and Ralph Mayer of Anderson Labs assisted in the preparation of this article. For more on tool steels, see* Tool Steel Simplified *by Palmer, Luerssen and Pendleton, Chilton Company; and* Tool Steels, *from the American Iron and Steel Institute, Washington, D.C.*

# A second opinion

by Paul Horgan

My initial interest in this article was as a technician. My background is in metals quality control, so I was suspicious of the high-flown claims in some tool catalogs. My intent in researching this article was to determine if the large differences in chisel prices were due to some measurable, physical difference in the tools. In my view, there is no measurable difference. The materials are all similar and the methods of manufacture aren't different enough to justify any substantial difference in price.

The lab rejected all tools softer than 59 RC, but I feel that this judgment is excessively harsh in the case of the Hirsch and Sorby chisels. The softer steel may require frequent sharpening, but in my view this is a minor consideration. Besides, differences of up to four points on the Rockwell C scale are not necessarily significant because of variables in hardness testing.

The laminated Japanese chisels we tested were made in a style once found in Virginia in the 18th century. Steel was scarce then, so only a small piece was used for the cutting edge of the chisel. Iron was used for the body because it was less expensive. The Japanese continue their traditional practice of laminating blades for what I see as two reasons. First, the Japanese respect and revere tradition. Second, they understand the interest we in the United States have for the Orient, and for very good business reasons they are exploiting the differences between our tool-making traditions. In selling laminated tools they are selling something different. These chisels are very well made, but their initial expense and the time required to maintain them makes them inappropriate for the beginner or the production professional, in my opinion.

My advice? Don't let the steel determine which chisel to buy. Pick any chisel that's reasonably priced and feels nice. Sharpen it as well as you know how. Any differences in the steel are so subtle that most woodworkers won't notice the difference. □

---

*Paul Horgan lives in Torrance, Calif.*

## Sharpening skew chisels

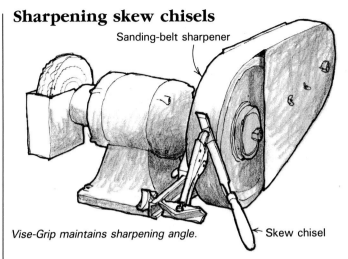

Sanding-belt sharpener

*Vise-Grip maintains sharpening angle.* ← Skew chisel

Some sharpening setups have a special tool rest to support the butt of the tool's handle, which keeps the cutting edge at the proper sharpening angle. The idea works great for straight plane irons and chisels, but presents problems for skewed tools. To put the skewed tool at the proper angle on the sharpening belt, the handle must be pulled to the side and held in midair, unsupported.

To solve the problem, I clamp a pair of Vise-Grips to the tool as shown in the sketch. I protect the chisel blade with a wrap of duct tape. If I have to disconnect the Vise-Grips during the grinding process, the imprint on the tape allows me to place the grips in the exact position again to complete the job.

—*Norman Vandal, Roxbury, Vt.*

## Adjustable protractor

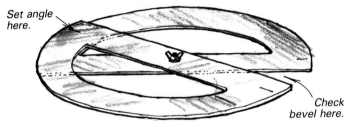

Set angle here.

Check bevel here.

An accurate adjustable angle gauge can be made quickly and inexpensively from two identical dime-store plastic protractors. With a tiny bolt and wingnut, fasten the two protractors together by enlarging the holes already made at the center. I find the device quite useful when cutting angles and also for checking the bevel angles on chisels and turning tools.

—*John Roccanova, Bronx, N.Y.*

## Recipe for razor-sharp carving tools

During my 50 years of carving I have collected some 280 edge tools which, for the kind of carving I do, must be kept sharp enough to shave with. To prepare the edge, I use three grades of progressively finer India stones. But the real trick is to strop the edge to a mirror finish. For this you'll need a couple of pieces of sole leather from the local shoe shop and an abrasive product called Cloverleaf Abrasive Compound, which was originally manufactured for grinding engine valves on Model T Fords. It is a smooth-cutting abrasive suspended in a Vaseline-like jelly. Cloverleaf is still manufactured today in seven different abrasive grades and can be bought in most auto supply stores. You will need two grades—I use one up from finest and two down from coarsest.

First soak the pieces of sole leather in light lubricating oil. Then rub about a teaspoon of the finer abrasive into the smooth side of one piece and a like amount of the coarser abrasive into the rough side of the other piece. Bend the leath-er into the profile of the cutting edge and strop both the inside and outside of the carving gouge to produce an incredibly sharp edge. —*Ford Green, San Antonio, Tex.*

## Woodcarver's clamping system

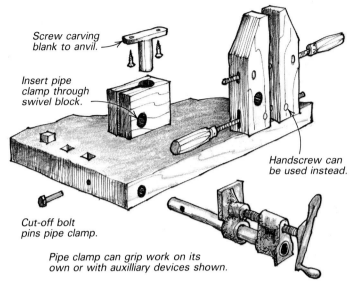

Screw carving blank to anvil.

Insert pipe clamp through swivel block.

Handscrew can be used instead.

Cut-off bolt pins pipe clamp.

*Pipe clamp can grip work on its own or with auxilliary devices shown.*

I originally designed this clamping system for holding half-size duck carving blanks. With a couple of additions, the system is quite versatile and can be used for many other woodworking jobs as well. The basis is a standard pipe-clamp head mounted on a stubby pipe, about 8 in. long. Drill a pipe-sized hole into the edge of your bench near the corner. If your benchtop is not thick enough to provide a strong lip above the hole, glue a block to the underside of the top to make the total thickness 2 in. or so. Now drill a ½-in. hole from the edge of the benchtop through the pipe and install a sawed-off ½-in. bolt to pin the pipe.

The clamp will serve quite well alone or with a bench dog as a light-duty vise. But two easy-to-build additions increase its uses. One addition, shown in the sketch, is a swiveling block and anvil for carving in the round. Insert the pipe clamp through the hole in the swiveling block before pinning the clamp into the bench. Then, work mounted on the anvil can be turned and swiveled to virtually any angle before the pipe clamp is tightened to lock it in place.

The second addition is simply a standard handscrew drilled so it can be slipped over the pipe. The clamping system can be set up or removed from the bench in just seconds.

—*Wallace C. Auger, Fairfield, Conn.*

## Chisel sheaths from old glove fingers

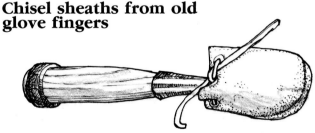

To prevent any chisels, knives and auger bits from damaging each other, I use the thumbs and fingers cut from old pairs of leather work gloves. I punch holes around the opening, and then add eyelets and a length of leather thong to tie the protector on the tool. I'm told that some leathers contain acids that encourage rust, so check your tools once in a while if you plan to try this method for long-term storage. With my everyday tools I've had no problems.

—*Craig S. Walters, Forest Ranch, Calif.*

# Body Mechanics and the Trestle Workbench

## Some appealing virtues, with nary a vise

by Drew Langsner

**Fig. 1: Trestle bench**

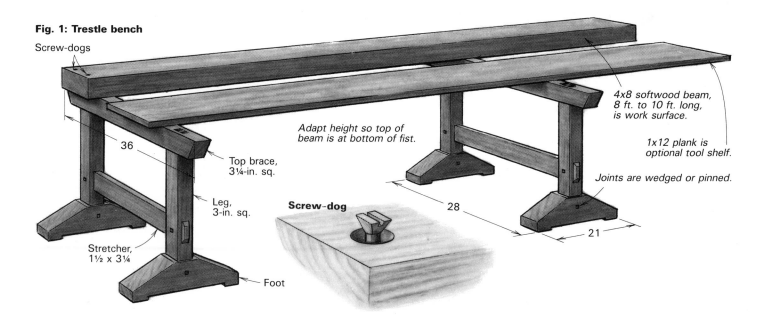

Screw-dogs

4x8 softwood beam, 8 ft. to 10 ft. long, is work surface.

1x12 plank is optional tool shelf.

Adapt height so top of beam is at bottom of fist.

36

Top brace, 3¼-in. sq.

Leg, 3-in. sq.

**Screw-dog**

28

Joints are wedged or pinned.

21

Stretcher, 1½ x 3¼

Foot

For the past two summers Carl Swensson has been teaching a five-day course in Japanese woodworking at Country Workshops, the series of hands-on seminars I offer at my home in the North Carolina mountains. Up to that time, Country Workshops had specialized in my own main interests—traditional American crafts and the European roots they sprang from.

For several years I had also been attracted to Japanese woodworking but was reluctant to get involved. It seemed an exclusive realm for specialists, craftsmen who dedicated years to perfecting their skills. Western-style woodworking, to me, had been providing enough challenges, and I wasn't sure I was ready for further complications. But I also had a strong intuition that Japanese woodworking had much to offer. The opportunity for a hands-on introduction came when I learned about a Baltimore-area woodworker named Carl Swensson. After working for several years in a conventional cabinet shop, Swensson began to look for a more challenging and personal way of working wood. His initiation in Japanese woodworking began with eight months of work with Kieth Mesirow. Swensson then came under the tutelage of master tea house builder Makoto Imai, for one-and-a-half years. Makoto's students learn by observation and personal trial—the master discourages questions. As a result, Swensson had to translate traditional ideas and methods into western concepts that he could identify with.

Although many Japanese woodworkers work on the floor at

very low horses (5 in. to 8 in. high), Makoto uses a trestle bench almost as high as a western workbench. It consists of two horses crossed by a heavy bench beam (the work surface) and an optional plank (the tool shelf), both about 8 ft. to 10 ft. long.

One prominent aspect of traditional Japanese woodworking is the absence of bench vises and dogs. During this century, Japanese craftsmen have adopted lightweight bar clamps, mostly for marking out or sawing multiple units of stock, such as *shoji* rails. But in general, Japanese woodworkers regularly accomplish very complicated tasks using only the body, the force of gravity and a pair of simple trestles to support the work. With practice, Japanese holding methods can be a lot faster than using vises and clamps. At a western workbench, you waste a lot of time loosening and tightening vises and repositioning dogs. At the trestle, you simply flip a board over or change your body position.

The trestles, shown in figure 1, are of straightforward construction. Joints are through mortise-and-tenon, and are wedged or pinned as appropriate. The beam is typically a surfaced 4x8, but can be smaller. It's usually fir or another softwood, which doesn't become as slick as the hardwood top of a typical western bench. This aids the craftsman in holding the material with his body because the material is less liable to slip. A trestle bench is usually sized so that the beam is at the height of the standing woodworker's fist. Swensson's beam is 30 in. above the floor.

Woodworkers who work flat materials with hand tools will

probably benefit from the trestle bench, especially when using Japanese tools. If you're tempted, you can make up a quick version using a pair of cut-down sawhorses. The beam's weight and mass are important. If a 4-in.-thick beam isn't available, laminate one to the approximate thickness.

During his workshop, Swensson demonstrated the use of the trestle bench for chiseling, planing and sawing. The first thing that struck me was the variety of body positions he employed. He doesn't maintain any working stance long enough for it to become tiring. What I didn't fully realize at the time was that all the movement had two more important and interrelated purposes—first, to direct the tool so that it would cut most effectively; second, to combine the tool's cutting action with the most efficient way to hold the work.

Japanese craftsmen use gravity as a work aid. The Japanese believe that one's center of gravity is just below the belly button. As you extend arms or tools away from this center, control becomes more difficult. One reason for pulling a saw or plane to your body is that each stroke becomes more controlled as you finish it. Also, any body (or structure) loses stability with increased height. This is partially why Japanese craftsmen often sit on the floor, and why many Japanese tools tend to be low or short.

Many tools, western as well as Japanese, are easier to use if you keep in mind some of the following rules of gravity and balance. When you can, situate your body with a wide, low base, such as by kneeling on the floor or sitting on the bench with legs forward and spread well apart. When you need control and accuracy, position the tools and the wood close to your body.

Learn to limit movements to the required joints and muscles. Large, more stable lower-body muscles are suited for comparatively slow and powerful movements, such as hogging wood with a plane. Small muscles of the upper body, arms and hands are best suited for detail work, which requires accuracy and subtle adjustments, or speed with less power (i.e. fast sawing).

Whichever set of muscles and joints you use, the other parts of your body should be immobile, but relaxed. Your work stance does not have to be tense if your center of gravity is well within a stable base. Extraneous tension is tiring and a waste of energy. Facial grimacing is a good example of this. Hanging over a workbench with a bent back is tiring and can lead to injuries. If you need to get over your work, extend one leg forward to support the shift in the center of gravity. When bending from the waist, support the weight of your upper body with an arm, thus taking strain off your back and also widening your support.

**Chiseling**—The cross-trestle leg should be directly under the chiseling area of the work beam, so that chiseling force goes directly to the floor instead of being wasted in bending or vibration. To immobilize the stock, Swensson usually sits on the piece, generally side-saddle, with at least one foot well based on the floor. The idea is to maintain at least a three-point base. You can vary the amount of weight taken by any one of these points. A simple shift in weight will dramatically increase "clamping pressure" on the work. Shorter boards are sometimes secured by folding a leg across the bench, with the piece under one's shin. Problems with very short pieces can often be avoided by chiseling before sawing a board to final size.

I was surprised to learn that Japanese woodworkers use steel hammers instead of wooden mallets. After trying this, I became a convert. A mallet absorbs striking shock that could be transferred to the chisel. The compact hammer head allows better visibility. There's also a greater range of balance adjustments since the

*Swensson clamps the work with his thigh and shin (top photo) as he begins to tap out the waste from a dovetail. Heavy paring cuts can be driven by chin pressure (photo above), using the strong muscles of the upper body. This provides good control.*

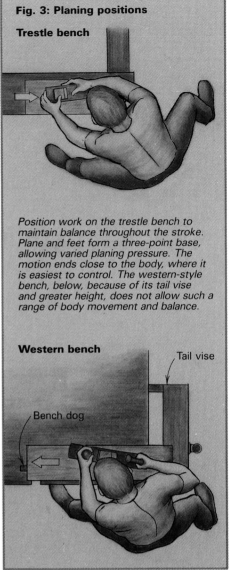

*Position work on the trestle bench to maintain balance throughout the stroke. Plane and feet form a three-point base, allowing varied planing pressure. The motion ends close to the body, where it is easiest to control. The western-style bench, below, because of its tail vise and greater height, does not allow such a range of body movement and balance.*

*Fast, flattening or hogging work is done with the large muscles of the legs and back, while the rest of the body remains relaxed. Balance is ensured by keeping the body's center of gravity inside the broad stance of the feet.*

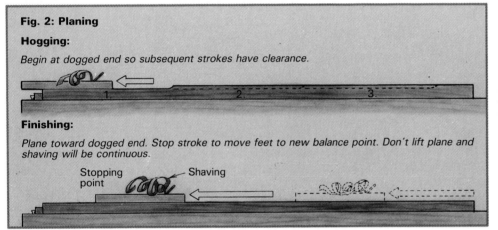

**Fig. 2: Planing**

**Hogging:**

*Begin at dogged end so subsequent strokes have clearance.*

**Finishing:**

*Plane toward dogged end. Stop stroke to move feet to new balance point. Don't lift plane and shaving will be continuous.*

Stopping point — Shaving

Western bench

Tail vise

Bench dog

weight ratio of the head to the handle is much greater than with a wooden mallet. Learn to grasp chisels lightly. A tight grip absorbs the hammer blow and wastes energy. If a chisel is sharp, it will go where it is pointed without your having to choke it.

**Planing**—Most planing is done with the work pulled toward two adjustable bench stops. Swensson's bench stops are a pair of ordinary countersunk wood screws, located about 6 in. apart, about 1 in. from an end of the bench beam. He has filed their heads square to provide more bearing surface against the work. Height adjustment is by screwdriver. A small cleat of scrap wood is often set between the bench stops and the work to prevent marring.

During the workshop, Carl likened planing to playing a violin. There are countless methods and nuances dictated by grain and shape of the board. There is no *best way* to plane, but there are general methods that can be used as starters. I'll describe the motions for pulling a Japanese plane. In general, the same ideas work in reverse for pushing a western one.

Fast, flattening or hogging work is generally done with strong leg movements and a locked torso and arm position. Each stroke begins with the forward (left) leg bent and the rear leg extended. The stroke ends with the forward leg extended and the rear leg bent. Long boards are flattened with a series of leg and lower body passes as shown in figure 3, working forward from the dogged end of the board so the plane has clearance.

For finish planing, the legs and body are held steady. The plane is pulled by the arms. To finish plane long boards, you can walk the plane with distinct, controlled steps. Unlike hogging, start at the far end of the board and work backward. Each planing stroke is taken with both legs well based. At the end of the stroke, the plane is held flat on the board, hands and lower arms frozen in place. From this position, take a "two-step" backward, so that arms re-extend for the next plane pass. Because the plane is not lifted from the board, it will take a continuous shaving.

Very thin boards that can't be dogged at the bench stops require a different planing technique. The near end of the board is held flat with downward pressure from the left hand, while the right hand begins the planing stroke. At mid-stroke the plane is frozen, not lifted. The left hand is then repositioned at the far end of the board so that the right hand can finish.

For edge work use a narrower plane, which is easier to steady on a narrow surface. Set the board on the other edge, with the near end pushed against a cleat and the bench stops. To guide and steady the plane, wrap your fingers far enough around the plane block so they can touch the sides of the board being planed. Boards to be edge-jointed can often be positioned side-by-side, so that common edges are planed simultaneously. This will cancel variations in angle; straightness requires care and practice.

When crosscutting, as in the photo at left and the drawing below, rotate the work so the saw's pull is down against the beam, helping to clamp the work. As shown above, rip cuts are best started by resting the work at an angle against the trestle. The left hand, gripping the work, is part of the basic three-point stance. With the body in balance, the arm is free to saw with easy, rapid strokes.

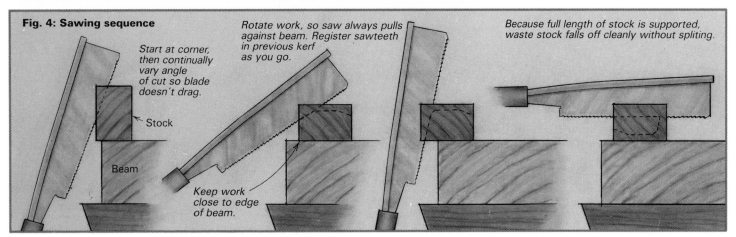

Fig. 4: Sawing sequence

Start at corner, then continually vary angle of cut so blade doesn't drag.

Stock

Beam

Keep work close to edge of beam.

Rotate work, so saw always pulls against beam. Register sawteeth in previous kerf as you go.

Because full length of stock is supported, waste stock falls off cleanly without splitting.

**Sawing**—Most sawing is done from a kneeling position, as shown in the photos above, with the left hand used as a body support and to hold the work. Locate your body in a position where you won't need to move your head or shoulders during the cut. Your eyesight should align with the saw and the layout lines on the edge and face of the board simultaneously, creating a single, flat plane. This method works well with western-style saws as long as they are sharp and the cut is straight. There will be no need for a tightly clenched hand or the use of force. With a light grasp you'll feel telling vibrations and, therefore, develop subtle control. A light grasp also minimizes physical fatigue. Rapid, light cuts are preferable to slower, heavier sawing. Swensson changes the angle of attack every few strokes, as shown in figure 4, so that he is constantly cutting at a "corner" inside the kerf, not dragging the sawteeth along a flat, full-length cut.

For long timber rips, rest one end of the board across the bench or trestle, and the opposite end on the floor. The prop angle can range from 30° to 90°. If the timber is light, steady it with one foot. Swensson works barefoot or in socks, as shoes may force grit into the wood. Long power rips are usually made holding the saw with two hands. In my experience, kneeling with straight back posture is much less stressful than standing in a bent-over position. You can finish up a rip cut by standing the board on one of the trestles.

**Summing up**—In my opinion, the Japanese trestle bench is not a substitute for, or necessarily superior to, a western workbench. Both are tools available to the contemporary woodworker. The trestle bench has become my choice for hand work such as mortise-and-tenon joinery and planing. It's fine for sawing, especially with a Japanese saw, if the stock isn't too short. I definitely prefer it for most architectural scale work.

For me, the trestle bench does have its shortcomings. It's too low for doing layout work without bending over at an awkward angle, unless you want to kneel or sit on a stool. Also, the 8-in.-wide beam is too narrow for some assembly work, but you can easily add other pieces up to the full width of 36 in. When I'm building a Windsor chair, or working on very small stock, I prefer the western bench with its extra height and built-in vises.

Working at a trestle bench can become an excellent introduction to the principles of how body mechanics and tool design affect each other. Swensson is quick to point out that there are innumerable sound ways to apply the ideas. Some techniques come quickly, but learning to get the most from the trestle bench is like peeling an onion—many layers and some tears. □

*Drew Langsner's Country Workshops take place in Marshall, N.C. Carl Swensson will be teaching Japanese woodworking again September 23 through 27. For information call (704) 656-2280.*

# Block Planes
## *What are they really for?*

by Maurice Fraser

The familiar little block plane is something of an enigma. Its origins, function—even the meaning of its name—are a little obscure. The typical block plane has a cast-iron body 6 in. to 7 in. long with an adjustable blade bedded at 20° or, on a low-angle block plane, 12°. Unlike bench planes, the blade cuts bevel up and has no cap iron to add rigidity and serve as a chipbreaker. Some models sport an adjustable mouth that can be set to an ultra-fine opening to reduce tearout. The bulbous lever cap, which gives the plane it's characteristic domed top, clamps down the blade and fits into the palm, making the plane comfortable to use in one hand. The nose of the plane has a dished-out knob or machined dimple as a rest for the index finger.

Small, one-handed planes have been around since medieval times, but the block plane, in the configuration we know, seems to be an American phenomenon a little more than a century old. It wasn't until 1873 that Stanley produced the small Model 9½ block plane, much like the one still being made today. Earlier "block" planes were larger, two-handed affairs.

**The block plane is an odd jumble** of assets and liabilities. Small size and light weight are its greatest assets. It's comfortable to use in one hand, especially on small pieces that would get lost under a large plane. A block plane can be useful for hundreds of small jobs: softening sharp edges, trimming small miters, fitting drawers, trimming excess plywood edging tape or projecting veneer, trimming finger joints or dovetails on small boxes and any time you need to hold work with one hand and plane with the other.

Over the years, Stanley has offered some fifty-odd models of block planes. Today, Stanley and Record, the major manufacturers, make only a handful of models (they differ mostly in the number of possible adjustments) in two basic types: standard (20°) and low-angle (12°). Footprint also makes a few models. Two small German-made wooden planes on the market are in the block plane size category but their blades are bedded at 50° and mounted bevel down like a bench plane.

The No. 9½ made by Stanley, Record and Footprint, is the stan-

*Small and light, the block plane is the choice for one-handed planing jobs. Unlike a bench plane, block plane blades cut bevel up. Top of the line models, like these Stanleys, have adjustable blades and mouths. Blade angle on the No. 9½ (right) is 20°. The low-angle No. 60½ has a 12° blade angle.*

dard 20° block plane with all the adjustments. I haven't tried the Footprint, but either the Record or Stanley No. 9½ is a good, honest, no messing-around tool for general one-hand planing.

The other conventional block is the low-angle (12°) No. 60½ made by both Record and Stanley. I prefer the Record 60½ to the Stanley because it has a wider blade (1⅝ in. to Stanley's 1⅜ in.) and it's heavier. And, at the time I wrote this, the Record plane cost a bit less than the Stanley. The quality of machining, however, is inconsistent. Sometimes the Record plane seems better made, sometimes the Stanley. Anyway, never buy a tool sight unseen unless you can return it if it's not right.

**The textbook myth is that a block plane's** low blade angle makes it the best plane for working end grain. Best? Well, they're OK. It isn't that a well-made block plane, perfectly tuned, can't make a decent end-grain cut, it can, if you set the plane for a very light cut, have the blade extra sharp, tighten the hold-down screw (not so tight that the blade can't be adjusted) and use a narrow mouth setting. But more often, my students get chatter on end grain that they wouldn't get with a sharp smooth plane. The low-angle blade doesn't hurt anything, but a low blade angle does not guarantee a low cutting angle. A look at cutting geometry shows that things aren't always what they seem.

As figure 1 shows, with the plane-blade bevel facing up, the 25° bevel angle contributes to the cutting angle. It's common to hone a 5° microbevel which increases the bevel angle to 30°. The standard block plane bed tilts the blade up another 20° for an actual cutting angle of 50° Compare this to the bench plane shown in figure 2. Since the bevel faces down, bevel angle doesn't affect the cutting angle. Standard pitch bench plane blades are seated at 45°, and the cutting angle remains 45° regardless of the bevel angle. So, a 20° block plane really cuts at 50° while a smooth plane cuts at only 45°. The 12° low-angle block plane with a 25° grind and a 5° microbevel has a cutting

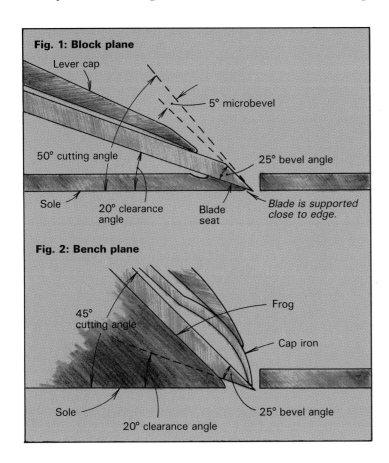

**Fig. 1: Block plane**
Lever cap
5° microbevel
50° cutting angle
25° bevel angle
Sole
20° clearance angle
Blade seat
*Blade is supported close to edge.*

**Fig. 2: Bench plane**
Frog
Cap iron
45° cutting angle
Sole
25° bevel angle
20° clearance angle

*Entrepreneur Tom Lie-Nielson has brought two vintage Stanley specialty block planes back to life in flashy, manganese-bronze incarnations. Shown here with the cast-iron Stanley originals are (left) the No. 95 edge-trimming block plane and (right) the No. 140 skew-rabbet block plane.*

# Specialty block planes reincarnated

Flipping through old tool catalogs can make a plane buff long for the good old days when specialty planes abounded. Stanley and Record seem to discontinue another hand plane each year. There's still a market for these tools and, though it may not be large enough to keep the big guys interested, small entrepreneurs may be able to fill the gap by reproducing the plane classics.

Tom Lie-Nielson has been doing just that in West Rockport, Me. He's making reproductions of the pre-World War II Stanley No. 140 low-angle, skew-rabbet block plane and the Stanley No. 95 edge-trimming block plane. Unlike the cast-iron originals, the Lie-Nielson repros are cast in manganese bronze because it's easier to machine and not likely to break if dropped.

The Lie-Nielson No. 140 skew-rabbet block plane is wondrous to behold. Like the originals, one side is removable, allowing the skewed blade to trim a rabbet. The bronze body and lever cap are quite heavy, providing useful damping against chatter. The blade bed offers rather solid support by block-plane standards. In ordinary use it planes well; the optional fence (unique to the Lie-Nielsen re-creation) is a fine idea, but not for making rabbets from scratch. For that you would want the cross-grain spurs and depth gauge of a regular rabbet plane. The fence and the skewed blade are useful for smoothing fielded panels that were begun on a tablesaw. The skewed blade cuts nicely across the grain. With the fence, the plane costs nearly $140— no casual purchase (available from Garrett Wade, 161 Avenue of the Americas, N.Y., N.Y. 10013).

The Lie-Nielson version of the Stanley No. 95 edge-trimming block plane holds up well to the original. It is a skewed low-angle block plane with an integral 90° fence. It will trim a straightened edge up to ⅞-in. thick and square it to the face while doing so. But its 6 in. length is inadequate to establish edge-joinable straightness on anything much larger than a bread box. Surely the name implies no such ability. The danger lies in the beholder's eyes: it looks as though it could do anything. It would serve well as a veneer or edging trimmer. At about $125 I would rather receive than give one (available from Garrett Wade and Lee Valley Tools, 2680 Queensview Dr., Ottawa, Ont., K2A 1T4, Canada). —M.F.

*The Achilles heel of block-plane design is the skimpy blade support. A small nub on the depth adjuster supports the rear of the blade and a machined flat at the mouth supports the cutting edge. Between these points the blade is unsupported, and likely to chatter.*

angle of 42°, only 3° lower than most bench planes but a full 8° lower than the standard block plane.

Any advantage the lower cutting angle may offer on end grain is nullified by a weakness in the block plane's design. The block plane can chatter because it lacks the rigidly-supported blade and substantial body mass of the bench plane. Compare a block plane blade with a smooth plane blade. The frog/bed on the smooth plane supports the blade for several inches underneath, plus a cap iron and a thick lever cap atop the blade. The block plane blade is supported underneath only by a raised nub or two in back and a milled ridge at the mouth, under the blade edge. The bevel-up blade is supported very close to the cutting edge, which could be an advantage if the blade had more support further back, but this skimpy arrangement leaves most of the blade unsupported. This is the Achilles heel in block-plane design and the most significant structural cause of chatter. Other defects—thin blades, improper bevel angles, warped soles—can be corrected by the owner, or manufacturer quality control, but the atrophied blade seat seems inherent in the tool's design as it's now being made. Superior machining in pre-war block planes mitigated this defect somewhat but even they rarely exhibit the rock-solid feel of a good bench plane with it's cap iron and continuous blade bed.

The blade seat problem is exacerbated by feeble lever-cap toggle clamps, a perennial block-plane problem. This design supplies inadequate and uneven clamping pressure on the blade. Much better blade-locking methods—especially the hinged knuckle-joint cap—can be found on some old block planes.

**To properly set up the block plane,** mount the blade bevel up and advance the adjusting knob until the blade edge can barely be felt along the plane mouth. Clamp on the lever cap handle; if the blade can easily be pressed sideways, tighten the clamping screw by very tiny increments until the blade can only be moved with difficulty. If the blade isn't perfectly parallel to the mouth opening, tilt the blade by means of the lateral adjustment lever. For planes without an adjustment lever, grasp the lever cap and the blade and wrest them left or right a trifle as needed.

If the plane has an adjustable mouth, loosen the finger-rest knob to unlock the mouth adjusting lever. Turn the plane upside down and observe the opening while you slowly shift the lever sideways: a mouth opening of about 1/32 in. is good for most hardwoods and a scant 3/64 in. for mild woods. Avoid zapping the blade's edge with the front portion of the mouth piece when narrowing the mouth. □

---

*Maurice Fraser teaches woodworking at the Craft Students' League in the 53rd St. Y.W.C.A. in New York City. He was woodworking consultant for the book* Crafts & Hobbies *(1979, Reader's Digest Press).*

*For most cuts, a block plane cuts best when it's skewed to the work. With a low-angle block plane skewed to the work (top photo) Fraser trims tablesaw marks from a miter. Scrap clamped to the board's edge prevents split out of end grain. Author relieves a sharp edge with a low-angle block plane (photo above).*

# The Spokeshave
## How to choose and use one

by Michael Sandor Podmaniczky

The spokeshave is a marvelous tool. Compact and comfortable to use, it can, with care, perform admirable service in a diversity of jobs. I find myself using one nearly every day for cleaning up drawknifed chair spindles, shaping and fairing curved parts, chamfering anything...and on and on. The spokeshave isn't without its quirks, though, and unless you learn to live with them, it's hard to get the tool working just right.

First of all, you've got to decide which spokeshave to use for which job or, if you don't have any spokeshave at all, which to buy. A glance at the spokeshave section in my favorite wishbooks reveals an armload of choices priced between $4 and $24. You could buy them all, but the collection would leave too little room in your toolkit and too much room in your wallet. Most mail-order catalogs offer several sizes of metal spokeshaves in two generic types: flat-soled and curved-soled.

As its name implies, the working face of a flat-soled spokeshave is machined flat, and apart from its extended handles, it looks and works like a plane with a very short, narrow sole. A round-soled spokeshave has a straight blade, like a plane, and when viewed from the front its sole appears flat. Viewed from the side, however, the sole is curved to a radius of about 1½ in. A half-round spokeshave is different altogether. It shows a concave sole from the front and has a blade curved along its width. A convex spokeshave is similar, but as the name implies, the sole is curved in the other direction.

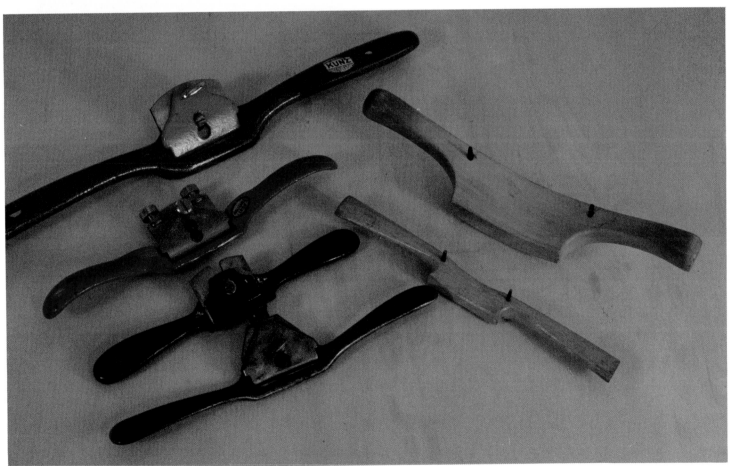

*Bought from a mail-order catalog or at a fortuitous yard sale, there's a spokeshave for every purpose. Reading counterclockwise from lower right: flat-soled wooden shave; shopmade convex for shaping chair seats; cooper's spokeshave; flat-soled metal with dual screw adjusters; author's favorite 9-in. Kunz (painted black); metal shave with single adjuster.*

Which you buy depends more on how much you want to squeeze out of your tool dollar than it does on the kind of woodworking you do. I whittle the selection down to manageable size by first deciding what I can do without. The half-round spokeshave, meant for shaping cylindrical parts like banister rails, is useless on work whose radius is larger than that of the tool's sole. On work of lesser radius, you'll do just as well with a smooth or block plane or a flat-soled spokeshave—after all, tangent is tangent and there's no point cluttering up your toolbox with a single-purpose tool when a more versatile one will do. Combination spokeshaves are round- and flat-soled shaves married by a single handle—good in theory, not so good in practice.

A cooper's spokeshave is big and beefy, and some boatbuilders like it for wearing down the inside surfaces of heavy, sawn ship frames. I've learned to work close and accurately with the bandsaw or drawknife, then touch up with a flat- or round-soled spokeshave. Another sucker-born-a-minute tool is the adjustable-mouth spokeshave. I rarely need this capability, but if I do, I slide one or two bits of shimstock or aluminum flashing behind the blade to close the mouth down, and I'm all set. Infinitely variable settings I don't need. Fine and rank will do nicely. A chamfering spokeshave—a flat shave with two adjustable fences mounted on the sole—is as specialized as an overbred show dog and I'm happy to do without both. One word about handle styles: those gull-winged spokeshaves which look like a 1960 Chevy in retreat are not proper. Having your hands up in the air, away from the line defined by the blade edge makes it very difficult to control the tool.

So it all boils down to this: Equip yourself with two simple straight-handled spokeshaves—a flat-soled for general-purpose smoothing or shaping of flat and convex or shallow and concave surfaces, and a round-soled for working tight inside radii. If you can find one, I'd recommend an old wooden-bodied type of flat-soled shave—and I don't mean the adjustable rosewood models you see in the catalogs these days. I'm talking about one of those dime-a-dozen beechwood jobs (sometimes fitted with a brass foresole) that always turn up in junk shops and yard sales. These are light, well-balanced and compact; the only tool for getting into that hard-to-shape curve on a Windsor chair seat, just forward of the arm post. Make sure the blade has a little life left to it and that the blade tangs fit tightly enough into the wooden body to hold the depth setting.

If you can't find a wooden shave, the best metal ones also happen to be the simplest. I like the 9-in. flat- and round-soled models made by Kunz (Garrett Wade's #19P02.01 and 3.01). Besides being inexpensive, these tools have another important advantage: you adjust the blade by loosening a single screw that holds the cap iron in place, instead of by the cumbersome thumbscrews found on more expensive spokeshaves, like the Record. Screw adjusters just get in the way and, worse, they rattle. There's something evil about anything loose on a hand tool, and unless I can stop the rattle with, say, beeswax to clog the threads, I just won't use the thing. For me, using a fancy Record spokeshave is like hopping into a Delta 88 after years of driving a Rabbit. No thanks, I'd rather soup up the Rabbit.

Being an inexpensive tool, the Kunz needs some tuning. The frog, the surface against which the back of the blade bears, should be filed flat to minimize chattering. Hollow-grind the inside edge of the cap iron so it bears against the blade only along its leading edge, and set it about ⅛ in. back from the blade's cutting edge. True an out-of-flat or poorly curved sole with a file

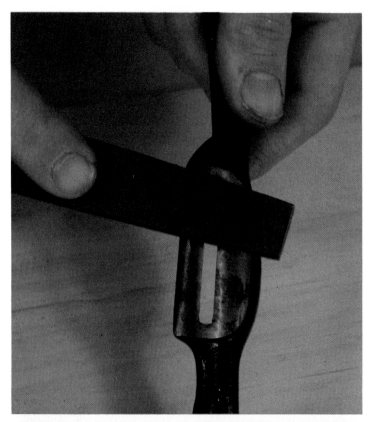

*Dressing a metal spokeshave's sole with a file improves its performance. To keep it from rocking, file the sole flat across its width. The Kunz, above, has no adjusters so author ground pockets on either side of the frog. A screwdriver inserted into both the pockets and the corresponding notches filed in the blade edge aids depth-setting.*

as well, as shown in the photo above. Remember, since the spokeshave rides on the leading and following edges of the sole, you'll want to file these edges straight across so the shave won't rock from side to side. To make blade setting a little easier, I ground small pockets in the casting adjacent to the blade with a Dremel tool. By inserting a screwdriver blade, which bears against nicks I filed in the blade, I can finesse the cutting depth I want.

Sharpen a metal spokeshave blade as you would a plane iron. Using an aluminum-oxide wheel, grind the bevel to about 25° or so—you don't need to get your protractor out, just eyeball it close. Next hone a bevel with a fine India stone, following that with a touchup on a hard Arkansas. A wooden spokeshave usually won't need grinding. But if it does, the metal, like a drawknife

## How spokeshaves work

### Wooden spokeshave

*A wooden shave cuts bevel-up. Contact points are the leading edge of the sole and the forward portion of the back of the blade.*

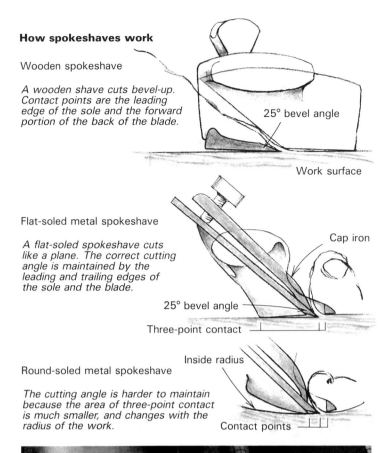

25° bevel angle

Work surface

### Flat-soled metal spokeshave

*A flat-soled spokeshave cuts like a plane. The correct cutting angle is maintained by the leading and trailing edges of the sole and the blade.*

Cap iron

25° bevel angle

Three-point contact

### Round-soled metal spokeshave

*The cutting angle is harder to maintain because the area of three-point contact is much smaller, and changes with the radius of the work.*

Inside radius

Contact points

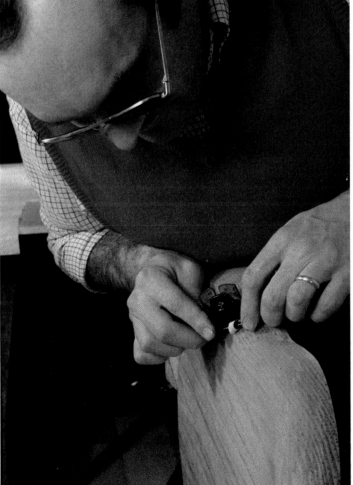

*The spokeshave's short sole makes it perfect for shaping and smoothing curved wooden parts, such as the Windsor chair seat Podmaniczky is making here. Best results come when the blade is kept at the correct angle to the work; control achieved by pushing rather than pulling the tool.*

blade, is often soft enough to file. Keep in mind that the blade pushes rather than slices through the work. This means that the blade should not have the micro-serrations left by a fine India but the polished microbevel produced by a hard Arkansas or comparable stone.

To get a spokeshave to do what you want it to, it's helpful to understand what makes it tick. Although it works like a plane, a spokeshave is really just a jig, a holder for a chisel blade. You could conceivably "plane" a surface dead-flat with a chisel, but the job would require a personality most unwelcome at an intimate evening over dinner. That's where the sole of a plane comes in. It orients the blade to the wood surface, allowing the plane to smooth a board by removing material and flatten it by bridging the peaks and valleys of the wood surface. Thanks to the plane's frog, the cutting bevel is always positioned at just the right angle.

It's not so straightforward with a spokeshave. While a plane both smooths by removing material and flattens by virtue of its long sole, the spokeshave is primarily a material remover. The sole is far too short to bridge surface irregularities of any size and is not as self-jigging, so you, the operator, have to keep the blade at the right cutting angle by holding the spokeshave correctly. As you work away with the spokeshave, you must deftly check your progress, shave some more and check again until the surface is just right. To get a consistent cut, position the tool to contact the work at three points—the sole's leading edge, the cutting bevel, and (just barely) the trailing edge of the sole. The drawing at left gives some idea of the angles involved. If you rock fore or aft on the sole, the cutting angle will be wrong and the spokeshave will skid over the wood instead of cutting. A wooden spokeshave works a little differently: since it cuts bevel-up, the forward portion of the back of the blade, rather than the sole, serves as the reference surface. To get the right feel of either type, you'll have to sharpen the blade and try it.

I sometimes pull my spokeshave for various reasons, like grain direction or body position (I *hate* standing on my head while working at the bench), so I'd never say don't pull, but these tools are designed to be pushed. And with just a little practice, you'll get far greater control by pushing. A nice feature on some spokeshaves are the cozy little thumb rests on either side of the frog. Fingers need not be wrapped around the tool handles. If the surface being worked is quite broad and one or both handles don't hang out over the edge, grab whatever is comfortable around the frog and cap iron with thumb and forefinger and push on the handles with the palm of your hand. Since *proper* handles are straight in line with the blade edge (*not* gull-winged, up and away), even without a firm hand grip, there is no tendency to roll or trip up. This grip is really helpful with round-soled spokeshaves, as they can be friskier than the flat ones.

If, no matter how you hold it, the spokeshave skids without cutting, either the blade is dull or it isn't set far enough below the sole to pull a shaving. Raise the blade a little if your spokeshave digs in and stops cold. Don't give up in frustration if the tool misbehaves at first. Starting off with the right tool, setup and procedures for use will eliminate most of the hangups that could discourage you from using it. As time goes by, you'll develop quite an affection for that versatile little fellow who lurks down in the corner of your toolbox. □

*M.S. Podmaniczky is a professional woodworker and boatbuilder who lives in Thomaston, Maine.*

# MACHINES

# Small Thickness Planers
## *We test six machines*

by David Sloan

A thickness planer can make life in the small workshop a lot easier. Most woodworking begins with a straight, flat, uniformly thick board, and while it's nice to know how to dimension a board with hand planes, it's also nice to have a machine that can do it for you. A planer can do the job in seconds, and since you can make boards any thickness you want, it frees you from having to design around the standard commercial thicknesses. In a busy production shop, a planer will soon pay for itself because it saves time and expands the range of work your shop can handle.

My first choice for a production-shop machine would be a big, heavy planer with an 18-in. to 24-in. wide bed. The massive cast-iron frame damps vibration, and a big heavy-duty machine can stand up to the hardest continuous use. Most important, the wide bed can accommodate glued-up carcase panels. But large production planers can cost and weigh more than a new car. A new 24-in. Powermatic with a 10-HP motor, for example, sells for about $15,000 and weighs in at almost 3,000 lb.

As an alternative, machine manufacturers have come up with much smaller, less expensive planers that are appropriate for the pro and hobbyist alike. There are a dozen or so of these small planers on the market—enough choices to give the potential buyer a headache. Since the average woodworker can't take a new planer out for a pre-purchase spin to see if he likes it, we chose six small machines with price tags under $2,000 and tested them in the *Fine Woodworking* shop. We already owned a 13-in. Delta (formerly Rockwell) RC-33 and a 15-in. Makita 2040. We borrowed the other four—the 12-in. Parks 95, 15-in. Grizzly G1021, 7-in. Williams & Hussey, and 12-in. Foley-Belsaw 985—from the manufacturers, and I put them to work on pine, poplar, red oak and hard maple. The ultimate test was bird's-eye maple, which is notorious for tearout.

Before reading on, take a moment to look at the box on the facing page, which explains the parts of a generic planer. The planer evaluations that follow refer frequently to the parts.

Prior to planing wood, I sharpened the knives of each planer on a Hitachi watercooled 1,000-grit knife grinder and set up the knives and rollers following the instructions in each respective manual. Then I surfaced roughsawn boards of different widths and lengths, taking heavy cuts to see how much the machines could take and light cuts to see how smooth a surface they could produce. I planed a few boards down as far as possible to see how thin each planer could go. To really strain the motors, I surfaced a hard-maple panel the full width of the bed, taking the heaviest cut possible.

Needless to say, none of these small machines has all the fea-

tures of the big production planers. To keep the price down, the manufacturers had to make compromises. None of the small planers is wide enough to be much use surfacing glued-up panels. No machine has variable-speed feed, although optional sprockets will change the feed rates of the Makita and Foley-Belsaw.

All six of the small planers performed adequately. Each was capable of surfacing 10-ft. long, roughsawn 8/4 hard-maple boards, although it isn't practical on the Williams & Hussey machine. All six planers produced a surface ready for hand-planing or sanding on every wood except the bird's-eye maple. Even on the lightest cut, with freshly sharpened knives, all but the Williams & Hussey tore out little chunks of bird's-eye. That said, there were significant differences between the machines in both design and convenience. Some duplicated features found on larger, more expensive machines, while others were designed from scratch to be relatively portable and as inexpensive as possible. In this article I'll describe the planers and mention any noteworthy characteristics—good or bad. Detailed specifications for each machine are given in the chart on p. 80.

**Parks 95 12-in.**—Cast iron is the first thing you notice about this planer—lots of it. The Parks comes closest to being a scaled-down version of a heavy-duty planer. The 95 was designed in 1935 and hasn't changed since. It's a well-crafted machine, solid and straightforward. The cutterhead, for example, has been carefully drilled for balance. None of the other machines showed any evidence of cutterhead balancing.

Our Parks 95 was mounted on a sheet-steel stand which houses the motor. The cast-iron cutterhead cover functions, in the closed position, as a chipbreaker. Instead of springs, its weight holds it against the board. The steel bed and feed rollers are all adjustable. The infeed roller is corrugated and there's also a pressure bar—standard features on the expensive planers. Rollers and pressure bar are easily adjusted with big nuts right on top

*The 12-in. Parks 95 planer, with optional sheet-steel base and magnetic starter, is a comfortable 37½ in. floor to table.*

# How a thickness planer works

A planer simultaneously reduces the thickness of a board and makes opposite faces parallel. The drawing shows the workings of a standard design. The powered infeed roller grips the board, flattens it down against the planer bed and pushes it into the rotating cutterhead. The spring-loaded chipbreaker helps hold the board flat against the table and minimizes tearout by breaking the chips lifted up by the knives, similar to the action of the cap iron on a hand plane. As the newly planed surface emerges from under the cutterhead, the pressure bar and outfeed roller keep the board flat against the table. The powered outfeed roller propels the board past the cutterhead and out of the machine.

A planer won't remove warp, twist or cup, so one face of a board must first be flattened on a jointer. If you feed a warped or cupped board through a planer, the feed roller will just flatten it out against the table. When the board comes out the other end, it will spring back—thinner, but still warped or cupped.

The surface produced by a planer appears flat, but is actually made up of tiny ridges—although they aren't actually true arcs. The larger the diameter of the cutterhead, the larger the arc that the knives traverse and the shallower these ridges will be. The number of cuts per inch, however, is the most significant factor in producing a smooth surface. The more cuts per inch, the smoother the surface, and this is achieved with a slow feed rate combined with a high cutter RPM. —D.S.

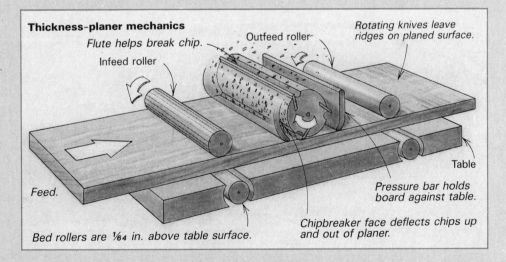

**Thickness-planer mechanics**

Flute helps break chip.

Infeed roller

Outfeed roller

Rotating knives leave ridges on planed surface.

Table

Feed.

Bed rollers are 1/64 in. above table surface.

Pressure bar holds board against table.

Chipbreaker face deflects chips up and out of planer.

Drawing: Kathleen Creston

*The only difference between our two-year-old Rockwell and the new Delta RC-33 is the knob that cuts power to the feed rollers. On the older machine (shown), the knob protrudes from the right side; on the new Delta, it's on the top. Table and cutterhead assembly are cast iron. The cutterhead assembly moves up and down on four steel columns.*

*Three flat steel springs bear down on the Delta chipbreaker to hold it tight against the stock. The chipbreaker adjusts with setscrews that rest on the steel bar shown.*

of the machine. The knives were easy to install and adjust. While I could install the knives standing up, I had to squat on the floor to set them accurately. Two V-belts power the cutterhead, which drives the feed rollers through a network of massive gears. A panic lever on the top of the machine can stop power to the feed rollers if necessary.

Because of its height—37½ in. to the table in its highest position—the Parks 95 was the most comfortable to use of all the machines. To change depth-of-cut, the table travels on two vertical screws, one at the center of each long side. The planer's thickness capacity is only 4⅜ in.—the smallest of all the machines.

Except on the very lightest cuts, the Parks I tested didn't feed perfectly. When the infeed roller grabbed a short board, the tail end of the board lifted up in the air, causing the bottom front edge to catch in the bed-roller slot and stop. I had to hold down the tail end to keep the board from hanging up. No adjustment to the infeed roller or the bed roller seemed to help. Perhaps a larger-diameter bed roller would solve the problem. I soon became accustomed to this little quirk, and kept a hand on the tail end of the board until the front end was well under the infeed roller. Other than that, the Parks performed admirably. With a 2-HP motor it had plenty of power and planed both thick and thin stock well.

**Delta RC-33 13-in.**—The Delta is a well-made, heavy-duty, cast-iron machine. To keep costs down, Delta makes this, its smallest planer, in Brazil. The machine I tested is two years old and carries the Rockwell label, but the Delta planers being sold today are identical, with one exception: a knob that cuts power to the feed rollers has been moved from the side to the top of the planer. In the 16 months that I've worked with this planer, I've never found a need to cut power, so I can't say whether the relocation is an improvement.

The motor is mounted on top, instead of in the base. When you adjust the depth of cut, the cutterhead assembly, not the table, moves up and down on four screws, one in each of the steel columns. There's a lot of cast iron in this assembly, plus the weight of the motor, so it takes some muscle to turn that handle. I like this arrangement. Because the table height doesn't change, you can support long stock with outboard rollers without resetting them for every cut. Three V-belts drive the three-knife cutterhead, which in turn drives a roller chain to power the feed rollers. A phalanx of anti-kickback fingers in front of the infeed roller eliminates any possibility of kickback.

The chipbreaker is a sheet-steel fabrication held down against the stock by three flat springs. There is no pressure bar. Knives are spring-loaded and very easy to set with the new bridge-type gauge supplied with the machine, although my sliced-up fingers can attest to the fact that the edges of the cutterhead are almost as sharp as the knives.

It isn't easy to adjust the height of the feed rollers. First you have to make a beveled wooden gauge block, which you then place under the cutterhead with a feeler gauge between the block and a knife. It's hard to maneuver the block, the feeler gauge, your fingers and your eyes in a very confined space in close proximity to very sharp knives—all this while kneeling on the floor. The adjusting screws themselves are in an awkward place on the underside of the frame.

In use, the Delta atones for the agony of set-up. Feeding was consistently smooth and effortless. The machine hogged through rough stock with ease, yet left a respectable finish on fine cuts. Neither thick nor thin stock posed a problem.

**Grizzly G1021 15-in.**—The success of the Delta design spawned this Taiwanese knockoff, which sells for about half the list price of the Delta planer. Place these two machines side by side, and the only obvious differences are the elevating wheel and the color: Grizzly green vs. battleship gray. A closer look reveals that the Grizzly isn't quite a carbon copy. Its bed is 15 in. wide instead of 13 in.—a definite improvement. When you turn the wheel, the table, not the head, moves on four screws. The Grizzly also sports extension rollers that bolt onto the cast-iron table. In most other features it duplicates the Delta. Even the pulley covers are interchangeable, though the bolt holes don't quite line up. The amusing similarity was the owners' manual. The Grizzly manual is the Delta manual practically verbatim. The paragraph that refers to the Delta's moving head had just been whited out.

All right, so the Taiwanese copied the Delta, but is it as good? Based on the two days I spent with this machine, I'd say no, but it's close. The castings are excellent. The Grizzly has a cast-iron base assembly that the Delta doesn't have. This machine is heavy—480 lb. with stand and motor, outweighing the complete Delta by nearly 200 lb. Where the Delta has sheet-steel gears to drive the feed rollers, the Grizzly has nicely machined castings—no great improvement functionally, but a nice touch. A dust hood for collection-system hookup is standard. The Grizzly has the same set-up virtues and vices as the Delta since the cutterhead and feed-roller designs are the same. On the other hand, the Grizzly I tested had only one weak, flat spring holding down the chipbreaker, while the Delta has three strong springs.

There was a problem. When I was setting up the machine, I found that the chipbreaker couldn't be adjusted anywhere near specifications. Closer examination showed that the fabricated sheet-steel chipbreaker was warped, possibly from the heat of welding. This meant that when the chipbreaker was mounted in the machine, the left side could bear down against a board, but the right side was about 1/16 in. above the surface. Boards would catch on the left side, slew over to the right, and go through the planer at an angle. Boards as thin as 1/4 in. disintegrated because they could lift off the table, but the quality of the cut on thicker stock didn't seem to be affected. I probably could have fixed the chipbreaker with a day's worth of filing, hammering and fiddling, but I ordered a replacement chipbreaker over the phone. It arrived within a few days, and took about 45 minutes to install and adjust. Boards no longer slewed to one side. Thin boards still disintegrated, but only about 40% of the time, with the worst damage occurring to the last few inches of the board. Stronger springs on the chipbreaker would probably solve this problem.

Although the design is the same as the Delta, feeding the Grizzly wasn't as easy. Boards needed a push to get started. The Delta hogged off more wood—3/16 in. vs. 1/8 in. for the Grizzly. The Grizzly is beefy enough that it could probably handle a much heavier cut, but the frame interferes and the stock won't feed if you try to cut more than 1/8 in. This is a major nuisance when you're rough-planing. Several boards that were thicker at the back end than at the front jammed against the frame halfway through. I had to stop and lower the table to finish the cut.

Since I spent only a few days with this planer, durability is something I can't predict. The Grizzly *looks* good and planed adequately on all but thin stock, but it's hard to judge the quality of motors or bearings from only a few hours of use. It's three-month warranty is the shortest of any of the planers. The importer says that replacement parts are available and defective parts will be replaced for the cost of shipping during the warranty period.

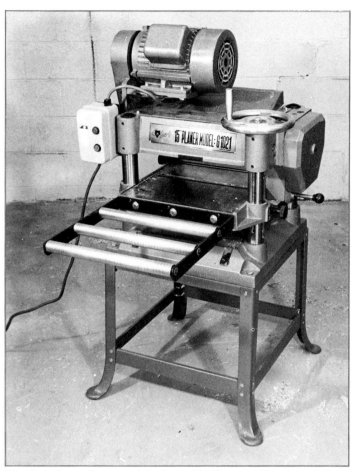

*The Grizzly as shown weighs in at 480 lb.—the heaviest of all the small planers. Extension bed rollers are standard equipment, front and back. The table moves up and down on the four steel columns. Base, table and cutterhead assembly are cast iron.*

*Almost identical to the Delta in design, the Grizzly sports one chipbreaker spring, where as the Delta has three.*

**Makita 2040 15-in.**—Like the Delta, the Makita I tested is one that we've had for about two years. The 2040 bears little resemblance to an industrial machine, although it does have a pressure bar. Its castings are aluminum instead of iron. The cutterhead has only two knives, and changing them was a snap. A shaft lock holds the cutterhead in position when you're unbolting and setting the knives—a nice feature. A plastic handwheel turns a central screw that elevates the table from underneath, and the table corners ride on four steel columns.

The 2040 is designed to take light cuts. It's the only machine that comes with a 110V motor, which is a small, 2-HP, high-RPM, universal type similar to those found in routers and electric drills. The motor slows noticeably on hardwood, especially when taking the maximum cut on wide stock. All the other planers have induction motors—the type common on tablesaws and other woodworking machines.

The bed rollers are steel, but the feed rollers are rubber. All are adjustable, but the current owners' manual doesn't explain how to adjust feed-roller height (our old manual did). This omission is due to Makita's concern that misadjustment might overstress the cast-aluminum frame of the machine. Anyone who uses the 2040 seriously will need to know how to adjust the feed rollers. Roller height is set by means of screws on the top of the planer at the ends of each roller, and is adjusted with a slotted, threaded ring that surrounds the spring-tension screw. This arrangement could be improved upon. Trying to turn the large out-

*The Makita 2040 needs a boost. Without blocks, the table is only 20¼ in. from the floor in its highest position. A small, high-RPM, 110-volt, universal-type motor is concealed in the base.*

*The Williams & Hussey is a benchtop machine. The motor pivots on a special mount and its weight tensions the V-belt. The add-on power-feed kit bolts on the side of the cutterhead assembly.*

side ring is impossible with a regular screwdriver, and I finally resorted to using a big cold chisel as a screwdriver.

The Makita has the fastest feed rate of the small machines—25 FPM, which works out to a very low 37 cuts per inch (CPI). According to accepted planer theory, the more cuts per inch, the smoother the planed surface. The Makita, however, with the lowest CPI of all the planers, gave a smoother cut than any of the other power-feed machines. This *shouldn't* be possible, but it is. So much for theory. A feed-speed reduction kit is available, although this couldn't improve much on the smooth finish that our Makita produced, except perhaps on highly figured wood.

There were some things I didn't like about the Makita. It's loud—by far the loudest of the small planers. Ear protection is a must. The table, at its highest, is only 20¼ in. from the floor—far too low for comfort. Our 2040 rests on 4¾-in. wooden runners, but it's still too low. More than once, I found myself kneeling on the floor to view the depth-of-cut gauge. The machine won't take a cut heavier than ⅛ in. on narrow stock or ¹⁄₂₅ in. on wide stock. As with the Grizzly, the frame interferes and prevents stock from feeding if you try to take a heavier cut. A board that's thicker at the tail end will jam against the planer frame halfway through the cut.

In spite of these problems, I liked this machine because of its smooth cut and wide, 15-in. capacity. I also liked the depth-of-cut gauge that lets you preview the amount of stock the planer will remove. The 2040 can't do fast, heavy hogging on roughsawn stock. It can handle big stock, but a little at a time. Its small size makes it a good choice for a cramped shop and it's light enough that you can slide it across the floor without breaking your back.

**Williams & Hussey 7-in. molder/planer**—This is a small, benchtop machine that doubles as a molder (I didn't test its molding capabilities). The basic machine comes in three models: W-7, which is a hand-feed model; W-7PF, which has a powered infeed roller; and W-7S, which has powered infeed and outfeed rollers like the larger planers. An add-on kit converts the hand-feed machine to either of the power-feed models. For the test, we got the W-7 hand-feed model and converted it to the W-7S.

This is a very nicely made planer. The bed and cutterhead assembly are cast iron, and machining is of the highest quality. Two ¼-in. thick knives, the thickest of any of the machines, are mounted on the square cutterhead. The heavy cast-iron cutterhead cover also serves as a chip deflector. (It's set too far in front of the cutterhead—2½ in.—to function as a chipbreaker.) There is an unpowered steel outfeed roller on the hand-feed model, but no infeed roller of any kind. The W-7S power-feed model has both rubber infeed and outfeed rollers. There are no bed rollers on any of the models.

Stock up to 7½ in. thick will fit through the planer. You have to remove the chip deflector to raise the head past 6 in., however, because the handle bangs into it.

I set up the planer on a table of 2x4s and particleboard. A 3450-RPM, 1½-HP Sears motor provided the power. Williams & Hussey sells an optional motor mount, which I recommend. With this setup, the weight of the motor keeps tension on the V-belt.

The knives don't require adjustment, as the knives on all the other machines do. You simply butt each knife against a shoulder in the cutterhead and tighten the bolts. This always sets the knives to the same height, even after sharpening, because the bevels aren't supposed to be ground unless they're badly nicked. To sharpen, you're supposed to simply stone the flat back of each knife. If you do grind the bevels, it's easy to set the knives by placing a shim between the knife and the cutterhead shoulder. Don't look for any help from the owners' manual—it's the worst I've ever seen with a woodworking machine. I frequently found myself winging it as I set up and used the W&H.

The hand-feed model is just that—fed by hand. You push the board into the planer with your hands and/or a push stick and pull it out the other end. It takes a little more effort than ripping on a tablesaw. The chip deflector and outfeed roller help hold the board down on the table, but since there's no infeed roller, it's easy to inadvertently lift up the tail end of the board and badly snipe the front end.

One side of the planer is open, so by flipping a board end-for-end and running it through again, you can plane boards up to 14 in. wide on the hand-feed model. Reversing a board means cutting against the grain, which may cause tearout. This method is okay for rough work, but the two cuts never match up and the resulting ridge must be hand-planed. The little machine seems most comfortable with narrower stock. The manufacturer sells optional steel guide bars that clamp to the table and prevent stock from wandering out the open side. I didn't test these, but they're probably a worthwhile investment. For cutting moldings, they're essential. The open side is a boon for molding because you can mold up to 7 in. from the edge of any size board or panel.

The hand-feed model gave the best cut of any of the small planers. Because you can feed the board at a snail's pace, the number of cuts per inch is extremely high. The surface feels as if it's been hand-planed. The Williams & Hussey hand-feed model was the only planer that didn't tear up the bird's-eye, no matter in what direction I fed the board. While the W-7 can plane boards as thin as $\frac{3}{32}$ in., I also managed to hog off $\frac{3}{8}$ in. in one cut on a 4-in. wide pine board by feeding very slowly—though the machine bucked and groaned in protest.

The power-feed kit takes about 30 minutes to install. Off comes the steel outfeed roller and on go the rubber rollers, roller chains and an oil-bath gearbox. The power-feed model has a 15-FPM feed rate.

The power-feed was disappointing. Roller tension is adjustable, but roller height isn't. The rubber feed roller just didn't bite hard enough. I had to push and cajole, and sometimes the board would just slow down and stop in midcut. No longer could I take a heavy cut—$\frac{1}{8}$ in. was the maximum on a 4-in. yellow-pine board. I tried taking $\frac{3}{16}$ in., but the motor jumped back on its mount, the belt slipped and the planer ground to a halt. The power-feed could handle cuts $\frac{1}{8}$ in. or thinner on 7 in. of hard maple, but I no longer got that hand-planed surface and the bird's-eye occasionally misbehaved. For a hefty $340 extra, the power conversion kit raises the price of the W&H almost as high as one of the larger, more powerful planers, but doesn't deliver the same capacity.

The W&H is not well suited for long, wide boards. For small-scale work or highly figured woods, however, the hand-feed model is excellent. The molding capability will appeal to frame-makers or contractors who need custom moldings. In addition to carrying stock molding knives, the manufacturer will make custom knives. If you're so inclined, you could also make your own.

**Foley-Belsaw 985 12-in. planer/molder**—This dual-purpose machine not only planes, but also can make an impressive variety of moldings. A fancier model, 984, even comes with a built-in ripsaw so you can both rip and plane or mold at the same time.

Compared to the Parks, Delta and Grizzly, the 985 is a lightweight, lacking almost all of the features of what I consider to be the ideal planer. While the table is cast iron, the rest of the

The Foley-Belsaw 985 planer/molder has a beefy 3-HP motor tucked under its sheet-steel frame. The top hinges up to expose the working parts.

frame is made of $\frac{1}{8}$-in. thick sheet steel. Tension can be adjusted on the rubber feed rollers, but roller height can't. When the rollers wear, they must be replaced, but at less than $20, this is no great expense. The cutterhead turns on ball bearings, while the feed rollers turn in lubricant-impregnated bronze bushings. The three knives are held in the cutterhead by wedge-shaped gibs, and it takes a hefty whack to break the grip of the cast-aluminum gibs. There are no bed rollers or pressure bar, and the chip-breaker is not adjustable. The table elevates on four screws.

Our test planer came with a beefy 3-HP motor that lives down in the sheet-metal base and drives the cutterhead with two V-belts. This monster caused the sheet-metal 985 to rumble and shake like an old flivver when I threw the switch, but on wide maple boards it was nice to have all that power. Foley-Belsaw offers a 5-HP motor as an option, but I don't think the machine's lightweight construction warrants it.

The owners' manual was the best of the lot, and the optional knife-setting gauge is the best design I've ever come across—a real pleasure to use. Another nice feature is the elevation handle: one turn moves the table exactly $\frac{1}{16}$ in.

Just by eyeballing, it was hard to judge the depth of cut. With most of the small planers, you can tell roughly how much of a cut you're taking just by glancing at the space between the board and the frame. Not so on the 985. With the cutterhead touching the board, there's still a big gap between board and frame. On the other hand, the frame couldn't interfere with boards that were thicker at the tail end, as it did on the Makita and the Grizzly.

As planers go, this is a no-frills machine. For example, the table had the roughest surface of any of the small planers and the edges of the casting were sharp enough to cut. I can't fault the 985 on short-term performance—it planed well on both thin and

## Planer characteristics

| | Parks 95 (United States) | Delta RC-33 (Brazil) | Grizzly G1021 (Taiwan) | Makita 2040 (Japan) | Williams & Hussey W-7 and W-7S (United States) | Foley-Belsaw 985 (United States) |
|---|---|---|---|---|---|---|
| **List price: Complete as shown; planer only** | \$1620; \$1050 | \$1802; \$1445 | \$844.95; | \$1780; | \$470 Hand-feed (W-7)* <br> \$740 Power infeed and outfeed (W-7S) | \$1095; \$825 |
| **Weight (pounds): Complete; planer only** | 410; 244 | 295; 260 | 480; | 254; | ;73 | 370; 252 |
| **Table size (inches)** | $12\frac{1}{8}$ x $20\frac{1}{8}$ | 13 x $19\frac{3}{4}$ | 15 x $20\frac{1}{8}$ | $15\frac{1}{2}$ x $23\frac{5}{8}$ | $8\frac{1}{2}$ x $14\frac{1}{8}$ | $12\frac{1}{4}$ x 27 |
| **Minimum stock thickness** | $\frac{3}{32}$ in. | $\frac{3}{16}$ in. | $\frac{3}{16}$ in. | $\frac{3}{16}$ in. | $\frac{3}{32}$ in. | $\frac{5}{32}$ in. |
| **Heaviest cut possible: 4-in. board; full width** | $\frac{3}{16}$ in.; $\frac{3}{16}$ in. | $\frac{3}{16}$ in.; $\frac{3}{16}$ in. | $\frac{1}{8}$ in.; $\frac{1}{8}$ in. | $\frac{1}{8}$ in.; $\frac{1}{25}$ in. | $\frac{3}{16}$ in.; $\frac{3}{16}$ in. (W-7) <br> $\frac{1}{8}$ in.; $\frac{1}{8}$ in. (W-7S) | $\frac{3}{8}$ in.; $\frac{1}{4}$ in. |
| **Maximum stock width** | 12 in. | 13 in. | $14\frac{7}{8}$ in. | $15\frac{5}{8}$ in. | 14 in. (W-7)** <br> 7 in. (W-7S) | $12\frac{1}{4}$ in. |
| **1-PH motor included in complete price** | $1\frac{1}{2}$-HP, 220V *** | 2-HP, 220V *** | 2-HP, 220V | 2-HP, 110V, universal type | None *** | 3-HP, 220V *** |
| **Switch included in complete price** | Magnetic | Magnetic | Magnetic | Mechanical | None | Magnetic |
| **Cutterhead dia.; no. of knives; RPM** | 3 in.; 3; 4200 | 3 in.; 3; 4500 | 3 in.; 3; 4500 | $3\frac{5}{16}$ in.; 2; 6500 | $1\frac{1}{8}$ in. square; 2; 7000 | $3\frac{1}{4}$ in.; 3; 4500 |
| **Feed rollers** | $1\frac{1}{2}$ in.; steel; corrugated infeed | 2 in.; steel; corrugated infeed | 2 in.; steel; corrugated infeed | $2\frac{1}{2}$ in.; rubber | $1\frac{1}{2}$ in.; steel; unpowered outfeed (W-7) <br> $1\frac{1}{2}$ in.; rubber; height not adjustable (W-7S) | $1\frac{1}{2}$ in.; rubber; height not adjustable |
| **Bed rollers** | 1 in.; steel | 1 in.; steel | 1 in.; steel | $1\frac{1}{8}$ in.; steel | None | None |
| **Feed rate** | 16 FPM | $11\frac{1}{2}$ FPM | $11\frac{1}{2}$ FPM | $29\frac{1}{2}$ FPM (reduction kit available) | Infinitely variable (W-7) <br> 15 FPM (W-7S) | 12 FPM (optional sprocket increases speed) |
| **Cuts per minute; inch** | 12,600; 66 | 13,500; 97 | 13,500; 97 | 13,000; 37 | 14,000; infinitely variable (W-7) <br> 14,000; 78 (W-7S) | 13,500; 94 |
| **Hood for dust-collection attachment** | Optional, \$70 | Optional, \$44 | Included | None | None | Optional, \$25 |
| **Warranty** | 1 yr. parts & labor | 1 yr. parts & labor | 3 mo. parts | 1 yr. parts & labor | 1 yr. parts & labor | 1 yr. parts & labor |
| **Miscellaneous** | Cast-iron frame; pressure bar | Cast-iron frame; anti-kickback fingers | Cast-iron frame; anti-kickback fingers | Cast-aluminum frame; pressure bar; segmented chipbreaker | Cast-iron frame; doubles as molder; bench-mounted. Power conversion kits available, \$235 and \$340. | Sheet-steel frame; doubles as molder |

* \$645 power infeed (W-7PF); ** by reversing board; *** other motors available.

thick stock for the few hours I used it. It can also take a bigger cut than the other power-fed machines. The Foley-Belsaw's sheet-metal design, however, cuts too many corners to suit me. But if you can make use of the machine's extensive molding capabilities, it's worth a closer look. The price is right, and it can do things no spindle shaper can. Foley-Belsaw stocks a number of knife patterns and will make custom knives to order.

**Conclusions**—No machine was perfect. So, weighing the good against the bad, here's how I'd rate the planers:

My first choice for an all-around planer would be the Delta RC-33. Adjusting the rollers was a nuisance, but it's a well-made, smooth-operating, reliable planer for both heavy and light work.

The Parks 95 is a close second. The feeding problem was the only thing that kept it out of a tie for first place. Its ease of adjustment and simple, solid construction were unmatched. It's a hard-working planer that will probably outlast several owners.

The Makita 2040 isn't built for the ages, but it should give years of service. It isn't fast at removing stock, but if a smooth surface is more important than a heavy cut, the Makita may be for you. Often heavily discounted, it is a good value for the money.

The Williams & Hussey W-7 hand-feed planer would be my choice for small-scale work. It's expensive for its size and weight, but it's very well made. Forget the power-feed models—the cost outweighs the convenience.

The Foley-Belsaw works very well, but I'd consider it only if I wanted the molding capability. Because it skimps on mass and conventional planer design, I wouldn't buy it as a planer alone unless I couldn't afford one of the cast-iron machines.

The Grizzly appears to be made well but assembled without much fine-tuning. It has all the adjustment hassles of the Delta, without the same smooth performance. It is, however, a usable planer at a very low price. Long-term durability is a gamble, but you can wear out two Grizzlys for the price of one Delta. □

---

*David Sloan is an associate editor at* FWW. *Since this article was published, Williams and Hussey has fitted its planer with a serrated-steel infeed roller and a rubber outfeed roller, thus improving feed problems. Also, Grizzly added two springs to its planer's chipbreaker.*

# Bandsaw Your Own Veneer

## *All it takes is patience and a sharp blade*

by Brad Walters and Richard Barsky

Anyone who has worked with commercially cut veneer knows that it can be tricky stuff to handle. Because it's so thin, sliced veneer doesn't gracefully suffer the dings and dents of hard use, and the margin for error—especially where two veneered panels adjoin—is quite small. One alternative worth trying is bandsawing your own thick veneer, a method that has several advantages over buying thinner stuff. Prepared veneers usually come in thicknesses between ⅛ in. and ⅟₃₂ in., but when you saw your own, you decide the thickness—in our shop, we usually aim for a ⅛-in. finished thickness.

Because sawn veneers are thicker, they work and feel more like solid wood, yet still retain the stability of veneer. Gluing the veneer to the substrate is easier, too—none of that curling, bubbling, splitting and the like to contend with. You'll also have more material to scrape, plane and sand when flushing up adjacent surfaces, so you won't have to worry about going through the face veneer and exposing the substrate.

Sawn veneers are cut by resawing (standing a board on its edge and bandsawing through its thickness), in this case into a number of thin slices. To resaw veneer, you'll need a bandsaw of adequate size and power. We use an old 26-in. cast-iron Silver bandsaw with a 5-HP motor. With a sharp 1-in. wide blade, it will handle anything we feed it, up to its 10¾-in. depth of cut. While a big bandsaw makes this job easier, don't be discouraged if you own a smaller machine. All bandsaws have limitations, but if you work at it, you might discover that your little saw will do just fine with narrower boards. Experimentation is the rule; try some scraps to find out just how wide your saw can go.

Before doing any cutting, check over your saw—there are some things you can do to improve its performance. The drive belt(s) should be tight and in good condition. The blade must be sharp and well-tensioned (¼ in. of flex with light finger pressure is good), and it should track smoothly. Make sure the bandsaw's tires are in good shape, and if they are glossed over with pitch from sawing softwoods, remove the blade and clean the rubber with lacquer thinner. Adjust ball-bearing thrust guides so they barely touch the back of the blade as it's running with no cutting load. Set fiber (or steel) guide blocks to bear lightly on the blade just behind the bottom of each tooth's gullet.

For resawing, we've found that a wide blade with a lot of set works best. We use a 1-in. skiptooth blade with four teeth per inch. If your machine won't accommodate this width, you can use a narrower blade; the wider the better, though, as the stiffness of the wider band makes for straighter cuts. Go ahead and experiment with other tooth patterns and sizes, but keep in mind that a coarse blade will cut more aggressively and may take a

With a sharp blade, well-adjusted guides and a stout fence, any bandsaw can cut veneers. Guided by a shopmade single-point fence, the authors' 26-in., 5-HP machine will saw boards up to 10¾ in. wide.

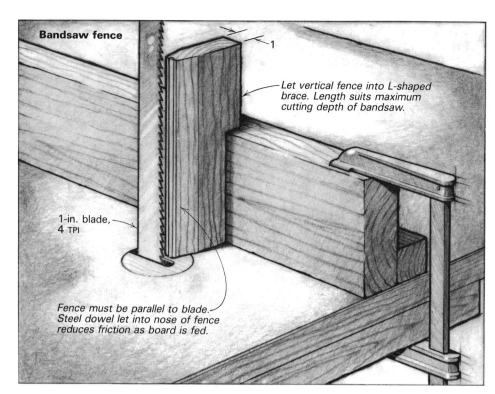

**Bandsaw fence**

Let vertical fence into L-shaped brace. Length suits maximum cutting depth of bandsaw.

1-in. blade, 4 TPI

Fence must be parallel to blade. Steel dowel let into nose of fence reduces friction as board is fed.

With the trailing edge of the fence positioned ⅛ in. in front of the blade, begin the cut by pressing the board against the fence just ahead of the blade. Follow the marking-gauge line (pencil-darkened for clarity) by pivoting the board on the fence.

wider kerf. A finer blade will yield a smoother if slower cut, but it will dull more quickly.

Once your bandsaw is ready, you need a fence to steady the wood so you can resaw veneer of uniform thickness. There are two kinds of fences: single-point and straight. We use the single-point, but each type has its own merits and drawbacks. As the drawing above shows, our single-point fence consists of a 10¾-in. high vertical member attached to an L-shaped brace that we clamp to the saw's table. Where the fence's pointed nose bears against the stock, we epoxied a ⅛-in. steel dowel into a groove, which reduces friction as the board is fed. This allows the stock to be "steered" as it's cut, which is helpful because the angle of feed can change slightly as the blade gets duller, and with variations in the hardness of the wood. Also, even a sharp blade will often have "lead," a condition where the teeth on one side of the blade are sharper than those on the other side, causing the cut to drift off toward the sharper side. You'll need to adjust the feed angle to compensate.

The straight fence is similar to a tablesaw rip fence, and because it supports the board along its length as well as across its width, cutting can proceed more quickly—if your stock is flat and straight. If the board is at all irregular, you won't have room to steer it to make corrections as the cut proceeds. Also, you can't make the steering adjustments for blade lead.

Before you set up the fence, decide what thickness to cut your veneer. This will vary, depending on the board you begin with and how many veneers you want out of it. We usually plan on one veneer leaf per ¼ in. of original thickness. This is generous and may seem wasteful, but it assures us of getting finished leaves of ³⁄₃₂-in. to ⅛-in. thickness. If we want more mileage out of a board, we may try for more leaves—four out of a ¾-in. board, for instance. With smooth, straight cuts we can still get a good finished thickness, but with bowed, warped or wide lumber this is risky. Experience will teach you the limitations.

Rather than set your fence for a standard thickness, look at your board and decide how many veneers you want from it, then divide the thickness into that many sections. Since the saw takes

a kerf each time you slice off a veneer, you have to account for this loss in your figuring. Multiply the kerf size times the number of cuts (one less than the number of veneers you want) and subtract that from the total thickness. Divide the remainder by the number of veneers you're going for, and you'll arrive at the actual thickness of each leaf. For instance, if we had a ¹⁵⁄₁₆-in. board and decided to get four veneers out of it, it would take three cuts to do it. Our saw takes a ¹⁄₁₆-in. kerf, so the total loss would be ³⁄₁₆ in., leaving ¹²⁄₁₆ in. to divide between the four veneers, or ³⁄₁₆ in. per veneer. If this is cutting it too close, you can go for one less veneer so you'll be less likely to wind up with a useless cutoff.

To set up, position the single-point fence so that the board contacts the fence about ⅛ in. before the cut begins. Use a steel rule to measure from the fence to the *inside* (closest to the fence) set of the blade, and measure from the top and the bottom of the fence to be sure it's parallel to the blade. This is important and should be accurate to within ¹⁄₆₄ in., otherwise you will cut wedges. Clamp both ends of the fence securely and check the measurement again. Usually you will need to loosen the clamps and make slight adjustments, or, if your saw has one, adjust the tilting table. If all else fails, place a small shim where the fence meets the bandsaw table to bring it parallel to the blade. Simply shifting the position of the clamp may also do it.

To prepare your board for sawing, surface it so the faces are flat, then joint and rip both edges square to the face and parallel to each other. If you plan to bookmatch, leave the length generous (especially if the grain is a cathedral pattern) because you'll often have to shift the veneers quite a bit to get them to line up. To give yourself an accurate reference for measuring the cut's progress, scribe a line along the top edge of the board with a marking gauge set to the thickness of cut. Also mark the butt end of each board with a bold V as a reference mark for matching later on. Now you're ready to go.

In sawing veneers, it's important to hold the face of the board firmly against the fence at the cutting point. You do this by pressing on the outside face of the board, just in front of the blade. Feed with one hand, and apply a steady but gentle pressure with

Drawings: Gary Theriault

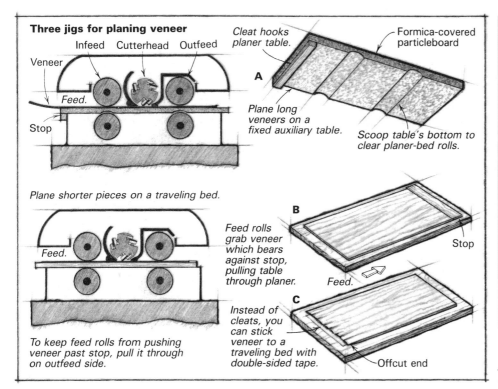

**Three jigs for planing veneer**

Infeed Cutterhead Outfeed

Veneer

Feed.

Stop

Cleat hooks planer table.

Formica-covered particleboard

A

Plane long veneers on a fixed auxiliary table.

Scoop table's bottom to clear planer-bed rolls.

Plane shorter pieces on a traveling bed.

Feed.

Feed rolls grab veneer which bears against stop, pulling table through planer.

B

Stop

Feed.

C

Instead of cleats, you can stick veneer to a traveling bed with double-sided tape.

Offcut end

To keep feed rolls from pushing veneer past stop, pull it through on outfeed side.

*Thick veneers are stiff enough to be glued up just like boards. Flush up the show surfaces, and alternate clamps top and bottom so the leaves won't buckle.*

the other. As you saw, make sure you maintain this contact, but focus most of your attention on the top edge of the board, where the blade should be cutting just outside your scribed line. Go slowly at first. If the cut wanders, make gentle steering corrections. It's better to drift over the line a little and correct gradually than to over-correct larger wanderings. Once you've established a good cut, feed the board steadily, using a push stick to finish. The key is concentration, and with practice, it's not difficult.

If your first cut is good, mark another line on the top edge and make the second cut with the bandsawn surface against the fence. You'll get the most mileage out of your board and the best grain matchup if you resist the urge to resurface between cuts. If you are taking just three veneers out of a board, make the first cut, then flip the board and make the second with the other surfaced face against the fence.

Don't be discouraged if things go badly at first. It takes practice to get the hang of it. Here are a couple of pitfalls to watch out for. If you have to force the board, the blade is probably dull. If you push hard enough, the blade can heat up and twist as it passes through the wood, and may exit the board's face—which is a good reason to always keep your pressure hand in front of the blade. Also, the blade is liable to break under such stress. It's not worth ruining your composure and your veneer by trying to squeeze a little more life out of a blade. Save yourself time and grief by changing it. If your saw bogs down with a new blade, it may be underpowered. Try reducing the width of stock you're resawing, or switch to a coarser blade. Aside from a lack of experience, inaccuracies in the cut will likely be due to your setup. Shut the machine off and try to analyze what is happening. Patience and precision will pay off.

After the cutting is done, you have the pleasure of working with what James Krenov calls "real veneer." If you've gotten smooth, true cuts, you can use the veneer as is, gluing the bandsawn surface to your ground material, then sanding, planing or scraping the top. We find it worthwhile, however, to take our veneers to a neighboring shop where they are passed through a wide-belt abrasive planer. Local millwork or cabinet shops some-

times have these machines and will usually rent time on them. You can expect to lose about ¹⁄₁₆ in. to the sander, depending on the regularity of your bandsaw cut. Using an auxiliary feed table as shown in the drawing, you may be able to pass veneers through a thickness planer. But be very careful, particularly with figured wood. It's dismaying to see a beautifully figured veneer come out of the planer in pieces.

When we're assembling veneers into larger panels, we do so before taking them to the sander. That way we have a fully prepared, flat panel ready for pressing as one sheet. Veneers at least ⅛ in. thick are thick enough to be jointed and edge-glued just like regular boards. Alternate the clamps top and bottom and use light pressure—just enough to squeeze out a tiny bead of glue. Concentrate on flushing up the show face so irregularities in thickness will be on the back side—usually the sander will flatten them out. One word of caution here: Veneers sawn from thick boards may be relatively moist. To keep them from cracking later, give them a couple of days to reach equilibrium moisture content.

We won't go into the particulars of pressing here. For that, see Ian Kirby's article in *FWW #47.* In veneering the back side of a panel, which you should do for stability, you have a couple of options. The best procedure is to cut additional veneers of the same species (although not of face quality) and of the same thickness. We've gotten good results, though, by using commercial veneers on the back side—usually mahogany veneer, which is available in wide pieces and is reasonably priced. We haven't had problems with the veneers being of different thicknesses.

Once resawing is added to your repertoire of skills, you'll find other uses for it. The technique will allow you to cut bookmatched panels for frame-and-panel work, or to get two matched ¾-in. boards or three ½-in. solid-wood drawer sides out of an 8/4 board. Essentially, you need no longer be restricted to the milled thicknesses available at the lumberyard. □

---

*Brad Walters and Richard Barsky operate Dovetail Woodworks in Boulder, Colo.*

# Jointer Talk

## Getting along with home-shop machines

by Jim Cummins

There are two jointers in my shop, a fairly new 6-in. Rockwell and an old 4-in. Sears. Neither one has an adjustable outfeed table, so setting the knives has been a trial-and-error chore that I used to put off as long as I could. Three years ago, I decided to set up the Sears for finishing work, particularly to get some good surfaces on a series of small boxes I was making in my spare time (*FWW* #43, pp. 32-38).

Following directions I'd read somewhere, I set each knife a hair higher than the outfeed table, then turned the jointer on. I put a fine, flat India stone on the outfeed table and slowly passed one end of it over the whirling cutterhead. This process, called jointing, removed a tiny bit of metal to lower each knife edge exactly even with the outfeed table. Of course, it blunted the knives at the same time, leaving a little hairline flat instead of a cutting edge. To resharpen each knife, I lowered the infeed table and laid an 8-in. hard Arkansas stone on it so that the stone rested on the knife bevel. Then I clamped the cutterhead so that the stone, moved by hand in a series of tight circles along the length of each knife, was at the proper angle to hone the flat away, as shown in the photo at the bottom of the page. The infeed table was protected by a sheet of paper under the stone.

This procedure forms a small secondary bevel. The cutting edge has a little more steel behind it than a single-bevel knife, and is, therefore, a little more durable. It took almost an hour to set, joint and hone the knives, but it proved worth it—the edges lasted much longer than they ever had before (partly, I'm sure, because I had more respect for the machine and took some care about what I was feeding it). One benefit came as an unforeseen bonus. The machine was set up so well that I began to sense how my own work habits subtly influenced its performance.

After a while I could walk up to that venerable, rackety old jointer with absolute confidence. On my good days I can surface bird's-eye maple box lids without tear out—I double-tape the lid to a heavier piece of wood that damps out vibration and acts as a push stick. Then I feed ever so slowly, imagining each knife taking a separate delicate slice, getting maybe three hundred cuts per inch. The waste box under the jointer slowly fills with slivers of wood as fine as featherdown.

With anything but super-sharp blades, such a method would be all wrong. In general work, if the feed rate is too slow the blades will rub the work and cause friction that burnishes the wood, as shown in figure 1. Such a surface may look all right, but it won't finish well or glue reliably—the surface fibers will have been pounded flat, overcompressed and overheated. A really dull set of knives can leave burn marks, but the wood can be damaged and chemically altered long before that point.

Usually, the first sign of dulling comes when I'm trying a slow feed on a hard wood, and the work rides up, resulting in a tapered cut. This is the point where I have to decide what's most important: a flawless surface or a straight joint. The blades are probably still sharp enough for general work, but I'll have to feed the work harder and faster. This usually cures the problem for a while. The surface will show some washboard marks, but at least glue joints will be straight and chemically unaltered.

The other choice is to change the blades. Nowadays, since I discovered the gadget described in the box on the facing page,

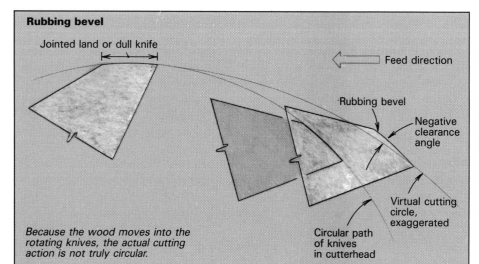

**Rubbing bevel**

Jointed land or dull knife

Feed direction

Rubbing bevel

Negative clearance angle

Virtual cutting circle, exaggerated

*Because the wood moves into the rotating knives, the actual cutting action is not truly circular.*

Circular path of knives in cutterhead

*To double-bevel knives, first level the cutting edges with a stone placed flat on the outfeed table and the jointer running, then hone them sharp as shown, with the cutterhead clamped steady. This gives a lasting edge.*

this is no great chore. But it wasn't always that way. I went through the stone-and-hone routine once with my 6-in. jointer, but within half an hour one of my helpers put a nick in the knives and I swore: "Never again." Instead, I devised a method that uses a pane of glass to set the knives. Coincidentally, the same idea appeared in Methods of Work in *FWW* #41, submitted by Joe Robson of Trumansburg, N.Y.

First you set the infeed table level with the outfeed table, checking alignment with a straightedge. Then you put a new knife in position, tightening the locking screws just enough to allow the knife to slide if pushed. You pull the knife up a little higher than the table and span the cutterhead opening with a pane of glass, holding the glass flat against both tables. Rotating the cutterhead backwards by hand brings the knife in contact with the bottom surface of the glass and pushes it down exactly the right amount. Then you remove the glass and tighten the screws, snugging each one down a little at a time, working from the center out, until all are evenly tight (otherwise you can bow the knife). Talking about distortion, don't take all the old knives out at once, but change one at a time so the tensions in the cutterhead stay balanced.

As a final check when all knives are set, you can press the glass down directly over the cutterhead as you turn the machine by hand. The glass will flex enough to let you feel each knife "drag" on it. If one knife drags more than the others, you should reset it. The accuracy of this method depends on how carefully you set up the sliding fit of the knives. Too loose, and they'll be pushed down too far. Too tight, and they'll be too high. The screws must be set evenly across the width of each knife, too, or one corner will end up higher than the other. The drag test will show you where adjustments are needed, and they usually are.

If your jointer has an adjustable outfeed table, you can set knives entirely by drag. Take a straight, light piece of scrap about 1 ft. long and lay it over the cutterhead. Rotate the cutterhead so the knife grabs the stick and moves it forward onto the infeed table. Mark the distance on the stick. When all knives move the stick the same distance, tested at various places across their width, their height is the same. You then adjust the height of the outfeed table to get a straight cut. The method is accurate, though tedious, and it won't work very well on jointers with fixed outfeed tables—unless you want the knives set high.

High knives do have one application, they produce what's known as a sprung joint, one slightly open in the middle. A tabletop joint with the right amount of spring would let you slip a cigarette paper between the boards at the middle. At glueup, the clamps easily pull this tight. The advantage is that the joint at each end of the tabletop is slightly overcompressed and therefore less liable to crack open in a dry spell. You can get a sprung joint either by setting the knives a few thousandths high in the first place or, on some jointers, by loosening the outfeed-table clamp screws, which causes the table to sag a bit.

Never having had an adjustable outfeed table myself, I have never been able to take advantage of the feature—when I want a sprung joint I take a pass or two with a block plane. Yet I know people who subscribe to arcane and magical outfeed table settings. Me, I like the machine to be level and parallel, with the knives exactly flush with the outfeed table. As long as the machine is at the same setting all the time it will be predictable.

The first step in jointing is to check the stock. The edge of the wood has to be roughly straight before a jointer can do its job. If the edge is severely convex, I take a pass or two just in the middle. Then it will ride right. The same goes for a badly concave edge, or a board with too much taper—I nip away the offending

*This new magnetic jig sets knives accurately, holding each in alignment as the gibs are tightened. A set of knives can be changed and set perfectly in less than ten minutes.*

## Magna-Set makes it easy

In a book once, I saw a photo of a man adjusting jointer knives with a large horseshoe magnet. He laid the magnet on the outfeed table, with the poles above the cutterhead. Next he rotated the cutterhead so that the cutting edge of a knife was at top dead center, and the magnet held the knife up in position while he locked the gibs. "Bingo!" I said, and started looking all over for a large horseshoe magnet. But such magnets are obsolete, and I eventually gave up the search, falling back on my old methods and putting off changing knives as long as I could.

Yet an ingenious inventor, George Hessenthaler of Quest Industries (Box 7768, Murray, Utah 84107), has come up with a $40 gadget that, instead of one large magnet, uses six small ones to imitate a giant, adjustable horseshoe. I tested the device, called Magna-Set, on my 6-in. Rockwell the other day, using it to move two of the knives sideways a little in opposite directions (this trick misaligns the little nicks in the knives and gives a smooth surface again). The job took just five minutes, and the jointer works great.

Here's the procedure: First, you figure out where top dead center is. The easiest way to determine top dead center is to look straight down at the cutterhead, and rotate it until the cutting edge is centered over the cutterhead shaft where it enters the bearings.

With top dead center as a reference, you scribe permanent lines on your jointer to index the jig. The jig is held flat to the outfeed table by four of its six little magnets, and the other two hold the blade in alignment while you tighten up. It's dead easy. Without affecting accuracy, you can even slide the two arms of the jig sideways if you need more room for your tools. The standard jig will slide open to span a 6-in.-wide jointer table, and there are optional rods that extend the reach as far as 12 in.

Can you use Magna-Set to set the knives a little high to make a sprung joint? Sure, there are two ways: either raise the jig with a sheet or two of plastic wrap, or experiment with different jig positions until you find one that works, then scribe a second reference line (any position other than with the knives at top dead center will leave them high).

This invention is so simple, straightforward and accurate that I may start changing jointer knives for the sheer fun of it. George Hessenthaler deserves as much credit as the guy who invented the self-piloting router bit. —*J.C.*

ends before taking a full-length cut. I check the quality of these roughing cuts to see if I've guessed right about grain direction.

When jointing faces, except when feeding very thick or very thin pieces, I use the push blocks that came with the Rockwell. They have comfortable hand grips and a flat, non-slip bearing area. I begin a full cut with controlled pressure on the infeed table, trying to guide the work level over the cutterhead onto the outfeed table. As soon as enough of the work is over the outfeed table I apply downward pressure directly over the cutterhead with one push block (to help prevent vibrations), and with the other block I press down just beyond the cutterhead. The idea is to register the cut against the outfeed table as soon as the jointed surface is long enough to bear properly. As the work moves along, I simply keep exchanging hand positions, taking care to keep the feed rate even and not to let the work ever stop.

If you are routinely getting edges that are concave or convex even though your knives are sharp, first check that your tables are parallel, and correct them according to your owners' manual if they're not. Then think about knife height—if knives are too high, you'll get a concave cut, and vice versa. But if your knives are level with the outfeed table, try adjusting the way you feed the work before you experiment with different settings.

Be conscious of the back pressure from the knives as they cut; if it diminishes, it means the stock is riding up and you'll have to take another pass at a faster feed rate. Listen for telltale "snick" or "pop" noises caused by thick chips tearing out ahead of the cut; if you slow the rate of feed your final surface may still be all right. Take note of everything: When a jointer is working right it sings a harmony of knives whacking away, motor shouldering the load, feathery chips flying against the chute and bearings humming under pressure. It pays to listen for such music—I've found that sharp senses are as important as sharp blades. □

*Jim Cummins is an associate editor of* Fine Woodworking.

# Face bevels

by Galen J. Winchip

If you experience tear out and chipping on your jointer (or planer), even though the blades are sharp, here's an idea borrowed from industry that may eliminate the problem.

Most jointers are designed to handle both hardwoods and softwoods and have a rake angle of about 30°, as shown in the sketch. For softwoods, such an angle works fine, but it's too acute for many hardwoods—when you cut against the grain, the wood splits ahead of the cut, chipping and tearing the surface. Hardwoods are best worked with a steeper rake angle, in the range of 10° to 20°. This more scraping cut leaves a smooth surface.

Rake angles in this range can be achieved by a process called back-beveling or face-beveling, and there's no major surgery

required on the machine. All you need is a thin bevel on the flat face of each knife. It doesn't have to be any deeper than the thickness of the chip you're taking—realize that this is not the depth of cut, but the thickness of the individual chips that go into making a full cut. A bevel of 1/64 in. will certainly do the job, and a bevel half that wide would probably work fine.

To determine the proper bevel angle, you will need an accurate drawing of the cutterhead and knives in your machine. After you have worked out the necessary angles, you can ask your sharpening shop to grind both the sharpness bevel and the face bevel. I do not recommend that anyone grind jointer knives without special wet-grinding equipment. Dry-grinding

in the home shop produces microscopic heat fractures at the cutting edge. Even home-shop honing can be done wrong. It is best to work the stones perpendicular to the edge, not parallel to it, otherwise the cutting edge is weakened by the scratch lines.

Cutting speed, surprisingly, has no effect on the cutting process in wood—think what a good job a hand plane can do. High speed tools such as routers make smooth cuts not because the cutter is moving faster, but because the faster speed means that the chips are thinner. The same applies to a jointer. Chip thickness depends on cutterhead speed, the number of knives, the depth of cut and the rate of feed. The thinner the chips, the less tear out.

Face beveling your

jointer knives is the same idea as choosing a cabinet scraper instead of a hand plane. Some woods are more prone to chipping and tearing than others, but for most work, you'd probably want the plane. Consequently, face bevel your knives only if you have chipping and tearing problems. There is no optimal rake angle for all work, unless it's the 30° angle that manufacturers already use. While you can modify this for special cases, don't overdo. For example, a rake angle of 5° will let you surface bird's-eye maple with no tearout, but the tradeoff is that it will take a lot of force to feed the machine, you'll have to take a shallow cut and reduce the feed rate, and the process will be noisy as well as a large load on your jointer. These drawbacks will apply to any other woods you may run over the machine, but there won't be any corresponding gain in surface quality.

Lastly, for good jointer performance, learn to feel your jointer work. The human being is the most variable and important part of the cutting process. □

*Galen Winchip teaches computer-aided design and manufacture at Illinois State University, Normal, Ill.*

**Face beveling**

Jointer knife — Cutting circle — 30° machine angle — Cutterhead

*The factory rake angle (left) can be modified by face grinding (right) to reduce tear out.*

1/64 — 10° net rake angle — 20° face bevel

# Making and Modifying Small Tools

*Small-shop methods for those special cuts*

by Howard C. Lawrence

T here are times, especially when making period furniture and trim, that a woodworker can't conveniently find a commercial molding cutter, router bit or shaped lathe tool that will produce the exact profile the work calls for. Sometimes we make do with the nearest stock cutter, and often regret it after the piece is finished—a period reproduction just doesn't look right unless its details are authentic. Yet the problem is easily solved. Even a weekend woodworker probably has enough equipment already to be able to make a tool that will do the job right, either by modifying an existing cutter or by starting from scratch.

There are two different approaches to working tool steel, regardless of whether you are reshaping an existing cutter or making a new one. You can choose to work the steel in its hardened state, which requires that you do all your shaping with grindstones (much as you would sharpen a hardened tool's edge), or you can work the steel in a softened state. This second method allows fast, precise shaping with files, and there's no danger of overheating the cutting edge. It does, however, involve some heat-treating to harden and temper the tool for use.

**Working hardened steel**—For small changes or fine detail, simply touch up the shape with a high-speed hand-held grinder such as the Dremel, using some of the variously shaped stones available. This technique makes it relatively easy to modify router bits such as the ones shown in the photo at right. For larger jobs, you can use your regular bench grinder, or you can use the sort of stones that fit an electric hand drill. These stones are inexpensive and come in a variety of shapes and widths, and you can shape the stones further with a grinding-wheel dresser (available from most stores that sell grinders). Hardened tool-steel stock can be cut to size, and some shaping done, with an abrasive cutoff wheel mounted on a grinder or a tablesaw. Such wheels occasionally shatter, so exercise care—don't stand in line with the wheel, and be sure to wear heavy gloves and goggles.

Basically, for hardened steel, that's it. If you take the same care to avoid overheating that you would when grinding a cutting edge, you won't affect the temper of the steel. As soon as you've honed your edge sharp, you can go put it to work.

**Working soft steel**—When you have a lot of steel to remove, I think it is much easier to work the steel in its softened state. If you don't want to learn heat-treating, you can buy soft tool steel and file it to the shape you want, then have it hardened and tempered by a local machine shop, which will have special ovens, temperature-measuring equipment, hardness testers, etc. But

*Standard router bits can be quickly modified with small stones in a hand-held grinder; larger tools can be heat-treated, then sawn and filed to shape.*

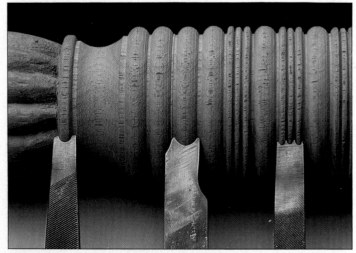

*Shopmade scrapers simplify repetitive patterns. The once-brittle file steel was toughened for safety by tempering with a propane torch. Most of the reeding was cut with a reshaped router bit.*

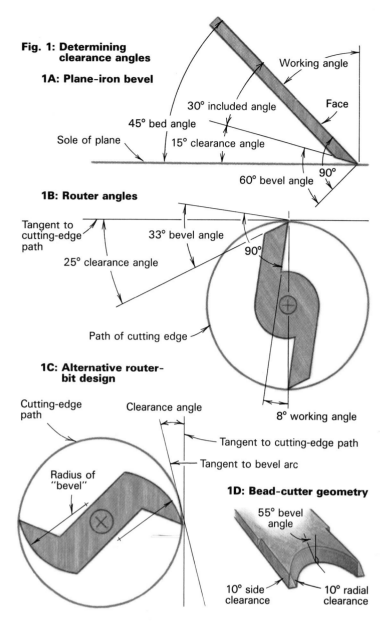

**Fig. 1: Determining clearance angles**

**1A: Plane-iron bevel**

Working angle
Face
30° included angle
45° bed angle
15° clearance angle
Sole of plane
60° bevel angle
90°

**1B: Router angles**

Tangent to cutting-edge path
33° bevel angle
25° clearance angle
90°
Path of cutting edge
8° working angle

**1C: Alternative router-bit design**

Cutting-edge path
Clearance angle
Tangent to cutting-edge path
Tangent to bevel arc
Radius of "bevel"

**1D: Bead-cutter geometry**

55° bevel angle
10° side clearance
10° radial clearance

---

bevel angle represents the material being ground away from the tool. Woodworkers, on the other hand, usually measure the included angle—the amount of steel left in the blade—and call this the bevel angle. The two different viewpoints sometimes cause confusion between woodworkers and machinists, though a good drawing will solve the problems.

To determine the clearance in a rotating tool, first draw it accurately to scale. Around its axis, draw a circle to show the path of the cutting edges, as shown in 1B and 1C. The work will lie on a tangent to this circle, and the working angle of the cutting edge is the angle between the face of the cutter and the radius. In 1B, the face of the cutter is offset 8°, and to get a 25° clearance angle you must grind at 33°. In 1C, the back of the cutter is ground as an arc, and the clearance is the difference between the tangent of this arc and the work surface. This second design has the advantage of allowing a stronger cutter, but if you are modifying such a tool, it is much easier to grind a straight bevel than to try to match the curved one.

Provide a side clearance angle of about 10°. One of my bead molding cutters, for an old molding head, is shown in 1D. Note the clearance angles on the outside edges of the tool and on the nearly radial parts within the bead. Keep in mind that what I've labeled as a 55° bevel angle is from a machinist's viewpoint; most woodworkers would call it a 35° bevel.

**Cutter profiles**—Shaped lathe tools, such as those shown in the photo of the table leg on p. 87, are used as scrapers: after most waste has been cut away, they are held perpendicular to the work. Thus their cutting edges are essentially the negative of the desired finished shape. Other tools, such as molding heads, router bits and plane irons, cut at an angle to the wood, and it is necessary to first draw a projection of the desired wood shape on the angled tool to determine the profile of the cutter itself. Draw the molding shape as shown in figure 2A, and show the blade in cutting position. This view shows the true cutter width, but since the working blade is not perpendicular to the molding surface, it doesn't show the true edge profile. To determine the true profile, next draw a side view of the cutter, 2B, at its working angle α, which can be determined as shown in figure 1.

View 2B shows the cutter's true thickness. It is possible to use views 2A and 2B to determine the actual shape of the cutter's face, which is shown in 2C. Begin view 2C by drawing the left and right edges of the cutter. The edges should be parallel to the face of the blade in 2B, and at the same width as in 2A. Next draw horizontal lines from 2A to 2B to show the locations of the cutter's corners on the face in 2B. Working perpendicular to the face in 2B, extend these lines over to 2C to show the corners of the blade in this view. For example, point *1* in view 2A has been transferred along the line drawn in red to point *1* in view 2B, and from there over to point *1* in view 2C.

Plot additional reference points along the cutter's profile in view 2A and draw a series of vertical lines from the molding profile up to the top of the cutter. The lines need not be equally spaced, but they should start at points important to defining the shape. Draw the lines on 2C with the same spacings they have in 2A, and transfer each point as you did for the corners. In the illustration, 12 points were used in all. The more reference points, of course, the more accurate the cutter profile will be. After all points have been transferred to view 2C, sketch in the full shape.

When the shape of the tool has been determined, paint the surface of the steel with machinists' layout fluid, a quick-drying

---

unless such a shop is close by, it is usually more convenient to do the heat-treating yourself, using simple procedures that were once the general practice for all toolmaking. You don't even have to begin with soft steel. You can take a hardened-steel tool, soften it yourself, file it to shape, and then reharden and temper it, all with the low-tech methods and equipment described in this article. Admittedly, a metallurgist or a precision toolmaker could come up with a long list of "buts." Yet for a small shop, the old methods are adequate.

**Determining clearance angles**—It's best to work out cutter designs on paper before starting to grind or file. The edge of the cutter must have a bevel behind it to provide clearance to the wood surface as the leading edge makes its cut. If you are modifying an existing cutter, it's usually best to keep the original bevel angle. If you are making a new tool, you should aim for a clearance angle to the work surface (not to the tool surface) of somewhere between 15° and 25° (for hardwoods and softwoods, respectively). Figures 1A, 1B and 1C illustrate how to determine the grinding angle. In 1A, for example, a plane iron is set at an angle of 45° to the work surface—this is called the working angle. A 15° clearance angle to the work surface therefore requires a bevel angle of 60°. Notice that I'm using machinists' terminology. Machinists measure bevel angles from a line perpendicular to the face of the tool. To a machinist, the

Drawings: Lee Hov

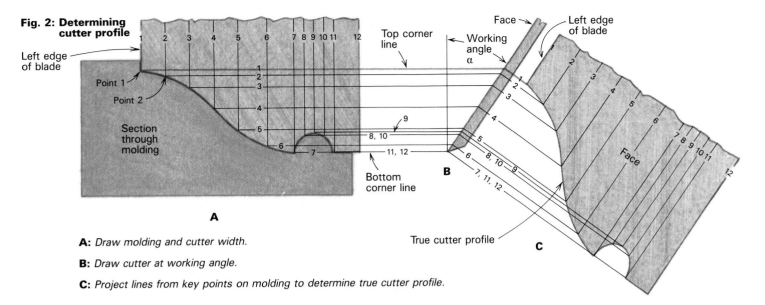

**Fig. 2: Determining cutter profile**

Left edge of blade

Section through molding

Point 1

Point 2

Face — Left edge of blade

Top corner line

Working angle α

Bottom corner line

True cutter profile

**A**

**B**

**C**

Face

**A:** *Draw molding and cutter width.*

**B:** *Draw cutter at working angle.*

**C:** *Project lines from key points on molding to determine true cutter profile.*

blue or purple paint that can be purchased in an aerosol can from an industrial hardware store, or made by coloring a little alcohol with a piece of carbon paper and adding a small amount of shellac. When the paint is dry, scratch in the pattern with a fine-pointed scriber.

**Shaping the cutters**—I usually rough in the shape with a saw and bench grinder. If the profile has intricate curves, much of the waste can be removed using metal-cutting blades in a jigsaw, provided that you are working softened steel. To refine the shape, clamp the part in a vise and work with a hand-held grinder or files (depending on whether the steel is hard or soft). I use Swiss pattern needle files to get into tight places, plus whatever other files conform to the shapes. Double-cut files remove metal quickly when roughing out, and single-cut files leave a smooth surface.

Keep in mind that it is not necessary to make the entire cutter from tool steel. The plane blade in the photo on p. 87, for example, consists of a tool-steel cutting edge brazed to a mild-steel tang. The large router bit is similarly brazed, making it much easier to fabricate. But don't plan such brazed joints in a part of a tool that will be under much stress in use.

First shape the profile of the cutting edge square to the face of the tool, then add the bevel. If grinding, keep the metal cool by dipping it in water frequently or by spraying it.

When grinding or filing the final touches, after you've roughed in the bevel, position the cutter in the vise at an angle such that you can see both the back and the face. Work carefully from the back toward the face, holding a piece of white paper against the face periodically as an aid to seeing the edge. When you've almost reached the face, position a light to give a reflection from the unfinished edge, and carefully file until the reflection just disappears.

**Keeping cutters uniform**—If you have to make more than one identical cutter blade (for a molding head, for example), first make a template out of thin brass or aluminum and scribe around it onto the blanks. Shape all the profiles square, then bevel each one in turn. Repeating the steps this way helps ensure uniformity. A single bit with matched cutters, such as the average router bit, is an exception. I find it best to grind one blade to shape, bevel and sharpen it, then scribe its shape on a piece of thin brass or aluminum cut to fit so it bears against both the

face of the cutter and the shank at the same time. You can then use the template as a gauge to check the length and profile of the other cutter.

It is not always necessary to have matched blades. If you plan to run only a small amount of wood, you can shape just one blade to cut, and grind back any other blades so they don't cut. Be careful to maintain balance in the cutter by leaving enough steel in the short blade or blades so that each weighs about the same as the blade that is cutting. With only one blade cutting, of course, the work must be fed to the cutter more slowly. Don't use the cutter if it is so out of balance that it vibrates.

**Heat-treating**—If you heat tool steel hot enough, it glows, and the color gives a rough idea of its temperature. Once the steel is heated above a certain critical temperature and then cooled very slowly (a process called annealing), it is left in a relatively soft state and can be worked with saws and files. If cooled quickly, the steel is hardened. It will be too brittle to make a good cutting edge, but if it is then reheated to just the right temperature (a step called tempering), it is slightly softened again to arrive at a balance that gives a good, tough tool edge. You can gauge tempering by colors, too: if steel is polished and heated, colored oxides that form on its surface indicate the temperature.

You can judge the hardness after any of the heat-treating steps by trying to file an edge with a sharp smooth file. The file will easily cut soft steel, will slide over very hard steel, and will just barely cut tool steel tempered to the desired hardness.

Keep in mind that we are talking about tool steel. You can't harden and temper mild steel such as I-beams and angle irons in this way. But if you start with a tool-steel blank or with an existing tool, regardless of which particular tool-steel alloy it is made from, you should succeed using the following procedures.

Flat-ground tool steel, sometimes called die steel, can be purchased soft in various sizes from an industrial-hardware or other machine-shop supplier. Its chemical analysis and heat-treatment requirements are shown on the wrapper or can be supplied by the seller. A typical temperature for both hardening and annealing is 1450°F to 1500°F. At this temperature, the steel glows a light red color, a little brighter than full cherry.

You can heat-treat small tools with a propane torch. Larger tools require more heat, but a MAPP gas torch, sold by Sears and others, will handle most small woodworking tools. In borderline cases, reduce air drafts by placing fire brick, pieces of asbestos shingle or other high-temperature insulating material around the tool as it is heated. Large tools may require an acetylene torch with a large tip.

Figure 3 lists two color spectrums: one for hardening steel, the other for tempering. Nobody would claim to be able to tell exact temperatures by observing colors, but the range is close enough for most small tools. Experience helps. The chart lists the glowing colors as seen in moderate light. In bright light or in very dim light, different temperature/color relationships apply. Higher-than-necessary temperatures may distort thin sections, so be sure to direct the flame at broad surfaces, not at sharp edges. Brazed cutters, like the two shown on p. 87, should be held at the brazed point with pliers while heating to lower the temperature there so that the braze will not melt.

**Annealing**—If you want to modify an existing tool by filing or sawing, the steel must first be softened by annealing. Heat the steel with the torch, hold it at a temperature of about 1450°F for a minute or so and then cool it slowly. If the steel is cooled too rapidly, it will not be softened. Test it with a file, and if the file won't cut easily, try again.

For most complete softening, the steel should be held at the elevated temperature for as much as an hour and then cooled in a container filled with ground soapstone, fine sand, ashes from which all carbon has been removed, or a similar insulating material that will keep air away and cause the steel to cool over a long period of time, perhaps 10 hours. Large tool shops have special ovens for this. For softening small tools, it is usually adequate to heat the steel to a light red for a minute or so, and then slowly reduce the heat by gradually withdrawing the flame. When no color can be seen in dim light, the temperature is below 1000°F and the tool can be set aside until cool enough to test with a file. You can now shape the tool.

**Hardening**—Hardening is accomplished by heating the steel to above its critical temperature (the same temperature as for annealing) and then quickly cooling it, usually by plunging it into a liquid. This is called quenching. The rate of cooling affects the hardness, the depth of penetration of the hardness, and, especially in large tools, the possibility of cracks forming. The most

common quenching liquids are water and oil. Water cools the steel faster than oil, but because of this faster cooling, water is more likely to cause cracks and distortion. Cracking isn't often a problem with small tools, though. Oil-quenching gives a softer core to the tool, and thus a tougher tool. Any kind of oil can be used for quenching, as long as it is thin and does not become gummy. Kerosene was often used in the past. Common salt (NaCl) added to water, making brine, also reduces cracking.

The quenching solution should be warm, 125°F, although for small parts the temperature is not critical. Just make sure there is enough solution to allow you to completely immerse the part without appreciably raising the liquid's temperature. When the steel glows at the desired temperature, plunge the part into the quenching solution, cutting edge first, aiming to wet both sides of the tool at the same time. Agitate the tool and keep it in the solution until the bubbling stops.

The cutter will now be so hard and brittle that a smooth file won't cut it. In use, such an edge would soon chip.

**Tempering**—When a hardened tool is reheated to a particular temperature, it is softened to a predictable degree, toughening it. You can control the temperature by heating the tool in a household oven, or you can estimate the temperature by observing the oxide colors. The degree of tempering is partially a preference of the person doing the tempering. If the tool is too hard, it will chip easily; too soft, and it will dull too soon. Tools are usually drawn to between a light straw color (quite hard) and a dark blue (softer). A sharp file will just barely cut steel drawn to a light straw. I prefer a light straw for shaper blades, and have never had one chip.

Polish the face of the tool with fine sandpaper or emery cloth. Holding the tool with pliers as far back from the cutting edge as possible, apply low heat from the propane torch well back from the cutting edge. The polished metal will show a sequence of colors as the flame heats it, starting with a light yellow. As this color moves toward the cutting edge, it will be followed by darker shades of yellow, straw colors, purple, blue, etc. When the desired color reaches the cutting edge, plunge the blade in water to prevent the edge from absorbing any more heat from the body of the blade. The plane iron in the photo on p. 87 shows what a typical tool will look like at this stage.

When tempering, heat the steel slowly to ensure even penetration into the tool and to prevent the color progression from moving to the cutting edge so fast that it would be difficult to stop it at the proper time. The desired final temperature is only about 450°F for straw, 560°F for blue. When the edge is properly tempered, a smooth file will be just barely able to cut it.

**Further reading**—For more about modern toolmaking as done in industry, consult the *Tool Engineers Handbook* (American Society of Tool Engineers, published by McGraw-Hill). Some of the older tool engineering books, such as *High-Speed Steel* by O.M. Becker (published by McGraw-Hill in 1910), discuss in greater detail the simpler, then more often used methods. These and other useful and interesting books can be found in the industrial-arts reference section of a large public library, or in the reference section of an engineering college library. ☐

### Fig. 3: Colors observed in heat-treating

**Glowing colors:**

| Lowest red visible in light 890°F | Dull red 1020–1160° | Full cherry 1300° | Light red 1550° | Full yellow 1750–1830° | Light yellow 1900° |
|---|---|---|---|---|---|

**Oxide colors:**

| Faint yellow 420°F | Light straw 440° | Medium straw 460° | Dark straw 490° | Purple 530° | Blue 560° | Pale blue 600° |
|---|---|---|---|---|---|---|

Approximate hardness, Rockwell C scale

| 60 | 59.5 | 59 | 58 | 57.5 | 57 | 56 |
|---|---|---|---|---|---|---|

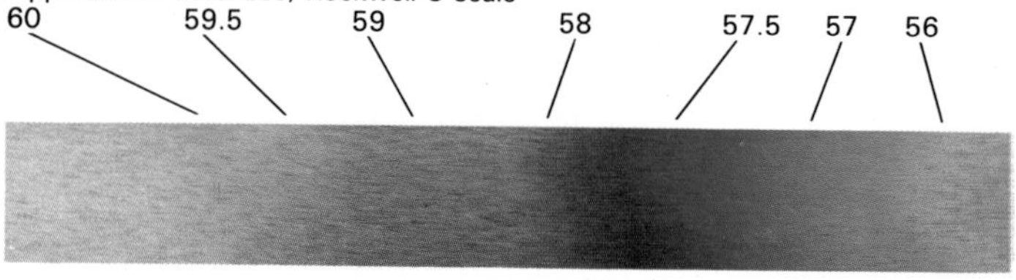

*Steel glows in the temperature range required for annealing and hardening, and the colors progress as in the top table, providing a built-in approximate temperature gauge. The temperatures required for tempering are much lower, and can be judged by observing the colored oxides that form on polished steel when it's heated. Colors are listed as they appear in moderate light—bright or dim light will change the relationships, and you may find that other authorities have their own names for the colors. No matter, hardness is easy to test, and experience brings consistency.*

*Howard Lawrence is a retired aerospace engineer whose avocation was house and small-boat building and who now makes period-style furniture. He is a member of the Society of Philadelphia Woodworkers.*

# Drill-Chuck Reconditioning
## *Overhaul cures lockjaw*

by Richard B. Walker

**B**inding, sticking, hard-to-operate drill chucks rank high on most woodworkers' pet-peeve list. Yet few of us do anything about them. A hoary myth is floating around that balky chucks can't be repaired. And since new ones aren't cheap (name-brand half-inchers are nudging $45 these days), most of us opt to struggle along with the same old cantankerous chuck year after year.

But the truth is, chucks can be readily field-stripped for servicing. Knowing how is the key. Like interlocking Oriental wooden block puzzles, a chuck's disassembly procedure is not immediately apparent. But once you find out how to get one apart, chances are excellent that just cleaning, deburring and lubricating will cure its problems. And, should any components turn out to be worn, replacement jaws, nuts and sleeves are available for most name-brand chuck models. Even a badly worn chuck can be totally rebuilt to like-new condition for roughly half the price of a new one.

I'd advise doing one thing before commencing any overhaul. Carefully inspect the gripping surface of the jaws. If the jaws are badly flattened, scored or unevenly worn, you'll probably need new ones. If that's the case, check to see if replacement jaws are available for that particular brand and model of chuck. If not, it makes no sense to do an overhaul, and you might as well resign yourself to buying a new chuck.

**Removing the chuck**—Thread-mounted chucks are used on portable tools and a few drill presses. Taper-mounted chucks are standard on the majority of drill presses, mounted either directly onto the machine spindle or via an intermediary adapter arbor, as shown in figure 1.

Usually you can remove taper-mounted chucks with wedges or a drift as shown, but if in doubt, consult your owners' manual for directions. For thread-mounted chucks, first open the jaws completely and check inside for a retaining screw. All reversing drills plus a few fixed-rotation models use them. Take care in selecting the proper size screwdriver to avoid damaging the slot. . .which could preclude ever removing the chuck. Retaining screws are always left-hand thread, so remember to turn *clockwise* for loosening. Sometimes factories apply a dab of thread-locking compound, and cracking it loose takes some force.

**Disassembly**—Almost all key-operated chucks fall into one of two families. Each type requires a different disassembly procedure, as shown in figure 2 on the next page. Determine which type you have by inspecting the sleeve area immediately behind the ring gear. Separate sleeve-and-ring gear models (the B type)

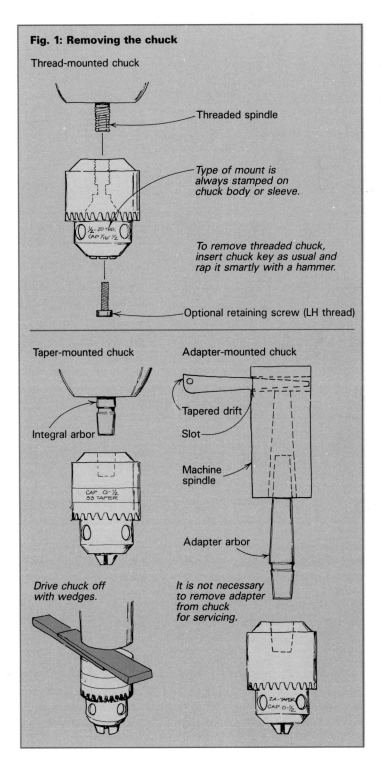

**Fig. 1: Removing the chuck**

Thread-mounted chuck

Threaded spindle

Type of mount is always stamped on chuck body or sleeve.

½-20 THD.
CAP ⅕₆-½

To remove threaded chuck, insert chuck key as usual and rap it smartly with a hammer.

Optional retaining screw (LH thread)

Taper-mounted chuck

Integral arbor

CAP O-½
33 TAPER

Drive chuck off with wedges.

Adapter-mounted chuck

Tapered drift

Slot

Machine spindle

Adapter arbor

It is not necessary to remove adapter from chuck for servicing.

2A-TAPER
CAP O-½

## Fig. 2: Two types of chucks

**Type A: Integral ring gear and sleeve**

*Jaws should be about two-thirds extended so as not to bind on sleeve.*

Sleeve presses off in this direction.

**Type B: Separate sleeve**

Sleeve presses off in this direction.

## Fig. 3: Pressure points

**Type A: Disassembly**

*Apply pressure with shopmade V-blocks or as shown in photos, facing page.*

**Type B: Disassembly**

**Type A: Reassembly**

**Type B: Reassembly**

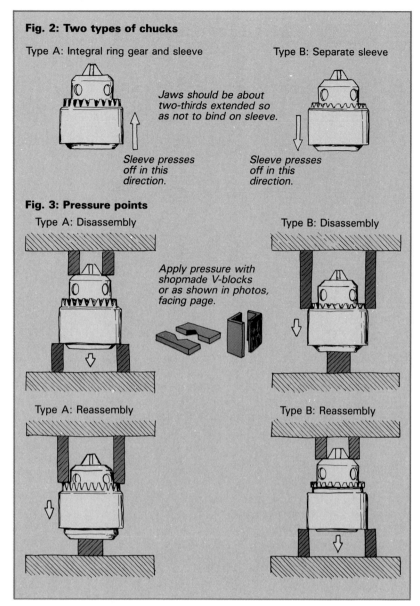

*In the type A chuck (most Jacobs chucks are type A), the ring gear is part of the outer sleeve. A separate split nut works the jaws. Note that it's not necessary to remove a tapered spindle adapter to disassemble a chuck.*

*In the type B chuck, the ring gear is part of the split nut that works the jaws. Pressure must be directed against the narrow outer edge of the sleeve, not against the ring gear, to slide the sleeve off.*

show a faint joint. Integral sleeve-and-ring gear units (the A type) have no demarcation line. Except for their economy consumer line (which is just about impossible to get apart without destroying the sleeve), Jacobs brand chucks are all A type, Supreme brand ones type B. Up until about 15 years ago, most chucks were made by these two companies. The recent flood of imports has changed this. And they're as apt to copy one type as the other, so you really have to check carefully. If you get it wrong, not only will your chuck fail to press apart, but you run the risk of damaging it as well. Both types are shown disassembled in the photos above.

Typical medium-size shop vises can press apart most ¼-in. and ⅜-in. capacity chucks plus some ½-in. ones. In the case of a really stubborn fit, you can resort to a gear puller or an arbor press. If you can't talk your corner gas station owner into letting you use his, most auto parts stores will rent pullers or the use of their bearing press for a few dollars.

Pounding the chuck apart isn't usually recommended because it may damage the sleeve or the body. But on a chuck that's in marginal condition, it may be the way to go. Choose a thick concrete slab or large block of timber as your base. Wield a heavy hammer. Scraps of aluminum or brass are preferred over steel for use as bushings/spacer blocks because they won't cause damage.

Quite often the hardest part of an overhaul is finding the appropriate-size metal bushings for pressing the sleeve off or on. Various sockets from U.S. or metric socket sets usually will work on up to ½-in. capacity chucks. For larger chucks, metal spacer blocks can be substituted. Positioning becomes more tricky, however, especially when you're using a vise. A pair of straight bars will serve, but V-type spacer blocks work a little better, providing four points of contact instead of two. You can easily make homemade V-blocks by hacksawing them from scraps of ⅜-in. to ½-in. thick steel plate or flat stock. Thick aluminum will also work (you can saw it on the bandsaw), but it will get quickly chewed up if you overhaul more than just a few chucks. Or you can saw two short, equal-length segments from an appropriate-size length of angle iron and use them upended.

Before pressing, close the chuck jaws about two-thirds. When they're open too far, they project into the path of the sleeve as it slides off, and damage can result.

Since you wouldn't be disassembling your chuck if it wasn't sticking, the jaws probably will be quite stiff to slide out of their channels. Try rotating them off-center a little while pushing and pulling. If that fails, pry them free, one notch at a time, using an old screwdriver as a lever. Jaws are keyed to their particular channels, so mark each as you remove it. Using the sharp edge

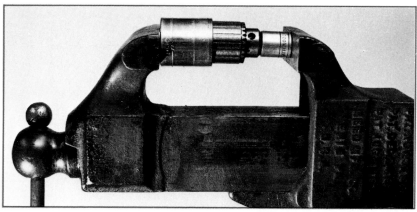

*Three setups for disassembling a type A chuck: For small to medium chucks, a vise can often do the job as shown above, using SAE or metric sockets as bushings. For stubborn chucks, a gear puller usually works (below left). Note that it bears against a bolt placed in the partly open chuck, not against the chuck's jaws. Really stubborn cases may require a hydraulic press, a tool your local gas station may let you use.*

*Burrs, which cause the jaws to bind, can form at sharp edges inside the chuck. Typical trouble spots are shown by arrows in the photo above. To remove existing burrs and help prevent reoccurrence, chamfer such edges with a knife, round needle file or stone.*

of a grinding wheel, I slightly nick the jaw tops once, twice, three times, respectively, and scribe corresponding lines on the chuck body.

**Reconditioning**—An old toothbrush and small wire brush will clean away any old lubricant or dirt from chuck components. If the grease has congealed and is stubborn, soak the parts in a pan of solvent and try the brushes again.

Now assess if replacement parts are required. Check the nut threads, jaw threads, jaw gripping surfaces and ring-gear teeth. Except in cases of severe abuse or extreme usage, these parts are usually quite durable, at least in name-brand chucks. But, some imports are a different story.

Most sticking and hard-operation problems are caused by internal foreign matter or burrs on the chuck body. Especially susceptible to burrs are the areas receiving thrust loads from the nut, and the jaw-cavity areas near the tip of the body, as shown in the photo above right. Some chuck bodies are hardened steel, and you will have to use slipstones to remove burrs. On unhardened bodies, you can use round files or even chamfer sharp edges with a knife. Work on rough areas until you have all the jaws sliding smoothly throughout their normal operating range, but don't change the overall size and shape of the channels.

**Reassembly**—Lubricate the components sparingly with oil or, better, a light grease. Oil will allow you to quickly spin the chuck open and closed, but grease gives a more solid feel to its operation and lasts far longer.

Position the jaws so all project the same distance, then replace the split nut. You can now manually turn the nut to check the chuck's operation throughout its entire range. As with disassembly, remember again to close the jaws about two-thirds. Double-check to make sure all jaws are projecting the same amount (it's easy to get one a notch out of place), and press the sleeve back on. The trick is to initially slide the sleeve over a *vertical* chuck body, thus ensuring the split nut remains in its proper position. Should anything bind or not feel right, press the sleeve off and start over again. Also take care that you're pressing straight and not slightly cocked.

When reinstalling taper-mounted chucks on spindles or adapters, clean both mating surfaces and always assemble dry—never use grease or oil.

Finish off your reconditioning job by purchasing a new chuck key. Chances are you could use one, and you've earned it. □

---

*Richard B. Walker is an Irvine, Calif., citrus grower who writes about metalworking and also makes guitars. Photos by the author.*

# Machining Stock to Dimension
## Start right to finish right

by Roger Holmes

The process of accurately dimensioning lumber lacks the romance of cutting beautiful joints, but is fundamental to quality woodworking. If you want precise joinery, easy assembly and a good finish, you must begin every job by making your cupped, twisted and bowed boards flat, straight and square—the accuracy of all future operations depends on straight, square stock. Before the advent of stationary power tools like the jointer, planer and tablesaw, woodworkers prepared their stock by hand. Today it's possible to sidestep all that handwork and rely on the speed and, to some extent, the built-in accuracy of power tools.

You can check for cup and bow by sight or straightedge, looking across the width for cup and along the length for bow. When placed on a flat surface, a twisted board will rock on the low corners. Sighting over winding sticks (identically dimensioned lengths of wood) placed across both ends of the board will also indicate twist.

Before doing any flattening or thicknessing, it pays to lay out and cut pieces to the rough width and length your project requires. Smaller pieces are easier to handle and less wasteful. A badly bowed 12-ft. board, for example, may make three relatively straight 4-ft. pieces, and the same logic applies for reducing width, as shown in figure 2 on the facing page. You can start with thinner rough stock because you'll need to remove less wood to flatten it. Of course, if you need four 2-in.-wide pieces, it may make more sense to dimension, then rip a 9-in.-wide board, and so on. If you'd rather not lay out the pieces before finding what's hidden beneath the rough surface, skim both faces in the planer before you cut it up.

Regardless of the size of the pieces, you must start by flattening one face of each on the jointer. Resist the temptation to skip this step and go right to the planer. A planer can't remove twist, bow or cup because the machine's rollers will flatten the board before it reaches the cutterhead. The board will lose its rough-sawn exterior, but the defect will spring back as the board leaves the planer.

**A jointer is basically** an upside-down, motor-driven handplane. It has two adjustable tables flanking a cutterhead. Each table should be perfectly flat, and, across its width, parallel to the cutterhead. The outfeed table is set at the same height as the highest point in the arc of the cutterhead. This alignment is critical—if the table is high, the board will taper end-to-end; if it is low, the end of the board will be gouged by the cutterhead as it leaves the infeed table. Moving the infeed table up or down sets the depth of cut. When flattening wide boards, I usually align the jointer's fence with the end of the cutterhead, allowing

maximum width of cut. For narrower boards, you can set the fence to use the sharpest part of the cutterhead. Rub paraffin or pastewax on the tables so the board will slide easily—the less force required to push a board across the cutterhead, the better. Before running a board over the jointer, remember that the most finely-wrought machines you'll ever see are attached to your wrists. Be careful.

If the board is badly cupped or bowed, I flatten the concave face, which is more stable on the tables than the convex face. It often doesn't matter which face of a twisted board is flattened first, but if the board is also cupped or bowed, plane the concave face first. Once you've picked a face, check the edge of the board to determine grain runout, as shown in figure 3, to avoid tear out. Set the infeed table for a shallow first cut, about ⅟₃₂ in., then feed the board into the jointer so the grain is rising into the cutterhead. If there is much tear out on the first pass, turn the board end-for-end. If the grain changes direction along the board, taking light cuts or angling the board across the cutterhead to produce a shearing cut will help.

Once you've determined the grain direction, increase the depth of cut, if necessary (I find ⅟₁₆ in. is usually plenty), and continue. Place your left hand near the front end of the board, and make sure that all four fingers and your thumb are touching the top face, not hanging over the end or edge. Sometimes I put my right hand on top of the board to push; on longer boards I grasp over an edge to begin the cut, then move my hand on top of the board or to a push stick.

As the face passes over the cutterhead, push it down on the outfeed table with your left hand. The contact of the newly planed face with the outfeed table ensures that the remainder of the face will lie in the same flat plane. Keep pressure on the board over the outfeed, not the infeed table. When 6 in. to 1 ft. of the board has moved across the cutterhead, I often move both hands over the outfeed table to feed the remainder of the board through. If you need more horizontal force, or if the board is short, push the end through with a push stick, not the end of your fingers. Be especially careful with thin or narrow pieces.

Work all the stock for a particular job in one batch—face it all at once, thickness it at once, and so on. Stack the boards by grain direction as they come off the jointer. An arrow on the flattened face helps for future reference. Keep the piles straight for all remaining operations and you'll save time and avoid frustration and torn grain.

When flattening cupped or bowed boards, try not to push down too hard as the board goes over the cutterhead—the board will spring back, thinner, but still bowed. For long, badly bowed

**Fig. 1: Board defects**

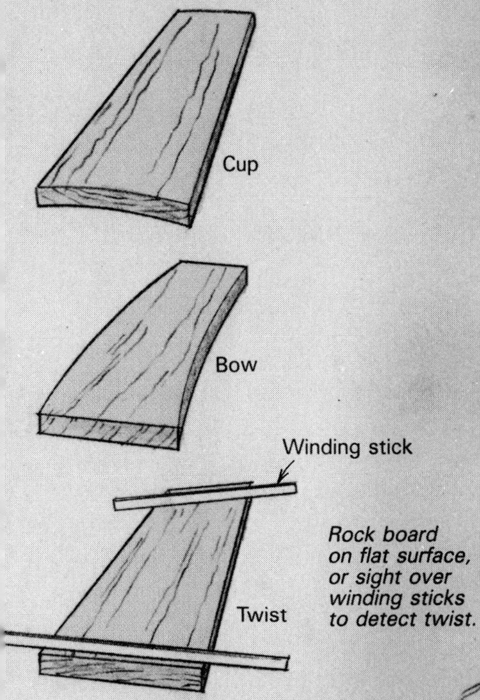

Cup

Bow

Winding stick

Twist

Rock board
on flat surface,
or sight over
winding sticks
to detect twist.

**Fig. 2: Efficient material use**

*To use material more effectively, lay out and cut pieces
roughly to size before flattening and thicknessing.*

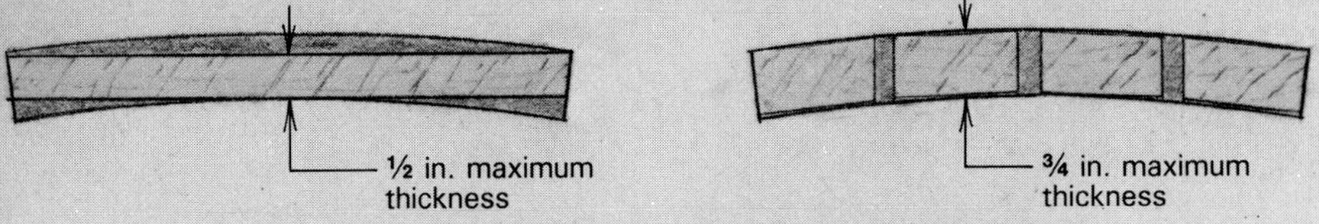

½ in. maximum
thickness

¾ in. maximum
thickness

**Fig. 3: Jointer**

*Feed rising grain into cutterhead to avoid tear out.*

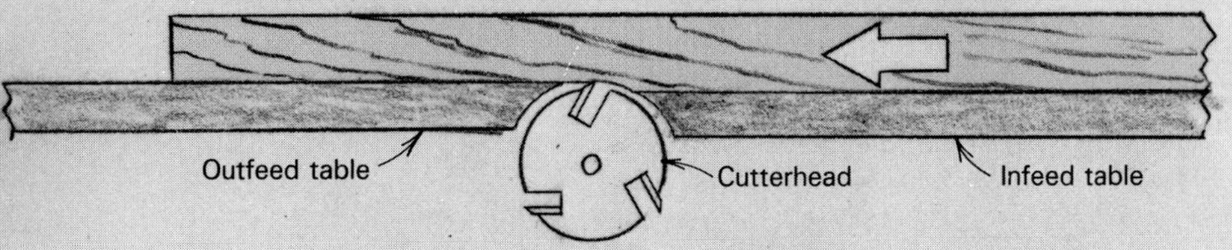

Outfeed table

Cutterhead

Infeed table

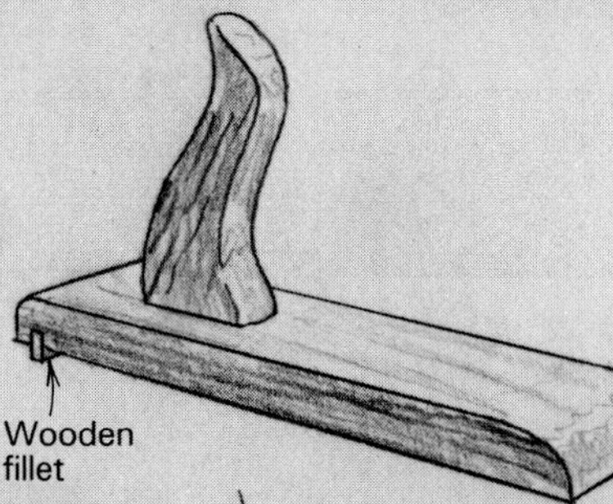

**Fig. 4: Hand positions**

**Fig. 4a: Push stick**

Wooden
fillet

*Push the end of a
short board through
with a push stick.*

B. When 6-in. to 1-ft. of the board has moved
across the cutterhead, you can move both hands
over the outfeed table to complete the cut.

A. To start the cut, push the board down on the table
with your left hand, feed with your right. As the
board passes over the cutterhead, shift the
downward pressure to the outfeed table.

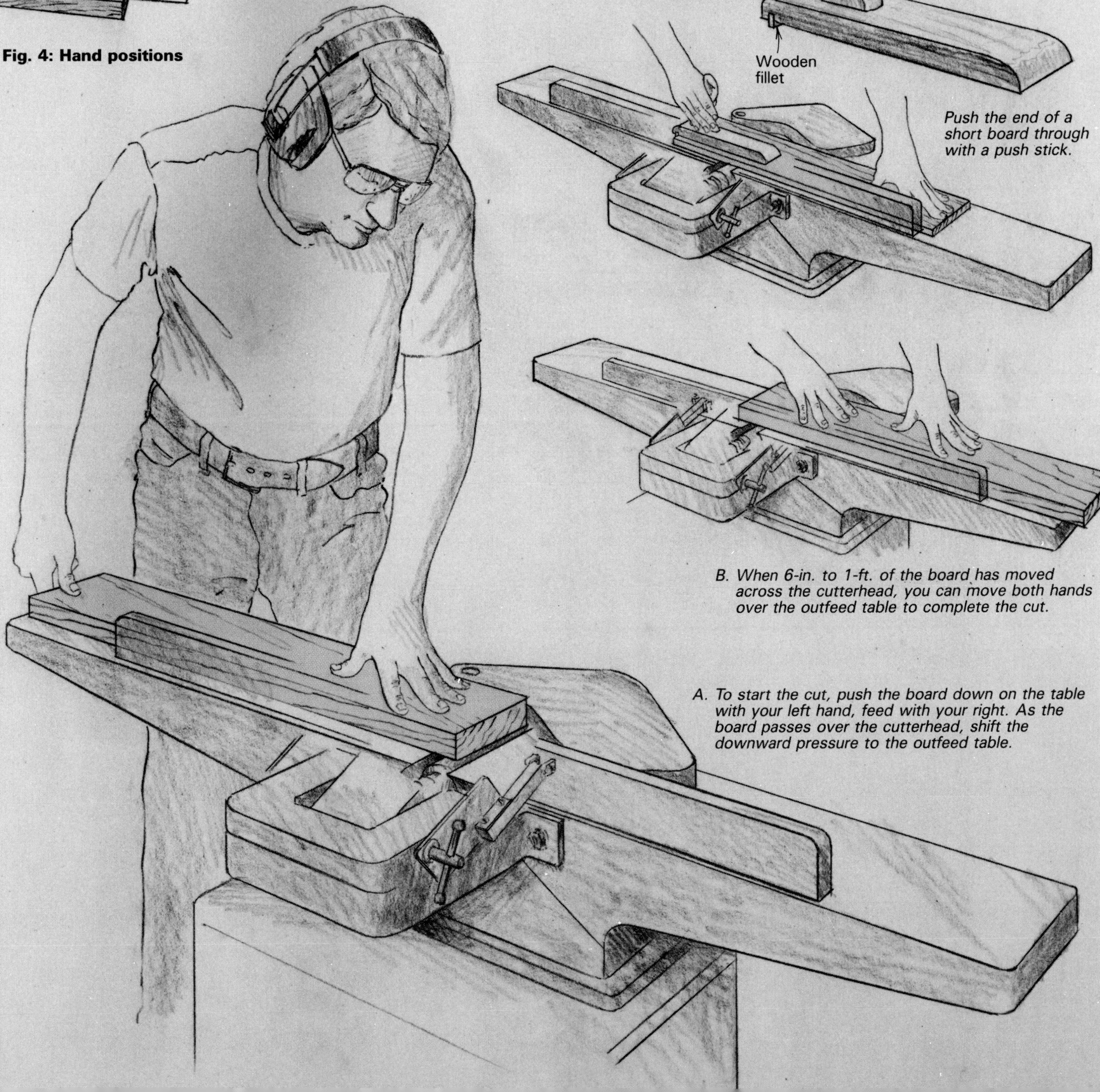

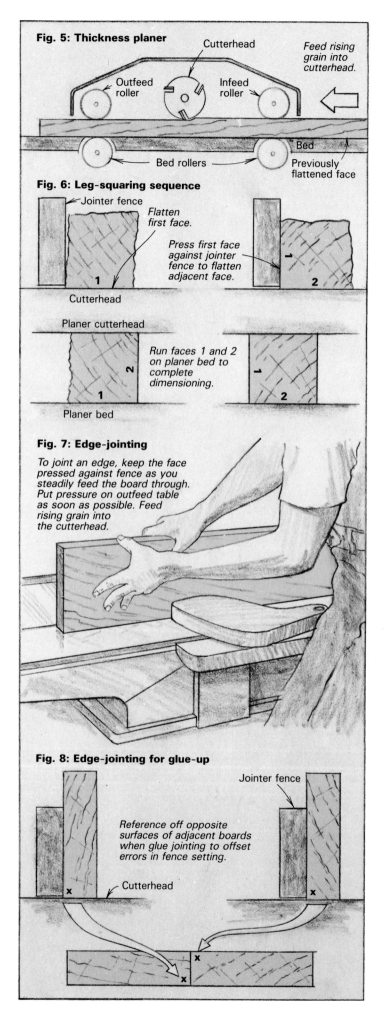

**Fig. 5: Thickness planer**

Cutterhead

*Feed rising grain into cutterhead.*

Outfeed roller

Infeed roller

Bed rollers

Bed

Previously flattened face

**Fig. 6: Leg-squaring sequence**

Jointer fence

Flatten first face.

Press first face against jointer fence to flatten adjacent face.

1

2

Cutterhead

Planer cutterhead

Run faces 1 and 2 on planer bed to complete dimensioning.

2

1

1

2

Planer bed

**Fig. 7: Edge-jointing**

*To joint an edge, keep the face pressed against fence as you steadily feed the board through. Put pressure on outfeed table as soon as possible. Feed rising grain into the cutterhead.*

**Fig. 8: Edge-jointing for glue-up**

Jointer fence

*Reference off opposite surfaces of adjacent boards when glue jointing to offset errors in fence setting.*

Cutterhead

x

x

x

x

boards, lower the middle of the board over the cutterhead and joint the trailing end, then reverse the board and repeat the process. Continue until the board looks straight, then make a pass from end-to-end.

Flattening a twisted board is a little trickier, and you can waste a lot of wood if you're not careful. You can see why by first balancing the board on its two diagonally opposed high corners, so that the corners are an equal distance above the surface. This distance indicates the amount of wood that must be removed to eliminate the high spots and flatten the face. Now, push down on one end of the board so the board is resting on three corners, and note how the gap increases at the fourth corner. This difference in height indicates how much more wood must be removed to flatten a board pushed over the machine balanced on three corners. The trick, then, is to balance the twisted face on two corners as it is fed into the cutterhead until there is enough flattened surface to support the piece. Don't rock the board as you push it through; this will just create another twist. When the board looks flat, make a single pass over the whole face.

Dimensioning table legs can cause headaches—it's maddening to end up with a rhombus instead of a square section. The solution is simple. Rip the legs roughly to size, flatten one face, then press that face firmly against the jointer fence and joint a second, adjacent face square to the first. Check to make sure the faces are at 90°; adjust the fence if necessary. Move to the planer to finish, alternating the two flattened faces on the bed.

Flattening a board wider than your jointer is always a problem. The safest solution is to rip the boards as wide as the jointer will take, flatten and thickness them, then reglue to make the wide, flat pieces needed. If you're loathe to rip that beautiful width of walnut, a less reliable and more risky method is to run first one half of the face, then the other over the jointer. Set the machine for a light cut and don't worry if the surfaces don't match each other exactly. If you can flatten the face, you can clean it up on the planer.

Pushing a board over a jointer always removes wood; whether it's the right wood depends on you. Pay attention to defects in each board as you try to remove them, and make a mental note when something goes right or wrong.

**The planer excels** at two jobs the jointer is not intended to do. It can create a flat surface that is parallel to an already existing flat surface, and it can uniformly reduce the thickness of stock. The planer is also one of the few woodworking machines that requires very little skill to operate, beyond organizing the boards so the machine cuts with the grain.

Most planers consist of a cutterhead and one or more powered rollers suspended over, and parallel to, a machined table (called the bed), which can be moved up or down to set depth of cut and thickness of board. Lay the flattened face down on the table, engage the end of the board with the powered roller and the machine does the rest. Remember, a planer won't flatten a bowed or twisted board, it will just make it thinner. (If a board is thick enough to resist the roller pressure, a planer may slice off the high spots of a cupped board enough to flatten it.)

I always run the thickest boards first, planing the whole batch at one setting before changing it. Add thinner boards into the batch as you raise the bed. Run the entire batch through at the same setting on the final pass to ensure uniform thickness. Take light cuts, not more than $\frac{1}{16}$ to $\frac{1}{8}$ in. If you must remove a lot of wood, alternating the faces after the second face has been flattened will reduce the possibility of warping.

# Saw it straight

by Larry Montgomery

As an apprentice boatbuilder, I was taught a method of straightening long, bowed edges that is much more efficient than repeatedly jockeying 12-ft. boards over a jointer.

The method is simple, as the drawing shows. Tack a perfectly straight piece of ⅜-in. plywood about 8 ft. long and 4 in. wide along the concave edge, leaving the nail heads about ¼ in. proud, for easy removal. Run the package through the tablesaw with the plywood guide against the fence. Pull the nails, flip the board, set the fence, and run the newly trued edge against it for a second edge parallel to the first. For longer boards, splice two pieces of ⅜-in. by 4-in. by 8-ft. plywood, end-to-end, with an overlapping backing piece.

If you don't have a tablesaw, or don't want to nail into FAS walnut, you can clamp a length of ¼-in. by 2-in. by 2-in. aluminum angle (available from building supply houses ) to the board for a guide, and rip along it with a circular saw and a combination or rip blade. If all else fails, snap a line and bandsaw the edge. ☐

*Larry Montgomery is a professional boatbuilder and writer in Port Townsend, Washington.*

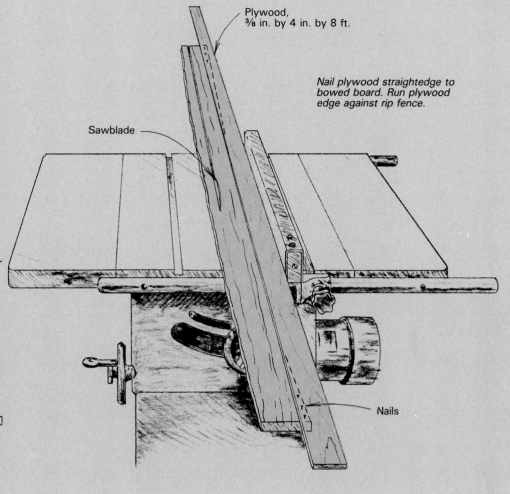

Plywood, ⅜ in. by 4 in. by 8 ft.

Nail plywood straightedge to bowed board. Run plywood edge against rip fence.

Sawblade

Nails

---

For thin stock, say ¼ in. or less, lower the bed rollers flush with the bed, or place an auxiliary bed of plastic-laminate-covered plywood or chipboard on top of the planer bed, to prevent the knives and rollers from distorting the piece. I find using an auxiliary bed as long as the pieces being planed works even better. The bed travels through the planer with the thin piece and cuts down on chatter. Wear good ear protectors, and don't ever attempt to reach or look into a planer while it is on.

**Edge jointing involves** straightening and squaring the edges of the board to its now-parallel faces. Use an accurate try square to check that the first board's edge is square to its face and adjust the fence as necessary. I push the board firmly against the fence with my left hand and push it along with my right. Keep the fingertips of your left hand in contact with the board and at least a couple of inches above the table and behind the cutterhead when starting out, and keep it on that same spot on the board as it passes over the cutterhead onto the outfeed table. When your left hand is over the outfeed table, a few inches beyond the cutterhead, leave it in that position and slide the board between it and the fence. As soon as possible, the downward pressure should be on the outfeed, not the infeed, table. When you need to reposition your right hand on the top edge, keep the board moving by pushing with your left. The whole operation should be smooth, the two hands working in unison so the edge doesn't

stall over the cutterhead. Don't do all the work with your arms, but shift your weight as the board goes over the cutterhead. A slower feed produces a smoother edge.

If necessary, make a couple of passes to straighten the edge, taking off ¹⁄₁₆ in. or so, then a final, slow, shallow pass for a smooth edge. If possible, feed the board in the direction of the rising grain. If you must go against the grain, feed very slowly and take a shallow cut. If the faces are flat, the machine will more-or-less automatically correct all defects in the edge, except bowing along the length. Bowing can be remedied by flattening increasingly larger sections on the ends of a concave edge or the center of a convex edge. Lower a concave edge over the cutterhead, as described for face flattening. If you've cut the pieces roughly to width, joint one edge, then rip the other to exact width. For glue-joint edges, reverse adjacent boards, as shown in figure 8 on the facing page, to compensate for slight inaccuracy in the fence setting.

Those are the basics of dimensioning stock. I tend to treat precise cutting to length as part of the joinery or assembly, because it makes more sense to me to lay out the finished length of a piece at the same time I'm laying out the location of a through-mortise or some dovetails. The shop is quiet, I get myself in a meticulous mood, sharpen my pencil and get to work. ☐

*Roger Holmes is an associate editor of* Fine Woodworking.

# Hollow-Chisel Mortising

## Strategies for boring accurate square holes

by John Leeke

If you have to chop more than four mortises at a time, a hollow-chisel mortiser is faster than the traditional hand methods of chopping directly or of drilling out most of the waste, then using a chisel to square up the hole. When I started using my mortiser, I found it quick and easy to cut clean mortises, but they were often out of square and the bits burned. After a while, I realized the problem was the way I was using and maintaining the tool, not a defect of the tool itself.

My mortiser consists of a cylindrical cast-iron bracket that bolts to the quill of my drill press. The chisel itself—actually a hollow, square tube held in the bracket by a setscrew—encloses a specially designed auger. When the chisel is plunged into the wood, the auger bores away most of the waste and the chisel's four sharp bevels square off the hole's round corners. Boring several square holes side-by-side produces a mortise.

Getting a hollow chisel to work as advertised is a lot like coaxing the most out of a hand plane—you need to sharpen and set it up correctly. To me this means grinding away the rough outside surfaces of the chisel to reduce friction, enlarging the notches and grooves inside the chisel for more efficient waste removal, and honing the chisel and the auger until they are razor-sharp.

Modifying the chisel to eject chips freely is important because the chips dissipate heat. If they jam in the corners or on the auger spirals, the added friction will quickly overheat the mortiser. Use a *fine* triangular file to deepen and smooth the notches and grooves on each inside corner, as shown in figure 1, but be careful—if you cut them too deep, you'll weaken the corner. Next polish the chisel's coarse, outside surfaces with a flat, hard Arkansas oilstone. Keep the chisel flat on the stone and don't dub over the cutting edge. This polishing will make it easier to plunge the chisel into the wood and to produce a sharper edge, since the cutting edge is the intersection of the outside walls and the inside bevels. I grind the bevels with a mounted stone chucked in the drill press and hone them by hand with a cylindrical slipstone. When you're satisfied with the chisel, use a fine triangular file to sharpen the auger, as shown in figure 2. I do most of the sharpening on the top surface.

Now mount the chisel on the drill press and insert the auger through the chisel into the drill chuck. The hard part here is setting the bit so it doesn't rub too hard inside the chisel, causing excessive heat and wear. I have a Jacob's chuck on my press, and I push the bit right against the end of the chisel. Tightening the chuck drops the auger down just enough to clear the chisel. With another chuck, you may have to drop the bit slightly before tightening it. You'll hear a very high-pitched squeaking if the auger and chisel rub too much. If this is the case, loosen the chuck and lower the bit slightly. A rattling sound is okay—even a properly adjusted auger rubs slightly against the curved bevels, wearing them away and turning slight burrs on the outside of the chisel. As long as you hone off the burrs, this wear is helpful since it lengthens the corner points, giving you more steel for sharpening the cutting edges.

Once the bit is chucked, you're ready to start mortising. You can make either a full cut, where the chisel is surrounded by wood, or a side cut, where at least one side of the chisel is open and unsupported, as when you cut right next to an existing hole. A full cut goes straight because the chisel is supported on all four sides, but a side cut will likely drift toward the open side and not be square. This is no problem if you're wasting away the middle of a mortise, but it could throw a joint out of alignment if the out-of-square cut is on an outside wall of the mortise. Also, the drift can damage the mortiser.

To overcome both of these problems, I make a series of full cuts, leaving a section of wood slightly narrower than the width of the chisel between each cut, then I go back and clear out the waste with open cuts. You can expand this method to mortises that are wider than your chisel.

Regardless of your cutting strategy, push the chisel through the work at a constant rate, with as few pauses as possible, to produce a steady steam of chips and a continuous cooling effect. Never stop the chisel inside a mortise where heat will be trapped. If you have a compressed-air setup or a vacuum system, rig it up to cool the bit and to help remove the chips.

If you do clog the chisel, the pressure of the chips from the next cut may clear the chips. If it doesn't, quickly shut down the machine, pull out the auger, and cool it and the chisel in a cup of water. I clear the clog with a narrow, bristled brush sold by kitchen-supply houses for cleaning coffee-percolator stems. Most of my clogging problems involve ¼-in. chisels.

When cutting through-mortises, remember to back up the bottom edge of the workpiece, or the chisel will tear the wood as it passes out through the wood. You could use a wooden block, but I prefer to make a ¼-in. thick aluminum backup plate that can be attached to the press table before the workpiece is clamped down. Drill the plate and file a square hole slightly smaller than the chisel, then lower the chisel through the soft metal to cut the final opening. Also, once you've tuned up your chisel, don't neglect it. Keep it sharp and don't put it away filled with soggy chips that can cause rust. Rusty chisels clog easily. □

*John Leeke makes furniture in Sanford, Maine. Photos by the author.*

Drawings: Christopher Clapp

## Fig. 1: Chisel tune-up

Bevels are curved to fit around auger.

Grind and hone cutting bevel as shown in photos below.

Deepen and smooth notch from groove to just below point.

Deepen groove for improved chip clearance.

Chips are ejected through chisel slot.

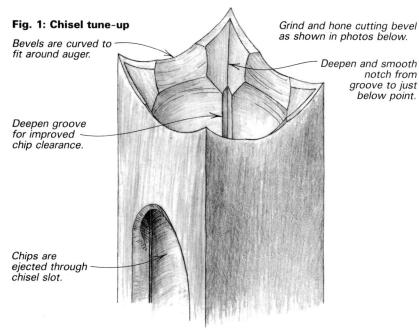

## Fig. 2: Sharpening the auger

File and smooth two bevels forming each cutting edge.

Maintain original angles on spurs and cutting edges.

Top bevel

Bottom bevel

Touch up spur on inside only.

Use rounded slipstone to hone inside edge of spiral.

*Plunge the chisel into the wood for a series of full cuts, outlining the mortise as in **A**, then clear out the waste. Using full cuts to outline large mortises (**B**) ensures square walls. A mortiser clamp holds the wood on the table. Use horizontal clamps or your hand to hold the piece against the fence.*

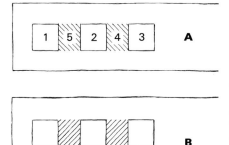

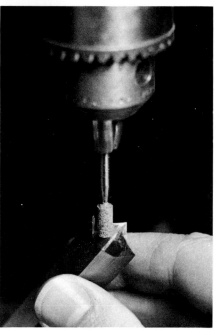

*To sharpen the chisel, chuck a ³/₁₆-in. dia. stone, and set the chisel so its bevel meets the stone at 40° (left). Grind the first bevel freehand at low speed, align the next side and repeat. With the chisel supported by a notched dowel set into a hole bored into the bench (above), twirl a round slipstone to hone the bevels. Polish the outside surfaces with a fine stone.*

*Don Strong, left, cuts a sliding dovetail on the Joint-Matic, a router joinery machine he invented and manufactures in his garage machine shop. He subcontracts foundry work, then does final assembly himself. A similar small-scale manufacturing setup turns out the Wirth Machine, a sophisticated joinery tool developed by former aerospace engineer John Wirth, right.*

# Two New Joinery Machines
## *And a look at their backyard beginnings*

by Paul Bertorelli

"Look here," says Don Strong, reaching into a plastic milk crate heaped high with small, gray iron castings, "this is the kind of problem you run into building your own machines." Pointing with a pencil, Strong shows me how sloppy pattern work mislocated a dimple needed to center a machinists' bit. At Delta or Powermatic, they'd probably toss the lot back into the furnace, then dispatch a stiff memo to the pattern foreman. Not Strong. He's devised a positioning jig for his drill press so the hole can be bored true, correcting the mistake.

Remedial engineering is all in a day's work for Strong, who in his garage workshop manufactures a machine called the Joint-Matic, a router-based joinery tool he invented nine years ago. The casting we are inspecting, a bracket for the Joint-Matic's cutter guard, is one of six that go into each machine. Recasting them would be costly and might delay shipment of the new ma-

chines, neither of which Strong's budding business can afford. So, to keep things rolling, Strong improvises.

He's ideally positioned to do so. As chief designer, manufacturing supervisor, quality control inspector and customer relations rep of Strong Tool Design, he's a one-man show, with a little help from his wife Bonnie, who handles the books. Strong is part of a tiny network of cottage-industry manufacturers sprung up during the past 10 years to service—and in part create—a demand for woodworking tools that the bigger companies don't make. He and John Wirth, another small-fry tool manufacturer I visited for this report, are true inventor-entrepreneurs, inveterate machine tinkers who've channeled their compulsive thingmaking into the manufacture of genuinely new tools. Wirth's machine, which bears its inventor's name, cuts many of same joints that the Joint-Matic will, but operates differently enough to provide an interest-

*The Joint-Matic makes quick work of the sliding dovetails used in this leg-and-apron table joint with corner bracket. A compound miter gauge available as an option positions the bracket to cut the angled pins.*

ing look at how a tool design can be approached in distinct ways.

Strong's Joint-Matic represents the direct approach. It was born out of the peculiar ingenuity of a woodworker accustomed to modifying machines to do what some workers might accomplish by handtools. "I had been building a little set of shelves...nothing really fancy, but it seemed a shame just to dado the corners," recalls Strong. He had in mind a sliding dovetail, an excellent carcase joint but a nuisance to cut by hand or machine. His Shopsmith and a new router offered a solution. If he could cobble up a bracket to hold the router, he could feed the work on the Shopsmith's horizontal table past the bit, cutting first the dovetail's socket, then the pin. After much trial and error, Strong got the arrangement down well enough to suggest commercial potential and two more weeks of night-time work refined it enough to produce the Joint-Matic prototype. The production machine looks a bit crude at first glance, but a shrewd design rationale lurks beneath its coarse exterior.

Essentially, Strong took the idea of a router table—an upright cutter past which the wood is fed via fence or miter gauge—and flipped it 90°. The Joint-Matic has two metal tables, one horizontal and one vertical. The vertical table, which holds the router, rides on two steel ways, allowing it to travel up and down, thus positioning the router bit relative to the work instead of the other way around, as with a router table. Wood is fed free-hand past the bit on the horizontal table or gripped in a tablesaw miter gauge that rides in a groove milled in the table surface. Borrowing a trick from metal-working machinery, Strong added a pair of steel lead screws synchronized by a bicycle chain and sprocket to crank the vertical table up and down.

**Strong's design has notable advantages** over a router table. For one, the lead screws have 16 threads per inch so they move the table (and bit) up or down $\frac{1}{16}$ in. per turn, where it stays put. Fine adjustments are made by cranking the screws through a portion of a turn. This is far better than fumbling with an imprecise shop-made fence and it gives the Joint-Matic remarkable accuracy, expanding its repertoire of joints. Using the miter gauge or an optional compound gauge for angled parts, you can grip the wood positively and feed it without slipping or skewing. The Joint-Matic solves one other router table shortcoming, as well: the router is mounted horizontally to one side of the cutting face instead of vertically beneath the cut so it doesn't suck sawdust into its guts, ruining the bearings and armature.

Originally, Strong had no intention of building the Joint-Matic himself. "I knew I had a great idea and that a lot of them could sell," says Strong, "but I thought I could make more money at it if I sold it to someone else." Strong offered his invention to Sears, Black and Decker, and Porter-Cable, all of whom turned it down as having too little sales potential. Rather than see the project wither, Strong began producing the Joint-Matic on his own, financing its development with income from his job as a millwright at an auto plant. "Every time I'd get $1,000 ahead, the money would go to pay for something...one week it might be patterns for castings, the next week it was the patent lawyer." By the time the Joint-Matic was ready for demonstration, Strong had spent more than $100,000.

To keep costs down, Strong used as many off-the-shelf parts as he could. The lead screws and table tracks, for instance, are standard industrial-hardware items. The sprocket and bicycle chain come from a Belsaw planer's depth-setting mechanism. Strong has castings poured at three foundries and subcontracts most of the machining and assembly work. Final inspection, testing, and shipping is done in his garage machine shop. The Joint-Matic

retails for $778, which includes a Bosch 1¾-HP router. Two options, a stamped-steel base and a compound miter gauge, cost $79 and $119.95, respectively. Strong sells a universal mounting plate so another router will work, so long as it has at least 1¾ HP and a ⅜-in. or ½-in. collet.

I experimented with the Joint-Matic for a couple of days, and I found that it's easy to set up and that it generally performs as advertised, without much fuss. It will cut basic carcase and frame joints like the mortise-and-tenon, box joints, several kinds of dovetails plus grooving and dadoing operations that yield various drawer corner joints. I think it's best at sliding dovetails, though. I usually don't bother with this joint for the same reasons that led Strong to invent the Joint-Matic. But his machine makes fast and nearly foolproof work of it. To make the socket, you chuck a dovetail bit in the router, set it to the desired depth, then position the bit by cranking the lead screws. The wood—say the side of a small carcase—is held upright on the horizontal table, fed into the bit and backed out once the socket is long enough. To cut the pin, you feed the wood held flat on the horizontal table, assisted by the miter gauge if the board is narrow.

**Now the lead screws do their stuff.** By referencing the initial bit setting from the same surface, usually the top face of the stock, you can accurately keep track of the bit's position by counting turns. If, for example, the wide end of the pin is to measure ½ in. and be centered in ¾-in.-thick stock, you simply crank the cutter down two turns (⅛ in.) and make one pass. Flipping the board edge for edge for the second pass automatically centers the pin. I got pins to fit perfectly by cutting them a little fat first, then trimming with partial turns of the crank. Increments as small as $\frac{1}{16}$ of a turn are practical, and move the bit about 0.003 in. At those tolerances, and because the Joint-Matic references off two surfaces, good results come only with accurately milled and square stock.

Mortising on the Joint-Matic is like mortising on a router table. You set the router to the desired mortise depth, center the bit in the stock thickness by counting turns, then plunge the wood onto the spinning bit, feeding it against the rotation as you go. Using spiral end mills (regular flute cutters don't seem to plunge as well), I got controlled, clean mortises on the Joint-Matic. The Bosch router has power enough to cut ⅜-in. wide mortises to about 1¼-in. deep in one or two passes. Anything wider or deeper gets a bit hairy. A ½-in. bit I tried grabbed and chattered unless I nibbled away at the mortise by tedious step cutting, which seemed more trouble than it's worth. Tenoning is done with the same bit set at the same depth. Using the miter gauge, the end of the stock is fed into the bit, cutting one cheek and one shoulder simultaneously. Flipping the board does the other half, centering

*Wood to be mortised on the Joint-Matic is plunged onto the bit then advanced against rotation. Mortises up to 1¼-in. deep and ⅜-in. wide are practical. Tenoning is done by feeding stock with the aid of a miter gauge, cutting cheek and shoulder simultaneously. Flipping the stock edge for edge automatically centers the tenon in stock thickness.*

the tenon. Again, I found it easiest to make a test tenon overlarge then trim to a perfect fit by tweaking the lead screw crank.

Through dovetailing is not the Joint-Matic's strong suit. If I hadn't actually done it, I wouldn't think it possible to cut both pins and tails, but Strong has devised a method that involves chasing one dovetail cut with another made at 90° to the first. At the end of all this, you're left to clean up the pins with a chisel, making me wonder why I hadn't started with a chisel in the first place. Half-blind dovetailing is more rewarding, the results looking like the round-bottomed jobs a Sears router-dovetailer produces. You can vary the pin-tail spacing, if you remember the correct number of cranks for each drawer front or side. On a carcase full of drawers, I'd prefer to use the Joint-Matic in the box-joint mode, at which it beats any of the tablesaw or router jigs I've used before.

Overall, I liked the Joint-Matic. Its forthright design reminds me of a mid-'60s station wagon: homely, but no hidden vices and rugged enough to last into the next century. The Joint-Matic's capacities and price are well-suited to an amateur woodworker's needs and, by dint of a first-rate owner's manual, anyone comfortable with a router should get good work out of it.

**John Wirth's joinery machine**, on the other hand, is an edge-of-technology counterpoint to the Joint-Matic's dowdiness. Where Strong's machine has a crank and bicycle chain, Wirth's has a complement of templates, gizmos and adjusters that make it a machine junkie's dream come true. In a way, the Wirth Machine's complexity reflects the background of its inventor. During the 1960s, Wirth worked as an engineer for McDonnell Aircraft, developing and testing airplane electronics systems in New Mexico. The climate appealed to Wirth so he settled there, founding Woodworker's Supply of New Mexico in 1972. His joinery machine is as much a result of his habitual need to engineer, as it is new product for Woodworker's Supply.

Wirth's experience parallels Strong's. He tried to interest Delta in a prototype at a time when that company's former parent, Rockwell, was selling its stationary power tool division and wasn't in a new-product mood. Powermatic nibbled too, but later declined to buy the design. Wirth ultimately invested some $70,000 of his own to put his machine into production. Like Strong, Wirth farms out the all-aluminum castings and major machine work. In a well-equipped machine shop in a corner of his retail store and warehouse in Albuquerque, Wirth makes the machine's accessories and does the painting, assembly and fine tuning. The day I visited, six machines in various stages of completion sat on long work tables while he experimented with jigs to produce variable-spaced

dovetails. In its current evolution, the Wirth Machine sells for $2,095, which includes a 1½-HP induction motor stepped up by belt and pulley to spin the bit at 20,000 RPM. A less expensive model, using a router instead of the induction motor, is being developed and is expected to sell for about $800.

**Wirth's invention is an intriguing hybrid** of a woodworking slot mortiser and a metalworking horizontal mill. It consists of an aluminum sliding table mounted to a base via bearings and a pair of steel tracks. The tracks and bearings allow the table to move along two axes, one perpendicular to the bit (y) and the other toward or away from it (x). Sounds like a slot mortiser so far, but Wirth added a twist. He mounted the cutter on a pivoting-arm arrangement which permits it to move up and down in the z-axis, then connected a template follower on top of the arm. By fastening a template where the follower can get at it, the machine functions as a part-reproducing pantograph.

In principle, the Wirth Machine is fathomable enough, but it requires undivided attention to set up, especially for operations involving the templates. All the basic joints are possible: the mortise-and-tenon, dovetails (except half blind), box joints, plus horizontal boring for doweling and neat, angled mortises for fixed-louver shutters. It'll also reproduce in wood any part capable of being traced by the template follower. If the base is bolted to a stout bench, the Wirth Machine can grasp and joint long stock, providing it's supported with roller stands.

I found the Wirth Machine to be a splendid mortiser, the operation for which it seems best suited. As with a slot mortiser, you first clamp the wood to the table with a fast-action clamp, then center the cut in the stock thickness, which, on the Wirth Machine, is done by locking the bit in its z-axis. Grasping a handle bolted to the table, you plunge the work onto the spinning bit by sliding the table in the x-axis. Moving the table back and forth in the y-axis completes the cut. Adjustable stops limit table travel, controlling the mortise depth and length. The Wirth Machine's cutting action is evener and quieter than you'd expect from a router, and mostly chatter free, chiefly because the induction motor doesn't bog down under load as does a router. By step cutting in three or four passes, I milled ½-in. mortises up to 2-in. deep and probably could have gone deeper with a longer bit. Mortising on this machine feels very safe because manipulating the table keeps your hands well clear of the cutter.

Every mortise deserves a tenon and at that, the Wirth gets involved. Tenoning is done by using the machine's one-to-one pantograph capabilities. Wirth provides Delrin tenon-shaped templates, each corresponding to a specific tenon size. One size, ⅜ in. by 2 in., comes with each machine, others are sold as accessories for $21.50 each. You screw the template onto an aluminum plate mounted on the machine's frame, then adjust the follower—a steel rod with a bearing threaded into one end—to contact the template. To cut the tenon, trace the template's profile with the follower by grasping one handle, which moves the bit up and down, and the other, which moves the table in both axes. This requires coordination not unlike rubbing your head and patting your belly at the same time, but it's not hard to get the hang of it and, while you concentrate on template tracing, the bit chews away all the wood that isn't tenon.

**I got acceptable tenons easily enough** but had trouble putting them where I wanted them. An index indicates how the template's position relates to what the bit will actually cut, but I found it time-consuming to adjust everything so that the tenon was accurately centered in both the thickness and width of the stock. Trial and error finally got the job done, but test tenons sliced off the end of my ever-shrinking scrap littered the floor under the radial-arm saw. The templates are made slightly undersize to compensate for a bit whose diameter has shrunk after sharpening. To fatten the tenon to a snug fit, you wrap a turn or two of tape around the follower. If it seems ludicrous to trim a $2,000 machine with a 29-cent roll of tape, the method does work and I can't think of a better way to do it. One nice thing about the tenons is that their radiused edges match the mortise, thus solving the nagging dilemma of whether to round the tenon or square the mortise.

Two other templates I tried, for dovetails and for angled shutter-louver mortises, were faster to set up. Both are 12 in. long, but the stock can be repositioned to allow for wide boards or long shutter stiles. The shutter template works particularly well, simplifying what would be a daunting task on a slot mortiser or a router table. Using this template, I was able to produce a 12-in.-long shutter start-to-finish in about 20 minutes.

The Wirth Machine's facility at shuttermaking suggests that its real potential is as a specialized joinery and shaping tool rather than as a general, jack-of-all-joints shop machine. If you want an odd-shaped tenon or one that's angled relative to the board's thickness, the Wirth Machine can accommodate. My joinery tastes are more straightforward, so except for mortising, I wouldn't have the patience to fuss with it unless I needed a dozen or so of one particular joint—which isn't always the case in the amateur's shop. But the sliding table is readily jigged and the template holder can accept all kinds of shop-built templates, making the Wirth Machine ideal for reproducing small or odd-shaped wooden parts, say in a pattern or model shop. An attachment Wirth sells for $325 converts the machine into a duplicator, which can reproduce long three-dimensional objects up to about 8-in. in diameter, a capability that ought to interest gunstock makers.

Wirth believes that's market enough to justify his investment and I for one would like to see him succeed. The major manufacturers introduce new products cautiously and then only if sales in the thousands are predicted. Wirth (and Strong) represent an innovative, less hidebound alternative source of new tools and there ought to be room for them in an expanding market.  □

*Paul Bertorelli is editor of* Fine Woodworking. *For more information, write Woodworker's Supply of New Mexico, 5604 Alameda N.E., Albuquerque, N.M. 87113 or Strong Tool Design, 20425 Beatrice, Livonia, Mich. 48152. We welcome comments from owners of machines described in this report.*

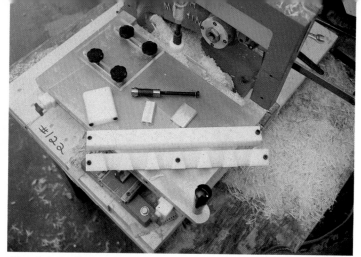

*About two dozen templates are available, including those for various sized tenons and for dovetails. The templates are made of a tough plastic called Delrin. The Wirth Machine's collet, top of photo, is drawn into a hollow tapered spindle by a long bolt.*

*The Wirth Machine set up for tenoning. The template follower, top, traces the template, guiding the bit to reproduce its profile on the end of the stock. As the bit cuts, the wood is held firmly against a plastic plate, setting the shoulder depth.*

# Variable-Arm Milling Machine

## Exploring the router's sculptural potential

by Stephen Hogbin

I've always been interested in exploring machines that are capable of making more than one letter of the visual artist's alphabet. The weaver's loom, the potter's wheel and the woodturner's lathe are all machines that allow tremendous variations within limited configurations. The variable-arm milling machines described in this article are another example.

These machines grew out of a request I received from an architect in 1974. At that time, I had been making turnings, some of quite large scale, which I would then cut in half and glue back together in another order, revealing the progression of the turning's cross section (see *FWW* #21). The architect had seen a small screen fashioned from one of my segmented turnings and wondered if I could make a larger one for the Metropolitan Toronto Library. This seemed reasonable enough, until I discovered that the screen he had in mind was up to 200 ft.

long and 7 ft. high. Conventional woodturning, even at large scale, was clearly not the best approach for this job. Rather than swinging a huge mass of material on the lathe, it seemed appropriate to hold the material and pass a cutting head across its surface. This action is similar to that of a milling machine.

When faced with such a technical requirement, I usually think about precedents—what existing machine might do the job? I don't want to start from scratch unless I have to and I don't want to become a designer of machines which are an end in themselves rather than a means to an end. However, this was not to be the case. For the screen project, the router seemed a good choice, both for basic shaping and for texturing. With its wide selection of bits, the router is among the most versatile—and I suspect underused—tool available to the woodworker. It can cut a hole or a groove; multiple grooves

generate a ribbed or fluted surface that brings a flat surface into the third dimension. The practical and visual uses of this language are numerous, from functional hollows in which objects are stored to decorated surfaces which wrap around functional things such as furniture. The trick is to identify a relationship that works and apply it.

As the drawing on the facing page shows, the machine I developed is essentially a pivoting horizontal arm that rotates about two axis. The arm, a steel I-beam, supports a 2-HP router which travels on a roller carriage. For regulated work, the router carriage can be precisely positioned by means of a lead screw that runs the length of the arm. The router is fitted with either a ¼-in. or ⅜-in. collet to accept bits of ¼-in. to 2-in. cutting diameter. A simple template at the end of the arm or beside the work, allows me to reproduce and repeat a profile as of-

*Hitched to an I-beam trammel arm, the router reveals itself as a sculptural tool of rich potential. To regulate the cutting, Hogbin attached his router to a carriage which slides along the arm to be precisely postioned by a long lead screw threaded through the carriage. He used this variable-arm milling machine to create a massive red oak room divider for the Metropolitan Toronto Library, above.*

ten as I want. To make most things, and perhaps to make anything worthwhile, it takes considerable time to learn the techniques which relate to the forms desired. Once the machine was built, I began experiments to discover its potential. I need to understand technique before I can move to the biggest challenge: putting my experiments into a cohesive visual statement. First I cut and milled a number of blocks individually to learn what basic cuts could be made, and the relationship of one cut to another. Whether individual pieces worked visually or had any application was unimportant at this stage. The idea was not to make art but to develop an alphabet of possibilities which would later become visual poetry.

As I progressed, I discovered both the potential and the limitation of my machine. The arm weighs about 50 lb. when held at its outside end but feels progressively heavier as you move closer to the axis. Maneuvering the boom gave me tremendous back and neck pain. To relieve it, I inserted a piece of elastic into the rod that supports the arm. This gave me fingertip control at almost any point on the arm. The pain subsided, the forms improved and I could forget about the burden of process and move freely with the balance of form and material.

My initial attempts seemed rather stiff and lacked the subtle interpretation I could achieve at the lathe using a hand-guided chisel. The act of milling is part of the engineer's tradition rather than the artist's. Out of frustration from the weeks of tinkering, I dropped a large, irregularly shaped log beneath the arm and ran the router across the surface. The result was a vigorous patterning that had the qualities of crashing waves, wind-blown sand dunes and mountains. Finally, the form was evocative and challenging.

I applied this new-found language in making the library screen, shown on the facing page. The screen consists of 350 red oak boards set into a steel channel and stone base built on the floor. To allow light and air to pass through the otherwise solid wall and to impart a lively and evolving pattern, I placed the boards in a jig 50 at a time, edge up and face to face. Milling the edges, first on one side and then on the other by turning the boards over, produced a sequential texture with a semicircular effect. This process was repeated to get the necessary number of boards for the screen.

The last architectural-scale piece I

*Combined with the milling machine's versatility, off-the-shelf router bits impart striking texture to wood. This sculpture shows the tool's remarkable expressive potential.*

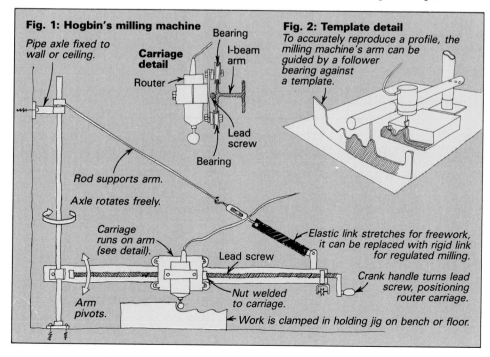

**Fig. 1: Hogbin's milling machine**

Pipe axle fixed to wall or ceiling.

**Carriage detail**

Bearing

I-beam arm

Router

Lead screw

Bearing

Rod supports arm.

Axle rotates freely.

Carriage runs on arm (see detail).

Arm pivots.

Lead screw

Nut welded to carriage.

Arm pivots.

**Fig. 2: Template detail**
To accurately reproduce a profile, the milling machine's arm can be guided by a follower bearing against a template.

Elastic link stretches for freework, it can be replaced with rigid link for regulated milling.

Crank handle turns lead screw, positioning router carriage.

← Work is clamped in holding jig on bench or floor.

*To make one version of* Calibrated Earth, *top, author built the small milling machine, right. The arm is less cumbersome and the work can be mounted on a turntable, making possible more the fluid, painterly compositions shown at far left and right. By painting the routed squiggles, Hogbin achieved an illusion of depth which suggests a cloud-filled sky or a flock of birds.*

made on the large milling machine was for C-I-L Inc., a Canadian chemical concern. The piece, which is called *Calibrated Earth*, makes reference to the image of earth. A small, painted derivation of it is shown above. The textured wood evokes clouds, water, sand, cracked mud, plowed fields or the desert. I used 11 different round-nosed cutters to produce the texture, but started the first groove with a V-cutter to give the finest start possible. The grooves were scraped with shaped cabinetmakers' scrapers and left without sanding.

For developing the models which eventually resulted in *Calibrated Earth*, I constructed a bench-sized version of the milling machine. By clamping the wood to a turntable beneath the arm instead of to a fixed holding jig, I expanded the ma-

chine's vocabulary, thus permitting the possibility of complex geometric carving much like that done by ornamental woodturners. However, I chose to explore forms that are freer. I achieved an elementary form of picture making by learning to organize these potentially disparate lines into a compelling whole.

Texture can be a key visual element of work produced on this machine. Spatial illusions can be produced. In *Calibrated Earth* the texture was cut from a flat surface but it appeared to be spherical because I used progressive sizes of cutters. Small cuts in the surface appear farther away than larger cuts. Optically, a cut can appear to be raised on the surface, especially if the hollow is lit from the bottom.

These kinds of effects are part of two-dimensional space and relief rather than

three-dimensional space. These qualities of surface led me more and more toward "picture making."

Relief surfaces are sensitive to light. If they are not properly lit, the subtle visual qualities are lost. One way to overcome poor light conditions is to add color in order to gain back the high contrast of hollow to flat surface. Initially I added color with caution, thereby evolving the vocabulary further. Now, three years later, the wood in my work is often completely covered with paint, even though its texture and the structure of the panel are still evident. I have also recently pulled prints from the surface—using the texture as the basis of the printed image.

Since 1974, and that initial request by the architect for a large screen, I have evolved from woodturning. machine

# Ted Hunter's router mimic

by Mary Hui

Finding a conventional lathe unsuitable for the large, textured turnings he wanted to create, Toronto sculptor Ted Hunter designed and built this machine, which is an adaptation of the mimic some machine shops use to duplicate parts.

Its chief mechanism is an arm which connects a template follower to a router suspended above the workpiece. The arm is capable of 30 in. of longitudinal movement, which equals the radius of the turntable. The turntable can be turned at 6 RPM by a motor, or it can be rotated by hand. A crank belted to a lead screw moves the center post along a track, mechanically translating the template's profile to the work. Once set up, Hunter finds that turning/sculpting proceeds very quickly.

"But in some ways," Hunter says, "the process has been slowed down. I have more time to think about what's happening."

Much of the machine's potential remains undiscovered. In his early experiments, Hunter found that a router bit left a textured surface which enhanced his work. "Before building the machine, I had ideas for shapes I wanted to create," says Hunter, "so I built the machine to create them. Now, using the machine, I come up with more ideas. With a chair, for instance, you know that when it's finished you're going to sit in it and that's partially how you know it's finished. The machine is part of a process [and] never finished because the end result is unknown." □

---

*Mary Hui is a Toronto free-lance writer.*

*Combining the shop-made milling machine, photo at top, with a lot of head scratching, Ted Hunter created the three-foot high hanging sculpture, above. He began with a 30-in. diameter mahogany blank made up of five brick-built discs. After routing the blank to the desired profile, he then sawed the turning into sections which he then reassembled into the final form.*

building, variable milling and now to printmaking. Although the techniques are different, in each process the wood surface is cut to produce different qualities.

This vocabulary-building activity—discovering similarities, making references and using one process as a metaphor for another—is a necessary part of giving form. This essay concentrates on technique and form; both are precursory to idea and content. Ultimately the poetry of any language is not contained in grammar, but in the spirit that motivates its form and content. □

---

*Stephen Hogbin, a designer and artist, lives on Owen Sound, Ontario. An exhibition of his recent work is to be shown in July at the Ontario Crafts Council Gallery, 346 Dundas St., Toronto.*

Photos: John Reck

# Low-Cost Dust Collection

## Cleans out your shop, not your wallet

by William S. Harrison III

I used to snicker every time some new fangled safety device hit the market. I'd give up woodworking, I told my wife, before strapping myself into gear more appropriate for moonwalking than woodworking. Then two years ago, I found myself cutting up redwood for hours each day in a closed, two-car garage. I began to feel a bit choked up, but that was only the beginning. I contracted a sore throat (from other causes) and kept on working. Despite all kinds of prescribed medicine, my throat got worse.

When my condition improved after five days away from the shop, it finally hit me that the fine sawdust was doing a number on my throat—and probably on my lungs, too. Donning a paint spray mask in the shop cleared my throat and confirmed my suspicions, so I immediately started work on a dust-collection system.

How serious is any sawdust problem? My gut feeling is that if you machine wood in an enclosed area more than one hour per day, you could be in trouble. The American Society of Heating, Refrigeration and Air Conditioning Engineers (ASHRAE) and the National Institute for Occupational Safety and Health (NIOSH) have standards for dust concentration, but what exposure is unsafe depends on the wood, particle size and so on (*FWW* #39, p. 36). The ASHRAE *Handbooks* (which you can find in major-city libraries, or ask an engineer friend) are crammed with information on dust control. If you're still uncertain about your dust-collection needs, ask an industrial-ventilation specialist or a sheet-metal contractor, many of whom fabricate exhaust systems.

I had eight machines that needed dust collecton: radial-arm saw, planer, jointer, tablesaw, bandsaw, stationary belt sander, drill press and shaper. I do quite a bit of industrial fume-collection design, so I dabbled with the thought of hooking all the machines up to a cyclone system with a bag on the outlet. (A cyclone separator creates two concentric helical air currents inside a cone-shaped collector. Centrifugal force separates dust and shavings from the airstream, and these settle out into a bin.) But a commercial cyclone system can cost $1500 and up, so I continued dabbling.

I surveyed my shop layout and my salvage collection, and decided that a single system would require too much piping and a larger blower than I had. So my best bet was to build three collectors: one for the planer, one for the radial-arm saw (these two machines share a separate room) and a multiple-port system for the rest of the machines. The multiple-port system (facing page) is the most complicated, so I'll describe it first.

Doyle Johnson's dust-collection system (*FWW* #12, pp. 76-78), comprising PVC drainage pipe, a ½-HP industrial collector and a 55-gal. drum, was my model. My system had to move enough air to handle two ports on the tablesaw at once, and I wanted to be able to hook up a machine quickly. A used 1-HP Cincinnati Fan #10 (a centrifugal fan) that I bought for $40 fit the bill for a blower. I replaced its three-phase motor with a single-phase (a $65 unclaimed rebuild at my friendly motor-rebuilding shop) and mounted it on a 55-gal. drum. I reinforced the thin metal drum lid with ¾-in. plywood to support the ductwork, which enters on the perimeter at an angle, creating a cyclone effect inside the drum. The heavier particles drop into the drum; lighter dust is caught by a bag on the blower's exhaust.

For the ductwork, I used Schedule 40 PVC pipe. (The name designates wall thickness—the higher the number, the greater the thickness. S-40 walls are about ⅛-in. thick.) S-40 pipe is readily available and isn't too expensive, and its inherent rigidity makes suspension easy. S-30 pipe is cheaper, but harder to find and the fitting selection isn't as great. (The box on p. 111 will help you figure the size blower and diameter and length of pipe you'll need.) PVC pipe glues together easily, and joints used for changing connections may be left unglued since they fit tightly. Where a machine joins the main pipe, I used an angled fitting called a sanitary-T (which is actually Y-shaped). These fittings restrict the airflow by friction losses less than right-angle fittings. You'll have to shape the pipe ends to fit some of the nozzles. PVC molds nicely when heated carefully over a gas burner, but be sure to clamp it while it cools.

Flexible tube is required for difficult connections under and around machines, but it's quite expensive, so I tried to use as little as possible. Industrial-grade runs about $1 per foot per inch of diameter in the 2-in. to 5-in. diameter range (2-in. pipe costs $2/ft. and so on). An adequate flexible tube called Ductall Vinyl costs about half as much and may be obtained from U.S. Plastics, 1390 Neubrecht Rd., Lima, Ohio 45801. It comes in sizes that fit snugly inside S-40 pipe of the same nominal diameter. You force the hose in the pipe with a screwing action, assisted by any vinyl tub-and-tile sealer to lubricate and seal the interface. I didn't bother with shutoffs or "blastgates" to block off machines not in use. I simply plugged the unused ports with bandsawn wooden plugs—cheap and effective.

Each machine required a different sort of nozzle. I made a few experimental nozzles before I reverted to my trusty *Industrial Ventilation, A Manual of Practice* for its tried and true solutions. (The book is published by the Committee on Industrial Ventilation, Box 16153, Lansing, Mich. 48902, and costs about $15.)

Two tablesaw nozzles—one above, one below the blade—may seem like overkill, but they do a super job. Depending on the number of blade teeth, depth of cut and so on, at least half the

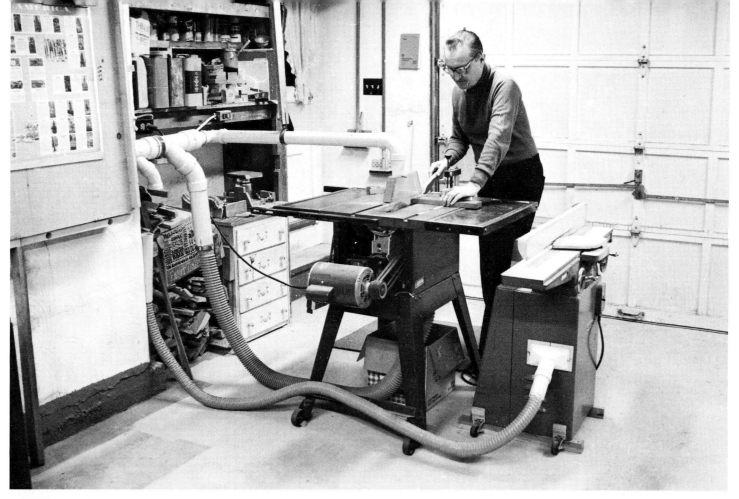

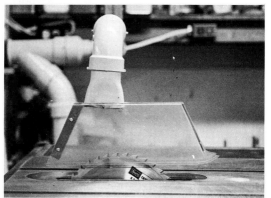

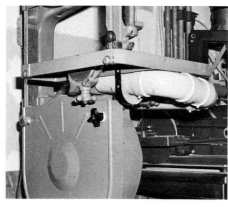

Harrison made his home-shop dust-collection system with PVC pipe, salvaged blowers and some ingenuity. The tablesaw (top) has nozzles above and below the blade. A modified vacuum-cleaner nozzle serves the jointer. The top tablesaw nozzle (middle left) is 2-in. PVC pipe shaped and bolted to a stock blade guard. The bandsaw nozzle (middle right) is PVC cut around the bottom blade guides. At the 55-gal. drum collector (bottom left), 3-in. and 2-in. trunk lines join a 4-in. PVC fitting, angled to create a cyclone in the drum.

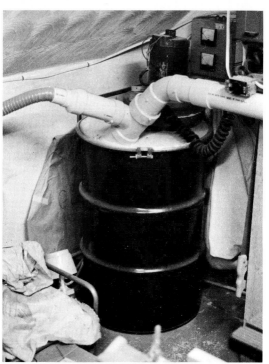

**Dust-collection layout**

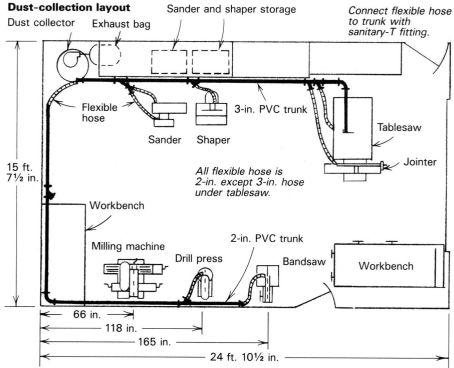

Dust collector    Exhaust bag     Sander and shaper storage     Connect flexible hose to trunk with sanitary-T fitting.

Flexible hose

3-in. PVC trunk

Sander    Shaper

Tablesaw

Jointer

*All flexible hose is 2-in. except 3-in. hose under tablesaw.*

15 ft. 7½ in.

Workbench

Milling machine

2-in. PVC trunk

Drill press    Bandsaw    Workbench

66 in.

118 in.

165 in.

24 ft. 10½ in.

109

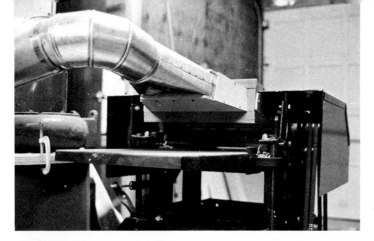

Four-inch metal duct, a 30-gal. drum and blower service Harrison's planer (above and left). The metal nozzle is extended under the planer's cover with ¼-in. plywood. A powerful vacuum cleaner collects from the two nozzles attached to the radial-arm saw's blade guard (below). An inner tube suspends the flexible hose from the ceiling, permitting the saw to travel easily.

sawdust is thrown down, the remainder up—and in your face if you don't have a top nozzle. Mine fits into a plastic Sears saw guard, which I shortened behind the blade to reduce the volume of air exhausted. The pipe is suspended from the garage-door track (the ceiling would do, too, of course) and the height of the guard can be easily adjusted by sliding the hanger along the pipe; the joints swivel since they aren't glued.

The bottom tablesaw nozzle consists of various bits of plywood and redwood fastened to each other and to the casting around the blade. Your saw, like mine, will probably require a trial-and-error nozzle design. The important thing is to make the nozzle as compact and leakproof as possible, otherwise your blower will be doing extra duty. Remember that the nozzle shouldn't interfere with tilting the arbor or changing the blade.

Nozzles for the remaining machines on the multiple-port system were fairly simple. My 6-in. Delta jointer has an outlet in the base to which I adapted an old vacuum-cleaner nozzle. The die casting on my Sears shaper fence has a hole right behind the spindle, into which I jammed the flattened end of some 2-in. PVC pipe. Some chips escape upward, so I intend to alter the

fence to accept a larger nozzle. The Sears belt and disc sanders come with nozzle attachments which work well. For the drill press, I used 2-in. PVC pipe held in place by a magnet bolted through the pipe. For the bandsaw, I cut 2-in. PVC to fit tightly around the bottom blade guides, then connected this pipe nozzle to the trunk with 2-in. flexible tube and a sanitary-T fitting.

As you can see, I kept my nozzles simple. Your machines may require different configurations. Just remember a couple of things. Try to take the shortest route from nozzle to dust storage. Make the nozzle as leakproof as possible, and position it to take advantage of the velocity of the particles imparted by the cutterhead or blade. At a distance of only one diameter from the intake pipe, the capture velocity (suction as measured by the velocity imparted to the particles by the exhaust system) drops to only 10% of its value at the intake mouth.

When you operate a multiple-port system, remember that blowers work best at their rated capacity. It is possible to starve the blower of air and make it work much harder than it needs to. My 1-HP Cincinati Fan #10 simultaneously captures dust very nicely from the 2-in. and 3-in. inlets on the tablesaw and the 2-in. inlet on the bandsaw. If I'm working on any of the smaller machines, I still leave both tablesaw ports open to feed air to the blower. An air-starved blower will whine about its problem; if your blower sounds shrill, try opening another port.

For my Sears (Belsaw) thickness planer, I mounted an old ⅓-HP Brown and Sharpe blower on a used 30-gal. drum. A piece of S-40 PVC pressed into the ¾-in. plywood lid with tub sealer connects with 4-in. metal elbows and clothes-dryer duct. I enlarged and extended an 8-in. metal Cincinnati nozzle with ¼-in. thick birch plywood. The conventional top location didn't work well because the blower isn't quite powerful enough. Mounted behind the cutterhead, the system picks up about 80% of the particles—abysmal by industry standards, but okay for my purposes.

Serving the radial-arm saw is an old Douglas (Scott and Fetzer) wet-and-dry vacuum cleaner, well made and powerful. I made the bin-type collector suggested by Sears, but it didn't work out, so I cribbed the rig shown in the bottom photo at left from the Industrial Ventilation manual, and it works great. For ductwork to the plywood nozzle, I used the vacuum cleaner's original 2½-in. rigid wand and flexible hose. An old Electrolux hose connects the nozzle on the front of the guard to a brush nozzle (without the bristles) carefully cut into the wand. Here, the shortest route from nozzle to dust storage isn't the best. You need the suspended loop and slack for minimum drag on the saw movement. The hose is hung from an old bicycle inner tube.

How much did it all cost? Forty-plus feet of S-40 pipe with a couple dozen fittings ran about $175; add flex at $40, motor, blower and drum at $120, a dustbag for $35 and miscellaneous stuff at $25, and that totals about $395. A commercial installation using 22-gauge metal duct with the same blower capacity would run about $2,000. I had most of the components for the radial-arm-saw unit, but a good estimate is about $110. The planer unit cost me about $120.

How efficient are these systems? Because of OSHA and NIOSH regulation, industry would strive for 99% capture of all airborne particles. The system shown here captures, on average, about 90% of all particles. This is sufficient to yield a very livable atmosphere in my two-car garage shop. When I plan a multi-hour ripping session, I add my face mask for insurance. □

Bill Harrison is an engineering director for a major company and has been an off-and-on serious woodworker for 30 years.

# Of pipe runs and pressure drops

Adequate dust-collection design depends essentially on matching your needs to a blower and correctly dimensioned pipe. Though expensive industrial-standard systems require elaborate calculations to achieve this, an effective small-shop setup needn't strain your wallet or your mathematics. The information here is simplified, but coupled with common sense and some trial and error in the shop, it should get you on the right track.

Start with a shop layout (like the one on p. 109), showing the position of the dust storage, blower and machines. Note which machines need one nozzle and which need two, and determine how many machines you want to collect from at one time. Check the chart at right for the cubic-feet-per-minute (CFM) extraction requirements for each machine.

The most important variables in the system are the blower capacity, the pipe diameter and length, and the losses to the system caused by friction in the pipe and other factors. A blower is generally rated by the volume of air in CFM it will move at a certain static pressure (SP), measured in inches of water. Pressure of 1 lb./sq. in. will raise water in a tube 27.5 in., and so on. (If the CFM and SP ratings aren't given on the blower, ask the manufacturer for them.) You can determine whether a blower is powerful enough by comparing its SP rating with the system losses, which are explained below. If the total losses don't exceed the blower's rated SP, it will move its rated CFM.

Velocity is as important as volume for our purposes. The recommended velocity for wood dust and chips is 3500 feet per minute (FPM). Too much below this speed and chips will settle out in the pipes. Knowing velocity and volume, you can calculate the pipe diameter you need using the formula $Q = AV$, where $Q$ is volume in CFM, $A$ is the square-foot area of a cross section of pipe, and $V$ is the velocity in FPM. Reducing the pipe diameter raises velocity, but also raises friction losses in the pipe. (Obviously, the formula can also be used to determine blower capacity for given diameters of pipe.)

Let's figure a simple system with a two-nozzle tablesaw and a one-nozzle bandsaw hooked up to a blower rated 700 CFM at $4\frac{1}{2}$ in. SP. Fourteen feet of 3-in. PVC pipe will run from the collector to a sanitary-T; a 3-in. flexible hose connects the T to the bottom tablesaw nozzle. The bandsaw will be hooked into the 3-in. PVC somewhere along the 14-ft. run.

First, pipe diameters. Plugging in the CFM figure from the chart for the top tablesaw nozzle and the recommended velocity gives 150 = $A$ x 3500; $A$ = 0.0428 sq. ft., or about $2\frac{3}{4}$-in. dia. pipe. I would push the lower limit and save some money by using 2-in. pipe. For the bottom nozzle, 200 = $A$(3500); $A$ = 0.0571 sq. ft., about $3\frac{1}{2}$-in. pipe. I'd use 3-in. The bandsaw calculation also yields $3\frac{1}{2}$ in., but the bandsaw is a long way from the blower and big pipe is costly, so I'll settle for 2-in. pipe and live with its high friction losses. Adding the airflow requirements for each machine, you get a collection system total of 550 CFM (150 + 200 + 200 = 550).

Knowing the pipe diameters and run, let's estimate the system losses and see if the blower is up to the job. Friction losses for straight pipe and fittings are shown in the chart, expressed as a loss in inches per foot of water SP. Losses for fittings are rated by equivalent losses for run of straight pipe of the same diameter. The figures are acceptable for a small shop, but they wouldn't meet industry standards.

Industrial-system designers figure losses for every component of a system—a terrifically complicated task. You can get a good idea of a small system's capacity, however, by calculating only the branch with the highest losses, which is usually the branch with a large nozzle located farthest from the collector; in this instance, the bottom tablesaw nozzle. Using friction loss figures

from the chart, and given nozzle and collector losses, you get this simplified calculation of losses in inches of water:

| | | |
|---|---|---|
| Bottom nozzle | (given) | 1.20 in. |
| Bottom hose, 6 ft. | 6(0.16 in./ft.) | 0.96 in. |
| 3x3 sanitary-T outlet | 6(0.16 in./ft.) | 0.96 in. |
| 3-in. main pipe, 14 ft. | 14(0.16 in./ft.) | 2.20 in. |
| Collector | (given) | 1.30 in. |
| | Total | 6.62 in. |

Determining nozzle and collector losses is complicated. The figures above are rough approximations for my own bottom tablesaw nozzle—a tight, 2-in. by 12-in. plywood funnel—and my collector—a 55-gal. drum, 4-in. intake fitting and blower. A smaller drum would lose less. If your nozzle and collector are different, a sheet-metal contractor might be able to help you with the calculations.

As it turns out, the blower's 4.5-in. SP rating is lower than the estimated losses. But because we're not aiming for high efficiency and the blower is rated 200 CFM greater than the load, I think it will be adequate. At worst, some dust will settle in the pipes, and the blower won't operate at peak efficiency. Increasing the pipe size will bring the system losses down. I use 4-in. pipe on my planer, but only a $\frac{1}{3}$-HP motor, so the tradeoff there is the other way around. (The chart also gives some rough rules of thumb for matching pipe diameter and blower capacity.)

A final example will demonstrate the tradeoffs between blower capacity, system losses and expediency. My 1-HP Cincinnati Fan #10 is rated at 700 CFM at $4\frac{1}{2}$-in. SP. It captures dust nicely from two 2-in. and one 3-in. inlet simultaneously. These openings correspond to a velocity of 7551 FPM, much in excess of the 3500 FPM recommended for wood dust. But numbers are deceiving. The actual velocity is much lower due to the numerous losses in the system. My sanitary-T inlets, for example, are far from ideal. Good practice would increase pipe size at every inlet and would assume how many inlets would be in use or just open drawing air only. But then, everything in life represents a compromise. —W.S.H.

---

**Friction losses at 3500 FPM:**
**Straight pipe**
4-in. pipe at 700 CFM will lose 0.14 in./ft. SP
3-in. pipe at 400 CFM will lose 0.16 in./ft. SP
2-in. pipe at 200 CFM will lose 0.16 in./ft. SP

**Fittings**
(SP loss equivalents in linear feet of straight pipe)
2-in. S-40 elbow = 4 ft. of pipe
3-in. S-40 elbow = 5 ft. of pipe
4-in. S-40 elbow = 6 ft. of pipe
2-in. or 3-in. sanitary-T outlet with 3-in. run (2x3 or 3x3) = 6 ft. of pipe
2-in. or 3-in. sanitary-T outlet with 4-in. run (2x4 or 3x4) = 8 ft. of pipe

**Pipe and blower matchups:**
2-HP blower, 1200 CFM at 6 in. to 7 in. SP—5-in. to 6-in. main pipe
1-HP blower, 700 CFM at 4 in. to 5 in. SP—4-in. to 5-in. main pipe
$\frac{1}{2}$-HP blower, 400 CFM at 5 in. to 6 in. SP—3-in. to 4-in. main pipe
$\frac{1}{3}$-HP blower, 250 CFM at 4 in. to 5 in. SP—3-in. main pipe

**Typical exhaust volumes, CFM**

| Machine | Recommended industrial std. | Home-shop compromise |
|---|---|---|
| Tablesaw, top | 300 | 150 |
| Tablesaw, bottom | 350-400 | 200 |
| Radial-arm saw, blade guard | 75-100 | 50 |
| Radial-arm saw, blade back | 350-400 | 150-200 |
| Bandsaw, under table | 350 | 150-200 |
| Disc sander, to 12 in. | 300 | 150 |
| Belt sander, to 8 in. | 400 | 200 |
| Jointer planer, to 8 in. | 400 | 200 |
| Planer, to 18 in. | 750 | 350 |
| Shaper, small, $\frac{1}{2}$-in. spindle | 400 | 250 |
| Shaper, large, 1-in. spindle | 800-1,000 | 400-500 |
| Drill press | 300 | 150 |

# Making a Panel Saw

*Sears saw serves as the basic machine*

by Larry Kellam

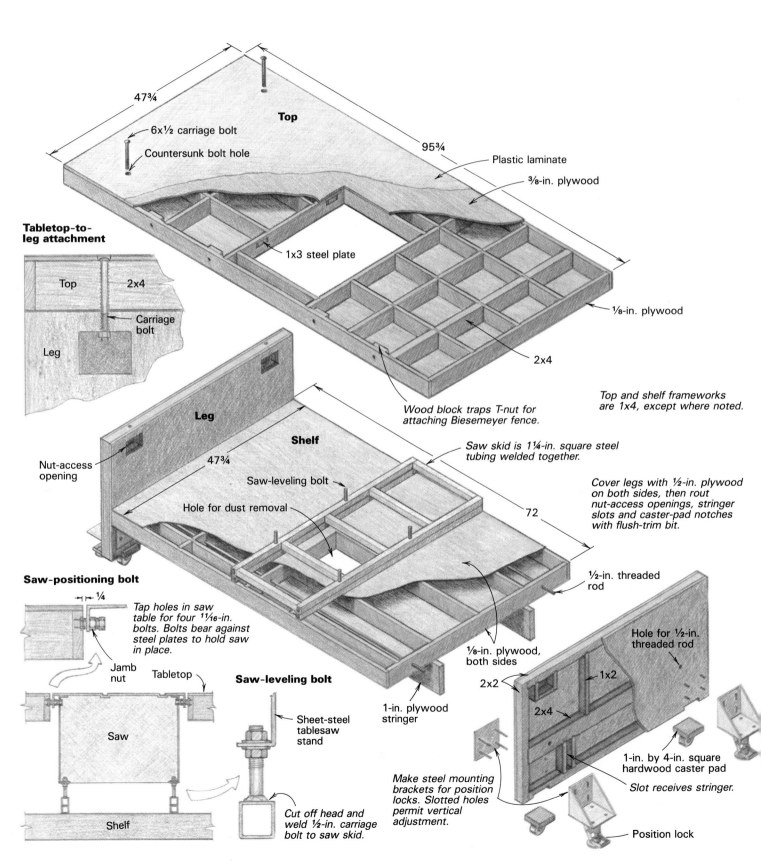

47¾

**Top**

6x½ carriage bolt

Countersunk bolt hole

95¾

Plastic laminate

⅜-in. plywood

**Tabletop-to-leg attachment**

Top

2x4

Carriage bolt

Leg

1x3 steel plate

⅛-in. plywood

2x4

Nut-access opening

**Leg**

**Shelf**

47¾

Saw-leveling bolt

Hole for dust removal

Wood block traps T-nut for attaching Biesemeyer fence.

Saw skid is 1¼-in. square steel tubing welded together.

Top and shelf frameworks are 1x4, except where noted.

Cover legs with ½-in. plywood on both sides, then rout nut-access openings, stringer slots and caster-pad notches with flush-trim bit.

72

½-in. threaded rod

**Saw-positioning bolt**

¼

Tap holes in saw table for four 1¹¹⁄₁₆-in. bolts. Bolts bear against steel plates to hold saw in place.

Jamb nut

Tabletop

Saw

Shelf

**Saw-leveling bolt**

Sheet-steel tablesaw stand

Cut off head and weld ½-in. carriage bolt to saw skid.

⅛-in. plywood, both sides

1-in. plywood stringer

Make steel mounting brackets for position locks. Slotted holes permit vertical adjustment.

Hole for ½-in. threaded rod

2x2

1x2

2x4

1-in. by 4-in. square hardwood caster pad

Slot receives stringer.

Position lock

In the ten years I've been building furniture, kitchen cabinets and store fixtures, my two biggest problems have always been lack of space and the absence of an additional pair of hands. To deal with the space problem, I've mounted each of my major power tools on casters so I can roll the machine I need to the center of the shop and go right to work.

Finding an extra pair of hands hasn't been as easy. I've always worked alone, which is fine until it comes to tossing around heavy 4x8 sheets of particleboard. You wouldn't believe the pain I used to put up with just to cut that stuff on my little 27-in. by 40-in. tablesaw. I tried some alternative solutions: roughing sheets with a circular saw and straightedge; ripping them on my radial-arm saw with cobbled-up extension tables. Then I got the idea of housing my tablesaw in a big, roll-around worktable. As the photo shows, my saw table is little more than a Sears 12-in. tablesaw, a Biesemeyer T-Square saw fence and a large table. Should the need arise, the saw can be completely dismantled.

While the Sears saw is by no means industrial-quality, I've never had any problems with it, so I couldn't see spending a small fortune on a better one. For about $60, I had the surface of the cast table ground to take out a nasty 1/16-in. warp. The Biesemeyer T-square saw fence is the backbone of my design. The joy of being able to set a fence up to 48 in. from the blade in about two seconds borders on the euphoric. I'm consistently getting truly straight and square carcases, and the reason for this is that I'm getting truly straight and square cuts. Thank you, Mr. Biesemeyer.

**Basic construction**—The table consists of four large panels: the top, the shelf that supports the saw, and the two legs. Each panel is a torsion box—a light wooden gridwork skinned over with plywood (*FWW* #32, pp. 96-102). I positioned the saw to the right of center because, unlike most people, I rip with the fence on the left side of the blade. But you can suit yourself. Right or left,

what's important is that there's enough room to set the fence 48 in. away from the blade. This allows you to cut to the center of a 4-ft. by 8-ft. sheet. I use this saw only for cutting panels and ripping, so I didn't extend the miter-gauge grooves into the table. If you want to extend the grooves, use thicker plywood for the top.

I made the torsion-box frames from clear fir. If I were to do it again, I'd probably use 3½-in. wide pieces of ¾-in. ply, simply because it's straighter. So the grid parts would stay put during glue-up, I assembled them with ⅛-in. deep dadoes.

Before gluing on the plywood skin, I positioned the Biesemeyer fence's angle-iron mount on the front edge of the top. I drilled holes for the mounting bolts and inserted a T-nut on the inside of each hole. I glued a small block of wood over each T-nut to make sure the nut could never come off. Once the plywood is glued down, the T-nuts are inaccessible.

I glued plywood across the entire top and bottom of each grid, and cut the openings later with a router fitted with a flush-trim bit. The top is ¼ in. smaller than a plywood sheet, so I could neatly trim the edges with the router. Contact cement works fine for gluing the ⅛-in. plywood to the grid, and the plastic laminate to the top. You can fasten the thicker plywood with white or yellow glue and screws.

**Assembly**—The legs are held together by two 76-in. long, ½-in. dia. threaded rods that pass through the shelf. I had these made at a machine shop for about $30, but you could also couple shorter lengths of threaded rod. The two plywood stringers slip into their mortises (don't glue them) and the shelf simply rests on the stringers. The saw goes in place on the shelf, and rests on a frame made from 1¼-in. square steel tube, which a blacksmith made for $100. Oak or maple would also do, and cost less. Four carriage bolts welded to the frame are used to level the saw.

To position the top, I used the bolt holes through the top panel

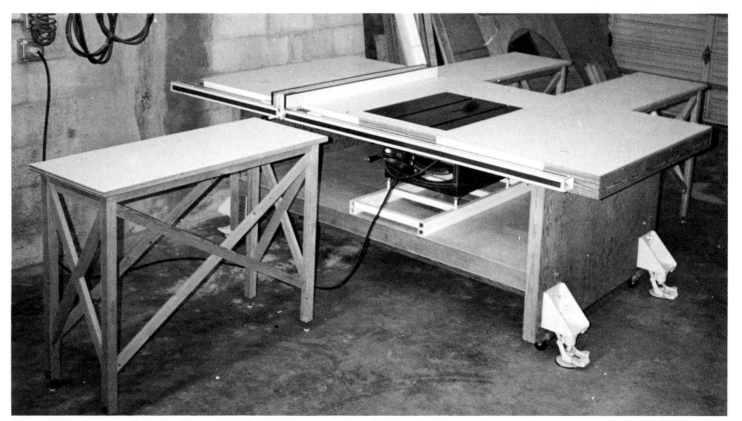

*Four torsion-box panels and a Biesemeyer fence convert a Sears tablesaw to an accurate, versatile panel saw. Outrigger-like position locks extend to hold the rolling table in place. Auxiliary infeed and outfeed tables can be positioned for more panel support.*

Photo this page: Larry Kellam; drawings: Lee Hov

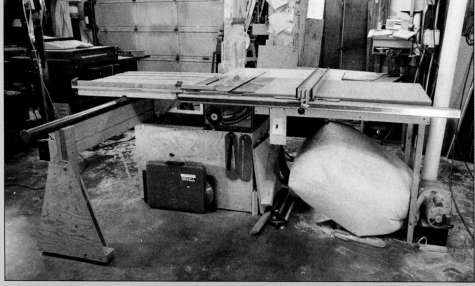

# Shopbuilt sliding table

by Rick Williams

I made a sliding table for my Sears saw from scrap plywood, and produced the ugliest saw in the world. It rolls on six ball-bearing nylon roller-skate wheels—four ride on top of the track, the other two on the vertical plywood track support. I made the track from a steel clothesline pole, but any sturdy, straight pole about 7 ft. long would do.

Everyone who sees my sliding table pushes down on the outside corner of the table, and when it moves up and down they ask, "Doesn't this cause any problems?" No. Since the workpiece itself must be on both the saw table and the sliding table at the same time, the workpiece actually holds the table in place.

I've made several other modifications to the 10-in. saw, such as replacing the metal legs with a plywood box. The box has a large drawer that wheels in from the end to catch the dust that used to fall on the floor and then rolls out for emptying. I've also made a safety guard that suspends from the ceiling. It combines an anti-kickback device and a dust-collection system.

I replaced the 1-HP motor with a 1.5-HP, 220-volt motor on a 24-volt relay. I've hooked up a three-way switch setup with one switch at the front of the sliding table so I don't have to climb under a 4x8 panel to turn on the saw, and one switch on the front of the saw for when I'm working on smaller pieces.

I'd estimate the total cost of the project (including saw, new motor, and sliding table) at $500. Every time I lay a piece of ¾-in. ply on the thing and slide it through a cut, I'm amazed that anything that looks so strange could cut so well. □

*Rick Williams is a cabinetmaker in Stanley, Kans. Photos by the author.*

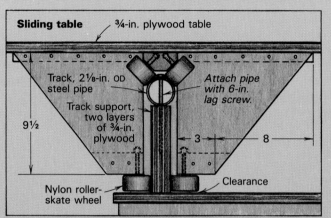

**Sliding table** — ¾-in. plywood table
Track, 2⅛-in. OD steel pipe
Attach pipe with 6-in. lag screw.
Track support, two layers of ¾-in. plywood
9½
3 — 8
Nylon roller-skate wheel
Clearance

*This homely setup is a Sears tablesaw outfitted with a sliding table cobbled from scrap plywood, a metal clothesline pole and six nylon roller-skate wheels. The plywood saw stand contains a wheeled drawer that slides in to collect sawdust and rolls out for emptying. The plywood and acrylic blade guard (below) is connected to a dust-collection vacuum system. The guard swings up and away when not needed.*

as a guide and drilled through the top 2x2s in the legs. Then I secured the top to the legs with four ½-in. dia. carriage bolts. Lastly, I fastened the Biesemeyer fence to the top.

The height of the saw is adjusted with the leveling bolts. When the saw is flush with the top, tighten the bolts in the table casting against the steel plates mortised into the saw opening.

To keep the table from rolling around in use, I attached four position locks (made by Bassick Div., Stewart-Warner Corp., 960 Atlantic St., Bridgeport, Conn. 06602) to the legs with steel brackets. The bolt holes in these brackets are slotted, so it's easy to level the table on an irregular floor.

Frankly, I'm a little embarrassed about the amount of money I've channeled into this project. All told, I've invested about $1,000. That includes the $300 I paid 10 years ago for my saw—today the same saw costs more than $600. Was it worth it? Yes. Every nickel. Besides, anything I build for the shop, I build to last a lifetime. I look upon my shop as a reflection of me and my work—a showroom, so to speak—and therefore I feel that everything that goes into it should be efficient, neat and well thought out. It's good for business. □

*Larry Kellam is a professional cabinetmaker in Miami, Fla.*

# Shop-Built Moisture Meter
## Printed circuit guides you through electronic maze

by Rick Liftig

Even though I've occasionally had problems with wood warping and cracking or joints coming loose because of moisture-related wood movement, I never could justify spending $100 or so to buy a moisture meter to check my stock before I used it. I've always been interested in electronics, so I decided to build my own meter. My home-built version, shown in the photo on the next page, cost $30. I've relied on fairly simple electronic procedures, so even if talk about soldering and circuits makes you uncomfortable, you should be able to build the meter.

The moisture content of wood can range from 0% for oven-dried samples to more than 100% for soaking-wet green wood, where the water in the wood weighs more than the wood tissue itself. Traditionally, technologists determined the moisture content by weighing a wood sample, oven-drying it until it was bone-dry, then weighing it again. The weight difference divided by the oven-dry weight, multiplied by 100, gives you the percentage of moisture content. This time-consuming method requires such an extremely accurate scale that it's impractical in most shops.

My meter, and many commercial models, bypasses drying and weighing by taking advantage of the fact that wet wood conducts electricity, while dry wood, a good insulator, resists the flow of electricity. By measuring this electrical resistance (expressed in units called ohms) and comparing your reading with standards developed by the U.S. Forest Products Laboratory and other agencies, you can determine wood's moisture content. The system works fine if the wood moisture content is in the 6% to 30% range, which is fairly common. Depending on the season and locale, most air-dried wood has 12% to 15% moisture content. Properly kiln-dried wood should be 6% to 10%. The electrical resistance in very wet or very dry samples is too erratic to give accurate readings.

Since we are measuring ohms, you might think that any off-the-shelf ohmmeter could measure resistance in wood. Wood is such a good insulator, however, that only a high-range ohmmeter capable of measuring in megohms (one million ohms) can be used. Early instruments used vacuum tubes and expensive high-voltage circuits, but my unit uses a modern, integrated circuit called an operational amplifier which can be wired to compare the wood's resistance to known resistances in the meter circuit. The details aren't too important; what's important is that the meter is sensitive enough to measure the moisture in a wood sample. Once I worked the bugs out of the system, I modified my meter dial to

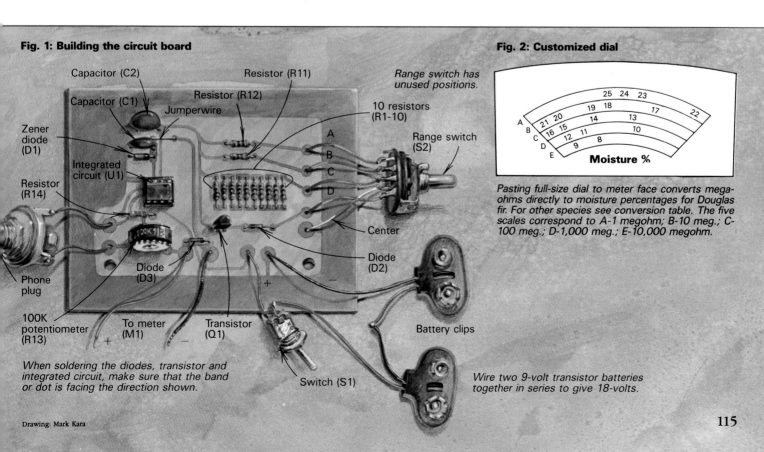

**Fig. 1: Building the circuit board**

Capacitor (C2)
Capacitor (C1)
Jumperwire
Resistor (R12)
Resistor (R11)
Zener diode (D1)
Integrated circuit (U1)
Resistor (R14)
10 resistors (R1-10)
A
B
C
D
Center
Range switch has unused positions.
Range switch (S2)
Diode (D2)
Phone plug
100K potentiometer (R13)
Diode (D3)
To meter (M1)
Transistor (Q1)
Switch (S1)
Battery clips

*When soldering the diodes, transistor and integrated circuit, make sure that the band or dot is facing the direction shown.*

**Fig. 2: Customized dial**

25  24  23
19  18  17  22
A  21  20  14  13
B  16  15  12  11  10
C  9  8
D
E
**Moisture %**

*Pasting full-size dial to meter face converts megaohms directly to moisture percentages for Douglas fir. For other species see conversion table. The five scales correspond to A-1 megohm; B-10 meg.; C-100 meg.; D-1,000 meg.; E-10,000 megohm.*

*Wire two 9-volt transistor batteries together in series to give 18-volts.*

Drawing: Mark Kara

115

show percentage directly, as shown in figure 2 on the facing page, so I wouldn't have to keep checking resistance charts. Just glue figure 2 to your dial face with rubber cement and you're ready to go. I find my readings, based on Douglas fir standards, are accurate enough for most uses, but if you want more accurate readings that account for the physical differences of each species, use figure 5. If the species you are testing isn't listed, you can assume its readings would be much the same as one of the listed species from the same geographic area and with similar density and structure. The values are probably within 2% of each other. Even within one board, you may find that much of a variation because of wood structure, uneven drying and contamination.

**Construction**—The simplest way to build the meter is to make a printed-circuit board from the pattern shown, drill holes to accept components, then solder the components on. The completed board, along with its gauge and switches, can be housed in any type of box—I used a cherry case fitted with a ¼-in. walnut deck. The printed circuit is not as mysterious as it looks—it's just a way of replacing wiring with thin copper lines drawn and etched on a board. All you have to do is buy a printed circuit kit from Radio Shack, or some other supplier, and follow the instructions in the package to the letter.

The probe is a 1¼ in. dia. piece of Plexiglas rod drilled to accept the probe leads, which are soldered to the steel points (taken from a cheap drawing compass) epoxied into the rod. I spaced the electrodes about ¾ in. apart, but the spacing isn't critical. Make the probes long enough to penetrate one-fifth to one-quarter the thickness of the boards you want to test. If you don't want to bother with a probe, drive a pair of nails into the wood and connect them to the meter with alligator clips.

**Calibration and use of the meter**—The meter must be calibrated before use. Solder four 10-megohm resistors together in a four-unit "daisy chain" series. Touching the ends of the chain to the probe tips, adjust R13 (the 100-K potentiometer) to read 14% moisture content, with the meter set to scale C. Do not touch the

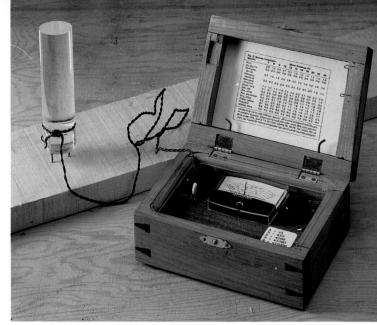

*A few common electronic components, a plastic probe and species chart let you gauge moisture levels and anticipate wood movement for about $30. Jazz the unit up with a custom made box.*

| Fig. 5: Species corrections | | Meter Readings (%) | | | | | | | | | |
|---|---|---|---|---|---|---|---|---|---|---|---|
| Species | 7 | 8 | 9 | 10 | 12 | 14 | 16 | 18 | 20 | 22 | 24 |
| Birch | 0.9 | 1.0 | 0.8 | 0.7 | 0.7 | 1.0 | 1.0 | 1.3 | 1.4 | 1.6 | 1.6 |
| Douglas Fir | 0.0 | 0.0 | 0.0 | 0.0 | 0.0 | 0.0 | 0.0 | 0.0 | 0.0 | 0.0 | 0.0 |
| Mahogany, African | 0.7 | 1.4 | 1.6 | 2.0 | 2.8 | 3.2 | 3.6 | 3.8 | 3.8 | 3.8 | 3.8 |
| Mahogany, Honduras | 0.3 | 0.3 | 0.3 | 0.4 | 0.6 | 0.5 | 0.2 | 0.0 | -0.5 | -1.0 | 1.5 |
| Mahogany, Philippine | -1.2 | -1.2 | -1.5 | -1.9 | -2.4 | -2.8 | -3.3 | -3.7 | -4.5 | -5.2 | -5.8 |
| Maple, hard | 0.7 | 0.7 | 0.4 | 0.1 | -0.2 | -0.1 | -0.2 | 0.0 | 0.2 | 0.5 | 1.0 |
| Oak, red | -0.4 | 0.0 | 0.0 | 0.0 | 0.0 | 0.0 | 0.0 | 0.0 | 0.0 | -0.2 | 0.0 |
| Oak, white | -0.1 | -0.2 | -0.4 | -0.5 | -0.5 | -0.5 | -0.8 | -1.1 | -1.5 | -1.8 | -2.0 |
| Pine, ponderosa | 0.4 | 0.6 | 0.7 | 1.0 | 1.4 | 1.6 | 1.6 | 1.4 | 1.2 | 1.2 | 1.6 |
| Pine, white | 0.0 | 0.1 | 0.2 | 0.3 | 0.7 | 1.1 | 1.3 | 1.3 | 1.2 | 1.1 | 0.4 |
| Poplar, yellow | 0.1 | 0.6 | 0.7 | 0.7 | 1.2 | 1.6 | 1.6 | 1.6 | 1.7 | 2.0 | 1.7 |
| Redwood | 0.0 | 0.0 | 0.0 | 0.0 | -0.2 | -0.5 | -0.8 | -1.0 | -1.0 | -0.2 | 0.0 |
| Walnut, black | 0.5 | 0.6 | 0.4 | 0.4 | 0.4 | 0.5 | 0.3 | 0.2 | 0.0 | -0.2 | -0.4 |

*Conductivity varies with different species. All species compared with Douglas fir standard. Example: When testing birch and meter reads 10%, look opposite Birch under 10%. Add 0.7% to meter reading for 10.7%. For woods not on chart, use figures for species of similar hardness and grain configurations.*

Adapted from *Furniture and Cabinet Making* by John L. Feirer ©1983, Bennett & McKnight, Peoria, Ill.

## Fig. 3: Printed circuit

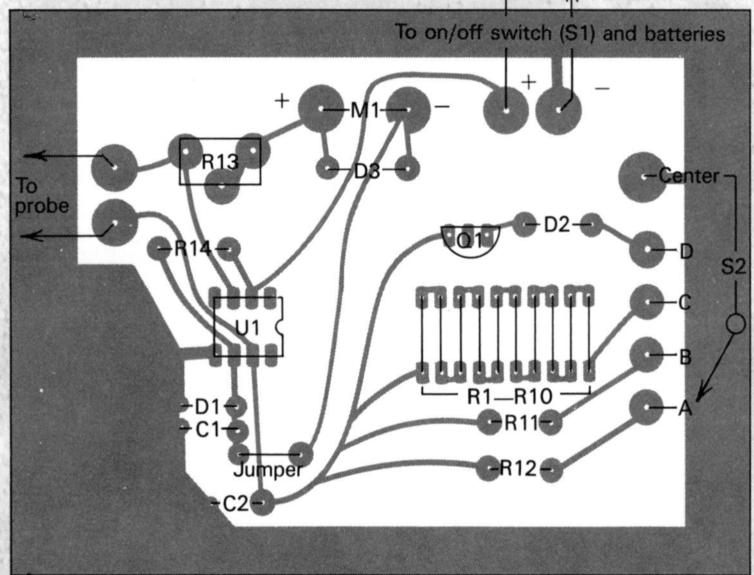

To on/off switch (S1) and batteries

+ —M1— —
R13 —D8—
To probe
—R14—
U1
Center
—D2— —D
—Q1— C
B
R1—R10
—D1— —R11— A
—C1—
Jumper —R12—
—C2—
S2

*Use diagram to layout printed circuit and add components. Black lines are connections on the top of the board. Grey patterns are circuits printed on underside of board. Underside of board is shown here. The parts are coded and refer to the parts list at right.*

## Fig. 4: Parts list

| Qty. | Radio Shack Part Number | Diagram Code | Description |
|---|---|---|---|
| 1 | 270-1752 | M1 | 0-1 milliamp DC meter |
| 1 | 276-561 | D1 | 6.2 volt, 1 watt zener diode |
| 1 | None | U1 | LM308 N Op Amp |
| 1 | 276-2009 | Q1 | MPS2222 Transistor |
| | 276-1576 | | Printed circuit fabrication kit |
| | 276-1577 | | Direct etching dry transfers |
| 2 | 276-1620 | D2 & D3 | 1N914 Silicon diode |
| 1 | 271-220 | R13 | Printed circuit potentiometer 100K |
| 15 | 271-1365 | R1 - R11 | 10 Megohm resistors ¼ watt |
| 1 | 271-1325 | R14 | 2200 ohm resistor ¼ watt |
| 1 | 271-1356 | R12 | 1 Megohm resistor ¼ watt |
| 1 | 275-625 | S1 | On-off switch (SPST) |
| 1 | 275-1385 | S2 | One pole 12 position rotary switch |
| 2 | 270-325 | | 9-volt transistor-battery clips |
| 1 | 274-252 | | Phone Plus |
| 1 | 274-256 | | Phone jack |
| 1 | 274-414 | | Knob for switch |
| 2 | 272-134 | C1 & C2 | 0.05 UF disk capacitors |

*Misc: 5 in. section of 1¼-in. diameter Plexiglas rod, 22-gauge wire, solder for electronics.*

*Parts available from Radio Shack; Jameco Electronics, 1355 Shoreway Road, Belmont, Calif. 94002; or Digi-Key Corp., P.O. Box 677, Thief River Falls, Minn. 56701. Unless you're very familiar with electronics, don't try to substitute electronic components.*

# Gauging wood movement

by Tom Liebl

Many people will tell you woodworking is a simple enough craft—the right tools (with plenty of horsepower), the right glue, no problems. Then, when your beautiful table-top cracks even though you glued and screwed hefty cleats across its underside, you wonder if maybe there's more to it.

"That's wood movement for you," the pros say as they scan your cracked top, but what does that mean? With a careful reading of Hoadley's *Understanding Wood*, the fundamental characteristics of wood will become clear, but in the workshop we are more often interested in how much movement than why. Few of us can get too excited about searching out just the right book, wading through a bewildering mass of data aimed at scientists, not craftsmen, then tracking down a pocket calculator just to figure out how much slack to build into a set of drawerfronts.

You could wing it, but cutting it too close could bring a summertime house call and a tarnished reputation. Leaving a ¼-in. gap would be playing it safe, but doesn't do much for looks. To solve this dilemma, I developed this chart on the movement and tendency to cup of most commonly used wood species.

I use the wood movement chart most, and when I combine potential movement with the cupping tendency of flatsawn lumber, I get a good idea of a species' dimensional stability. If I had a choice between red or white oak for a tabletop, I'd lean toward the white.

To use my chart, you must know three factors: the width of the piece, its annual ring orientation and the moisture content (MC) range where you live. The table is based on 12-in. wide boards, a convenient size for measuring expansion and contraction. Ring orientation may be either tangential (flatsawn) or radial (quartersawn). When in doubt, assume tangential since they move more than quartersawn.

After wood has been kiln- or air-dried to equilibrium with its environment, it will continue to shrink and swell with any change in relative humidity. You can determine your annual moisture range by monitoring local conditions or by consulting a moisture-change map, like the one in Hoadley's book.

I feel that for my area (and much of the midwest and the northeast), a 7% change in MC (5% to 12%) is appropriate for wood that has been treated with a moderately moisture resistant finish, like polymerized oil. Wood with a highly resistant finish (lacquer, shellac or varnish) might change as little as 3%. For many coastal areas, plus much of the south, a 3.5% range would work nicely.

Think of the measurements in the table as baselines, which you can adjust for changes in width, MC, or both by simple arithmetic. For example, take an 18-in. flatsawn red oak door panel. The table gives a movement of .31 in. over a 7% MC cycle for a 12 in. width. Since movement is directly proportional to width, the calculation is simple—18 is 1.5 times 12, so the movement for an 18-in. board is 1.5 times the movement of a 12-in. board or $1.5 \times .31 = .46$ in.

The MC range is figured in the same way. If you live in a 3.5% area (half of our 7% baseline), simply halve the result of your movement calculation.

For best results, you also must determine the current moisture content of the wood, usually with a meter like the one shown on page 116. If we want to install the 18-in. panel in a frame, our answer of .46 means that we must allow for at least a .23 in. movement in each side slot, but we must know the panel's current moisture content to decide whether to fit tight or loose.

Fitting tight in the summer and loose in the winter is a general rule. In any case, it's best to allow a little extra for movement, especially if you can't determine the current MC or face conditions that could produce extreme variations—say, furniture built in the dry southwest being shipped to the Pacific northwest. Once you understand how moisture affects wood movement, almost any situation can be anticipated. □

*Tom Liebl designs and builds furniture and boats in Madison, Wisc.*

| Dimensional changes | | | |
|---|---|---|---|
| Species | Movement of 12 in. wide board over 7% change in moisture content | | T/R¹ |
| **Hardwoods** | Radial | Tangential | |
| Ash, white | .14 in. | .23 in. | 1.6 |
| Basswood | .19 | .28 | 1.4 |
| Beech | .16 | .36 | 2.2 |
| Birch, yellow | .22 | .28 | 1.3 |
| Butternut | .10 | .19 | 1.9 |
| Cherry | .11 | .21 | 1.9 |
| Elm, American | .12 | .28 | 2.3 |
| Hickory | .22 | .35 | 1.4 |
| Locust, black | .13 | .21 | 1.6 |
| Maple, sugar | .14 | .30 | 2.1 |
| Oak, red | .13 | .31 | 2.1 |
| Oak, white | .15 | .31 | 1.8 |
| Sassafras | .12 | .18 | 1.6 |
| Sycamore, American | .14 | .25 | 1.7 |
| Walnut, black | .16 | .23 | 1.4 |
| Willow, black | .09 | .26 | 2.6 |
| Yellow, poplar | .13 | .24 | 1.8 |
| **Softwoods** | | | |
| Baldcypress | .11 | .18 | 1.6 |
| Cedar, Alaska | .08 | .17 | 2.1 |
| Douglas-fir (coastal) | .14 | .22 | 1.6 |
| Pine, eastern white | .06 | .18 | 2.9 |
| Redwood (second growth) | .08 | .17 | 2.2 |
| Spruce, Sitka | .12 | .22 | 1.7 |
| **Imported Woods** | | | |
| Khaya | .12 | .17 | 1.4 |
| Lauan, Dark red | .11 | .22 | 2.1 |
| Mahogany | .14 | .20 | 1.4 |
| Teak | .08 | .16 | 1.8 |

**Decimal equivalents**
.03 = ¹⁄₃₂-in.   .125 = ⅛-in.   .31 = ⁵⁄₁₆-in.   .44 = ⁷⁄₁₆-in.
.06 = ¹⁄₁₆-in.   .25 = ¼-in.   .38 = ⅜-in.   .50 = ½-in.

¹ *Ratio of tangential to radial shrinkage (green to oven-dry) indicates tendency to cup in flatsawn lumber. Higher ratio means a greater chance of cupping.*

---

probe tips or resistors with your hands as this will change the reading. The meter is now calibrated for all ranges, and should remain accurate as long as the batteries are good.

To use the meter, jam the probe straight into a clear area of the board's face, so that an imaginary line between the points runs parallel to the grain. For the most accurate reading, measure the wood at room temperature. Also, don't insert the probe towards the end of a sample, which will probably be drier than the rest of the board. When measuring, switch the meter ranges from lowest to highest (i.e. A to E) and stop at the position that gives a mid-range reading, usually the most accurate and easiest to read. If you can't get a reading, the sample probably has a moisture content of 6% or less. Readings may vary from one part of the board to another due to improper drying, abnormalities in grain structure, dirt and other surface contamination. If you have any doubts about a reading, probe several other areas of the sample.

I've found that having such a useful and inexpensive instrument in the shop is a real plus. If you're contemplating working with wide panels it would be wise to determine the moisture content of the stock before you begin work. The time and trouble you'll save is well worth the effort. □

*Rick Liftig lives in Meriden, Ct., where he dabbles in woodworking and electronics.*

# FINISHING

# Catalyzed Lacquers
## Creating a rich finish that's tough as nails

by David E. Shaw

If you want a clear wood finish that you can tap dance or iron a shirt on, try catalyzed lacquer—it's as tough and strong as baked enamel, more resilient than polyurethane, and doesn't look like plastic. Rather, it has that lovely sheen that only lacquer can produce, and it can be rubbed to a myriad of looks, from a rich gloss, to a mellow satin, or even dead flat.

Catalyzed lacquers also penetrate well and resist everything from intense cold to paint stripper. I prefer them for kitchen and bathroom cabinets, anything for a kid's room, and for tables, floors and other surfaces that are subjected to excessive moisture, temperature variations and plain old physical abuse.

Chemically, catalyzed lacquer is a nitrocellulose base blended with alkyd resins and urea formaldehyde. Hardening is induced by a phosphate ester catalyst, which reacts with the ingredients to form tough, chemical bonds. The amount of catalyst needed is critical and varies from brand to brand, so make sure that you get precise instructions. You should also heed safety warnings—any lacquer will give off fumes, but catalyzed lacquer gives off urea formaldehyde as well. I don't feel this is any more dangerous, but it does smell worse and will quickly give you a headache that can linger for days. If you do not have a good double-cone, organic-vapor respirator and can't provide fans or some other type of forced ventilation, don't use catalyzed lacquers.

There are two distinct types of catalyzed lacquers. The one I prefer produces the toughest finish because the catalyst is added to each coat, from the sealer on. Both Maclac Chemlac (available from distributors of Maclac Lacquer Co., 198 Utah St., San Francisco, Calif. 94103) and Sherwin Williams' Sherwood Super Kemvar HS (Sherwin Williams Co., 101 Prospect Ave., Cleveland, Ohio 44115, and its local distributors) fall into this category. The other lacquer is Synlac, a "bleed through" type, in which only the top coat of lacquer is catalyzed and the catalyst bleeds into the sealer and base coats (available from Industrial Finishing Products, 465 Logan St., Brooklyn, N.Y., 11208). This lacquer goes over Synlac's special barrier-coat sealer, and you can apply it over any finish that the barrier coat will adhere to, which is just about anything. If you want to refinish a lacquered or varnished table without stripping it, for example, you could reseal it with the barrier-coat, then apply bleed-through lacquer.

**To use catalyzed lacquers,** you must first mix the right amount of catalyst into the lacquer. Since most brands recommend two to four ounces of catalyst to every gallon of lacquer, an ordinary shot glass is an accurate measure for quart-size spray guns. Too much catalyst leaves a greasy finish that may take days to dry and

gives off a disagreeable odor for five or six months. Too little catalyst produces a relatively weak finish.

Once mixed, catalyzed lacquers spray on and dry just like ordinary lacquer, or they can be mixed with thinner and lacquer retarder—an additive which slows drying—and brushed on. Most manufacturers recommend high-grade thinner, which dries slower than inexpensive types, giving the lacquer more time to flow out smoothly and resist the whitish-blue hazing that develops in humid areas. In a pinch, you can hype-up regular thinner by making a mixture of 90% to 95% thinner (by volume) to 5% to 10% retarder. For brushing the lacquer, you can add up to 25% retarder in the thinner mixture, then spread the lacquer with a soft brush, just as you would brush on shellac. Too much retarder gives a greasy finish that can be dried only with a good deal of steel-wool buffing and lots of elbow grease.

Whether you are spraying or brushing, you first must apply at least one coat of a catalyzed sealer, let it dry, then sand lightly with 320-grit wet/dry paper. For open-pore woods, you may have to sand down two or three consecutive coats of sealer until the grain is filled, since catalyzed lacquer cannot be used over wood filler or any oil-based stain. Next apply three or four coats of lacquer, sanding between each coat with 600-grit paper. While manufacturers recommend that you wait four or five hours between coats, I have sprayed three coats in less than three hours.

Once applied, catalyzed lacquer must cure seven to 10 days to develop its full strength. The finish gives off a slight odor as it cures, but if you mixed it right, the odor will go away within a day or so. The disappearance of odor doesn't mean the finish is fully cured. Wait the full 10 days. If you rub out the cured finish with rottenstone, you can create as high a gloss as you'll get with any finish. If you rub with 00 steel wool you can kill the gloss entirely. Use 0000 steel wool for a more satiny effect.

Occasionally, when I'm in the final stages of finishing, I must alter the color of a finish to produce what my customer ordered. You can do this by adding a colored glaze between the lacquer coats or by tinting the lacquer itself. In either case, use oil-based or oil-compatible color (I use so-called Universal colors, either UTC brand, Byzantine brand or Japan colors by Ronan, available by mail order from Industrial Finishing products).

For glazing, I mix color with mineral spirits to form a very thin, weakly-colored stain that I apply with a lint-free rag, wiping with the grain and feathering the glaze at the end of each stroke until I evenly color the entire piece. Let the glaze dry about an hour until it's evenly dull before applying more lacquer. To tint the lacquer itself, add color to thinned lacquer and test until you get the shade you want. There are no tricks here, except your

To ensure that the lacquer is free of all dust and impurities, filter each batch through a cone filter as you fill the spray gun cup.

*Shaw sprays catalyzed lacquer just like regular lacquer, with long, even, overlapping strokes, above. A double-cone, organic vapor respirator and fans or other forced ventilation are mandatory. Finishing the finish is the most time-consuming part of the job. To ensure a rich, smooth finish, each coat must be rubbed out with fine wet/dry paper. To check his work, right, Shaw examines the finish closely from a low angle where light reveals any defects.*

gun control must be perfect—an uneven coat looks horrible.

Catalyzed lacquers have many of the same problems as conventional lacquers, and the remedies are often the same. Fisheye, for example, is caused by contaminants, usually silicon, on the wood. Catalyzed lacquers will fisheye when applied over almost any contaminant, so I always assume that any refinished surface is contaminated and mix a fisheye remover into the lacquer. With new pieces, I test the sealer on some inconspicuous corner. If there is any trace of cratering, I use fisheye remover.

As with conventional lacquer, you can prevent hazing on catalyzed lacquer by adding enough retarder to slow the hardening process, giving the lacquer time to bleed off moisture before drying. The retarder also helps the lacquer flow out smoothly. To minimize air bubbles in the wet film, spray the catalyzed lacquer when the temperature is 75°F to 85°F, a much narrow range than for ordinary lacquer. If you must spray at higher or lower temperatures, add about 5% more retarder.

If something goes wrong, you can remove a catalyzed finish, but do it quickly before the lacquer cures or you're in for one miserable job. Paint stripper will remove partially-cured lacquer, but it takes an awful lot of stripper and even more elbow grease. If the finish has fully cured, straight lye (a can of Draino in a

quart of water) applied over and over works eventually, but it does not do the wood any good. After using the lye, you must rinse the wood with water and vinegar and usually have to bleach it with oxalic acid before refinishing. Make sure you wear your respirator and chemical-resistant gloves, and mix the lye in a plastic bucket—the solution can react with aluminum containers to produce harmful fumes.

Clean your brushes and spray gun immediately with lacquer thinner or acetone, or you will ruin them. Manufacturers claim the lacquer mixture will be usable for about three months, but I've found it must be used within a week if you want the strongest possible coat. Old lacquer won't turn into gelatinous ooze as long as it's kept in a sealed container. You can use it, but don't expect it to be any stronger than regular lacquer. In the last four years I have applied catalyzed lacquer to hundreds of pieces of furniture and numerous kitchen and bathroom cabinets, and have yet to hear a customer complain. So, for a finish that is as tough as nails, lovely to see and simple to apply, catalyzed lacquers are the only way to fly.                                            □

―――――――

*David Shaw is a writer, furniture finisher and restorer in Kelly Corners, N.Y.*

Photos: Elizabeth Jean Shaw

*Eighteen coats of clear lacquer produced the deep, glossy finish on this tray carved from* sen, *an elm-like wood.*

# Japanese Lacquer
## Urushi, *a traditional thousand-coat finish*

by Charles Roche

 When I began my apprenticeship in Japan, my teacher showed me one of his beautiful lacquered pieces. "How many coats does it take to achieve a finish like this?" I asked. When he didn't answer with a number, I thought it odd that a man who had spent most of his life doing this work couldn't, or wouldn't, directly reply to a simple question. That was not the last time I received a less than satisfactory answer. Gradually, through my own work with lacquer, I realized that part of the problem was my approach: I was trying to learn about lacquer the way I would learn about a commercial finish—by reading the can!

Lacquer, called *urushi* in Japan, must be approached differently. Craftsmen have been working for more than 2,000 years to learn how to use this viscous, brown sap produced by the Urushi tree (*Rhus vernificera*). They developed techniques to conform to its properties instead of modifying the natural substance to meet their demands, as can often be done with synthetic materials. Thus, a lacquer finish always has been as difficult to achieve as it is beautiful to admire.

Lacquer is not just a pretty finish, though. Its strength makes it perfect for frequently used bowls and trays, and for tables, chairs and cabinets. It is nontoxic and unaffected by hot liquids, food, oil, salt or mild acid. In fact, its durability is the stuff of legends. Some pieces reportedly have come through shipwrecks and months in the ocean as bright as if they were fresh from the maker's hands. I've seen a museum exhibit of ancient lacquerware bowls that had been unearthed in China—over the centuries the wood had completely rotted away, leaving only the thin red and black lacquer shell. Once I accidentally dropped a finished piece of lacquerware. The surface wasn't marred, but the wood underneath was dented, so I pierced the *urushi* film with a pin and steamed the wood back into shape with a wet cloth and hot iron. Except for the pinholes, the lacquer was unharmed.

Although lacquer finishes may be clear or colored, the materials for the opaque colored finishes are difficult to obtain outside of Japan. Also, a finish that enhances rather than covers wood grain seems to suit Western tastes best, so here I'll deal only with raw lacquer, which produces a deep brown, translucent stain. Ex-

Photos: Tsuyoshi Ito, Studio do-do

cept for the lacquer, which is sold in large tubes like toothpaste, the needed tools and materials are easy to buy or make.

I'll start with *fuki urushi,* the most complete method of lacquering and the process I used on the tray shown on the facing page. The term means "wiped lacquer" (excess lacquer is wiped off with a cloth), but it's usually translated into English as "clear lacquer" because the finish is translucent. My favorite colloquial name is *sen ben nuri,* which means "thousand-coat finish." Although this is a gross exaggeration, I've sometimes felt that I had at least approached that number before completing a piece.

I applied 18 coats of lacquer to the tray, sanding between coats with silicon carbide paper or charcoal powder. In addition, I sealed the wood pores with several coats of a paste filler made from pulverized Japanese waterstones, water and lacquer. The actual color and gloss of a finish depend on the number of coats of lacquer, the amount of sanding between coats, and the way the paste filler is used. Almost any species of wood can be lacquered. Generally the final color of a lacquered piece ranges from a dark-walnut matte to a high-gloss, translucent reddish-orange.

**Before you begin working** with lacquer, there are a few things to keep in mind. First of all, *be careful* (see box below). Second, because lacquer hardens by a chemical reaction, not just by the evaporation of moisture or solvents, you'll have to build a "wet box"—a sort of humid incubator that encourages this chemical change. You can fashion any type of box, but just make sure it's big enough to hold what you plan to finish. To maintain the required 80% to 85% relative humidity range, I hang towels on the box's inside walls, dampening them daily with water from a plant sprayer. On cooler days I put one or two electric lights on the box floor to keep the temperature between 25°C and 30°C (77°F to 86°F). For objects too large to fit into my regular wet box, I build a simple frame and cover it with plastic. Inside the enclosure, I bend a gooseneck lamp over a pan of water to maintain the desired temperature and humidity.

If the temperature and humidity are too low, the *urushi* may not harden; if too high, the lacquer may harden too quickly and take on a milky cast or "burn." High heat and humidity may also make a thick coat of lacquer shrink and wrinkle. Fortunately, though, the required heat and humidity ranges are quite broad and not that difficult to maintain, at least not in a humid country like Japan. *Urushi* can be fickle, though, no matter what you do. Even under perfect conditions, I've had pieces remain tacky for days.

Conditions in your workroom are important, too. It must be as free of dust as possible, especially during the final coats, which magnify even the smallest trapped particles. Oil, even the oil from your fingerprints, can be more damaging than dust—it may keep lacquer from hardening. The room must also be warm and dry to keep the lacquer fluid and easy to spread.

**You begin the actual finishing process** by squeezing a small amount of *urushi* onto a lacquered work table called a *joban* or onto a sheet of glass. The lacquer is then taken from the smooth

> CAUTION: *Urushi* can cause a skin rash, which can be severe with susceptible individuals. The tree that produces *urushi* is akin to poison sumac. Some people are never affected, but others cannot even enter a room where it is being used without breaking out. It's best to assume you are allergic. Try not to get any on your skin. If you do get it on you, wash the spot immediately with alcohol. Although *urushi* has a pungent smell, it's nontoxic, so you don't have to wear a respirator.

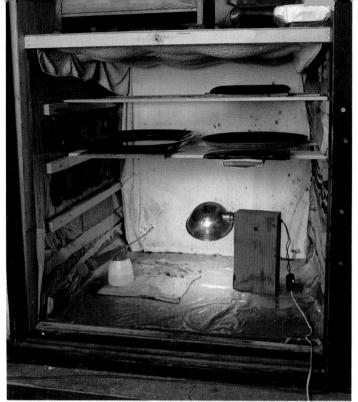

*This typical wet box, shown with its door removed, is a rough container equipped with a wet/dry thermometer to monitor humidity and temperature. Towels dampened with a plant sprayer provide moisture. Lamps supply heat when the box is sealed.*

*Apply the* urushi *with a short-bristled brush. The first, soaking coat creates a dramatic color contrast between the raw wood and the finished area. The glove keeps oily fingerprints off the wood.*

surface and applied with a short-bristled brush. Never squeeze it directly onto the workpiece. Lacquer is expensive and thus used conservatively—you don't want to expose large amounts to the danger of dust contamination or premature hardening. The *joban*'s sealed surface is easy to clean and does not absorb lacquer.

There's no formula for determining how much lacquer to squeeze out at one time, but you'll want enough to cover the piece you're doing. For the 15-in. tray used in this demonstration, a daub the size of a walnut would be enough for a generous first coat of lacquer. I use brushes made from a combination of human hair and horsehair, but any firm brush that does not shed bristles will do. Leave the first coat on for a few minutes, allowing the wood to absorb it freely. Then remove excess lacquer with a wooden spatula (called a *hera* in Japan), and thoroughly wipe the surface with a clean, dry, lint-free cotton cloth. Next place the piece on the smooth wooden slats inside the wet box until the lacquer has hardened, which may take as long as three days for the first coat. Until the stone-paste filler is applied, both sides of the piece are worked at once. After adding the filler, I

Cut hera from any clear, straight-grained wood. Their exact size, flexibility and shape depend on the job, but for a start split out a blank 27cm long by 6cm wide and plane it to a thickness of 6mm to 7mm. Cut the blank diagonally to yield two hera. Mark the top—all further shaping will be done to this face. Taper the blank thickness from 6mm at the handle to 1mm at the edge. Continue to thin the handle by planing the top face along lines A-D and A-B. Don't remove much from the centerline A-C.

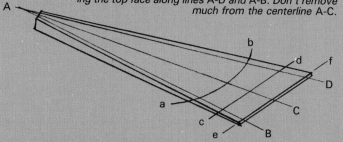

Next feather the area from arch a-b to edge e-f so that there are no abrupt changes in thickness. To ensure uniform thickness at the edge, make the final taper from line c-d to the edge with one slice of a sharp knife. Finally, cut off the edge e-f at any angle that suits you.

*To make a wood filler, use a hera (wooden spatula) to mix pulverized stone powder with water, then work in a small amount of lacquer until the paste can be smeared easily.*

*Holding one end of a nylon cloth filled with stone paste in his teeth, Roche twists the other end with one hand and uses the hera to pick up the paste as it is filtered through the cloth. Then he uses the spatula, right, to smear stone-paste filler over the wood and into its open pores.*

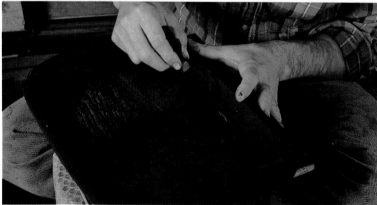

*Removing hardened stone paste is tedious. Wet-sand the layer to create a mud-like slurry, above, then wipe the area with a wet cloth. Wood grain is visible through the semi-transparent areas. Sandpaper is too rough for final coats, which must be polished with powdered charcoal dust and a cloth wrapped around a cotton pad, right. The polishing motion resembles that associated with French polishing.*

work on one side of the piece at a time. At this point, I wrap the slats with soft paper so the finish won't be scratched.

When the first coat has hardened, wet-sand the surface with 240- to 280-grit wet-or-dry silicon carbide paper over a sanding block. Always use water as the lubricant. As you sand, you'll see the high spots become lighter in color as the lacquer is removed, while the low spots remain dark. These spots usually are so slight that you can't feel them with your fingers, but they would be obvious in the glass-like surface of the finished piece, so you must eliminate them. Don't try to remove all the irregularities in one step. After sanding with 240-grit, apply another coat of lacquer as before, allow it to dry, then wet-sand with 320-grit. Then add a third coat of lacquer and wet-sand with 360-grit paper. Be careful not to sand through the lacquer completely, or you'll damage the wood cells and they'll absorb lacquer differently than will the undamaged areas. When your sanding lightens the entire surface evenly, all the surface irregularities have been removed. Apply a final coat of lacquer to finish the smoothing process.

Next seal the surface with stone-paste filler. To make the filler, place roughly equal parts of stone powder and *urushi* on your work surface. Add a small amount of water to the powder and mix thoroughly with a sturdy spatula until you have a barely damp paste. Now gradually work the *urushi* in with a kneading, smearing motion. Before using newly prepared stone paste, mix it with some left over from a previous project. If you don't have any old stone paste, don't use the new stuff for a day or two to ensure that the ingredients have settled into one another.

You must strain the paste before using it. Put a gob of it on a piece of fine mesh nylon (used for silk-screening), then twist the nylon. With a wooden spatula, skim off the paste that squeezes through the mesh and smear a thin coat over the entire project. Press firmly to force it into the open pores and fibers of the wood. When the piece is covered, place it in the wet box until it has hardened. Usually this takes from three days to a week or more. The piece is ready to work when you can make whitish scratches by running your fingernails back and forth across the surface.

Removing the dried paste from the surface is one of the more difficult parts of lacquering. Attach 400-grit wet-or-dry paper to blocks shaped to fit the object and wet-sand until you can't see any paste on the surface. Don't remove any of the underlying coat of lacquer, or the finished piece will have an uneven color and gloss. With a wet cotton cloth, remove the thick mud created by the wet-sanding. Wash the surface with water and apply a coat of lacquer before repeating the stone-paste process and sanding with 500-grit. On the second coat, you have to apply the paste only to patches you missed on the first application—these spots will be easy to see because they'll be dull compared to the rest of the surface. Usually two coats of stone paste are sufficient, but you might need a third coat on a broad-grained wood like oak.

After you've removed all of the hardened stone paste, thoroughly wash the entire surface with fresh water. Since the wood is, or should be, completely sealed by now, there's no danger of warpage. If the stone paste washes out of the grain, however, you probably didn't put enough lacquer in the paste mixture. Make a new batch and repeat the sealing process.

Now you are ready to begin laying up coats of lacquer to achieve the depth and brilliance typical of the finest work. These coats should be extremely thin—apply just enough lacquer to moisten the surface without building up any perceptible thickness. Brush on the lacquer, then spread it over the entire surface with a soft linen cloth wrapped around a piece of absorbent cotton. Move the cloth in a circular motion at first to ensure even

application, then run down the grain in long, even strokes. For hard-to-reach places, wrap the linen over a spatula. After lacquering, put the piece in the wet box again until it has hardened.

Sand the hardened coat lightly with 600-grit paper, just enough to remove any dust that may have settled on the surface and to ensure good bite for the next coat. Apply six to eight thin coats, allowing each to harden and sanding between coats with progressively finer paper—600-, 800-, 1,000- and 1200-grits.

After the eighth coat of lacquer, even the finest wet-or-dry paper would be too rough, so you must buff the surface with charcoal powder and water on a wad of absorbent cotton. Use a tight circular motion over the entire surface, then wash off the powder with clear water. The surface should show up evenly dull.

Now apply a thin coat of lacquer, using linen wrapped over absorbent cotton instead of a brush. Let the lacquer harden as before, but do *not* buff the surface with charcoal powder. Simply apply the final coat of lacquer directly over the previous one.

If everything has gone well, the piece should have a very high-gloss finish that is durable and extremely easy to care for. If for some reason the finish is uneven or you wish to refinish a piece, you must go back to the point where 400-grit paper was used and repeat the process.

To clean up, remove excess lacquer from your brush by "prying" it out with a hard wooden spatula. Then dip the brush in vegetable oil. Work the oil into the brush and squeeze it out with a spatula. Repeat until the oil comes out clean. Leave a little oil in the brush to prevent any residual lacquer from hardening. Before using the brush, you must reverse the cleaning process, using lacquer to remove all of the oil. Work tables are also cleaned with oil, then washed with alcohol. Excess lacquer and stone paste can be saved in a bowl covered with plastic wrap.

Time is the true test of the quality of any finish. If the process I've described seems too difficult and time-consuming, take another look at the results. A good lacquer finish will not dull, and it's easy to maintain—it can be cleaned with a soft, moist cloth and polished with a dry, cotton cloth. Even if you don't want to use the complete method, don't give up on *urushi*. You can cut the work in half by omitting the stone paste, and only have to give up some gloss. You can create a dark matte finish, much like a dark walnut stain, by letting the first coat soak in, removing the excess with a cloth and allowing the lacquer to harden. I especially like the soft, semigloss sheen achieved by applying three coats. Apply a heavy first coat as previously described, let it harden, then lightly dry-sand with 400-grit. Repeat the process for the second coat, then apply a final coat.

Working with *urushi* has been a source of both satisfaction and discouragement for me. New problems arise with every piece. But among the romantic ideals my teacher, Kuroda Kenkichi, has about craftsmanship is the belief that something made from a 300-year-old tree should last for at least 300 years. Some might call that philosophy and some might call it common sense. In any case, *urushi* is a step in the right direction. □

*Charles Roche operated a small furniture shop in Lexington, Ky., before going to Japan in 1978 to study woodworking and lacquering. He worked with Kuroda Kenkichi for three years before opening his own studio in Kyoto. For a price list and information on ordering* urushi *and stone powder, write to the author at Kamigyo-Ku, Muromachi Dori, Kamedachiuri Sagaru, Uratsukiji-Cho 81, Kyoto 602, Japan.* Urushi *can also be obtained from Woodfinishing Enterprises, 1729 N. 68th St., Wauwatosa, Wis. 53213.*

# Wood Stains
## Five ways to add color

by George Mustoe

Woodworkers often dismiss staining as an unpleasant, unskilled task that seldom produces natural-looking colors. That's to be expected. Retailers primarily stock semi-opaque stains, which can smother the wood if they are applied improperly. Manufacturers often encourage applications like "rosewood" stain on fir plywood, as if you could make drab wood exotic by tinting it a lurid shade. All this advertising hype ignores the real value of stains—they let you make a board's heartwood and sapwood a uniform color without fundamentally changing the wood's natural hue. Stains let you make six chairs and a dining table all the same color, without cutting a forest of trees to obtain matching boards.

Five basic groups of coloring agents are commonly called stains. *Semi-opaque stains,* the well-known oil stains sold in every hardware store, are surface finishes made by mixing transparent and opaque pigments with mineral spirits and linseed oil or varnish. *Transparent wood stains,* close chemical cousins of fabric dyes, are relatively color-fast aniline compounds derived from coal tars. The dye powder is dissolved in water or alcohol. These solvents carry the color deep into the wood cells. *Varnish and lacquer stains* are the conventional clear sealer coats tinted with transparent dyes. *Tinted penetrating oils* are billed as a complete finishing system that penetrates deeply into the wood to seal it, and provide a satiny "handrubbed" look. The oils, usually tung or linseed, are colored with dyes or pigments. *Chemical stains* are water-soluble inorganic compounds that react with the wood to create colorfast tints without dyes or pigments.

**Transparent dyes** are the best choice for hardwoods. More than 70 colors are available, ranging from subtle browns to spectacular bright colors. Their high degree of transparency means you won't hide the beauty of the underlying wood grain. Avoid these dyes on softwoods which absorb the watery solutions so rapidly that it's difficult to get even coloration.

Water-soluble aniline dyes are non-toxic (good for toys if you add a moisture-proof coat of clear varnish), non-flammable and very fade-resistant. Dissolve an ounce of dye powder in a quart of hot water in a glass, plastic or stainless steel container, then saturate a sponge or rag with dye. Wearing rubber gloves, squeeze out enough liquid to prevent dripping and splashing, then wipe on a generous coat parallel to the wood grain. To obtain a lighter shade, water down the dye rather than apply a skimpy coat, or you'll get uneven coloration. After wetting the surface, wipe off excess dye with a squeezed-out sponge or rag. The color will lighten as it dries, so leave the piece overnight before you decide if the shade is right. Apply a second dye coat for more intense color. Since water in the dye also swells the wood fibers, smooth the dried coat with fine 400- to 600-grit paper before adding a top coat of finish. An alternate method is to moisten the wood with water before adding any color, then sand the raised grain before dyeing.

Aniline dyes soluble in methyl (wood) alcohol are called "spirit stains." These are available as powders or pre-mixed liquids (Watco 5-Minute Wood Stain). Although not as fade resistant as water-soluble dyes, they produce sparkling clear colors. You apply them the same way as water-soluble dyes (the alcohol even contains enough water to raise the grain), but the solvent makes them potentially hazardous. Good ventilation is essential because respirators won't completely block out the fumes. Wear rubber gloves to prevent skin contact. These dyes are difficult to apply evenly on large surfaces because they dry so fast, usually within 15 minutes—if one section dries before the adjacent area is covered, you'll get a hard line between the two. The dyes are, however, particularly useful for touch-up work. The alcohol solvent lets them bind to oily woods or surfaces with traces of old finish that would repel water-soluble dyes. Adding a little shellac increases this ability.

You can avoid the grain-raising problems of water- and alcohol-soluble dyes by using NGR (Non-Grain Raising) dyes. You buy these pre-mixed in a water-free hydrocarbon solvent. NGR dyes are lightfast, but their fast drying rate limits them to small surfaces. The vapors are toxic, so good ventilation is essential.

**Oil stains** have done the most to give staining a bad name, but they can be good for enhancing the not-so-nice softwoods used in much interior carpentry. Go easy, though. The stains' high pigment content makes it easy to produce dingy-looking finishes, and the colors may be way off. "Mahogany" stains can range from red to brown to nearly purple, and maple can be anything from tan to orange. However, you can mix several colors to obtain a more pleasing shade; the formulas are so similar that even different brands can usually be intermixed.

Oil stains should be wiped on in the direction of the grain with a brush or a soft cloth. After waiting a few minutes for the wood to absorb the stain, wipe off the excess. If you want a darker shade, increase the waiting period or apply a second coat of thinned stain. Wiping the surface with mineral spirits will lighten the color. Again, good ventilation is essential because the vapors are flammable and toxic; oily rags are also a fire hazard.

Water-based stains, like those by Deft, are a fairly new product made up of opaque pigments suspended in a vinyl or acrylic base. Generally the colors are less intense than most oil stains, an advantage when subtle staining is desired. They are nonflammable and have no toxic vapors or bad odor.

**Tinted penetrating oils** are useful whenever an easy-to-apply, complete finishing system is needed. You apply the oil according to the package directions, then wipe off the excess. Additional coats can be applied before hand buffing the finish. Penetrating oils are not intended to be used with any other type of finish—some of these oils leave behind residues that may inhibit the drying time of varnish or lacquer. You can also make tinted oils by dissolving dye powders in tung or linseed oil, then thinning with 20% to 30% mineral spirits.

**Varnish stains** are synthetic or natural varnishes tinted with transparent dyes. This combination makes them highly transparent, and they intensify porous areas of the wood less than other stains. The first coat of varnish penetrates the porous area deeply, causing darker coloration, but then this coat blocks further absorbtion after it dries. Thus, subsequent coats will even out the color. Varnish stains have highly diluted tints, so you must apply several coats. The transparent color also makes it a good choice for softwoods such as pine and fir; inexpensive lumber can be livened up without ending up with the lurid colors and grain patterns that often result from oil stains.

Lacquer stain is similar to varnish stain but dries faster and has more toxic vapors. Ordinary clear lacquer can be colored by adding alcohol-soluble aniline dye, first dissolving the dye in a little methyl alcohol or lacquer thinner.

**Chemical stains** react directly with the wood and are somewhat unpredictable, so you must experiment with every species to see what color the chemicals will produce, especially if you want to reproduce the chemical stains on old pieces. Oak treated with ammonia turns a warm brown. Wood containing tannin becomes silvery gray when wiped with a solution of ferrous sulfate. Potassium dichromate, potassium permanganate and sodium carbonate (sal soda) will darken most hardwoods. The methods are simple: stir 1 to 2 tablespoons of chemical into a quart of lukewarm water in a glass jar (don't use metal, which may react). Except for ammonia, the chemicals are free of fumes, but they are poisonous if ingested. Wear rubber gloves and apply the solution with a rag or sponge. Let the stain dry overnight before sanding the raised grain.

Regardless of the product, staining can be a valuable technique in this age of high lumber prices and dwindling forest resources, when it's often necessary to salvage sap-streaked and bland boards. It's definitely not a sign of shoddy workmanship.  □

*George Mustoe is a geochemistry research technician at Western Washington University in Bellingham, Wash. Sources for stains include Sigma Chemical Co., P.O. Box 14508, St. Louis, Mo. 63178 (chemicals); Henningson & Associates, P.O. Box 6004, Rockford, Ill. 61125 (water-soluble dyes); Woodfinishing Enterprises, Box 10117, Milwaukee, Wisc. 53201 (stains and dyes), The Woodworkers Store, 21801 Industrial Boulevard, Rogers, Minn. 55374 (water- and oil-based stains, penetrating oils, NGR stains), H. Behlen and Bros. Inc., Route 30N, Amsterdam, N.Y. 12010.*

## Staining problems

Many staining problems are due to poor surface preparation, rather than a problem with the stain. No stain will work well unless it's evenly absorbed into the wood. Dull planer knives can glaze and compress the wood fibers enough to block stains. Thorough sanding parallel to the grain (to at least 120-grit) is essential. Even tiny swirl marks and scratches will absorb stain differently than smooth surfaces. Problems here can be cured only by sanding or hand-planing the wood to a fresh surface.

Dried glue won't absorb stain, so gluelines can show after staining, especially where the joint juxtaposes contrasting grain patterns. You can't fix these defects, so lay out stock so grain patterns match, and fit joints tightly so gluelines are thin.

The only way to remove ugly glue smears that appear after staining is to re-sand and restain the surface. If you suspect smears, you can make the glue temporarily visible before staining by dampening the wood with mineral spirits or lacquer thinner—use chalk or a pencil to mark areas that need more sanding.

End grain is highly absorbent and can sometimes turn almost black if you don't seal the open pores before staining. For oil stains, use linseed oil as a sealer. Shellac (3-lb. cut) diluted 1:1 with denatured alcohol makes a good blocking agent for most other stains. No matter how much sealer you use, large areas of end grain don't stain well unless you are trying to emphasize the contrasting textures.

Wood-patching compounds and fillers seldom absorb stain like the surrounding wood. Unless you have extraordinary luck, you must do a good deal of experimentation on scrap lumber to come up with a colored patching compound that dries to match the stained lumber. Some stainable compounds remain porous after drying, but if porosity of the patch differs greatly from that of the surrounding wood, these fillers may come out lighter or darker than you desire. Even if you get a good color match, the lack of grain patterns will reveal large patches. Instead of using synthetic patches, the best results often come from inserting a plug of matching wood. This means routing or chiseling out the defect to get smooth margins and thin gluelines. If synthetic patching compounds are used, hand-tint the repaired area with oil stains or artists' acrylic colors to match the adjacent stained wood. Apply the colors with a fine brush and streak them to follow the grain lines of the surrounding wood.

Wood fillers applied to smooth the surface of open grained woods usually work well with stains. The fillers come in many colors, so experiment to find one that matches the stain. Mineral-spirits based fillers can also be custom tinted with dry pigments or up to 30% oil stain. The paste-like filler is thinned to a creamy consistency with mineral spirits, then liberally brushed onto the stained wood, saturating the open pores. Wait a few minutes for the filler to dry to a dull luster, then rub with a coarse rag to wipe off the excess and smooth the surface. Let dry overnight, then sand lightly with 320-grit paper.

Once stain has been applied, don't let the colors bleed into later coats of finish. Your best precaution is to make sure the stain has a different solvent than the next coat of finish. For example, water-soluble dyes won't bleed into lacquer or varnish, but oil and spirit stains will. You could also let the stain dry thoroughly, then seal it with a thin washcoat of shellac.

Stained wood is vulnerable to surface damage because scratches and abrasions may penetrate the colored layer and expose lighter wood. You can't just restain a scratch—the microscopically rough walls pick up pigment and end up too dark. A better approach is to restore the color by applying a tiny brushful of diluted stain, tinted varnish or shellac colored with spirit stain. With extensively damaged pieces, it's better to strip off the finish and redo the whole piece.                    —G.M.

# Driftwood Finishes

*Weathered wood in an hour or two*

by Jim Cummins

When I got into the picture-framing business 19 years ago, most framers could dash off a variety of wood finishes. One of the most popular was the barnwood or driftwood finish, usually applied to common pine. Fresh from the lumberyard, kiln-dried pine can be textured and colored in an hour or two to imitate wood that has gracefully weathered 20 years. I've seen the same finish used on trim moldings and on rustic indoor furniture, on hardwoods and softwoods both.

If you're framing a picture, my article in *FWW* #35 will show you how to make many molding shapes on the tablesaw. The next step, for a driftwood finish, is to texture the wood. Then you add layers of contrasting stain and paint so that the darker color ends up in the low spots, the lighter on the high. You can vary the look quite a bit, so the final result may be dark or light, warm or cool.

Most framers today buy pre-finished driftwood moldings, and many of these don't look like wood at all. Some are garish, others dismal. I believe this happens because manufacturers try to imitate each other's successful products instead of imitating wood, and each imitation gets further from the truth. Yet a good driftwood finish isn't difficult. All you have to do is mimic nature's own weathering.

**Texture**—Wood has hard grain and soft grain in alternating layers. When wood ages, the soft grain on the surface breaks down and disappears, leaving a craggy texture. Finishers duplicate the process by removing the soft grain with a wire brush. I have a 6-in. dia. wire brush mounted on the shaft of a bulky, old ⅙-HP motor. When I have a lot of frames to do, I haul the motor out and clamp it to my workbench. But for just a frame or two, I usually use a straight wire brush or chuck a

small round one in my electric drill. In addition to the brush, I sometimes use an old table fork to incise long, wandering scratches that imitate surface checking. If you want a few wormholes, try an awl. Be sure to sand any sharp edges, as these break down quickly in natural aging.

If the surface gets fuzzy, I either sand it with a coarse grit or burn off the splinters with a propane torch, depending on whether I want to keep the wood light or allow it to become darkened by charring.

**Color and value**—Natural wood *color* ranges from hot reddish-browns to cold bluish-grays. Any color also has *value,* the degree of lightness or darkness it would have if seen in a black-and-white photograph. The final color and value of a driftwood finish can be anywhere in the natural color and value range.

Nature's palette is broad, but it's used with discretion. One side of a weathered board may age warm and very dark, while the other side is a pale silvery gray. But you're not likely to find such extremes on any one side exposed to the same conditions. This is a guideline for a successful driftwood finish: choose similar colors and values for both the bottom coat and the top coat. Don't try to put a cold gray top coat over a hot brown base—you'll end up with a finish that's visually "jumpy." And remember that a wood surface ages dark or it ages light, not both at the same time.

My general advice is that warm pictures look best in warm frames, and light pictures look best in light frames. Avoid too much contrast. As a rule, choose warm or neutral tones rather than cool ones, except for very cold pictures. But if you're planning to hang a warm picture on a cool wall, pick frame colors that will provide a transition, or the picture may look out of place.

To my eye, the most beautiful finishes,

whether light or dark in value, occur when one color is slightly warm and the other slightly cool. If neither is extreme, the two harmonize and sparkle.

**Painting**—The picture framer's standby used to be casein paint sold in quarts and gallons, but I haven't been able to get any for years. Milk paint, which dries too hard, is a poor substitute. I've tried artists' casein paints in tubes, but they aren't formulated to flow well from a large brush, and I mostly use them just for tinting. So, keeping up with the times, I've turned to latex paints, poster paints and watercolors. Almost anything will work. A wide range of grays can be made by mixing white or off-white latex with raw umber and yellow ocher artists' colors, either acrylic or casein. Watch out for black, though—it's deceptive. If you use any in making a gray, the color may look warm while wet, but it will dry cold.

The sample in the color photo was made with one coat of Minwax stain, followed by latex paint tinted with artists' acrylic color. I applied the stain to the textured wood, and blended in the latex while the stain was still wet. This simultaneously lightened the dark stain undercoat and darkened the latex coat, to reduce the contrast and bring the two closer together. The wet-on-wet method is somewhat hit-or-miss and takes some practice. But there's a more methodical way that guarantees good results every time: Give the textured wood a thin toning coat of paint or stain. When that's dry, seal it with a thin coat of shellac. When this is dry, apply a top paint coat that contrasts slightly with the base coat. Remember the advice about color and value, and choose colors that won't fight with each other.

When the top coat is dry, steel-wool through it, down to the base coat. The top coat will remain in the valleys, while

128

the base coat peeks through on the high spots, accentuating the grain. The shellac between the two coats will provide some luster and highlights.

That's really all there is to it, but here are some variations of the technique. After applying the base coat and the shellac sealer, lightly wax the high spots of the frame before you apply the top coat. While the top coat is still wet, use a rubber squeegee to force the paint down into the unwaxed fissures and wipe it from the waxed high spots at the same time, saving yourself the steel-wooling step. You could also use a dry-brush technique to apply the top coat: Wet the brush as usual, then spread the paint on a sheet of newspaper until the brush is nearly dry. Now lightly drag the brush over the frame so it hits just the high spots.

**Fine-tuning**—Now is the time to step back, compare the result with what you were aiming for, and add whatever last touches seem necessary. At the very end of the process, you can introduce a little strongly contrasting color and value to produce visual tension. If a warm brown finish looks dull, add a tiny bit of light green to the high spots. Or add orange to cool gray. But if the result draws attention to itself, it's too much. A decorative finish should sing, not shout.

If you're working on a picture frame, you can use children's crayons for the highlights. On a finish that needs more durability, you can use oil paints, barely touching the high spots. Coating the entire job with wax will make the top coat more transparent and thereby make the finish more uniform in color. Keep in mind that the finish will be seen, usually, from several feet away. □

*Jim Cummins is an associate editor at FWW. His shop is in Woodstock, N.Y.*

*A stiff wire brush can simulate the craggy texture that occurs in natural weathering. If the wood is still bland, add graining with a table fork. The sample at right shows progressive 'aging' of a molding stick, compared with a naturally aged block.*

## Finish repair

*When a wet tray remained too long on my 30-year-old cherry serving cart it removed spots of the beeswax finish. Can I repair this wax finish without damaging the patina?*
                                    —*Frank W. Hollin, Philadelphia, Pa.*
**Beau Belajonas replies:** You may be dealing with more than just a wax finish. There could be varnish, shellac or lacquer underneath the wax. If the water spot has only damaged the wax then the remedy is very simple. Mineral spirits dissolves wax. All you need to do is give the piece a good scrubbing with 000 steel wool dipped in mineral spirits and wash away the wax, dirt, grime and water spot. To restore the patina, make some tinted wax by melting Amber Butcher's paste wax and adding a dash of raw or burnt-umber oil color. Wax is highly flammable so be sure to do this in a double boiler so the heat source can't ignite the wax. (Keep a fire extinguisher handy and be careful; a wax fire recently destroyed my shop.) Let the wax cool overnight.

Apply a thin, even coat of this colored wax and allow it to dry for 24 hours. Rub the wax down hard with lots of paper towels or old cotton sheets to get an even sheen. Allow to harden overnight. Repeat this colored-wax application and rubdown process at least three times. Apply a final coat of regular Amber Butcher's wax.

If there's varnish, shellac or lacquer underneath the wax and the water spot has penetrated the finish, the repair is a little more difficult. You have to rub off a thin layer of the finish where the spot has penetrated. First remove the wax as described above. After drying with paper towels, dip 000 steel wool into a solution of 1 part boiled linseed oil to 1 part mineral spirits. Instead of steel wool, you can make an abrasive paste by mixing rottenstone or 4F pumice with the oil solution and carefully rub it on with a soft cloth.

Rub the water spot slowly and carefully. The oil solution gives you some body and acts as a lubricant so you don't cut into the finish too quickly. This process should remove most spots and is also a good way to level minor chips in the finish. If the spot doesn't come out it's penetrated too far and the entire finish must be removed.

After the spot has been successfully rubbed out, clean off any residue with mineral spirits and wipe the surface dry. Apply a thin coat of satin varnish (alkyd or urethane) diluted 4 parts varnish to 1 part mineral spirits. Tint the varnish lightly with raw umber if desired. Allow to dry for 24 hours then carefully rub it smooth with worn 400-grit wet/dry sandpaper and follow with a wax polish. To add more color and depth you can follow with the colored process described above.
[Beau Belajonas is a professional wood finisher who lives in Camden, Me.]

## Windsor chair finishes

*I'd appreciate an expert opinion on an appropriate finish for Windsor chairs. Is there a toner or stain that will even out the color of the different woods—pine, birch and red oak— that make up the rungs, legs, seat, back and spindles? I'd like to use Watco for a final finish.*
                                    —*Calen Fitzgerald, Grand Forks, B.C.*
**Michael Dunbar replies:** In the Federal period (1780-1810), when most American Windsor styles were developed, these chairs were always painted—green being the most popular color. It's often said that Windsors were painted only to cover the different woods that make up the chair but I disagree. Instead, I believe that the painted surface existed in the chairmaker's mind before the chair design did and that Windsors look the way they do because of this choice of finish. If the wood was meant to be seen, Windsor designs would be very different.

A lot of utilitarian furniture in the Windsor era was painted.

Wood was perceived simply as an abundant, versatile material. Today however, when so much of our furniture is made of chrome and plastic, our perception of wood is different. For us, wood is precious—a link to the natural world. The phrase "natural beauty of wood" has become a cliche and a clear finish has become an extension of that cliche. Painted furniture goes against current fashion.

To use a natural finish on a Windsor, however, is to try to separate the chair from the paint around which it was designed. Color coalesces the verticals, horizontals and curves of a Windsor into a whole and prevents the eye from being distracted as it moves along the lines of the chair. The different woods in a Windsor were selected, not for what they looked like, but for the physical characteristics of the species. When these woods are visible, the different colors of the oak, birch and pine are distracting, as you've already found. As a result, one tries to turn the chair into a uniform shade of brown with chemicals and stains. In other words, one tries to paint with dyes instead of paint.

I finish my Windsors with milk paint because it resembles the original lead-based painted finish (available from The Old-Fashioned Milk Paint Co., Box 222, Groton, Mass. 01450). [Michael Dunbar makes Windsor chairs in Portsmouth, N.H. He is the author of *Make a Windsor Chair With Michael Dunbar,* 1984, Taunton Press.]

## Finish for cypress paneling

*I've just finished a den in tongue-and-groove pecky cypress and need some suggestions on how to seal and finish the wood. I would like to end up with a warm and natural looking finish.*                    —*Kenneth E. Behnke, Edgewater, Md.*
**George Frank replies:** Once I had a living room paneled in pecky cypress. I considered the finish warm and natural looking. First I mixed half and half white and ivory water-based acrylic paint. Then I stirred approximately one part of it into 8 to 10 parts of water and painted all the paneling with it. When dry, I sandpapered off all the paint that I could, leaving some in the "pecks" of the wood, in the frame-corners and in the moldings. After a thorough dusting, I sprayed on a wash coat of orange shellac, followed by two or three coats of clear lacquer (not the water-white, but the amber-clear), sanding between coats. I steelwooled, waxed my finish and was pleased. [George Frank, a retired master European wood finisher, lives in South Venice, Fla.]

## Blushing lacquer

*What causes lacquer to blush when sprayed at high humidity? Why will a mist coat with a large percentage of thinner blush, while a coat of unthinned lacquer won't? When spraying a guitar body, you can often see the pattern of the internal bracing when blushing occurs; the braces seem to inhibit blushing, which occurs everywhere else on the thin soundboard and back. Why?* —*Abraham Wechter, Pau Pau, Mich.*
**George Morris replies:** Lacquer blushes when atmospheric water vapor condenses on the newly sprayed surface. When lacquer is sprayed, the sudden release of compressed air and the extremely high evaporation rate of the lacquer thinner combine to super-cool the surface, inviting condensation. The more thinner, the more cooling, which explains why the unthinned lacquer doesn't blush. The internal bracing in a guitar body acts as a heat sink, warming the lacquer and reducing the blushing effect directly over the brace.

To avoid blushing, avoid spraying on especially humid days. If you must, use a retarder to slow the evaporation rate. When blushing does occur, allow the lacquer to dry at least an hour, then wipe with 0000 steel wool.
[George Morris makes guitars in Post Mills, Vt.]

# An Oil and Varnish Finish

by Lothar Baumann

I mill a lot of my lumber from walnut logs and crotches, and can control the figure in the wood according to how I cut it. When I've uncovered a really fine feather figure, I go to the trouble of stretching it; I resaw the block several times, bookmatch the grain, and veneer the best looking wood over solid walnut for wall-cabinet doors and other furniture. When I've finally gotten a piece made, I aim for a finish that brings out the hard-won feather to best advantage.

Oil is my favorite. It penetrates the wood and makes the most of the wood's ability to reflect and bend light, creating depth and allowing the figure to shimmer. But a lot of my customers don't want pure oil—they grew up with durable polyurethane, and won't settle for anything else. Combining oil with polyurethane gives some of the benefits of both. The idea isn't new, and lots of people have different ways of mixing and applying the blend. I've settled on a system that takes more work than a lot of people seem willing to go to, but the results are worth it.

First, I sand the raw wood smooth, working up through progressively finer grits until I reach 220- or 240-grit garnet paper. In theory, each grit scratches the surface efficiently and uniformly, and the next grit size removes the first set of scratches, replacing them with slightly finer ones. You use one grit, say 100- or 120-grit, to remove major machine marks, fuzzy grain and other irregularities. (I use a 4-in. by 24-in. Makita belt sander, but occasionally turn to a hand plane or scraper.) You sand until the wood is completely even, then move up to the next finer paper, 150-grit, and sand until the first set of scratches is gone and the surface looks even. Work through the remaining grits in the same manner. If you skip grit sizes or start with too fine a paper, you'll waste a lot of time. Even worse, flaws you thought you'd sanded away will reappear in the finish. This whole initial-preparation process shouldn't take more than half an hour for a pair of cabinet doors.

Sandpaper is a precision tool and deserves to be taken seriously. Each piece of grit is bedded in a layer of adhesive that holds it to the paper backing and exposes just so much cutting edge. If you tear or fold the paper, you'll break into the layer of adhesive and expose more cutting surface than was intended on the grit particles along the edges, putting yourself back a grade or two if the edges hit the work. Grit can also become dislodged from the paper, and if you don't dust the wood between grits you can end up with wrong-size scratches that will mar the pattern. If this happens, it's best to resand with the previous grit. People who use power sanders often complain about swirl marks on the wood. These may not be the machine's fault, but the result of loose grit left on the work.

Beware of buying cheap stuff. I got a bargain on some paper not too long ago and bought hundreds of sheets, but I discovered that the 220-grit is full of larger particles that make the paper useless; it's too fine for coarse work, and too scratchy for finish-sanding.

I don't usually stain the wood because it already looks the way I want it to, nor do I apply fillers—the finishing process fills the pores as much as necessary. When the surface has been taken to 220-grit dry, I apply clear Watco oil as a primer coat, rubbing it in with 220- or 280-grit wet/dry paper wrapped over a block of Celotex. The Celotex distributes the pressure just as a cork block would, but it's cheaper. When saturated with the oil mixture, Celotex becomes spongy and may disintegrate. If you set aside damp blocks and allow them to dry, they will become harder and more durable. When I feel the sandpaper begin to slip on the wood instead of biting, I know that it's almost finished its job and that most of the 280-grit scratches are gone. I switch up to 320-grit and sand again, then repeat the process with 400-grit and 600-grit.

The wet-sanding produces a slurry of wood dust and oil, which is forced down into the pores. I wipe the slurry off the surface before beginning each new grit, but leave the 600-grit slurry on the surface until it begins to thicken. Then I wipe the wood across the grain until it's almost dry and set it aside for the oil in the remaining slurry to dry completely. This takes about three days in hot weather and up to a week and a half in the winter, when it's cool and damp. One test for dryness is to put the work briefly in the sun or near a heat source; if it bleeds oil, it's not ready yet.

When the oil is dry, remove the slurry film with steel wool, working in the direction of the grain. Polish the wood to remove any oil residue from the surface. If the surface quality is uneven, with dull spots where the oil has been absorbed, apply another coat. Work it in with 600-grit paper, sanding with the grain. Wipe off the excess with paper towels and let this coat dry. If you are determined to completely fill the pores, you can sand again to build up a slurry and let it dry again on the wood, repeating until the surface is flawless. I don't mind a few open pores because they keep the wood looking like wood.

I complete the process by applying an oil-and-varnish mix. The mix is 3 parts polyurethane, 2 parts boiled linseed oil and 2 parts mineral spirits, applied with a rag. I usually sand-in the first coat with 600-grit paper, just a little—too much sanding at this stage will only open up new pores. I apply two or three coats, although I have used up to eight, wiping each coat clean and almost dry, and allowing drying time between coats. I don't sand after the first coat unless there's an imperfection that I overlooked earlier. I have used several commercially prepared tung-oil mixtures, such as Hope's, Gillespie's and Formby's, instead of my oil-varnish mix, and they work equally well. The sanding of the finish into the wood seems to be the critical factor to obtain the results I want. Applying the top coats of finish takes time, but you can't call it much work. It's more like a reward for all the preparation that went into getting the wood ready for it. □

*Lothar Baumann is a woodworker in Berea, Ky. He uses the same finish when he works on the lathe.*

# TURNING

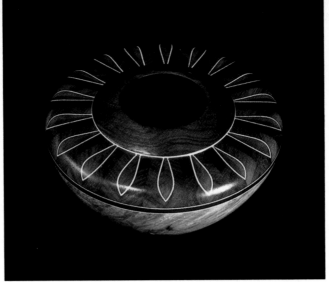

*Subtle or showy, the colors and textures of wood, burl and veneer interplay in authors' geometric designs. Glued up from bands of wedge-shaped segments, the lathe-turned bowls shown play on Indian-pottery forms and patterns from the American Southwest. Turnings shown range in height from 4 in. to 9 in. with an average wall thickness of ⅛ in.*

# Segmented Turning
## *Redefining an old technique*

by Addie Draper and Bud Latven

While exploring the art of woodturning we rediscovered and refined an old turning technique known as segmentation. This process involves gluing various shapes and colors of wood together then turning them to create lively, infinitely-variable designs. The method is time consuming and often complicated but worth it for the richness and diversity of designs it makes possible.

We've always savored the beauty of burl and we find that the regulated crispness of segmented designs contrasts nicely with the unpredictable burl figure. Once a year we go on burl-hunting trips to the West Coast. Some of our favorite species include walnut-root burl from the Sacramento valley, lilac burl from southern California and maple-root burl from western Oregon. The challenge is to devise patterns that complement each burl's unique character.

It's hard to say why we combine certain woods or why a particular pattern complements a particular shape. What works aesthetically and what doesn't is largely subjective but color, figure and density are the main things to consider in planning this kind of turning. If a burl's figure is subdued, a segment band of brightly contrasting wood—rich, red paduak on a field of ash—will liven up the piece. For accent, we might work contrasting or complementary-colored veneers into the pattern. As a rule, we avoid highly-figured woods in the segment band because too much figure is distracting. Woods of similar density turn and sand more easily. If you juxtapose a soft wood next to a hard, dense one, the finished surface may have an uneven feel. This isn't necessarily a liability—the contrast can produce some interesting tactile qualities—but it's something to consider when choosing woods.

The shapes we turn have evolved from many sources. Living in the Southwest, we've been influenced by the indigenous Indian pottery. Though these shapes were developed in clay, they have a directness and simplicity of line that translates nicely to woodturning. Other cultures have provided rich inspiration as well. The jar-like bowl in the top left photo, for example, owes much to the Greek hydria.

Whatever the shape, we usually begin a bowl by drawing it full-size on graph paper. We start with an elevation view including the segment pattern, then make a full-size plan view of each segment band, as shown in the drawing on p. 136. This is a critical step because it allows us to refine the shape and plan the segment pattern in minute detail. We can then measure the various angles and sizes of each segment right off the drawing instead of puzzling it out mathematically. We've found that it's a lot simpler to measure in millimeters and centimeters when working at this scale.

The basic building block for our designs is a segment with a truncated-wedge shape. A few of our bowls are turned entirely of segmented sections, but most consist of a burl blank onto which we glue one or more segment bands that make up the desired pattern. The segment patterns can become quite complex. It's impossible to describe in this article how we make every one, but by experimenting with the basics explained here, you'll be

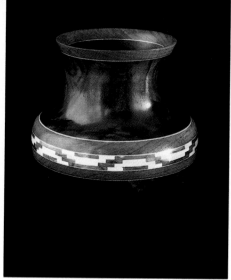

able to figure out the more complex patterns and invent new ones. We've developed different types of segments and several techniques for combining the segments into patterns. Solid-block segments and slant-line segments, both shown on p. 136, are the two basic segment types. Solid-block segments are cut from solid wood. Slant-line segments are sliced from a glued-up sandwich of multi-colored woods and veneers so that the laminates form a diagonal stripe across the segment face, as shown in the drawing. The apparently curved lines of holly veneer in the bowl, facing page, center, are simply a variety of straight slant-line segments. The lines appear curved because they traverse the bowl's radiused edge.

Solid-block and slant-line segments can be combined in many different ways, but there are two basic ways that we glue up the segments—single-angle and multi-angle patterns. A single-angle pattern, like a pie cut into equal slices, is made up of segments with the same angle, say 18 segments at 20°. A multi-angle pattern alternates segments with different angles, say 12 segments at 20°, and 12 segments at 10° spaced wide, narrow, wide, etc. Photo #11 (p. 137) shows a simple multi-angle pattern. Whether single-angle or multi-angle, the segment angles always add up to 360°.

By stacking bands of segments we create a multiple-row pattern. The complex Aztec design shown in the photo (facing page, right) is an example of a solid-block, multi-angle, multiple-row pattern.

Once you have drawn the design full-size, you are ready to make the segments. The diameter of the segment band should be 1cm larger than the finished diameter to allow for turning. You can measure the angle and width of each segment at it's heel and toe right on the drawing, or, if you are mathematically inclined, you can calculate the circumference with the formula $C = \pi d$ and divide this by the number of segments if all the segments are the same angle. This will give you the approximate segment width at the circumference. It won't be entirely accurate because it will be the arc of the end of the segment, so the segment itself will be slightly smaller. But since the segments are cut slightly oversize anyway, the measurement you get with this formula will be close enough.

We usually plan to cut the segments so that we don't have to turn end grain. The grain direction should run around the circumference of the turning. We cut the segments 2mm oversize on either side, then sand them to size on the disc sander with an 80-grit disc. Solid-block segments are crosscut from a board on the tablesaw. The sawing process for slant-line segments is two-step, as shown at the bottom of p. 136. Remember that slant-line segments are sliced from a glued-up sandwich of contrasting woods. First, on the tablesaw, we crosscut parallelogram sections from the sandwich. Then we square off the corners of the parallelograms on the bandsaw. For sanding the segments to size, we've tacked a wooden fence to our disc-sander table at 90° to the disc. A wooden push stick (one for each angle) with the end cut to the segment angle feeds the segment into the disc. To ensure consistency, use one segment, sanded to the proper size, as a pattern for the others.

Before gluing the segments to the burl blank, we level the turning blank with a custom-made sanding disc, as shown in photo #4 on p. 137. This 12-in.-diameter disc was machined from ½-in.-thick aluminum by a local machinist. It has a steel spindle with a morse taper that matches the drill press quill. After the segments have been trued up on the disc sander, they're ready to be glued to the burl. With a circular protractor, duplicate the radial "grid" from the full-size drawing directly on the burl blank. Accuracy is very important. Lay the segments on the grid and bring them in tight to check for a proper fit. If there is a total of more than 1mm of slop all the way around, the segments need to be touched up on the sander.

When the fit is right, apply glue to the bottom of a segment and rub it onto the blank moving it back and forth and applying downward pressure. We use Titebond glue for all our laminations. Line up one segment side along a radius line and lay a straightedge along the side of the segment. The straightedge should still follow a radius line on the opposite side of center. Allow the glue to set for five minutes. Glue the next segment and rub it into position against the first, but don't bump the already-glued segment out of position. Continue this process, gluing each segment in place around the circumference of the blank, taking care to align each segment on the "grid" lines. Continuous attention to accuracy avoids compounding problems. This is especially important in multiple-row and slant-line patterns where minute joinery errors add up to become major ones in the finished work. The photos on p. 137 show how we lay up a solid-block multi-angle pattern. When you've laid up ¼ circle, check it with a square. When you've laid up ½ circle, check with a straightedge. Make a third check with a square when you've laid up ¾ circle. We usually need to touch up the last three segments slightly on the disc sander for a tight fit. Once all the segments are glued up, let the work dry overnight. We find that it's not necessary to clamp when laying up the segments, but we do clamp the layers of veneer or other hardwood laminates that may be part of the piece. We have never had a piece fly apart on the lathe.

We usually glue a piece of hardwood to the bottom of the burl. This will be turned down later to become a very thin foot at the

# Making a segmented bowl step-by-step

**1. Draw desired shape full size on graph paper**

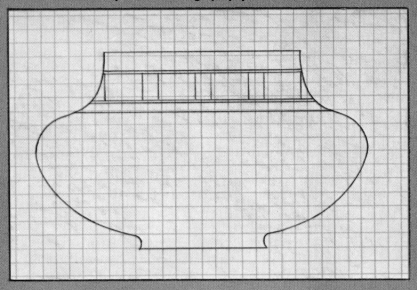

*Draw plan view of each segment band:*

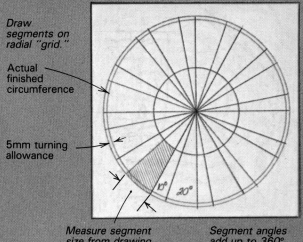

Draw segments on radial "grid."

Actual finished circumference

5mm turning allowance

Measure segment size from drawing.

Segment angles add up to 360°.

**2. Cut segments**

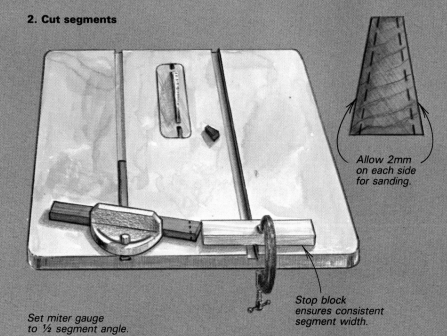

Allow 2mm on each side for sanding.

Set miter gauge to ½ segment angle.

Stop block ensures consistent segment width.

**3. Sand segments to size**

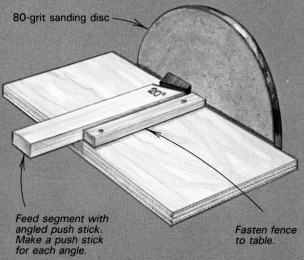

80-grit sanding disc

Feed segment with angled push stick. Make a push stick for each angle.

Fasten fence to table.

**Slant-line segments**

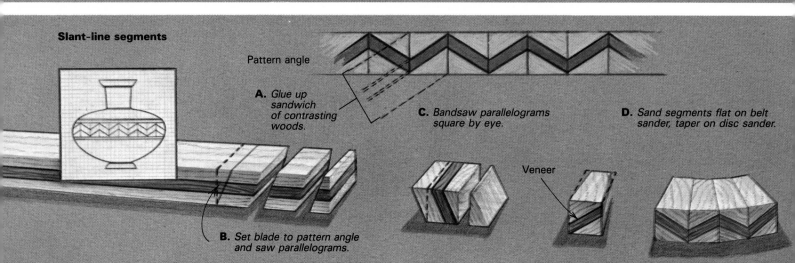

Pattern angle

**A.** Glue up sandwich of contrasting woods.

**B.** Set blade to pattern angle and saw parallelograms.

**C.** Bandsaw parallelograms square by eye.

**D.** Sand segments flat on belt sander, taper on disc sander.

Veneer

136

*Gluing up begins with a burl-blank bandsawed round then sanded flat with a custom-made sanding disk ( 4). After gluing on a layer of veneer, the pre-planned segment "grid" is drawn on the blank ( 5) and the segments glued in place one-at-a-time. Checks for square at 90° ( 6), 180° and 270° reveal cumulative errors in segment size and allow corrections. The completed solid-block, multi-angle segment band ( 7) is set aside to dry.*

*After gluing on a hardwood rim and foot, the blank is screwed to a faceplate. The center is drilled to depth with a ¾-in. multispur bit, then the tailstock is brought up for support ( 8). First the outside is turned to shape with scrapers ( 9), then the inside is scraped, leaving the tailstock in place ( 10) for as long as possible to support the work. After sanding, the bowl is parted off the lathe and the bottom sanded flat before finishing with Waterlox ( 11).*

bottom of the piece. We glue a piece of maple to the hardwood which is, in turn, screwed to a faceplate.

The blank can be quite heavy, so do as much of the turning as possible between centers. We do most of our rough turning at 1000 RPM to 1500 RPM and finish turn at 2200 RPM. First, we turn the outside with scrapers. For complex pieces we stop occasionally to check the drawing against the turning. If an interesting effect starts to happen during the turning process we don't hesitate to deviate from the drawing.

We sand the outside, first with 60-grit, then with 80-grit sandpaper before starting the inside. With a chuck in the tailstock, we bore to within ⅛ in. of the bottom of the burl using a ¾-in. multispur bit, then turn the inside with scrapers, striving for a wall thickness of ⅛ in.

We finish-sand down to 400-grit, and part the bowl off through the layer of hardwood, leaving only about ⅛ in. still attached to the burl. We sand this flat on a piece of 120-grit sandpaper fastened to the benchtop, working through the grits down to 400-grit. Six or more coats of Waterlox finish the bowl.

The segmentation process can be as simple or as complex as you choose to make it. Since the actual lathe work is often only a small part of the entire process, it's a good idea to develop turning techniques before plunging into segmentation work. You'll find, as you experiment with our techniques, that you'll discover new effects at the lathe that you just can't predict on paper. □

*Bud Latven and Addie Draper are professional woodturners in Tajique, N.M.*

# Turning a Lidded Box

## A centerwork project

by Richard Raffan

Lidded boxes may seem complicated, but the steps involved are really quite simple. Boxes demand more precise tool control than do bowls, and care, attention to detail, and a few tips on how to overcome all the little problems usually encountered make them readily achievable turning projects. Craftsmanship has less to do with the conception and birth of an object than with knowing when to be careful and what to do when things go wrong.

I've made boxes as large as 10 in. in diameter and 6 in. deep. These were turned on a faceplate with the grain running across the lid and base, but warping always spoiled the lid fit when the grain was aligned this way. Today, I make all my boxes with the grain running through from top to bottom. What little warping does occur is not much of a problem on a small box because the lid can be made thin enough to flex slightly without being too fragile. But I find warping is still a major problem in boxes over 3 in. in diameter, even with well-seasoned wood.

For turning boxes, I prefer what's known as a spigot chuck (available from Cryder Creek, Box 19, Whitesville, N.Y. 14897). This chuck grips a short tenon or flange turned on the end of the wood. A 3-jaw chuck may also be used for turning lidded boxes. I do not recommend screw chucks for boxes because they don't

Turn a ⅛-in. tenon or flange on each end of the cylinder to fit the spigot chuck. Hold the parting tool in one hand and the calipers in the other. Stop cutting when the calipers slip over the tenon.

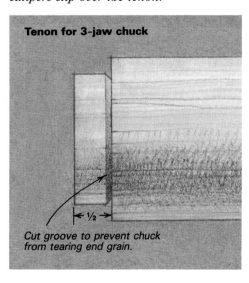

Tenon for 3-jaw chuck

|← ½ →|

Cut groove to prevent chuck from tearing end grain.

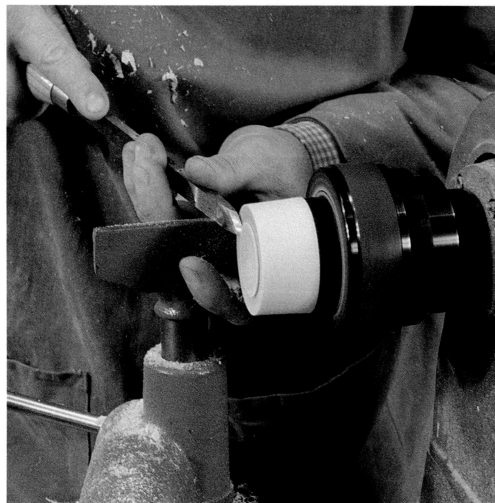

A second shearing cut with the skew chisel trues up the rim of the lid. Tilt the short point of the skew away from the wood to avoid a catch.

grip well on end grain unless the thread penetrates the wood an inch or more. This wastes wood and develops leverage problems that do not arise when working closer to the headstock. Neither do I recommend expanding collet chucks for boxes. As they expand into a recess they act like mini log splitters and tend to weaken the wood. If a tool should catch, especially at the point farthest away from the chuck, it will likely lever the blank away from the chuck and split the wood.

**To start, turn a cylinder between centers** with the lathe running no faster than 1200 RPM to 1500 RPM. A 2-in.-dia. cylinder 4 in. long is a good size. With a parting tool, turn a tenon on each end to fit your chuck. The size of the tenon will depend on the type of chuck. A spigot chuck will grip a ⅛-in.-long tenon. A 3-jaw chuck needs a ½-in.-long tenon with a groove cut in the corner where it protrudes from the main cylinder. This will prevent end grain being pulled by the jaws as they clamp in to grip.

Mark off the lid and bandsaw the cylinder in two, giving you separate blanks for the lid and base. Mount the lid blank in the chuck and true it by making shearing cuts along the cylinder and across the end grain with a small skew chisel. Take the opportunity to practice tool technique. Choose the technique you find most difficult and practice now, while a catch is not too disastrous.

Once you have trued the end grain, take a final cut ⅜ in. in from the rim before hollowing the interior, as shown in the photo on the facing page. Undercut this surface slightly so it fits flush with the shoulder against which it will eventually rest. With very hard woods such as cocobolo, African blackwood or Mulga, the cleanest surface will probably come from a very delicate scrape cut.

Next, I rough out the domed inside of the lid with a ¼-in. or ½-in. shallow-flute fingernail gouge. I use an old trade technique, cutting away from the center to 2 o'clock, as shown in the drawing at right. Position the tool rest so that the gouge point is at the center of the stock and begin the cut with the gouge on its side, flute facing away from you. Push the tool in at the center about ⅛ in., then pull the handle toward you and simultaneously rotate the tool clockwise to keep the bevel rubbing and the edge cutting. (The tool really does cut upside down on the "wrong" side of center.) Hollow the lid with a series of cuts, starting at the center and working outward with each successive cut until the walls are about ⅜ in. thick. Finish shaping the inside with a heavy roundnose scraper, taking light cuts.

You must now consider how the lid fits and how the desired suction fit between lid and base (see box at right) can be achieved. Two points here: first, the suction comes from the two cylinders sliding apart. The finished flanges on the lid and base must not taper. If they do, you'll end up with a lid that fits tightly, but you'll never enjoy the gentle resistance of the suction as you remove it. Secondly, all parts of the lid that will contact the base must be turned as accurately and cleanly as possible so that they fit true on similarly turned parts on the base. Sanding must be kept to a minimum to avoid eccentricity as softer grain is worn away. Cut the fitting parts well enough so that only a quick dab with 180-grit sandpaper is required for a smooth surface.

With a square-end scraper, rough out the flange leaving about ¹⁄₃₂ in. more than your finished surface. Take a final cut with the scraper to finish the flange. Be sure to grind a sharp left corner on the scraper edge. Check the flange with inside calipers to ensure that you have a true cylinder (no taper). This is the first part of the perfect fit.

During this stage your tool may catch and knock the blank off

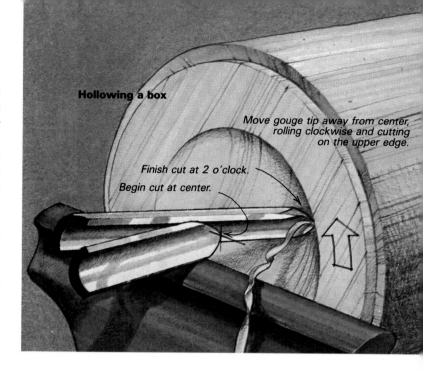

**Hollowing a box**

Move gouge tip away from center, rolling clockwise and cutting on the upper edge.

Finish cut at 2 o'clock.

Begin cut at center.

## About box design

I like box lids to fit so they pull off easily against the resistance of a slight vacuum and fit against a cushion of air created as they slide over the base. I sometimes test the fit by lifting the box by its lid. It should take about two seconds for the base to slide off a perfectly fitted lid. I like the interior of the box to be a different shape from the exterior, so that it might surprise the inquisitive. The inside contour doesn't need to follow the outside.

To disguise any movement in the wood, I detail the line where the lid and base meet with a groove or a bead. A smooth join on a freshly completed box will be hard to detect, but later (usually only minutes), the slightest eccentricity or warping will leave one edge jutting over the other to mar the surface for a caressing hand. Detailing the join eliminates this problem.

The line of the join affects the visual balance of the box. Mostly, I prefer to locate it between one-third and one-half of the way from either the top or bottom, but if I don't care for its position once I've cut it, I'll add other bands or grooves to balance the form. —R.R.

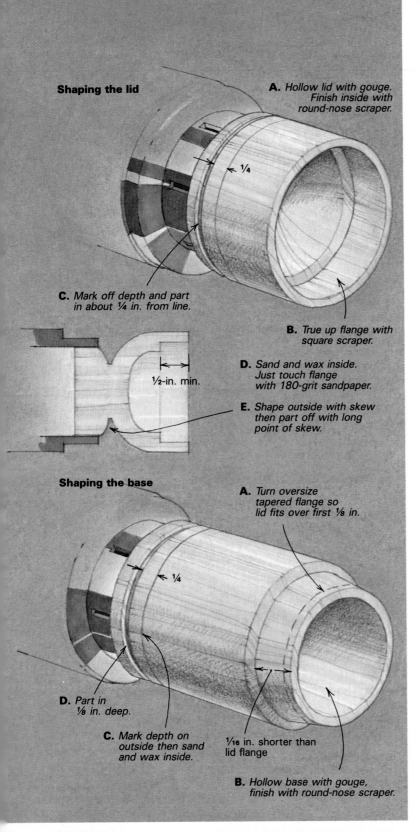

**Shaping the lid**

A. Hollow lid with gouge. Finish inside with round-nose scraper.

← 1/4

C. Mark off depth and part in about 1/4 in. from line.

1/2-in. min.

B. True up flange with square scraper.

D. Sand and wax inside. Just touch flange with 180-grit sandpaper.

E. Shape outside with skew then part off with long point of skew.

**Shaping the base**

A. Turn oversize tapered flange so lid fits over first 1/8 in.

← 1/4

D. Part in 1/8 in. deep.

C. Mark depth on outside then sand and wax inside.

1/16 in. shorter than lid flange

B. Hollow base with gouge, finish with round-nose scraper.

*After sanding and waxing the inside, trim the flange to fit the lid. Use the long point of the skew as a scraper.*

center. Don't worry. Remount it and true the inside dome of the lid, leaving the flange and rim until last. If you've cut the inside and still need to true the rim, don't use a shear cut because the grain will split away down the flange. Use a delicate scrape on the end grain.

Measure the depth of the lid and mark a pencil line on the outside. Sand and finish the domed inside of the lid. Be careful not to touch the flange, which should require only a dab of 180-grit sandpaper. I finish with soft beeswax.

To define the top of the lid, part in about 1/8 in. from the line on the headstock side. Rough out the exterior of the lid with a skew, then part off the lid with the point of the skew. You'll finish turning the lid later, when it's mounted on the base, but cut as much as possible now, while the blank is held firmly in a chuck.

Mount the base blank and true it with the skew. To rough-fit the lid, cut a tapered flange so that the lid fits just over the end. This is surprisingly easy to do by eye, but if you make the end too small, just extend the flange farther back into the blank. As the base revolves, fit the lid and apply just enough pressure for the lid to leave a burnish line. This line gives you the final flange diameter. Don't cut the rest of the flange to size yet. If you hollow the base first, you can afford a massive catch and get away with it. If you finish the lid fitting and then have a catch, you'll probably fail to get the base running true and will have to start over again.

Hollow the base with a 1/2-in. gouge followed by a roundnose scraper. Measure the depth and mark this on the cylinder, then sand and wax the inside. To mark off the bottom, part in 1/8 in. from the line on the headstock side. This gives you a 1/8 in. thickness for the base. (Make it 1/4 in. if you're really nervous.) Don't part in deeper than 1/8 in. at this stage. You need to know where the bottom is when you finish turning the exterior, but you still need the support of the wood running into the chuck.

Using the long point of the skew as a scraper, cut away the flange taper so that the lid fits tightly. If at this stage you discover the flange slightly off center, it doesn't matter. Turn it true. If you've overcut it, you can cut the flange shoulder farther back into the base and, if necessary, cut some off the rim. Cut the flange about 1/16 in. shorter than that in the lid, and cut the shoulder at the bottom of the base flange cleanly. Ideally, the fit between lid and base will be tight enough to prevent the lid from spinning on the base when you remount the assembled box for final shaping of the lid.

If you have a good suction fit, but not enough friction to prevent the lid from slipping and spinning on the base, try this: remove the lid and hold a lump of soft wax (beeswax is ideal) against the revolving flange so that a ring of viscous wax develops. Stop the lathe and mount the lid before the wax solidifies. You have only a few seconds to push the lid on but once there, the cooled wax will hold it fast unless you cause the lid to turn slower than the base by cutting or sanding too hard, in which case friction quickly melts the wax.

Turn the outside with a skew chisel. Depending on your skill and audaciousness at this stage, you can turn a delicate finial on the lid. This isn't difficult as long as you put no pressure against the axis. Arc the point of the skew down into the wood by pivoting the skew on the rest for maximum control. Don't merely push the skew forward into the wood.

Sand and finish the outside before fine fitting the lid. This is the stage that makes or breaks the quality of a lidded box—getting that suction fit just right. With practice and experience it can be done within a minute. Otherwise it takes time and patience.

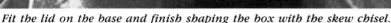

Shaping the bottom

**A.** Turn jam-fit chuck from stub that remains after parting off.

**B.** Mount base and use skew chisel to trim bottom slightly concave.

*Fit the lid on the base and finish shaping the box with the skew chisel.*

Proceed with caution. Too much enthusiasm at this stage and you could overcut and the lid will be loose. The best fit will come from a tool-cut surface with a minimum of sanding. I use the long point of my skew chisel as a scraper. This gives maximum control with minimum risk. After each delicate cut I can stop the lathe, try on the lid, and test the fit. Once it pulls off with reasonable ease, I sand the flange—a dab of 180-grit sandpaper is sufficient—and wax.

Once the lid fits satisfactorily, part off the base. Be careful to catch the box, not hold it, or the wood still attached to the chuck will spin a hole in the bottom.

On the stub that remains in the spigot chuck, turn a tapered jam-fit chuck, as shown in the drawing. Mount the base and true up the bottom with a skew chisel. I always turn the base slightly concave so that the box sits flat. I usually chamfer the corner between side and bottom using the long point of the skew. A sharp corner could easily be damaged or chipped.  □

*Richard Raffan is a professional woodturner in Mittagong, Australia, and author of the book,* Turning Wood with Richard Raffan *(1985, Taunton Press). He has just finished work on a woodturning video, available next year from Taunton Press.*

# Poured pewter inlay

by William Vick

I decorate my turned boxes with pewter inlays. Pewter, an alloy of tin, antimony, copper, and sometimes bismuth or lead, has a low melting point (420°F) and is easily poured into kerfs cut by lathe tools. One source for pewter is T.B. Hagstoz, 709 Sanson St., Philadelphia, Pa. 19106.

To inlay a flat lid, rough the outside to the final shape, then use a parting tool to cut kerfs at the desired locations. The kerfs should be at least ⅛ in. deep and slightly undercut. The undercut serves to anchor the pewter.

To inlay a band around the circumference, turn the area above the band close to the finished box diameter. Form the groove by cutting in at an angle with a parting tool, leaving a dam to contain the molten pewter.

To melt and pour the pewter you'll need a pouring ladle with a wooden or plastic handle (a ladle with a wooden handle and small spout is available from Dixie Gun Works, Union City, Tenn. 38261) and a propane torch. The box must be on a perfectly level, non-flammable surface. In a well-ventilated area,

away from combustibles, put a small piece of pewter in the ladle and melt it by heating the base of the ladle with the torch. Once it melts, continue heating for about 30 seconds more. The metal must be hot enough to flow completely around the inlay cavity. Pour quickly and evenly. If the metal hardens before the cavity is completely filled, you'll end up with defects in the finished inlay.

When the pewter has cooled, mount the piece on the lathe and take light cuts with a sharp tool to trim the piece to final shape. Cut the pewter and the wood together. Because pewter is so soft, the cutting edge will not dull quickly.  □

*William Vick teaches woodworking at Mills Godwin High School in Richmond, Va.*

*Pewter bands were poured in place.*

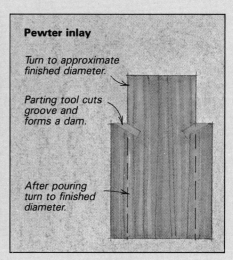

Pewter inlay

Turn to approximate finished diameter.

Parting tool cuts groove and forms a dam.

After pouring turn to finished diameter.

# Tips From a Turner
## *Make your own mini drive centers*

by Allan Turner Hedstrand

Ready-made spur centers are oversized, clumsy things if you're turning small work. About eight years ago when I was turning miniature spinning wheels and vases, I devised some mini-centers that don't get in the way. These are made from steel rod and are fitted into a Jacobs chuck at the headstock.

A standard spur center has a center point and four sharp prongs that grip the work. The center point has one main function: if you punch a centerhole into the

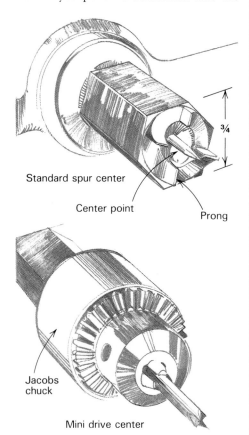

Standard spur center

Center point

Prong

Jacobs chuck

Mini drive center

end of a blank, the center point will slide into that hole as you snug up the tailstock and will keep the work centered until the drive prongs seat themselves. Some people think that the center point keeps the blank securely on the lathe as well, a little

insurance against the blank flying off and hitting someone. Well, I suppose this is true if you are a heavy-handed turner whose tactics force the prongs to tear loose from time to time. But with miniature work, such insurance isn't necessary. In the first place, cuts are light, and no decent turner is likely to tear the prongs loose. In the second place, the workpiece itself is so light that even if you do knock it off, it won't hurt you. The point of all this, if you will pardon one mild pun, is that you don't really need a point. It's optional.

I made my mini-centers from steel-rod scraps that I had around at the time. These happened to be ³⁄₁₆-in., ¼-in. and ½-in. diameters. The larger two have no center points. To make a center without a point, cut off a piece of rod about 1¾ in. long and file four cutting prongs as shown in the drawing below. The file alone works fine for the ³⁄₁₆-in.

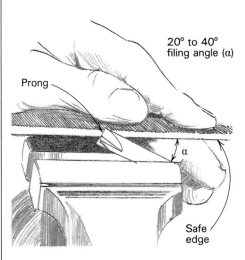

20° to 40° filing angle (α)

Prong

α

Safe edge

rod, but for the larger sizes you can speed the job by hacksawing most of the shape.

If you do want a center point, make it before you file the prongs. Chuck the rod at the headstock and drill a centerhole in the end. A ¹⁄₁₆-in. bit is large enough for rod sizes smaller than ⅜ in. Don't bother setting up the bit in a chuck in the tail-

stock—fit it in a spare chuck and hand-hold it while the rod turns. Next drive a nail into the centerhole until it's tight and you can't pull it out. If you don't have the right-size nail, fit an oversized one in the chuck on the lathe and turn the nail down with a file or a whetstone. If the nail is slightly loose in the centerhole, prick-punch around the hole to tighten it. Then clip it off so it protrudes about ⅛ in.

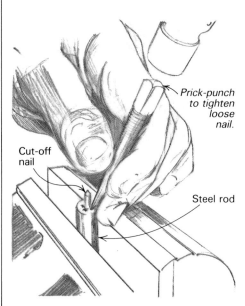

Prick-punch to tighten loose nail.

Cut-off nail

Steel rod

With the rod turning in the lathe, file or stone the center point until it runs dead true. If you're using a file, make sure it has a safe edge so you don't wear away the end of the steel rod. Then file the prongs, being careful not to mar the point. As a final touch, I mark one of the prongs with a small nick, as an aid in repositioning work that has to be returned to the lathe.

When mounting work, I usually saw two cuts into the end of the blank to seat the prongs, and if I'm using a drive center with a point, I poke a hole with an awl. This extends the life of the center. Mine, even though they're made of mild steel, have lasted a long time.

142

Drawings: Bruce Bulger

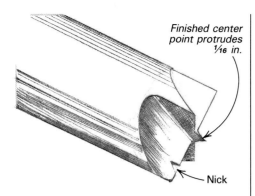

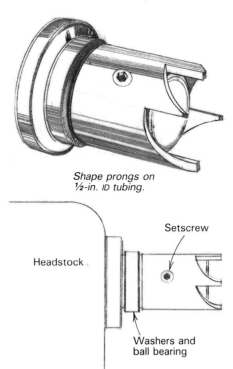

Finished center point protrudes 1/16 in.

Nick

Shape prongs on 1/2-in. ID tubing.

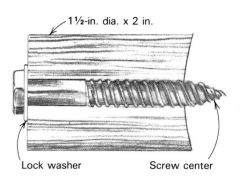

1½-in. dia. x 2 in.

Lock washer    Screw center

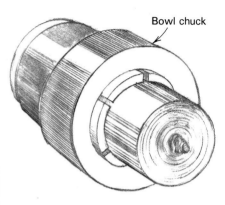

Bowl chuck

Frank Pain, in his book *The Practical Wood Turner* (Sterling Publishing Co., 1979), says that the production turners in his day had a two-prong spur center (which he calls a fork center). This design would be even easier to make than the four-prong design, but if you want to try one, be sure to include a center point. It's easy for these wedges to slide off center otherwise. And, as Pain points out, file a dead spot on each prong near the center, so the shape doesn't wedge itself too deeply into the work.

Another drive center that has proved useful in my shop fits over a ½-in. dia. mandrel on a wooden lathe I once made (altogether I've made six or seven). It's simply a ½-in. ID steel tube with four

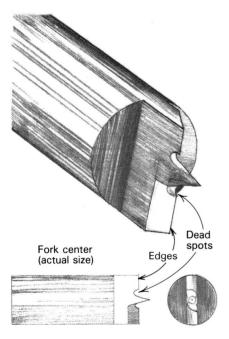

Fork center (actual size)     Edges

Dead spots

Headstock

Setscrew

Washers and ball bearing

prongs filed as shown. I drilled and tapped a hole for a setscrew to keep it in place, and slid two washers and a ball-bearing race over the mandrel to take the pressure against the tailstock. I've used this hollow center a lot because it grips well without penetrating deeply, so it minimizes waste when I'm turning tiny vases. Originally, I fitted it with a center point by drilling directly into the end of

the mandrel and banging in a ⅛-in. dia. steel pin. But I've never found the center point to be necessary.

For regular-size bowls, I bought a lathe chuck designed to grip a 1½-in. foot on a half-turned bowl so that you can turn the inside without having to screw a faceplate to the bottom. Many chucks operate on similar principles—they either grip a projecting foot or extend to lock into a depression. In theory, you turn the outside of the bowl (and the foot) while the blank is mounted on a faceplate or a screw center, then remove the bowl, fit the chuck to the bowl and to the lathe, and turn the inside. Well, I didn't like the idea of all that faceplate-and-chuck changing, and I devised a screw center to fit the chuck, so that I could do the whole job without ever removing the chuck from the lathe.

To make the screw center, I turned a piece of prickly-ash branch to a 1½-in. diameter and bored a ³⁄₁₆-in. centerhole clear through. Reversing the blank in the chuck, I enlarged the hole to ¼ in. partway to accept a lag-screw shank. With this size hole the wood grips the shank so tightly that usually I can center a bowl blank on the lag screw without even removing the screw chuck from the lathe chuck. A lock washer adds some extra resistance to turning. If the lag screw does turn when I'm screwing on a blank, I simply remove the screw center from the lathe chuck and hold the bolt head with a wrench while I screw the blank. But this seldom happens, not even when I've backed out the lag screw a little to prevent it from

going too deeply into thinner stock.

Of course, there are times when you want to reverse and recenter the work on a single faceplate. Here's another trick: Screw the blank to the faceplate and turn the outside of the bowl as usual, flattening what will be the foot. Without removing the blank from the lathe, glue scrapwood to the foot (with paper in the joint so you can split off the wood later) and bring up the tailstock to clamp things until the glue dries. Then recess the face of the scrapwood to the exact diameter of your faceplate. When you screw the faceplate into the recess, it will be exactly centered. This takes for granted that your faceplate runs true. If it doesn't, it's easy enough to true it with a file as it turns.

Here's one last tip that might help you someday. I once combined two lathes, because one had a fine bed and the other had a decent headstock. In the process, I went from a Morse taper #1 to a Morse taper #2, which meant that one of my old drive centers no longer fit. I made an adapter from seasoned persimmon wood by turning it to a taper—testing with chalk as I went along—until it didn't wiggle in the #2 taper swallow. I tapped it into place, then bored a hole in it and tapered that to accept the #1 taper on the old drive center. The adapter still runs perfectly true and doesn't slip, even after four years.    □

*Allan Hedstrand, 28, is a self-taught turner living in Brooksville, Fla.*

# Decorative Turning
## *Plunging right into a bowl's personality*

by Tom Alexander

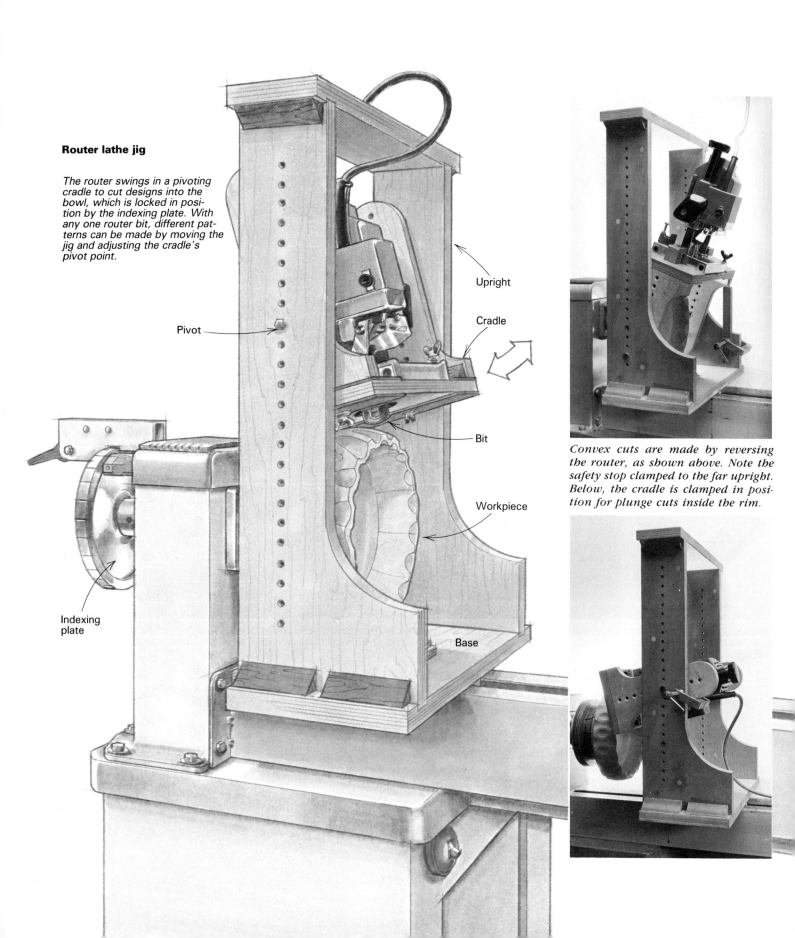

**Router lathe jig**

The router swings in a pivoting cradle to cut designs into the bowl, which is locked in position by the indexing plate. With any one router bit, different patterns can be made by moving the jig and adjusting the cradle's pivot point.

Pivot

Upright

Cradle

Bit

Workpiece

Indexing plate

Base

*Convex cuts are made by reversing the router, as shown above. Note the safety stop clamped to the far upright. Below, the cradle is clamped in position for plunge cuts inside the rim.*

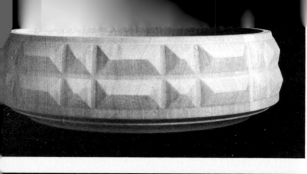

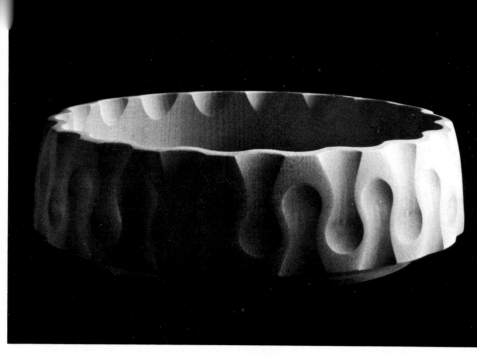

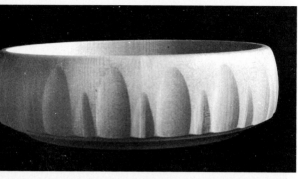

*These bowls were all stave-laminated on the same set-up jig before turning, a production process that keeps their basic size and proportions about the same. Yet the incised decoration makes each bowl unique. All cuts were made with the jig on the facing page, using the two router bits shown at right. Alexander grinds his bits from old planer blades and bolts them into a ½-in.-shank mandrel.*

The bowls shown here are about 9 in. in diameter, and the patterns on them were sculpted by a router. The process works something like turning on a Holtzapffel lathe: The workpiece is first turned to shape, then the lathe is stopped and the work locked so it can't rotate. A cutting tool, in this case a plunge router in a pivoting cradle, incises an arced groove into the bowl's surface. The piece is then rotated a fixed amount and locked again, and another groove is cut. One or more series of such cuts complete the pattern.

The bowls shown here were turned from stock that was stave-laminated, that is, glued up like a barrel. The technique saves wood, and various jigs make it suitable for production turning. One limitation of using jigs is that all the bowls come out about the same size and shape, but the router's surface treatment gives each one individuality.

You can adapt the methods to any size bowl and to whatever router and lathe you have. I make my own router bits, as shown in the photo above, but standard bits could also be used.

If your lathe doesn't have an indexing plate, you'll have to buy or make one to lock the headstock at various positions. An indexing plate is a perforated wooden or metal disc fastened to the headstock spindle. A pin goes through a hole in the disc and prevents the spindle from turning. The indexing plate can be outboard or inboard—the location depends on the lathe and on whatever locking-pin arrangement is convenient. Some lathes have locking-pin holes drilled right in the pulley. Another option would be to drill holes in the back of the faceplate.

To make an indexing plate, turn a disc from plywood and mark a series of concentric circles on its face. Around each circle, drill a series of holes at fixed intervals for the locking pin (divide the number of degrees, 360, by however many stops you want the circle to contain, then lay out the holes with a protractor so they're evenly spaced). You'll also need a router cradle. As shown in the drawing, the uprights are attached to a base that locks on the lathe ways and can be moved closer to or farther from the work. Inside the uprights, a pivoting cradle holds the router. A row of holes in the uprights allows you to position the cradle at various heights, and a similar row of holes in the cradle itself determines the radius of the arc of the cut. Fine adjustments are made by changing how far the bit extends beyond the baseplate, and most cuts are made in one pass.

In the drawing, the router is mounted inside the cradle and the cradle's pivot point is close to the router base. This arrangement results in a tight concave cut in the workpiece. For the opposite effect, a sweeping convex cut, mount the router as shown in the top photo on the facing page. The bottom photo shows the cradle locked by a clamp—in this setup, the router plunges forward to make patterns inside the rim. If your router doesn't plunge, you can make inside cuts by arranging the pivots so the router's swing is within the bowl instead of outside it, or by making a router cradle that slides rather than swings.

These variables, in combination with choice of bit, allow great versatility. In fact, it's unlikely that you'll ever make two bowls that look exactly the same, however hard you try. I try to visualize each cut before it's made, swinging the cradle to see the arc and sometimes substituting a dowel stub for the bit so I can better see its path. Even so, minor changes in depth of cut or in the profile of the workpiece add up to subtle differences from one bowl to the next. These surprises, fortunately, are usually pleasant ones. One final tip: It's a lot easier to deepen an existing cut than to try to make it a little shallower after the fact. So plan your cuts carefully. If you do go too deep, the only remedy is to turn down the whole bowl a little.  □

*Tom Alexander turns spinning wheels and bowls in Ashburton, New Zealand. Photos by the author.*

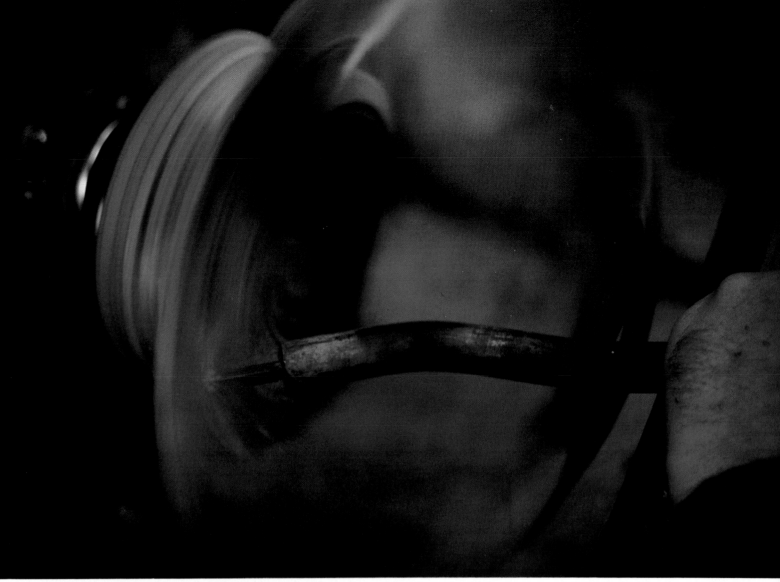

*As you turn a hollow log into a bowl, the open sides become a blur through which you can watch the tool at work.*

# Turning Mostly Air
## *Finding the hidden shapes in rotted logs*

by G.A. Goff

Did you ever find a piece of wood with just the right color and spalting pattern, only to be disappointed because it was rotten through the center or sides? Me, too. I just couldn't bring myself to throw these chunks away or burn them, so I eventually ended up with a lot of them lying around. Finally, I figured out a way to turn them on the lathe.

I had been turning hollow vessels for years, making just enough of a top opening to work the tool through and get the sawdust out. One day, while turning a block that had a hole in its side, I noticed that the sawdust flew out the side, which kept the cavity clean. I could also look through the hole as the wood was spinning to watch the tool work. I became curious as to how large a hole or combination of holes a turning could contain and still hold together. After breaking a few and learning from my mistakes, I soon found that I could relatively easily turn shapes

that were 50% air around their circumference. I was soon pushing some turnings toward 80% air and 20% wood.

I never intended these vessels to have any functional use, or even be a recognizable anything. I just wanted to see how far I could go. And yet, the wood is beautiful. It has character: spalting, hole patterns caused by termites, ants and grubs, and other discolorations and holes from insects, fungi and bacteria. To me, such wood is unsurpassed for natural beauty.

The turned shape is very much determined by the piece of wood you begin with. To turn one of these blocks, I first look for an area solid enough to attach to a faceplate, then I try to visualize what will result when the block is turned. Will it hold together? Will it stand without tipping over? Many details of the final turning will only be revealed along the way, but you have to consider structural soundness from the beginning.

*This 11-in.-dia., 4-poster bowl was turned from a hollow cherry log. The process is shown in the photos on p. 148.*

The job calls for special tools. Conventional gouges and chisels work with the bevel riding on the wood, acting as a fulcrum to control the depth of the cut. With open turnings, however, if the heel of the tool rides the wood, as soon as a hole comes by, the tool falls in, and the piece breaks. Some of my early turnings broke at ½ in. thick. To get around this problem, I've made the scraping tools shown in figure 1.

I call one bowl style, shown in the photo above, a 4-poster. The one pictured was turned from a hollow cherry log, in the same manner as the chinaberry one shown on p. 148. The log was 8½ in. in diameter, and the finished bowl is 11 in. in diameter. The bowl has a 34½-in. circumference, and the four posts contain a total of 6¼ in. of wood. That's about 18% wood, 82% air.

To mount a 4-poster block, I make a flat side on the chunk and epoxy-glue a ¾-in. plywood block, which I then screw to a faceplate. I turn between 430 RPM and 575 RPM. If the speed is too slow, the tool must wait too long before the wood comes back around; if it's too fast, the centrifugal force will move the wood out of the way or, worse, cause it to fly apart. Don't try this work without face and head protection.

Experience is important, so be prepared to break a few blanks. With each failure you will learn what speed is too fast or too slow, the best shape for the tools, and how much open space to try for. You will also develop the right touch. By sound and feel, you will know when to back off and change something.

Turning the outside is straightforward and relatively easy. Sometimes I lose a blank at this stage because of some hidden

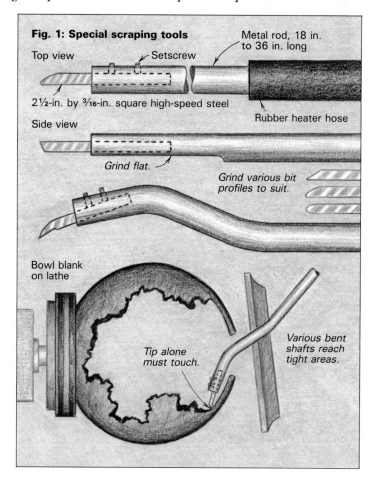

**Fig. 1: Special scraping tools**

Top view

Setscrew

Metal rod, 18 in. to 36 in. long

2½-in. by ³⁄₁₆-in. square high-speed steel

Rubber heater hose

Side view

Grind flat.

Grind various bit profiles to suit.

Bowl blank on lathe

Tip alone must touch.

Various bent shafts reach tight areas.

### Turning a 4-poster

*A 4-poster begins as a hollow log mounted on a faceplate (above). When the ends of the log have been roughed round (top right), they show the curves that will become the four posts as the inside is turned. To stabilize the wood for inside turning, Goff runs nylon filament tape up the posts and around the blank (left). Notice that the mouth opening has been scribed but not yet cut. The photo on p. 146 shows inside turning in progress, and the photo below shows the result. The wood is chinaberry.*

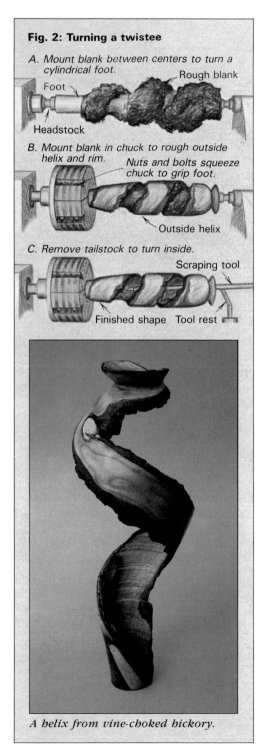

**Fig. 2: Turning a twistee**

A. Mount blank between centers to turn a cylindrical foot.

Foot

Rough blank

Headstock

B. Mount blank in chuck to rough outside helix and rim.

Nuts and bolts squeeze chuck to grip foot.

Outside helix

C. Remove tailstock to turn inside.

Scraping tool

Finished shape    Tool rest

*A helix from vine-choked hickory.*

defect, but mostly it is just like the early stages of roughing down any irregular blank. As I gradually make the log round, I check that the four posts are symmetrical. If they're not, I shift the blank a little on the faceplate until things are working out right.

When it comes time to turn the inside, I reinforce doubtful wood with nylon filament tape—for a 4-poster I run strips up each post. Then I make a complete circle around the middle of the four posts. This causes the other three posts to add some support to the one being cut. I reposition the tape as the turning progresses. It's important not to distort the flexible posts when first applying the tape, or when repositioning it. Otherwise when you restart the lathe, the posts won't be in the same relative positions, and therefore won't be cut uniformly.

To start the inside, I either drill a hole or just cut through to the rotted inside with the cutting tools. The opening in the 4-poster on the facing page is $1\frac{3}{8}$ in. in diameter. I then work down in shallow increments of $\frac{1}{4}$ in. to $\frac{1}{2}$ in. at a time. As in other turnings, this allows the lower material to support the portion being cut. It's important to get the post thickness right before moving lower, as there will be no support if you try to move back up to touch up a thick spot. I find it necessary to turn the inside in one sitting. If the work is left overnight, even the least amount of warping will cause enough distortion to throw the posts out of line.

Another shape, which I call a twistee, is a helix. The lower right photo on the facing page shows one of the first I made. The stock isn't from rotted wood, but from a branch or small tree trunk with a vine wrapped around it. Over the years, the shape gets more and more pronounced until the tree finally grows back over the top of the vine. Finding trees with the most pronounced helical bulges is the first step in turning a twistee. I look for sections about 5 in. in diameter and 14 in. long.

I mount the wood between centers, as shown in figure 2, and reduce the headstock end to 2 in. in diameter, forming a round tenon that fits a shopmade plywood chuck. With the blank in the chuck, I support the other end with the tailstock so I can reduce the outside with the scraping tools until I have a clean band of wood spiraling from the base to the rim.

After the outside is done, the fun begins. I remove the tailstock and position the tool rest at the top of the vase. Then I turn through the top opening as before, but without the reinforcing tape—there's nothing to attach it to.

One problem is gauging the thickness. When I first began turning air, I liked being able to see the tool on the inside. But as I got to pieces with less and less wood, it became difficult to see exactly where the wood was. The effect is similar to watching a ceiling fan, where as the speed increases, the blades become a blur. Once—when turning the twistee shown in the photo—I had the uncanny experience of having the wood seem to disappear. I could see the top of the vase, with the tool shank entering it, and I could see the tool tip itself perfectly well, but the middle of the turning was completely gone. It seems that I had reached the point where 90% of the circumference was air; I *very* carefully finished it.

Sanding on both the 4-poster and twistee is done with the piece stationary. I begin with a grinder, then a drill. Next I handsand, using the sandpaper to work oil into the wood. This helps to seal the pores with the sawdust and to penetrate and toughen the wood, adding strength that is greatly appreciated by those who handle these delicate turnings. I have tried many oils, but the thickest and stickiest I've found—and the toughest when dry—is called Val-Oil, made by the Val-Spar Company in Stone Mountain, Georgia. The oil, usually four to six coats, is sanded in

*This 7-in. dia. birch bowl was turned from an asymmetric hollow log with one open side. The author frequently prowls the woods in search of such potential gems. The trick is to imagine what curious shape lies hidden in a rotten log.*

*A 4-poster bowl from spalted apple, about 11-in. dia.*

with wet-or-dry paper, from 100-grit up to 320-grit. The outside surface gains a fine luster, but I frequently leave the tool marks on the inside. Skeptics sometimes need to see them before they will believe that the piece was turned.

All the wood I use is found, and part of the adventure is hunting through the woods with a hatchet, gently using it to probe the downed logs, looking for something that seems substantial. I have used about 35 different native southern species. Sometimes the logs are so far gone that it is difficult to tell exactly what wood I have in my hand.

Be forewarned that this sort of turning can have its unnerving aspects: Once, I stopped the lathe to reposition the tool rest, an operation I'd done five or six times already, and a scorpion jumped out and took off across the table. I was so stunned that I simply stood there and watched him scamper away. Scorpions, centipedes and black widow spiders all seem to like this sort of wood as much as I do. □

*Gil Goff's shop is in Athens, Ga. Photos by the author.*

# WOOD

# What Does "Grain" Really Mean?

## Some seventy meanings clarified

by R. Bruce Hoadley

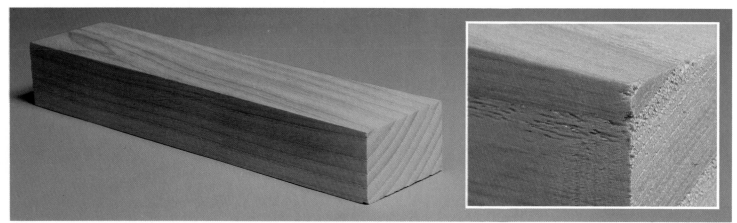

*What we commonly call grain is the result of exposing the tree's annual rings on the surface of a board. With a ring-porous hardwood such as ash, the large earlywood cells are sliced lengthwise, resulting in bands of distinct lines.*

Seldom can a discussion about wood get far without the use of the word "grain." Yet grain is such a versatile word that its many accepted meanings are often confusing, and sometimes even contradictory. A woodworker who says "I don't like the grain of that board" could be talking about any number of things. Most likely, he means the board's *figure,* the visual pattern on the board, but he could also be talking about the *slope of the grain* (too much slope weakens a board), or about the way the board grew in the tree—a luthier, for example, senses that an *edge-grained* piece of spruce is stiff enough for a guitar top, a *flat-grained* piece isn't.

Here are some seventy phrases involving specific meanings of the word grain. They are all the result of two variables: the way the tree grew and the way it was sawn.

**Planes, surfaces and direction**—"Grain," first and foremost, commonly designates the alignment of the longitudinal cells that comprise the bulk of wood tissue, as shown above. *Grain direction* is a better term when used in this sense. We speak of wood splitting *along the grain* or *with the grain,* meaning parallel to the fibers; *across the grain* means generally perpendicular to the fibers. Surfaces cut parallel to the grain direction are called *longitudinal grain* or simply *long grain,* as opposed to *end grain,* which is the surface perpendicular to the fiber direction.

Grain can also refer to the position of the growth rings with respect to both the plane of cut and the appearance produced. For example, a tangential surface—parallel to the growth rings—is said to have *tangential grain.* This term is also applied to boards whose widest surface has this orientation. Synonymous

with tangential grain are *flat grain, plain grain* and *slash grain.* If the surface is perpendicular to the growth rings, it is said to have *radial grain,* that is, the wide face of the board was oriented on a radius of the tree stem. *Edge grain, vertical grain* and *quarter grain* are flexible terms, but they all represent grain that is more radial than tangential.

Obviously, boards can be cut with varying degrees of grain orientation. In commercial lumber, *flat grain* includes boards with growth rings oriented at angles of 0° to 45° to the wide face; *edge grain,* 45° to 90°. *Bastard grain* indicates that the growth-ring placement is clearly neither flat grain nor edge grain, but somewhere in the 30° to 60° range. *Mixed grain* refers to a quantity of lumber that includes assorted edge, flat and bastard grain in any combination. *Side grain,* as the opposite of end grain, can mean any of the above long-grain surfaces, and it sometimes indicates, confusingly, flat grain only. In boards or panels, the better of the two surfaces is sometimes referred to as *face grain.*

It is generally assumed and expected that the grain direction is parallel to the long axis in boards, dowels and turnings. Such pieces are said to be *straight-grained.* Deviation from this ideal is termed *cross grain.* The degree of cross grain is expressed as *slope-of-grain.* A slope-of-grain of 1 in 12 indicates that grain direction deviates 1 in. away from the board's axis for every 12 in. along the surface. Severe cross grain is called *steep grain,* and pronounced deviation from the surface plane, especially in veneer, is called *short grain.* When the axis of a board is not parallel to the growth rings, the result is called *diagonal grain. Dip grain* indicates an undulation in the grain direction, as typically occurs in the vicinity of a knot.

A board may be cut straight along the axis of a tree, but grain direction in trees is not always straight up and down. For example, within a straight stem, the fibers may have a helical alignment, referred to as *spiral grain.* Any board sawn parallel to the stem (or log) axis will likewise have spiral grain. In some species the stemwood has spiral grain that alternates cyclically from right to left, producing *interlocked grain.*

Various other characteristic patterns of distortion in grain direction can develop in the tree. These result in distinctive patterns on machined surfaces. For example, *curly* or *wavy grain* produces a washboard surface when split radially, and the barred visual effect produced when the wood is machined smooth is also called curly or wavy grain. In maple it is sometimes called *tiger grain,* or *fiddleback grain* because of the traditional choice of such wood for the backs of violins.

**Grain and figure**—If we are speaking primarily of fiber orientation, as we have been, "grain" is the word to use; if we are referring to the wood's surface appearance, it is more meaningful to use the word "figure." The following grain patterns produce characteristic figures when the wood is surfaced.

Intergrown cell structure in the crotches of forked trees is called *crotch grain.* In certain species, such as black walnut, if the crotch is sawn down the middle into two Ys, the pattern is aptly called *feather grain.*

Bulged or bumpy growth layers are called *blister grain,* and produce blister figure when sawn tangentially. If the blisters grow elongated rather than round, the grain is called *quilted.* *Leaf grain* and *flame grain* are somewhat showy tangential cuts resembling their namesakes.

Sometimes wood grows in localized tight swirls and dimples. In maple, *bird's-eye grain* results. When a piece of bird's-eye maple is split tangentially, one surface will have numerous little peaks, and the other will have corresponding craters. When surfaced, the figure resembles lustrous, deep eyes. *Dimpled grain,* characteristic of lodgepole pine, splits similarly. Another spotlike figure occurs in burls, a result of dormant-bud proliferation.

*Interlocked grain,* surfaced radially, results in bands of light and dark that shift back and forth with changes in light direction. The resulting figure may be called *ribbon* or *stripe grain.* Roe figure is similar, and the grain, also interlocked, may be called *roey.*

More properly called "figure," some "grain" depends on the characteristic patterns produced by the rays when the tree is cut radially. When the ray flecks are conspicuous or particularly lustrous, the wood is called *silver grain. Rift grain,* occasionally called *needle-point grain,* is produced on a longitudinal surface oriented 30° to 45° to the rays, the term being used especially for white oak with its large rays; the term *comb grain* is used where the vessel lines are parallel to the board's edge and produce a uniform pencil stripe.

**Grain and surfacing**—When wood is being planed, it tends to split ahead of the cutting edge. On a board with cross grain, the splitting will follow the direction of the fibers, either running harmlessly up and away from the surface or running troublesomely into it. Thus we prefer to plane *with the grain* rather than *against the grain.* If we go wrong, *chipped* or *torn grain* results. In most wood with a pronounced figure, wood fibers are intergrown in various directions or at steep angles. This is why figured wood is more difficult to work.

When flat-grain surfaces at a high moisture content are machine-planed, or when knives are dull, denser latewood may rise above adjacent earlywood. This surface unevenness (which is most pronounced on the pith side of flatsawn boards of uneven-grained softwoods) is called *raised grain.* If the growth rings actually separate, *loosened* or *shelled grain* results. When we saw or plane wet wood, or hardwoods with reaction wood (tension wood), the fibers may not cut cleanly, and the frayed, fibrous surface that results is called *fuzzy* or *woolly grain.*

**Earlywood and latewood**—Visual contrast between earlywood and latewood is expressed as evenness of grain. Southern yellow pine and Douglas fir thus have *uneven grain* because of their distinct growth rings, while basswood has *even grain,* because its growth rings are barely discernible. In softwoods, visual contrast parallels workability—an uneven-grained carving block usually means jumpy cuts.

In describing growth-ring width (rate of growth), as in structural grading of lumber, narrow rings are termed *narrow grain, close grain, fine grain* or *dense grain.* Wide rings are described as *wide grain, open grain* or *coarse grain.* To add to the confusion, similar terms are often used to indicate relative cell size or permeability. We hear the terms "open-grained" and "coarse-grained" used to describe woods that have large cells and absorb finish readily, but the term "texture" is preferable in reference to relative cell size. Woods with large cells should be called *coarse-textured;* woods with small cells, *fine-textured.* Much of the confusion about grain can be avoided by using clarifying adjectives or by substituting a more appropriate term such as texture, figure, or growth-ring placement. For example, following popular usage, one might be tempted to describe a given piece of ash as being both close-grained (if growth rings were narrow) and open-grained (because of its large pores). It would be better to describe such wood as "slow-grown" and "coarse-textured."

Other miscellaneous uses of the word grain appear from time to time. Some are doubtless local in origin or use. *Short-in-the-grain,* for example, has been used in Britain to describe wood prone to brittle fractures. When an individual is lacking a specific term to describe a particular aspect of wood, the word grain is readily pressed into service to fit the situation at hand. An ambiguous term such as *tight grain* might be used by the cooper in reference to white oak (whose "water tightness" is due to tylosis-filled vessels), by the ébéniste in reference to maple (based on its fine texture), or by the violinmaker to describe fiddleback figure (where the bars are closely spaced). Various other uses seem to have been coined to fit the situation at hand—one reads of clear grain, wild grain, swirly grain, variegated grain, or grain character; these terms have little specific meaning to me. I've also heard people say, "The grain runs a bit," and "The grain is heavy." I'm not sure what these statements mean, either.

Getting to the end of my list, there is *graining,* which is the texturing or painting of surfaces to imitate natural texture or figure. At its best, graining is a fine art; on the other hand, the plastic cabinet on my TV set warns of "simulated wood-grain design," and I suppose this is part of the category, too. Other meanings of grain get us away from wood, and concern themselves with cereals, weight tables, and beaches. I suppose I've missed a few, but for now the thought of inventing any more uses for this overworked word sort of…well…goes against *my* grain.  □

*R. Bruce Hoadley is a contributing editor to* FWW. *An excellent pamphlet,* Figure in Wood: An Illustrated Review, *is available from Research Information, 101 Comer Hall, Auburn University, Ala. 36849 ($2.00 ppd.).*

*Ash's distinctive bark, with its neat, contrasty striations, makes the tree easy to identify at any season of the year. Its compound leaves, composed of leaflets on a central stem, are among the first to fall in autumn. A distinguishing characteristic of black ash is the leaflets' close attachment to the stem.*

# Ash
*Counterfeit oak or quality cabinetwood?*

by Jon W. Arno

A t a recent antiques show, I found a dozen or so turn-of-the-century commodes labeled "oak." The general public and a lot of antiques dealers seem happy enough to identify every light-colored, open-grained wood as oak at a glance. The oak label serves as a convenience for pricing and dating such pieces, but it isn't always accurate. Two of the commodes at the show were of mixed wood construction (predominantly elm); the three nicest were unquestionably ash.

Most people may not have much reason to care. Ash and oak are both open-grained woods, with similarly attractive and somewhat racy figures. Furniture made from either wood has a look of solid quality. Yet I think ash outclasses oak in several important ways, at least from a cabinetmaker's viewpoint—the two woods have decidedly different characteristics. For starters, oak is a

member of the beech family, *Fagaceae,* which includes the oaks, the beeches and the chestnuts. Ash belongs to the olive family, *Oleaceae,* and is related to lilac and forsythia.

**You don't have to be a botanist** to quickly separate oak from ash. Oak has prominent rays that are easily visible on the flat-sawn surface, where they appear as bold lines called ray flecks. In some species of white oak, these flecks may be more than $\frac{1}{16}$ in. wide and well over 1 in. long, while in the red oaks they are generally smaller and darker. In fact, the rays are such a dominant feature in white oak that it's often specially quartersawn to expose them as broad bands or ribbons. These are extremely hard and dense, and in stained wood you could call their appearance either fantastic or outrageous, depending on your taste. I person-

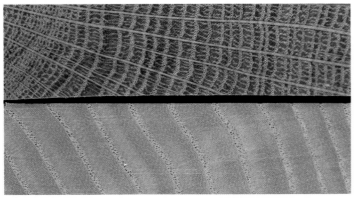

ally don't like the effect, but if you do, score one point for oak, because no matter how you cut ash, it will not produce this pattern. Like all woods, ash has rays, but they are almost undetectable with the naked eye. As a cabinetmaker, I view this as one of ash's great virtues, because flatsawn and radially sawn boards can be used in the same piece with no surprises when the stain goes on.

Oak contains tannic acid. If you expose the wood to strong ammonia vapor, a chemical reaction will turn it dark brown. This staining process is known as fuming, and it won't work on ash. Personally, I use ammonia only on windows, but if fuming sounds like a good idea to you, score another point for oak.

Oak's acid content is a mixed blessing at best. A friend of mine once left a green piece of oak on his tablesaw overnight, and by morning it had permanently etched its shape as a black rust mark, which is still there after four years.

**Ash's biggest advantage** is that it is generally less dense than oak. If we cabinetmakers accept our two premier domestic hardwoods as having nearly ideal density—black cherry with a specific gravity of 0.47 (green to oven-dry) and black walnut at 0.51—we find that the various species of ash straddle this range, while the oaks are all somewhat denser. Ashes run from 0.45 to 0.55, oaks from 0.52 to 0.80. Ash is by no means a soft wood in comparison to pine, basswood, butternut, poplar or aspen, but it is relatively soft when you consider its ability to withstand pounding and stress. Ash yields an end product with great strength relative to both its weight and the amount of energy expended to shape or fashion it. And what could be nearer and dearer to a cabinetmaker's heart?

Because of these advantages, ash was one of several favored woods in Grand Rapids factories during the so-called "Golden Oak" era. Oak got all the publicity, but ash often was the dominant species in those utilitarian and now quaintly obsolete mixed-wood pieces: the dry sinks, commodes, cupboards and wardrobes that were cranked out by the thousands in the late 19th century for America's growing middle class. I'm grateful that nobody thought to call the stuff "Golden Ash"—the lack of publicity helps keep ash at a reasonable price.

While keeping a low profile in cabinetry, ash has established a worldwide reputation as the wood for baseball bats and as one of nature's most perfect materials for tool handles. For these purposes, second-growth trees with straight, evenly spaced grain are selected and specially graded. The white-ash sample shown on this page was cut from a friend's woodlot and wouldn't make a bad bat. Such ash has great strength-to-weight ratio and rigidity. Also, once the surface is smoothed, ash polishes well. Whether this is achieved by constant contact with human hands, as in the case of a tool handle, or by the deliberate effort of a woodworker, the end result is a definite plus.

Within each annual ring, ash has a honeycomb of porous earlywood followed by a layer of dense latewood, making it a sort of natural laminate. The American Indians discovered that they could separate the layers by soaking the quartered log and pounding it vigorously. As the earlywood broke down, thin strips of strong, highly flexible latewood peeled off, which the Indians used for basket splints and ribs in their canoes.

There are over a dozen species of ash native to North America, but only a few of them reach timber size. Those that do all produce ring-porous woods. There are, however, some subtle differences that relate not only to the species of ash, but also to the environment in which the tree grew. Generally speaking, the

*Oak and ash are easy to tell apart. Oak has prominent rays, most pronounced when it's cut radially (top left), but also visible as a needlelike pattern on the tangential surface (bottom left). Ash's rays are hardly visible, allowing both radially and tangentially cut lumber to be mixed in the same piece of furniture. Brown ash is in the center, white ash on the right. The lower half of all samples has been oiled.*

*The rays, lines of cells extending from the pith to the bark, are much more prominent in oak (top) than they are in ash. Both woods are ring-porous: large cells produced in early spring are followed by more solid growth in summer.*

strong, straight-grained wood resulting from second-growth timber, which is so desirable for tool handles and sports equipment, is not the best for cabinetmaking. First-growth ash, or ash that has grown slowly for whatever reason, produces the nicest furniture lumber. For one thing, the ratio of heartwood to sapwood is greater in slow-growing trees. For another, these trees produce relatively more earlywood than latewood each season, which means that their wood is lighter in weight, more porous, and far more interesting in figure.

**In the lumber trade,** most of the wood marketed as "white ash" comes from two species: white ash (*Fraxinus americana*) and green ash (*F. pennsylvanica*), both of which are plentiful throughout the eastern United States. Although on the average white ash might be a little denser and tougher than green ash, variations in growing conditions make the two overlap considerably. Another species, blue ash (*F. quadrangulata*), is of little consequence in the lumber trade because of its limited and sporadic range (around the Ohio and Mississippi River basins). It produces a wood that is almost identical to green ash, and it too is marketed as white ash. Blue ash gets its name from a blue dye extracted from the bark, which was once used for dyeing cloth.

The so-called "white" ashes make nice cabinetwoods once the project is complete, but three other species of ash are noticeably softer and easier to work: black ash (*F. nigra*), pumpkin ash (*F. profunda*) and Oregon ash (*F. latifolia*). To my way of thinking, black ash is the connoisseur's choice. Native to the Great Lakes states, New England and Canada, its environment is a harsh one, which forces slow growth that results in a lighter, less dense wood with exceptionally pretty flatsawn figure. The heartwood is a beautiful soft brown in color (in some parts of its range, black ash is referred to as "brown ash" by lumber dealers) and produces a natural "fruitwood" tone with nothing more than a coat of clear varnish. Because of its narrow annual rings, black ash was the preferred species for basketweaving, and like all the ashes, its stratified nature makes it one of the better woods for steambending.

Pumpkin ash, a similar species, is found in the South. It's less dense than the white ash species and extremely variable as a result of environmental conditions. Pumpkin ash growing in swampy areas will produce a buttress-like base that yields light, soft wood, tending to brittleness. On the West Coast, Oregon ash produces a reasonably good cabinetwood. Its specific gravity of 0.50 makes it somewhat softer than any of the white ashes.

**Price and availability** of the ashes depend a little on how creative you are. Like the old saying "Water, water everywhere, nor any drop to drink," ash is abundant, but my favorite grades for furniture usually end up as shipping crates and pallets, not in retail lumberyards.

Until recently, local lumberyards didn't have much reason to stock ash. Customers always seemed to be asking for maple, cherry, walnut and oak—and if not these, then some exotic timber. Today, at least in my area of Wisconsin, times are changing. Without much trouble, I can get select, kiln-dried ash at between $1.40 and $2.00 a board foot. The problem is, the mills aren't always careful to identify the species, and lumberyards therefore don't always know what they have. Most of the time it's white ash, and of such high quality that it lacks character.

To find my favorite, black ash, I look around at the beginning of the distribution chain, either buying direct from a mill or going to a pallet manufacturer. The last time I did this, about a year

Michael D. Durante

*Turn-of-the-century pieces from the 'Golden Oak' era—like the author's commode above—often are not oak at all, but ash.*

ago, I got lucky. The pallet manufacturer said: "Yeah, I got some ash, but it's just that soft brown stuff from up near Rhinelander; you can have it for forty-five cents a board foot...." "Well, maybe I can make it work," I muttered. I took all he had, about 200 bd. ft., stickered and air-dried it for a few months (with its low stump moisture content, ash dries well and easily), then had it planed for 10¢ a foot. Sure enough, it's a cabinetmaker's dream: beautiful, slow-grown northern black ash, at 55¢ a board foot. How sweet it is!

To conclude from all of this that ash is somehow an undiscovered, world-class cabinetwood to be ranked with walnut, cherry, rosewood and teak would be driving a point beyond its credible limits. Ash is nice in comparison to many woods, but it also has its faults. After praising ash for its laminate qualities, I should point out that the flip side of this feature is that the wood splits easily, as anyone who has spent much time chopping firewood knows (and appreciates). Ash is also very splintery, and unless your hands are calloused from constant shopwork, you may pick up some slivers when cutting and coarse-sanding it. Once shaped, however, it smooths out nicely. Given its extremely open grain, ash must be filled before you can finish it to the kind of glass-smooth surface required for some surfaces, such as tabletops. And, finally, ash does not weather well when exposed to moist, outdoor conditions. Powderpost beetles and other wood-eating bugs absolutely love the stuff. If resistance to the elements is important to your project, score one last point for oak, white oak in particular. It weathers well. Especially in antiques shops. □

*Jon Arno is an amateur woodworker in Brookfield, Wis. He wrote about other domestic woods in* FWW *#25, #41 and #46.*

# Hardwood Lumber Grades

*There's a method to the madness*

by David Sloan

I 've bluffed my way through many a lumberyard. I learned young. When I was a kid, I wanted a big hunk of maple to make a rifle stock. At the lumberyard, the man in charge pointed to a pile of thick maple planks. "Come and get me when you've found what you want," he said. I did, and for years afterward, that's the way I bought wood. Whenever I'd hear lumberyard lingo like "FAS or number one common, sir?", I'd put on my poker face, give a knowing nod, and say, "Sure. Uh, do you mind if I look through the boards?" I didn't have the slightest idea what lumber grades like FAS or No. 1 common meant, but I knew a nice board when I saw one.

My bluff worked fine until I bought wood for a big job. I didn't have time to pick through a hundred oak boards, so I went with a grade called No. 2 common because it was cheap. Much to my dismay, there was a short, narrow, knotty board for every nice one that came off the truck. I suggested that the knots added character, but my customer didn't agree. I had to order more oak, and ultimately lost money on the job.

That lesson motivated me to learn about lumber grades. I picked up the basics from books. Recently I rounded out my education by attending a three-day log-, lumber- and tree-grading workshop in Indiana, where I even got to do a little grading myself. Purdue University and the Indiana Hardwood Lumberman's Association sponsor several of these workshops each year. Attending one is a good way to learn about hardwood grading. (For information, write to Daniel Cassens, Dept. of Forestry and Natural Resources, Purdue University, West Lafayette, Ind. 47907.)

Grades provide the basis for determining lumber quality and price. The *concept* of hardwood grading is simple: a high-grade board must have more clear, defect-free surface area than a low-grade board. The grading system provides standards for defects and board size, and equations for calculating clear surface area.

The standard grades of hardwood lumber are (from best to worst) firsts and seconds (FAS), selects, No. 1 common, No. 2 common, and No. 3 common. There are special grades for certain species, but in general the standard grades are what you'll find. The chart on p. 158 describes the top four standard grades. No. 3 common boards aren't suitable for furniture, and usually end up as pallets or shipping crates. Familiarity with the top four grades will get you through most situations, although lumberyards rarely stock all four. Some yards will have only FAS and No. 1 common; some will sell a mix of the top two grades and call it "selects and better"—it varies from yard to yard. Increasingly popular is a non-standard grade called "FAS one face" (abbreviated F1F). In this grade, one board face will

To choose the grading face, grader Wally Cole flips a red-oak board with his steel-tipped lumber rule. Cole marks a grade with his crayon-tipped wand and records the surface measure and grade in the logbook in his left hand.

157

## Calculations make the grade

The drawing below shows how a grader visualizes clear face cuttings on the board's worst face. To make the grade, the cuttings must exceed minimum size and contain enough cutting units to meet minimum requirements based on board surface measure (SM). One cutting unit = 12 sq. in. (i.e., 1 in. x 12 in., or 2 in. x 6 in.). Both boards shown have an SM of 8 (SM = [width in in. x length in ft.] ÷ 12; drop fractions under ½). The chart gives the minimum cutting sizes and maximum number of cuttings permitted. To determine minimum number of cutting units required, multiply SM by a conversion factor (10 for FAS and selects, 8 for No. 1 common, 6 for No. 2 common).

### Minimum standards for hardwood grades

| Standard grade | Minimum board size* (width x length) | Minimum size of clear face cuttings* (width x length) | Minimum % of clear surface area on graded face | Maximum number of cuttings permitted: SM | Cuts |
|---|---|---|---|---|---|
| **Firsts and seconds** or **FAS** (two separate grades combined and sold as one) | 6 in. x 8 ft. | 4 in. x 5 ft. or 3 in. x 7 ft. | Firsts: 91⅔% Seconds: 83⅓% | 4 to 7 | 1 |
| | | | | 8 to 11 | 2 |
| | | | | 12 to 15 | 3 |
| | | | | 16 and over | 4 |
| **Selects** (graded on best face) | 4 in. x 6 ft. | 4 in. x 5 ft. or 3 in. x 7 ft. | 91⅔% | 2 to 7 | 1 |
| | | | | 8 to 11 | 2 |
| | | | | 12 to 15 | 3 |
| | | | | 16 and over | 4 |
| **No. 1 common** | 3 in. x 4 ft. | 4 in. x 2 ft. or 3 in. x 3 ft. | 66⅔% | 1 | clear |
| | | | | 2 to 4 | 1 |
| | | | | 5 to 7 | 2 |
| | | | | 8 to 10 | 3 |
| | | | | 11 to 13 | 4 |
| | | | | 14 and over | 5 |
| **No. 2 common** | 3 in. x 4 ft. | 3 in. x 2 ft. | 50% | 1 to 3 | 1 |
| | | | | 4 and 5 | 2 |
| | | | | 6 and 7 | 3 |
| | | | | 8 and 9 | 4 |
| | | | | 10 and 11 | 5 |
| | | | | 12 and 13 | 6 |
| | | | | 14 and over | 7 |

*May vary for some species.

**Clear face cuttings**

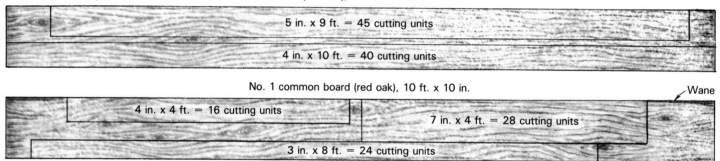

FAS board (red oak), 10 ft. x 10 in.

5 in. x 9 ft. = 45 cutting units

4 in. x 10 ft. = 40 cutting units

No. 1 common board (red oak), 10 ft. x 10 in.

Wane

4 in. x 4 ft. = 16 cutting units

7 in. x 4 ft. = 28 cutting units

3 in. x 8 ft. = 24 cutting units

grade FAS, and the other face No. 1 common or better.

Here's how grading works. Boards aren't graded by their overall appearance, as you might think. The system is based on the assumption that a hardwood board will be cut into smaller pieces to make furniture parts, flooring, etc. Boards are graded by overall length and width, and by the size and number of imaginary "clear face cuttings" (the furniture parts) that the lumber grader visualizes (no actual cutting is involved) in between knots and other defects on the board's *worst* face. One grade, selects, is graded on the best face; F1F is graded on both faces. No unsound defects, such as large holes, loose knots or wane, are allowed on the reverse side of the imaginary cutting. The higher the grade, the wider and longer the clear cuttings have to be, as shown in the drawing above.

In addition to the size of these clear cuttings, the grading rules also specify the number of cuttings a board must contain to make a grade. That's not all. When the surface area of all the clear cuttings in a board is added up, the total must exceed a specified minimum requirement. The surface area of the cuttings is measured in cutting units. One cutting unit equals 12 sq. in. of board surface. (To find the number of cutting units in a cutting, multiply width in inches times length in feet.) The total

number of cutting units required varies for each grade and also within each grade, depending on the board's overall surface area. Two boards that are exactly the same size with the same number of defects and the same amount of defect-free surface area could end up as different grades—the *location* of the defects could prevent a board from having large enough clear cuttings to make the higher grade.

The defects in between the clear cuttings can vary drastically from board to board within a grade. They could be tiny knots, but are just as likely to be holes or large knots. There are size limitations for knots and holes, but in general the grading system isn't concerned much with the defects, only the clear wood in between.

The actual rules for determining grade are ridiculously complex, but they work. To make things even more complicated, grading rules differ somewhat depending on the species. For example, in cherry the "clear cuttings" may contain tiny knots. The National Hardwood Lumber Association's pocket-size rule book ($3 from PO Box 34518, Memphis, Tenn. 38184) gives all this information. It reads like the instructions for an IRS tax form, but it's worth having if you want to understand lumber grading. And if you buy lumber in quantity, it's essential.

After reading all this, you may conclude that the grading system has little relevance to small-scale woodworking—a valid point, perhaps. The system was designed to meet the needs of the lumber and wood-products industries, not the individual woodworker; without the rules, million-board-foot lumber transactions would be impossible. But if you understand it, the system will enable you to buy and sell boards in quantity, sight unseen. When you specify a grade, you don't have to examine the boards to know, very specifically, what you're getting in a shipment. If there's a dispute between buyer and seller, out comes the rule book. The grade can be verified by measuring the board in question and making a few calculations.

Every decision in the lumber business, from the felling and bucking of the tree to the sawing and edging of the boards, is made with one thought in mind: produce as many high-grade boards as possible. The more high-grade boards a log yields, the greater the profit for all concerned. A wide board that would make some woodworkers swoon with delight will be ripped in two if doing that will raise the grade.

So how can you tell which grade to buy? If you need only a few boards, or you're concerned with a board's overall appearance, you're better off using my old trick of picking out what you want. (Be considerate. Ask permission before you pick, and restack any boards you move.) The best boards will always be in the FAS pile, but if you want to save money, look in the No. 1 common pile first. You'll find a few nice boards. The difference in retail price between an FAS board and a No. 1 common board is roughly 40% (for red oak), but sometimes the difference in appearance isn't that great. A knot that was a defect in the grader's eyes may be pleasing to yours.

When you need a quantity, say, 50 bd. ft. or more, the law of averages starts to work and you can buy blind by grade alone. Not surprisingly, the NHLA rule book ignores aesthetics. In the real world, however, any large single-grade order will contain nice boards, ugly boards, and boards in between. The larger the order, the more likely it is that you'll have an even distribution of nice, ugly and in between (remember statistics in high school?). So when buying by grade, it's always a good idea to order a little more wood than you'll need, to allow for waste. The lower the grade, the more waste you should expect. You'll have minimal waste with FAS or selects, but you'll pay more.

Even if you want perfectly clear stock, you may not always need to buy FAS for every furniture project. The chart gives the minimum sizes for clear cuttings in each grade. These are the smallest clear pieces that you can expect to get out of a board. Consider what size pieces of clear stock your project requires and buy the lowest grade that will give you that size. If only one side of the board will show, buy selects (or F1F) instead of FAS. The cuttings are the same size as FAS, but selects cost a little less.

What if your project requires long, wide, pretty boards and you don't need a lot of little furniture parts? Pick if you can. On a big job you may have to buy blind. The chart gives you the minimum percentage of clear surface area you can expect on the graded face. If money's no object, play it safe and buy FAS or selects. In these grades you'll have wider boards and fewer defects. But if, like me, you don't mind a few knots in the middle of your pet project, or gluing up narrower boards, you can usually save money by ordering No. 1 common. You'll get a few ugly boards, and roughly 17% less clear wood than with FAS, but each board foot will cost about 40% less. And besides, those knots add character, remember?                                                                    □

---

*David Sloan is an assistant editor at* Fine Woodworking.

# A grader in action

Grading requires a lot of measuring and a lot of math. When you're learning—juggling unfamiliar tools, rules and numbers—it seems to take forever to grade just one board. George Screpetis from Pineville, La., an instructor at the Purdue University grading workshop I attended, said that a pro spends only a few seconds with each board. Fumbling as I was at the time, that was hard to believe. It took me a few seconds just to get my grading rule book out of my back pocket. I decided to see for myself.

Wally Cole is a professional grader at Cole Bros. Lumber Co., a sawmill in Woodbury, Conn. He's an amiable young man, in his early thirties I'd guess. The afternoon that I stopped by, I found him standing on the grading platform armed with the tools of his trade: a lumber rule, a crayon-tipped wand and a logbook. As the newly sawn and edged red-oak boards shuttled along on the roller-chain conveyor that crossed the platform, he quickly eyeballed each board's length and measured its width with his lumber rule. A scale printed on the rule gave him the board's surface measure (surface area in square feet). Giving the board a quick flip with the steel-tipped rule and his boot, he chose the worst face for grading, mentally calculated the required number of cutting units and visually laid out the clear face cuttings. Then, with a flourish of his crayon-tipped wand, he marked the board with a grade symbol. As the graded board moved down the conveyor, he ticked off the grade and surface measure in his logbook. Two handlers working with him stacked the boards into piles by grade. The entire grading sequence took only a few

seconds for each board, just as George Screpetis had said.

A good grader like Cole can grade as much as 10,000 bd. ft. in an 8-hr. shift. Graders often get paid by the board foot, so speed is just as important as accuracy. Sometimes Cole seemed to do nothing more than flip a board with his rule before he marked a grade. In fact, he was so fast that I couldn't wind, focus and shoot my camera fast enough to keep up with him. "The best boards grade themselves," he explained. A defect-free board takes only a glance, because if it's large enough to make FAS, no further scrutiny is needed. It's automatically FAS.

Cole was grading to fill an order. The customer had specified standard FAS, F1F, No. 1 common and No. 2 common. If a customer's specifications differ from the standard grading rules, Cole will grade to meet those specs.

I asked if some species were more difficult to grade. Cole said that red oak is one of the easiest woods to grade green because it doesn't have unusual characteristics. Yellow poplar, also being sawn the day I visited, is tougher to grade because it has tiny burls that look like knots at first glance. The burls aren't considered defects in poplar, but knots are, so the grader must check each board carefully to avoid confusing the two.

Hardwood boards are often graded twice: once green, and again after kiln-drying. Since the boards are already graded when they go into the kiln, the dry-grader regrades only boards that have drying-related defects that would cause a drop in grade. Boards more than 10 in. wide are usually picked out at the second grading and sold at a premium.     —D.S.

159

# Quilted Mahogany
## *The tale of a magnificent mutant*

by Mark Berry

One of the pleasures of woodworking is often the story behind the wood itself. Some wood, specially selected for its striking grain or some other unusual characteristic, will raise eyebrows and interest in its origins. But on rare occasions a wood turns up that practically pops the eyes out of your head. Recently our woodworking firm, Hoddick, Berry and Malakoff, had the good fortune to work with the extraordinary mahogany you see pictured here. The wood was so amazing that I decided to track down its story. Here's what I found.

In 1965 in Honduras' Chicibul jungle, a party of loggers discovered a large mahogany tree—over 100 ft. high, 10 ft. in diameter at the base, 50 ft. to the first branches. The spiraled bark indicated that the wood might be highly figured. Felling and transportation to the mill almost 200 miles away was a daunting prospect, but loggers take pride in being able to fell these monsters, so down it came. Unfortunately it didn't fall where they intended, toppling backward into a large ravine instead. Even after the log was cut in half a D7 Caterpillar tractor couldn't pull it out, so there the tree rested for the next 18 years.

In 1971 Robert Novak, who was running a sawmill in the Chicibul jungle, first heard rumors of a giant figured mahogany tree stuck in a ravine. After Novak left to form his own lumber company, a mill approached him about purchasing the log and after some haggling, a crew was sent into the jungle after it. They quartered the two halves with chainsaws, then dragged and trucked the eight pieces 100 miles through the jungle to the river. The quartered logs were then sawn in half again, pushed into the river and floated 70 miles down river to a steam-powered sawmill—a vestige of early British logging operations.

When finally opened at the mill, the log was revealed to be the rarest of the figured mahoganies, technically known as "blistered" or "quilted." The exact cause of this grain pattern is not known, though it is believed to be due to a genetic defect. A 20-year-old desk made of mahogany with an identical figure sat in the mill office, and none of the millhands had seen anything like it in the interim. News of the rare log drew other buyers, and soon a bidding war ensued between Novak, who wanted to mill it as lumber, and two firms, one German, one

Robert Novak

*One-sixteenth of the original quilted mahogany log emerges (left) after a 70-mile float to a Honduran sawmill. Above, the freshly bandsawn boards, some almost 4 ft. wide, are sorted before being stacked for air drying. Berry and his partners resawed and laminated the mahogany to plywood for the carcase of the dresser (right and far right). The ebony border helps keep the wood's extraordinary figure from overpowering the piece. The end grain of the solid drawer fronts displays the same figure as the face.*

Fritz Hoddick

Fritz Hoddick

American, who wanted it for veneer. Novak won.

The huge pieces were pushed through the mill's 40-in.-throat bandsaw under Novak's close supervision, each log carefully positioned for the best possible cut. The entire milling operation took 12 days. The yield was nearly 12,000 bd. ft., of which about a third had true blistered or quilted figure, another third had more of a wavy, ribbon figure, and the balance was a combination of these two and about three other grain patterns.

When air-dried to 35%, the wood was shipped to Miami, and drying completed in an evaporator kiln. Mahogany usually takes approximately 11 days to kiln dry. This mahogany took 30 days because of its greater density and the special care and gradual drying required by the wavy grain. Half the wood remained in Miami, while the other half was shipped to Handloggers Hardwood Lumber, run by Tim Mahoney in Sausalito, California. Novak sold the rest directly to woodworkers around the country to whom he had sent a mailing.

A brochure printed by Novak preceded the shipment to Handloggers, stirring up interest in the woodworking community. My partners, Peter Malakoff and Fritz Hoddick, and I were among the first to see it. The lumber was incredible. Straight, flat, fully figured and without defect, the boards were over 1-in. thick, 10-ft. to 14-ft. long and 6-in. to 36-in. wide. The price: $10 to $30 a board foot, depending on width. As we went through the stack we were joined by a man who had heard about the wood and wanted to buy some and have furniture made from it. Peter Malakoff cleared his throat and mentioned that we happened to be woodworkers. A relationship quickly developed, and we soon found 250 bd. ft. of figured mahogany (the pick of the shipment) stacked in our shop.

Having got the wood and the client, we had to figure out how best to use it. Design is particularly crucial when using a highly-figured wood, as the wood can easily be overpowering. Eli Sutton, a free-lance designer with whom we often work, came up with a modern rendering of the classic Japanese *tansu*, a traditional chest with doors and drawers. The ebony frames the wood

like a picture; a simple and elegant solution. The client liked it enough to commission two, one for himself and one for a friend.

Because of the rarity and expense of the figured mahogany, we had the 1-in. thick boards resawn. The risk of the blade wandering in the 18-in. to 24-in. wide boards forced us to settle for splitting the boards in half. After resawing and thickness sanding (planing was out of the question), we were left with veneers slightly over ¼ in. thick.

We glued the ¼-in. veneers onto ½-in. Finnish birch plywood and then fit the ¾-in. panels in the frames. We couldn't bring ourselves to put ordinary backs on these pieces, so we installed figured-mahogany panels there, too. As I began working the wood, I noticed another amazing feature: the figure on the edge grain *and* end grain was almost identical to that of the face grain. The wood was also exceptionally dense and quite stable.

The solid quilted-mahogany drawer fronts form a pattern taken from a hexagram in the *I Ching* that has special significance for the client. The drawers, which slide on Accuride glides, are fitted with Tutch latches, so that no hardware mars the lines of the hexagram. Finished with four coats of Tungseal and a coat of Trewax, the quilted mahogany has matured with the passage of time to a deep, rich brown with a striking iridescence.

Having whetted your appetite for this extraordinary wood, I have to say that only about 1,000 bd. ft. remains at Handloggers (PO Box 1625, Sausalito, Calif. 94966), and Novak (PO Box 1365, Sausalito, Calif. 94966) also has some. But don't give up hope. When I last spoke with Robert Novak he was making plans to have the 12-ft. long butt of the log (about 3,000 bd. ft.) pulled out of the jungle. He also told me the following story. After his wood had been milled he took a sample to a friend at another Honduran mill. His friend called over his tree hunters and said, "I'll give anyone $1,000 who finds a tree like this." So with a cash incentive and a little luck maybe we won't have to wait another 20 years.  □

*Mark Berry works wood with his partners in San Rafael, Calif.*

# THINGS TO MAKE

## Fig. 2: A working bench

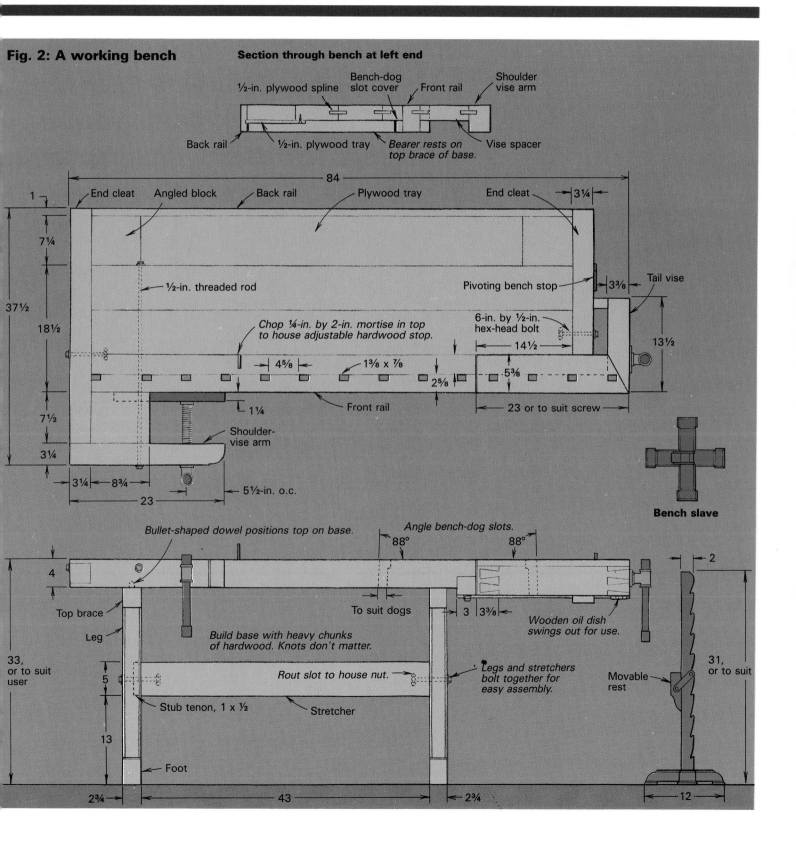

**Section through bench at left end**

½-in. plywood spline
Bench-dog slot cover
Front rail
Shoulder vise arm
Back rail
½-in. plywood tray
*Bearer rests on top brace of base.*
Vise spacer

84

End cleat — Angled block — Back rail — Plywood tray — End cleat — 3¼

1
7¼
37½
18½
7½
3¼

½-in. threaded rod
Pivoting bench stop — 3⅜ — Tail vise

*Chop ¼-in. by 2-in. mortise in top to house adjustable hardwood stop.*

6-in. by ½-in. hex-head bolt
14½
13½

4⅝
1⅜ x ⅞
2⅝
5⅜

1¼
Front rail
23 or to suit screw

Shoulder-vise arm

3¼ — 8¾
23
5½-in. o.c.

**Bench slave**

*Bullet-shaped dowel positions top on base.*
*Angle bench-dog slots.*
88°
88°
2

4

Top brace
To suit dogs
3  3⅜
*Wooden oil dish swings out for use.*

Leg

*Build base with heavy chunks of hardwood. Knots don't matter.*

33, or to suit user

5
*Rout slot to house nut.*
*Legs and stretchers bolt together for easy assembly.*
Movable rest
31, or to suit

Stub tenon, 1 x ½
Stretcher

13

Foot

2¾
43
2¾
12

# Flip-Top Table
## Double-duty design

by Robert March

*Ebony wedges accent the exposed mortise-and-tenon joints wh  
the rosewood legs intersect with the front and back stretchers a  
the dual side stretchers. A bridle notch carries the top stretcher  
to braces under the double-leaf top.*

**Fig. 1: Chinese flip-top table**

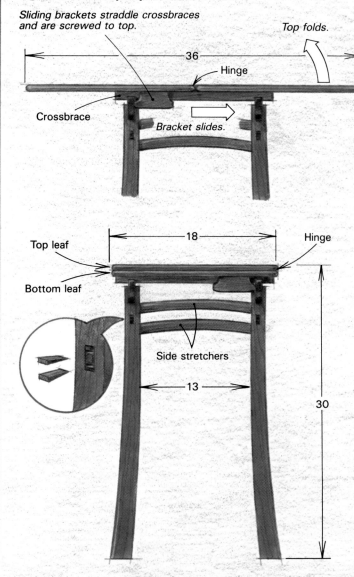

Sliding brackets straddle crossbraces  
and are screwed to top.

Top folds.

36

Hinge

Crossbrace

Bracket slides.

Top leaf

18

Hinge

Bottom leaf

Side stretchers

13

30

Like many contemporary woodworkers, I've been in-spired by the simple elegance of Chinese furniture of the Ming dynasty (mid 14th to mid 17th century). I es-pecially like the splayed-leg altars of the period and de-cided to design a multipurpose table based on this traditional form. The rosewood table I developed has a definitely Oriental flavor, but it has more exposed joinery and more curved compo-nents than the Chinese pieces. The open-up top adds a dash of versatility, allowing the table to convert from an 18-in. deep side-board/buffet to a 36-in. deep desk or dining table.

All the exposed joints are through mortise-and-tenon or bridle joints. Visually these joints are most important where the legs intersect with the long front and back stretchers and the dual side stretchers. Three stretchers tenon into each leg, while the uppermost long stretchers run through the notched legs out to braces under the overhanging top. To give the table a light, graceful feeling, I left open space between the stretchers and the top, and stopped the legs short of the upper edges of the front and back stretchers. This space also showcases the shaped brack-ets connecting the base to the top—two mitered frame-and-panel leaves joined with butler-tray hinges. The back leaf is stacked upon the front leaf when the table is closed. When you open the top, the brackets let you slide the top forward so that it always remains centered over its base and is unlikely to tip.

**I build the base of the table first,** then veneer the top while the glued-up base cures. Begin by making full-size ¼-in. Mason-ite templates for the legs and stretchers. Since rosewood is ex-pensive, I save wood by tracing the templates directly onto the rough boards, rather than squaring up pieces, cutting joints and then bandsawing the curves. Generally I cut the legs from 8/4 stock and the stretchers and frame pieces from 4/4 or 5/4.

Place the leg templates so that the wood grain will follow the curve of each piece. Ideally, you should shape the pieces so the annual rings in the wood run diagonally across the ends, as shown in figure 1. To cut the legs, bandsaw the front face, then trace the template over the adjacent, now-curved face, and band-saw that side. The final shaping is done by hand. Square up the top 4 in. to 6 in. of each piece with a smoothing plane and refine the curves with a compass plane. Next trace the stretcher tem-plates onto the rough stock and bandsaw these pieces before sur-facing their flat faces with a jointer and a thickness planer. After compass-planing their curved edges, I cut them to size on the tablesaw. At this time I also cut the crossbraces to size and sur-face them.

Before mortising the legs, I cut them to length on the table-

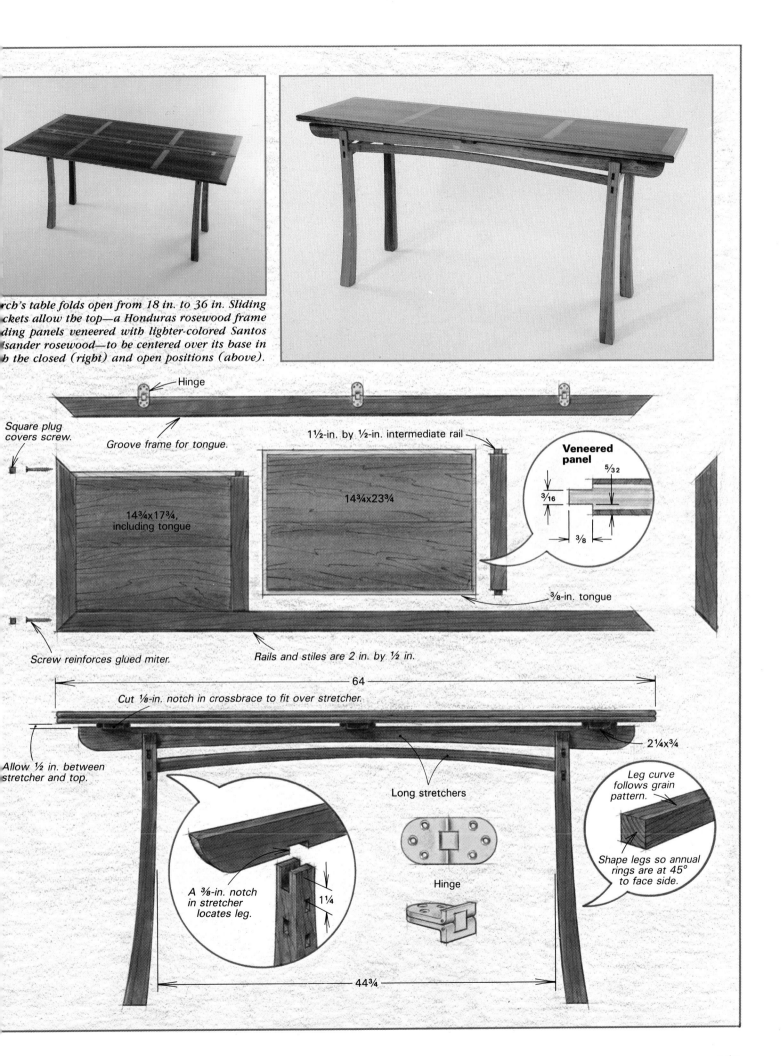

_rch's table folds open from 18 in. to 36 in. Sliding_
_ckets allow the top—a Honduras rosewood frame_
_ding panels veneered with lighter-colored Santos_
_isander rosewood—to be centered over its base in_
_b the closed (right) and open positions (above)._

Hinge

Square plug
covers screw.

Groove frame for tongue.

1½-in. by ½-in. intermediate rail

**Veneered
panel**

⁵⁄₃₂

³⁄₁₆

³⁄₈

14¾x17¾,
including tongue

14¾x23¾

³⁄₈-in. tongue

Screw reinforces glued miter.

Rails and stiles are 2 in. by ½ in.

64

Cut ⅛-in. notch in crossbrace to fit over stretcher.

2¼x¾

Allow ½ in. between
stretcher and top.

Long stretchers

Leg curve
follows grain
pattern.

A ³⁄₈-in. notch
in stretcher
locates leg.

1¼

Shape legs so annual
rings are at 45°
to face side.

Hinge

44¾

165

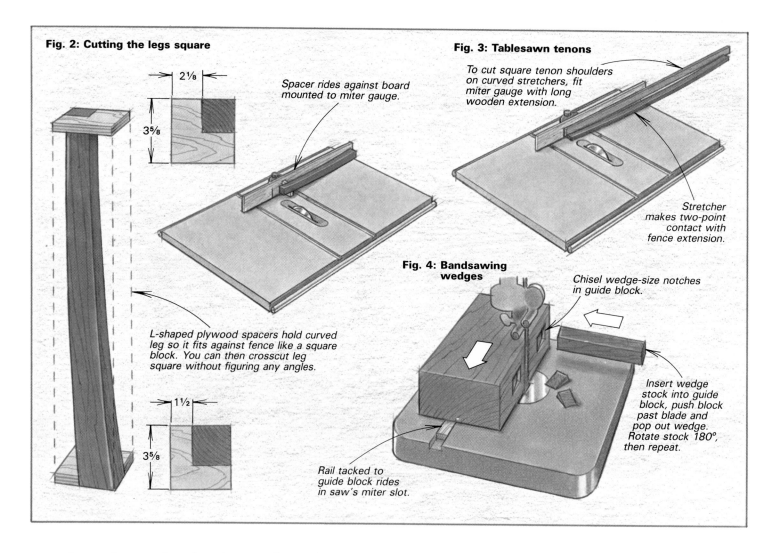

**Fig. 2: Cutting the legs square**

2⅛

3⅝

Spacer rides against board mounted to miter gauge.

L-shaped plywood spacers hold curved leg so it fits against fence like a square block. You can then crosscut leg square without figuring any angles.

1½

3⅝

**Fig. 3: Tablesawn tenons**

To cut square tenon shoulders on curved stretchers, fit miter gauge with long wooden extension.

Stretcher makes two-point contact with fence extension.

**Fig. 4: Bandsawing wedges**

Chisel wedge-size notches in guide block.

Insert wedge stock into guide block, push block past blade and pop out wedge. Rotate stock 180°, then repeat.

Rail tacked to guide block rides in saw's miter slot.

saw, using two homemade L-shaped spacers (figure 2) that hold the end of the leg against the miter gauge and parallel to the saw table so the leg can be crosscut. I cut the ⅜-in. by 1-in. mortises with a hollow-chisel attachment for a drill press (see pp. 98-99). The mortises must be cut from the outside face of the leg because that's the only way the piece will lie flat on the drill-press table. If you don't have a hollow-chisel mortiser, chop the mortises by hand. Next notch the bridle joint in the top of the legs by standing the leg upright in a tenoning jig and clearing the ⅝-in. by 1¼-in. slot with a dado cutter. Even though the stretchers are curved, you can cut the tenon shoulders on the tablesaw. Mount a long wooden extension on the saw's miter gauge (or use a large sliding table) and hold the piece face-down with the concave curve facing the extension to cut the first shoulder (figure 3). Then flip the piece to the other side of the blade to cut the second shoulder. Cut the tenons 1/16 in. to ⅛ in. too long—you'll trim them flush after assembly. After cutting the shoulders, stand the stretcher in a tenoning jig and cut the cheeks.

The narrow top and bottom tenon cheeks and their shoulders are bandsawn. I cut the shoulders about 1/16 in. shy of the line, then use a chisel to pare them flush with the shoulders I previously cut on the tablesaw. While I'm at the bandsaw, I cut two slots, each the width of the bandsaw blade, into the tenons for the ebony wedges, which taper from ⅛ in. to 1/32 in. (figure 4).

After scraping and sanding the base parts, assemble the two ends. You can use bar clamps to pull the joints together, but place them so you can drive wedges into the tenons before the glue hardens. Because yellow glue dries slowly on oily rosewood, I leave the clamps on overnight before trimming the ten-

ons flush. To complete the base, glue and clamp the tenons of the lower front and back stretchers into the mortises of the two ends. Be careful not to overtighten the clamps, or you'll bow the stretchers. The base is now rigid enough that you can position the top stretcher over the legs and scribe where the stretchers must be notched to fit into the leg. After cutting the ⅜-in. deep notch, I glue the pieces together and attach the cross supports as shown in figure 1.

**I begin the top** while the base is clamped and drying. Even though each leaf is really three separate panels held in a frame, I press one large sheet for each leaf, then cut it apart to ensure that the grain pattern will match on all three. I usually bookmatch two long, wide sheets of rosewood veneer for each side of the leaves. Since both sides are so visible, I use show veneers on both, with the flatter, "swirly" grain in the center and the more striped grain to the outside.

To joint the veneer, clamp two sheets between two heavy squared-up boards. Set the sheets so the mating edges protrude 1/16 in. to ⅛ in., then hand-plane the edges flush to the boards with a jack plane or a jointer plane. Next remove the veneer from the boards and tape the mating edges in two stages, first stretching 3-in. strips of masking tape across the seam on the inside face to pull the joint tight, then flipping the veneer sheet over and securing the face-side seam with veneer tape. Remove the masking tape before pressing the veneer. After preparing veneer for each face of the leaves, select a smooth, flat sheet of ½-in. thick Baltic birch or other high-quality plywood for the substrate. Cut these sheets 1 in. oversize all around and with the grain running across

Color photos: Jack Russell; drawings: David Dann

the short dimension. This makes the panel more stable, since the veneer grain continues the plywood's crossbanding, with the grain of each layer at 90° to the next layer.

I press the veneer with 16-in. 2x4 battens over four ½-in. thick chipboard cauls cut the same size as the plywood. Set two cauls on a pair of sawhorses and cover them with waxed paper to prevent the veneer from sticking to the chipboard. Put the veneer face-down on the waxed paper, roll a coat of urea-formaldehyde glue onto one side of the plywood panel and put the glued face onto the veneer. After rolling glue onto the top side of the plywood, put the second veneer sheet, this time face-up, on the plywood. Add another sheet of waxed paper and two more cauls to complete the package. Place the 2x4s in pairs, one on top of the package and another directly below it underneath the panel, and lightly clamp the sandwich together. Tighten the clamps, beginning in the middle of the leaf to squeeze out excess glue. The next day, unclamp the panels and use a handscraper to remove the dry veneer tape and to smooth both faces.

A tongue-and-groove joint holds the panels in the frames. Mill the frame pieces about ¼ in. thicker than the veneered plywood and slightly longer than their finished dimensions. Then, on the tablesaw, cut a ³⁄₁₆-in. groove into the inside edge of each piece. After cutting the intermediate rails to length, leaving enough for a tenon on each end, saw the veneered plywood to width, then into the three panels. Rout a centered tongue on the four edges of each panel and on the ends of the intermediate rails.

To assemble the top, arrange the pieces on your bench the way they will be clamped. For the outer frame (two rails, two long stiles), begin at one corner, cut the miter joint and clamp it up to mark the next corner for cutting. Once the second miter is cut, repeat the process for the third corner, and so on. I reinforce each miter with a screw. Before gluing the pieces together, I mortise a shallow ⁵⁄₁₆-in. square hole in the outside edges of each miter, then drill through the mortise for the screw. This allows me to cover the screws with square plugs that complement the table's angular look. If you've accurately cut the three plywood panels, you shouldn't have any problem clamping the leaf into a perfect rectangle. Then screw the miters together and plug the holes.

Planing the frame pieces flush to the veneer is difficult, especially at the corners—it's easy to tear the edge of a rail or stile or to nick the veneer. I plane in from the outside edges with a jack plane or a smoothing plane, using the veneered surface as a register for the nose of the plane to ensure that the frame pieces remain flat. I partially round the outside edges with a ½-in. quarter-round router bit set so that only the lower half of the bit cuts. Then I scrape the entire top and sand with 220-grit. I rout the mortises for the hinges with a template, and hinge the two leaves together. Before attaching the top to the base, I finish the table with at least six coats of clear Waterlox oil.

The three U-shaped brackets holding the top to the base (figure 5) should fit tightly around the crossbraces but still allow the top to slide. If the brackets are too loose, the center of the open table will pop up when someone leans on an edge. Properly installed, the brackets hit the back stretcher when the top is closed and the front stretcher when the top is open. Work out the adjustment by first clamping the brackets in place when the top is closed and moving them around as needed. When you're satisfied, fasten the brackets with round-head brass screws. □

*Robert March is a woodworker/designer and head of the woodworking program at the Worcester (Mass.) Crafts Center. Black-and-white photos by the author.*

With the veneer sheets clamped between boards so that the matched edges stand proud, March hand-planes the edges.

After joining the veneers with masking tape, March flips the sheet over and props a plank under one leaf to pinch the veneer seam tight. The seam is then secured with veneer tape before the masking tape is pulled off.

Each of the top's two intermediate rails is tenoned into the stiles. Tongues on the three panels slip into matching grooves cut in the table frame.

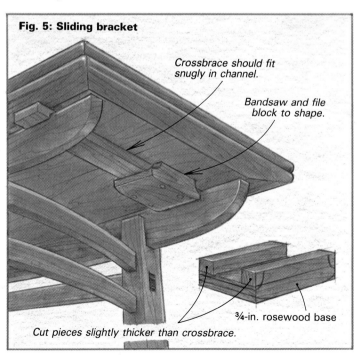
**Fig. 5: Sliding bracket**

Crossbrace should fit snugly in channel.

Bandsaw and file block to shape.

¾-in. rosewood base

Cut pieces slightly thicker than crossbrace.

# Making Period Bedposts

## Methods from the Deep South

by Asher Carmichael

A spinning beam 4 in. square and up to 7 ft. long has a lot of inertia, and turning one into a bedpost might seem a frightful task. Yet in the course of visiting several bed makers in the Mobile area, I discovered that proper planning and some ingenious jigs can take the risk and the mystery out of the job. Mobile is a bedmaking center, the home of one major bed manufacturer, Reid Classics, and a few one-man shops as well. The jigs and fixtures shown in this article can be used not only for bedposts, but for any long turnings.

The Reid Classics story began some 50 years ago, when Robert Reid went to work for Roy Blake, a cabinetmaker who specialized in restoring and reproducing the many antiques found in the Mobile area. After WW II, Reid and his brother Julian opened a general woodworking shop that in its early years made everything from horse-drawn carriages to tennis rackets. Because of demand, they eventually specialized in period four-poster beds. Over the years, they have devised machine-production methods that still maintain the uncompromising excellence of detail they had learned from Blake (who in his late seventies still does some work in a one-room shop in his home).

The Reids have, over the years, done their best to perpetuate their methods and the traditions that Blake started. Of the three other bedmakers in the area, two—Milton Collins and Glenn De-Gruy—worked for the Reids for years before starting their own shops, and the third, William Blake, learned his craft from his uncle Roy, the same old master who steered Robert Reid into woodworking so many years before.

Beds are knockdown construction so that they can be moved. A typical four-poster is shown in the photo on the facing page. End rails and side rails—usually 2 in. thick and 5 in. wide—are tenoned to fit into mortises cut in square sections of the posts, as shown in figure 1, then held in place with long bolts and embedded nuts. The standard hardware used in the 18th century is still available today from many local hardware stores, and if not, period-hardware suppliers such as Horton Brasses (Box 95, Cromwell, Conn. 06416) will have them.

The headboard is never glued in place. It is kept from loosening by the location of the bed bolts—the bolts securing the end rails are above the ones in the side rails, so that they constantly pull in on the posts and the headboard. The tester (pronounced teester, and often spelled that way in old records) is sometimes straight and rectangular, sometimes arched or serpentine. The top of each post carries a brass or steel pin that passes through

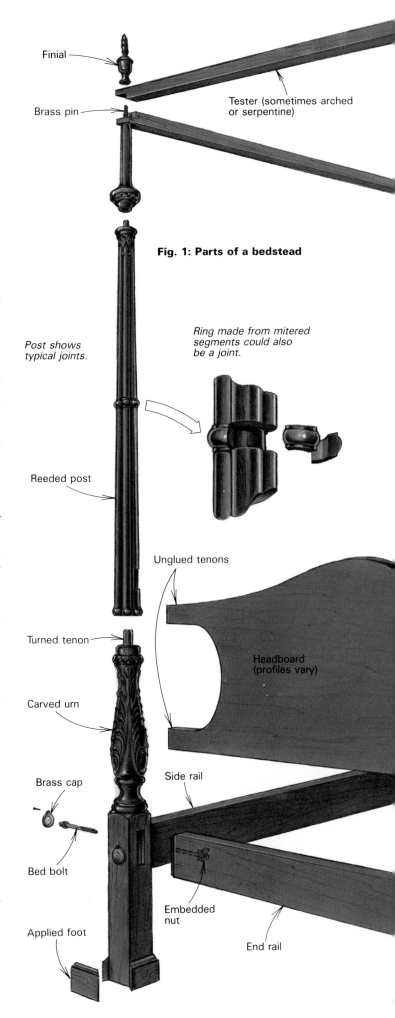

**Fig. 1: Parts of a bedstead**

Finial

Brass pin

Tester (sometimes arched or serpentine)

*Post shows typical joints.*

*Ring made from mitered segments could also be a joint.*

Reeded post

Unglued tenons

Turned tenon

Headboard (profiles vary)

Carved urn

Brass cap

Side rail

Bed bolt

Embedded nut

Applied foot

End rail

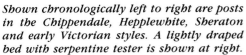
*Shown chronologically left to right are posts in the Chippendale, Hepplewhite, Sheraton and early Victorian styles. A lightly draped bed with serpentine tester is shown at right.*

the tester to hold it in place. The finial then slides onto the pin to conceal it. In Colonial days, testers carried the weight of voluminous side curtains of expensive imported fabric, which could completely enclose the bed and its occupants. A richly draped bed provided privacy and shelter from drafts, and showed off the family's wealth as well. One old document lists 56 yards of material ordered as bed "furniture," which is what they called the fabric. Today's four-posters are seldom so fully furnished.

Mattresses, filled with up to 40 pounds of down, were at first supported on thick stuffed pads laid directly on the floor, but methods of raising them up on webs of rope and canvas were soon devised, with the ropes secured through holes or pins in the rails. Reproduction beds are usually adapted to take standard box springs in the same ways used for regular beds.

The Reid shop makes scores of period designs by combining about thirty different posts with various headboards and testers. By studying bedposts in museums, and making templates of antique posts that come in for repair, the Reid shop has accumulated authentic patterns that span periods from early Chippendale to late Victorian. As a rough guide, Chippendale's influence shows in cabriole legs with ball-and-claw feet, and also in square posts with applied foot moldings. Hepplewhite's style had reeding instead of the earlier fluted designs and Sheraton introduced round, tapering legs. Such distinctions are not always easy to make because styles and influences overlapped. The tall posts favored up to around 1820 soon gave way to heavier designs with shorter posts, no drapery, and sometimes even fancy foot rails in addition to the structural members. Such changes marked the end of an era. As Wallace Nutting once wryly wrote: "A foot rail did not come in until good styles went out."

The furnituremaker in the 18th century often turned bedposts in one piece except for the finial. In those days, turning a one-

piece post had advantages. For one thing, their boring tools were probably not as efficient as today's, and it would have been difficult to drill accurate dowel holes to join a post made in sections. In addition, turners used manually powered lathes, which allowed them a range of slow speeds that took most of the danger out of turning long, heavy stock. This and the use of a steady rest diminished the tendency of slender work to whip and vibrate.

A few of the shops in the Mobile area have lengthened their lathes to accept longer than usual work. One approach is to remove the headstock and tailstock from a standard lathe, and then make new lathe ways from heavy angle iron. The headstock and tailstock are attached by whatever means is practical, and the whole assembly is raised up on a sturdy wooden stand. Another way to lengthen a lathe is to remove the tailstock from one and the headstock from another, and to bolt the two lathe beds in tandem atop a long support table.

Yet even though they have the means, no one in Mobile regularly turns full-length posts. Instead, area bedmakers have developed methods to join posts turned in shorter sections. These ideas can be used by any turner to join long work such as standing lamps and coat racks as well as bedposts. If you begin with full-length stock, as most bedmakers in Mobile do, you can make the grain in the finished work match from section to section. Yet this isn't absolutely necessary. Shorter stock may be much more available—and economical—and there is usually so much decoration around the joints that the continuity of the wood grain will be somewhat obscured in any case. A big advantage to working in sections is that your present lathe will probably be up to the job. Also, a post turned in sections will turn out straighter than a one-piece post.

The Reid shop rips post stock full length from 4-in. thick planks, and a typical blank will warp a little as it is cut from the

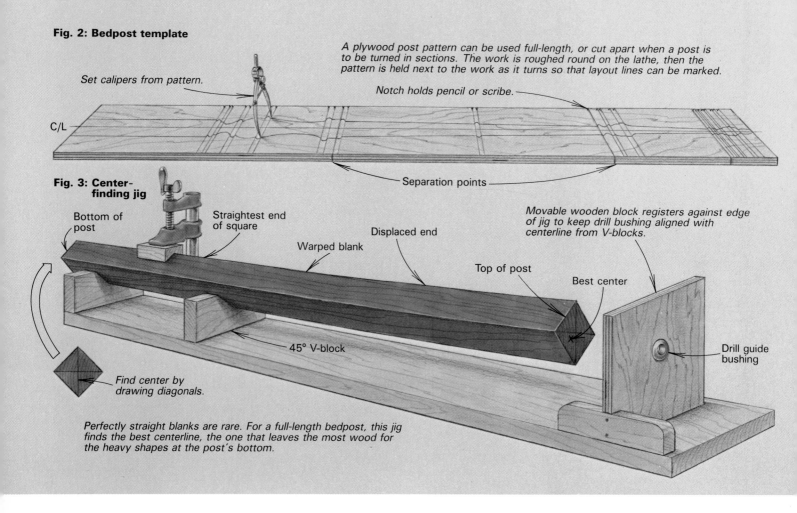

## Fig. 2: Bedpost template

*A plywood post pattern can be used full-length, or cut apart when a post is to be turned in sections. The work is roughed round on the lathe, then the pattern is held next to the work as it turns so that layout lines can be marked.*

Set calipers from pattern.

Notch holds pencil or scribe.

C/L

Separation points

## Fig. 3: Center-finding jig

Bottom of post

Straightest end of square

Warped blank

Displaced end

Top of post

*Movable wooden block registers against edge of jig to keep drill bushing aligned with centerline from V-blocks.*

Best center

45° V-block

Drill guide bushing

Find center by drawing diagonals.

*Perfectly straight blanks are rare. For a full-length bedpost, this jig finds the best centerline, the one that leaves the most wood for the heavy shapes at the post's bottom.*

board. If you are planning to cut a post into three or four sections, warp will not be too much of a problem, because you can square up the joints on the lathe, undercutting the endgrain a little for a perfect fit.

When working in sections, it's wise to consider which part of the joint should be tenon and which part mortise. There are often deep cove cuts either immediately above or below a joint, and the rule is to bore the mortise through what will be the heavier part in the finished post. It is a good idea to keep any joint mortises well away from the square mortises for the bed rails, in order not to weaken the post at this critical point. Bedposts typically separate as shown in figure 1, and an average tenon might be 1-in. to 1¼-in. dia., and about 3 in. long. Tenons are grooved to allow glue squeeze-out.

A crucial step in making a bedpost is to draw this sort of information, including the separation points, on a full length plywood pattern of the post, as shown in figure 2. If the post is to be turned in sections, the pattern can be cut apart and used to scribe separation points onto the stock, allowing extra length for integral tenons (at upper joints, where strength is not so critical, it is often possible to substitute a dowel, which conserves post stock and makes for better grain matching).

With the work in the lathe, hold the pattern next to it for marking the points where the profiles change. At the base of the post, and with the lathe turned off, mark the point where the square section ends, and scribe the lines around all four faces. Then round off the corners with the point of a skew chisel. Mark the other points on the work after it has been roughed round with a gouge—simply hold the pattern next to the stock as it turns and slide a pencil down the notch in the pattern. Then set calipers according to the pattern and transfer the di-

ameters to the work with a parting tool.

If you cut full-length stock into sections, be sure to mark their orientation on the end grain as soon as you cut the divisions, so that they can be turned and assembled in the correct order. You can mark the matching sections A (for the bottom of the post), then B-B, C-C, etc. These letters will serve to keep you from accidentally reversing a section when you put it in the lathe. These marks will probably be turned away when you square up the joint lines, but you can mark them again at that time so you won't intermix post sections later.

If you have a long-bed lathe and decide to have few separation points in your design, you will have to consider how much the stock is warped. In ordinary turning, a slightly warped piece of wood is simply center-marked at both ends, and the warp is turned away. But in a bedpost, such a procedure may cause problems. It is necessary for the square section of the stock to stand straight and to be perpendicular to the bed rails. This means that the blank must be chucked in the lathe with the square part of the post on-center—any warp in the blank must be confined to the length of the post that will be above the rails. Figure 3 shows a jig that finds the best centers for a full length post. The bottom of the post (the straightest end of the blank) is marked with diagonals to show its center, then is held in a pair of V-blocks. The warped end is allowed to go its own way. A movable wooden block with a drill-guide bushing in it then locates the "center" at the finial end. If you make a jig like this, locate the drill-guide bushing in the block according to the size of the V-blocks and the stock. To check that the bushing is correct, put the block at the base of the post (the end that will remain square); the bushing must align exactly with the marked center. Of course in stock that is too badly warped, you may not

*Robert Reid gauges a bedpost tenon to the right diameter, using calipers and a parting tool at several places along its length.*

be able to turn full length without running out of wood.

When the finial center has been drilled, the blank is usually divided into two sections before turning. Because the tenon is turned at the top of the square section of the post, the upper post section must have a mortise at its bottom end as well as one for the finial pin. It is no trick to center a turned tenon, but it would be almost impossible to accurately center the matching mortise if it were drilled after the stock had been turned. The solution is to bore the mortise before turning, then insert a steel plug in the hole, as shown in figure 4. One end of the plug is countersunk to match the 60° live center at the tailstock, which centers the pre-drilled mortise so that the post can be turned around it. When mounting the work in the lathe, the finial end goes at the head-stock, and is driven by a spur center that instead of having a point, has a center pin that fits the finial mortise. Both mortises, therefore, end up centered in the post.

The center-finding jig is also useful if you plan to make a pen-cil post bed, one with octagonal posts instead of turned ones. When the Reids make a pencil post, they first find the center and drill the hole for the finial pin, then they mount the blank on a sliding jig that runs past a commercial shaper, which cuts each face of the tapered octagon in turn. Robert Reid got the basic idea from Roy Blake, whose original jig worked on the bandsaw, as shown in figure 5. The jig indexes the finial mortise on a pin that allows the post to be rotated for successive cuts. The band-saw blade cuts a straight taper from the top of the post, but the taper ends above the square base of the post. Thus, the bottom of the post can be used to index each cut in turn, by resting first on a flat face and then on a corner. In order that the taper end grace-fully, the corner cuts must be stopped before the blade exits the work. The blade is then backed out of the cut and the waste

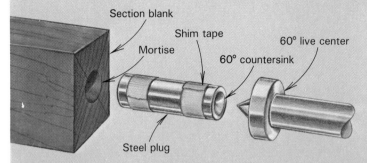

## Fig. 4: Aligning joints

*Tenons are turned on the lathe, which ensures that they are perfectly centered and parallel to the section's centerline. Mortises are bored in the square stock, then the post section is turned using a plug in the mortise to ensure that the post is centered around it.*

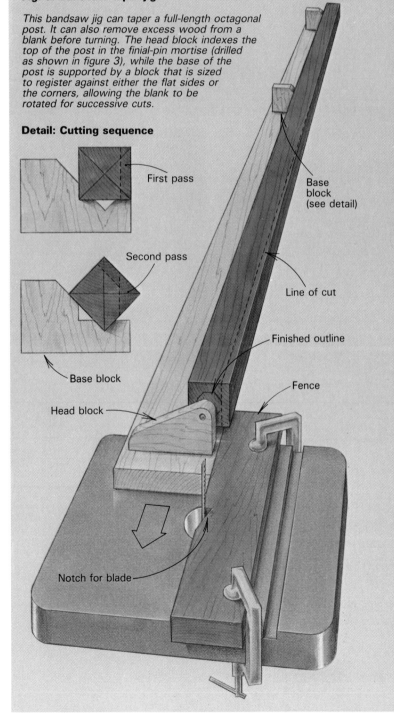

## Fig. 5: Bandsaw taper jig

*This bandsaw jig can taper a full-length octagonal post. It can also remove excess wood from a blank before turning. The head block indexes the top of the post in the finial-pin mortise (drilled as shown in figure 3), while the base of the post is supported by a block that is sized to register against either the flat sides or the corners, allowing the blank to be rotated for successive cuts.*

**Detail: Cutting sequence**

Julian Reid, above, operates a reeding jig—a carriage that rolls along the lathe ways carrying a router mounted on a pivoting arm. A bearing on the bit holder follows the contours of the work, which is locked in position by an indexing plate at the headstock. Mobile bedmaker William Blake, left, demonstrates his similar jig, which uses a simpler solid-pilot bit machined from tool steel (far left). The setscrew visible at the end of the bit locks the V-shaped cutter in place.

Reid's ingenious rope-twist machine, shown below, uses a bit similar to the straight-reeding machine (top), but in this case the carriage is attached to a cable arrangement that hooks up to the headstock spindle. As the operator moves the carriage along the ways, the work rotates a specific, adjustable amount for each inch the carriage moves.

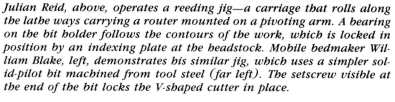

Robert Reid's shopmade duplicating router carves four knees at once, following a pattern mounted in the center.

The Reid shop shapes lamb's tongues on a pencil-post by pattern-sanding the curves on a belt-sander.

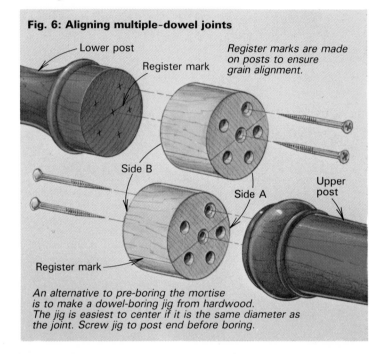

**Fig. 6: Aligning multiple-dowel joints**

Lower post

Register mark

Register marks are made on posts to ensure grain alignment.

Side B

Side A

Upper post

Register mark

An alternative to pre-boring the mortise is to make a dowel-boring jig from hardwood. The jig is easiest to center if it is the same diameter as the joint. Screw jig to post end before boring.

A bed with cabriole legs must have unusually heavy corner posts to withstand the strain put upon the rails. Note that this section of the post carries the tenon. If the tenon were on the upper section, the corner post would have to be mortised, weakening the construction.

nipped off, leaving enough wood for either a lamb's tongue or a simple cove. The Reid shop makes lamb's tongues by pattern-sanding, as shown in the top photo on this page. Lamb's tongues can also be shaped by hand with spokeshaves, carving tools or drum sanders in an electric drill. The tapered faces can be cleaned up with a few strokes of a plane.

An alternative method for aligning sections of a post is shown in figure 6. The joint is held together by four dowels, which are accurately located by means of a hardwood boring jig screwed to the end of the section. The jig is easiest to center if it is made the same diameter as the finished post. Grain alignment is accomplished by registering the jig on reference lines marked on the stock before it is turned. Posts can be clamped up by jacking them against a ceiling joist or by building an extra long clamp.

The jigs shown thus far are enough to make several authentic bedpost designs. But fancy ones call for reeding, fluting, carving and other decorations. In the old days, these chores were done by hand, but Robert Reid quickly found that handwork was too costly, and he soon invented some production methods. As he says: "Any time a machine can make a perfect duplicate of handwork, a man would be foolish to insist on doing the job by hand. But a 100% machine-produced object that arrives at only a 98% duplication of handwork is a compromise with integrity. What you want is whatever the machine can do—25%, 75%, 98%—plus whatever handwork it takes to finish the job right."

The four-man Reid shop can turn out about 125 beds a year, each one taking about two weeks through the system. Every bed is a custom order—the shop will make any combination of posts, headboard and tester. Machines do most of the roughing out, but the final touches still require handwork. There's a duplicating lathe, for example, that follows a pattern with four ounces of pressure on its stylus, and applies 400 pounds of pressure to cut the wood. The bedpost comes off the lathe clean enough that a lot of factories would then simply sand, stain and lacquer it, but Reid's remounts the work on another lathe and refines the shapes by hand-turning.

Similarly, Reid built a router jig, shown in the top photo on the facing page, for reeding bedposts. The work is locked in position by an indexing plate at the headstock. Then the carriage is moved along the lathe bed by hand, and a router mounted on a pivoting arm follows the contours of the work, piloted by the bit holder. Reid's uses a commercial bit holder, with a ½-in. shank and ball-bearing pilot. Bedmaker William Blake has adapted the idea using a bit machined from steel, with the cutter held in place by a setscrew from the end. Blake's cutter and jig are shown in the photos at far left on the facing page.

Reid also built a duplicating router (bottom left, facing page) that follows a carved leg and makes four simultaneous copies. These also get their share of hand carving before stain and lacquer go on. One of Reid's most ingenious machines (left, center) looks like a great-granddaddy of the Sears Router-Crafter. It's a router setup that makes helical rope-twist bedposts, and he cobbled it up from Model-A parts when he was only nineteen years old. Reid recalls the first Victorian rope-twist bed he made: "I had to carve each post by hand, and it seemed like I would never finish. If there's an easier way to do something, I'm going to do my best to uncover it." But it's a safe bet that he's not going to lower his standards to do so. □

Asher Carmichael, whose spider-leg carriage table was in FWW #40, works for Emperor Clock Co., in Fairhope, Ala. Black-and-white photos by the author.

# Adirondack Chair

## A fresh look at an old favorite

### by Bruce Beeken and Jeff Parsons

*Inspired by Vermont artist Janet Fredericks' painting of two old Adirondack chairs (top left photo, facing page), the authors designed their own updated version of this popular outdoor chair. Its straightforward construction lends itself to short-run production.*

For nearly a century, the familiar Adirondack chair has been a part of the north-country landscape. The classic version of these carpenter-cobbled chairs consisted of nailed-together pine boards that were usually given a coat of leftover house paint. Owing to joinery that didn't accommodate wood movement, many Adirondacks soon worked themselves into kindling. Nonetheless, the chair's simple and pleasing form has ensured its popularity as an outdoor chair.

Our interest in the Adirondack chair began several years ago, at a time when we were identifying our shop's emerging goals. We were interested in designing a functional, solid-wood object suitable for short production runs. An exhibit by Janet Fredericks, a local artist whose paintings of rural Vermont life include images of Adirondacks, catalyzed the project. The chair was ideal. It satisfied our requirements and provided us with an opportunity to

improve an already appealing design. The north country had contributed to our aesthetic sensibilities; by building an improved Adirondack chair, we could reciprocate and enjoy that landscape in comfort.

The first Adirondack was built by a Westport, N.Y., man in the early 1900s. It is said that he gathered his family on their lakeside lawn, where he mocked up chairs to test both seat and back angles, searching for a combination that would make the chair's flat boards comfortable. Shortly thereafter he patented the "Westport Chair," which, though popular, was notoriously uncomfortable. Despite this shortcoming and the chair's vulnerability to the weather, the design has proved to be aesthetically durable.

Our chair began at the drawing board. Using the comfort lines described in *Basic Design Measurements for Sitting* (Agricultural Experiment Station, Univ. of Arkansas, Fayetteville, Ark. 72701,

**174**

*Old Adirondack chairs were fastened with rust-prone nails, a shortcoming the authors improved with mechanically sound joints and shipbuilders' trenails.*

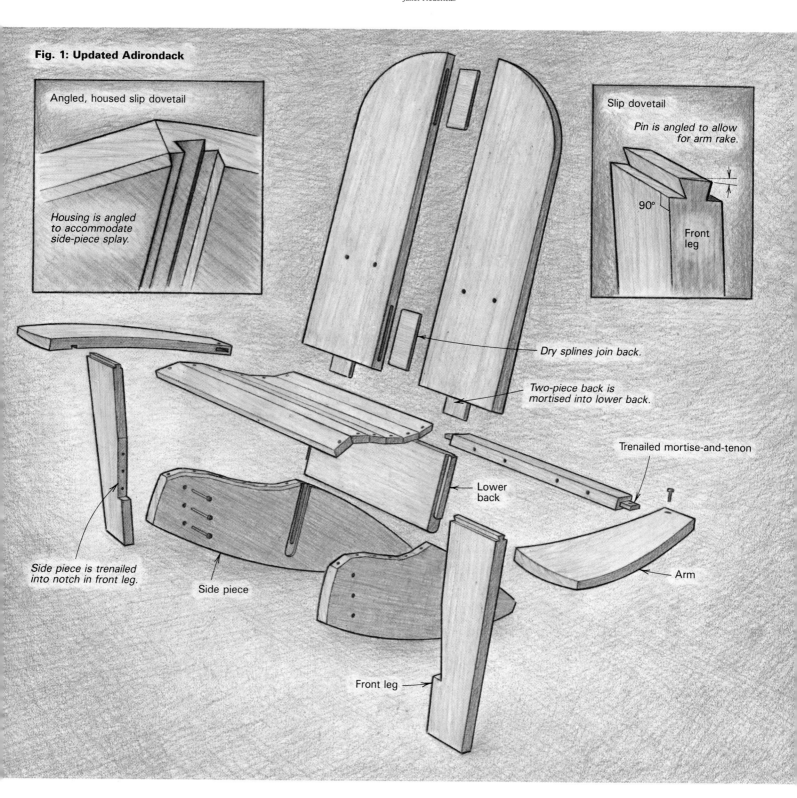

**Fig. 1: Updated Adirondack**

Angled, housed slip dovetail

Housing is angled to accommodate side-piece splay.

Slip dovetail

*Pin is angled to allow for arm rake.*

90°

Front leg

Dry splines join back.

Two-piece back is mortised into lower back.

Trenailed mortise-and-tenon

Lower back

Side piece is trenailed into notch in front leg.

Side piece

Arm

Front leg

# A jig sampler

Jig making, which comprised a large part of our Adirondack chair project, underlies the success of most production runs. The chief function of a production jig is to orient the wood blank so that the part can be reproduced precisely and safely. For efficiency's sake, a jig must suit the movement of both operator and machine. Orientation of joints means that many parts must be made as lefts and rights, thus left and right jigs are often required.

We designed three basic kinds of jigs to make the 16 wooden parts for our chair: jigs for profiling, tapering and joint-cutting. The photos and drawing offer a glimpse into our approach to jig making.

The chair's curved parts—the arms, side pieces and back—were made with a series of shaper profiling jigs. Two of the arm jigs are pictured in the photos at the top of the page. The jigs themselves mimic the specific part's shape. After the blank is bandsawn to within ⅛ in. of the finished profile, the part is mounted and both jig and part are passed through the shaper. The jig's edge guides against a bearing that is part of the shaper's knife collar, and the knives crisply cut the profile in much the same way that a router flush-trim bit works with a template.

Versatility can reduce the number of jigs needed. The six seat slats, for example, were all beveled on the shaper using one jig adjusted to each slat's different bevel angle by a plywood template. Often, though, clamping and machine limitations make one jig impractical. A single jig wouldn't do the arms for us because grain direction and anchor points for the

*The chair's curved parts were produced with shaper profiling jigs such as the two shown for the arms, above left. Two were needed for each arm because clamp anchor points keep the jig from being fed past the knives in one continuous motion. Parsons, above right, has bandsawn a rough arm blank and is shaping it to the final profile with the first jig. He'll mount the part in the other jig to finish the job.*

Bruce Beeken

*By tapering its arms and legs, the authors gave their Adirondack a lighter, more refined personality, while leaving enough wood for strong joints. Above, Parsons feeds the arm-tapering jig through the planer. The arm is tapered in three passes by raising the bed after each cut.*

*The authors' tablesaw doubles as router table, and the fence shown also does double duty. Above, Beeken uses one side of it to mill an angled dovetail pin for the chair's front-leg-to-arm joint. By reversing the fence, he can rout the straight pin for the lower back.*

bulletin 616), we developed overall proportions and the shapes and appropriate cross sections of the joined parts, at the same time considering how each part could be jigged for production. At this stage, it was important to introduce design changes without compromising the character that had first drawn us to the chair.

Functionally, an outdoor chair must be comfortable for extended periods of lounging. The sitter must have enough room to stretch, shift position, or curl up with a blanket. The original Adirondack had a fairly narrow seat and wide, horizontal armrests that tended to be unsympathetic to the elbows. We solved this problem by introducing a wider seat, sweeping curves on the inside edges of the arms, and a sloping arm. The original chair's back-to-seat angle was harsh, and the low-slung seat (6 in. off the ground) made getting out difficult. Seat height should make exiting the chair a simple affair, so we raised it slightly and applied a reverse curve for comfort. The curve also keeps the occupant's back from being jammed into the back/seat intersection and the knees from being clipped by the seat's front edge.

Traditionally, Adirondack chairs were nailed together, sometimes with galvanized fasteners. The problems that such fasteners present when exposed to water are well known to boatmakers. Water wicking along the fastener into the wood causes rapid deterioration. Moisture also swells the wood, and when the wood shrinks with drying, the fasteners become loose, turning the chair wobbly. White cedar's ability to resist rot made this preferred boat material an obvious choice for our chair.

We eliminated metal fasteners entirely, substituting interlocking joints with good mechanical strength at each stress point (figure 1), p. 175. The seasonal stress and movement about the yard to which an outdoor chair is subjected call for stout joinery at key locations, namely where the arms join the front legs and where the lower back joins the upper back and the side pieces, so we used mortise-and-tenons and slip dovetails here. To provide enough material for sound joinery, we made these components out of 6/4 stock. Where possible, we tapered the thick parts—in both length and width—to avoid visual clumsiness.

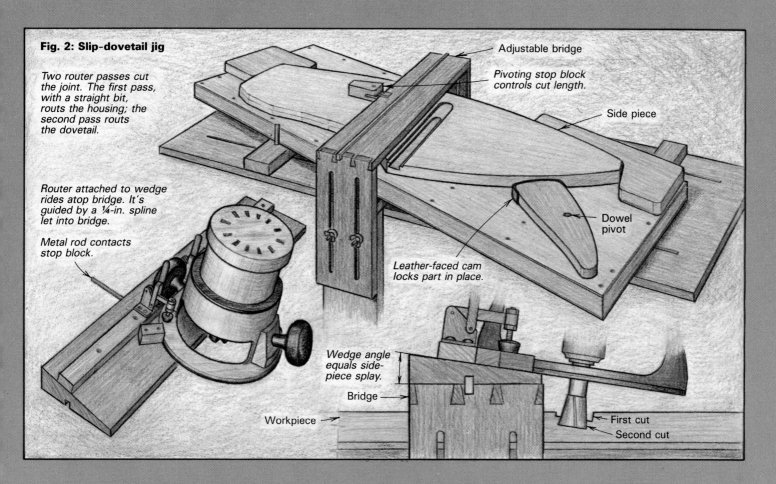

**Fig. 2: Slip-dovetail jig**

Two router passes cut the joint. The first pass, with a straight bit, routs the housing; the second pass routs the dovetail.

Router attached to wedge rides atop bridge. It's guided by a ¼-in. spline let into bridge.

Metal rod contacts stop block.

Adjustable bridge

Pivoting stop block controls cut length.

Side piece

Dowel pivot

Leather-faced cam locks part in place.

Wedge angle equals side-piece splay.

Bridge →

Workpiece →

First cut

Second cut

clamps prevent it from being passed by the spindle in one continuous motion. Double-spindle shapers and different mounting techniques can solve this problem. We have a single-spindle shaper, however, which spins counterclockwise. This requires jigs sympathetic to grain direction, and shaping must be done from both faces.

To give our chair a lighter, more refined look, we tapered the arms and legs in both width and length. This leaves wood where it's needed for strength and joint making,

while removing it where it isn't. The bottom left photo on the facing page shows the taper jig we built to mill the compound tapers. The jig bases are torsion boxes, which are lighter and more stable than solid wood or plywood and much easier to build compound angles into.

Probably the most involved jig is the one for the angled, housed slip dovetail that joins the lower back to the side pieces. (figure 1). In tapering the side pieces, material is removed from one side only, which encourages them to warp. By hous-

ing the dovetail (which is canted to match the angle of the side pieces), we avoided a lot of exasperation in fitting.

Routing the pins for the slip dovetail was simpler. By having the bottom of one of our tablesaw's extension wings machined flat and parallel to the top, we are able to bolt a router under the wing so the saw doubles as a router table. The bit projects through a hole bored in the wing. We clamped an angled fence to the wing, then milled the pins by feeding the stock vertically past a dovetail bit. —B.B., J.P

Where strength wasn't as important, we pinned the parts with trenails (pronounced "trunnels"), traditional shipbuilding fasteners that are really large wooden nails. Trenails are easily turned on the lathe, but we needed two dozen per chair in two sizes, so we found it more economical to buy them from Kisly Systems Inc. (18 Pearce Ave., Manasquan, N.J. 08736). After dipping the rot-resistant locust trenails in marine epoxy, we drove them into tapered, counterbored holes in the joined parts. Shipbuilders leave their trenails proud, flushing them up later with a sharp slick. To avoid cleanup on the finished chairs, we turned a domed head on our trenails and let them project slightly.

After drawings were completed (and the jigs shown on the facing page were designed), we made a prototype, which allowed us to figure production time and provided us with a sales tool. By multiplying the prototype production time by our hourly shop rate, we were able to establish a basis for pricing the chair. To test our business acumen, we presold enough chairs to comprise a run, printed a spec sheet and included a photograph of

the prototype, then sent about 30 flyers to prospective clients, architects and gallery representitives. This resulted in enough sales to proceed with the first run of 18 chairs, a number sufficient to test our economics yet small enough to minimize potential losses. When the last chair was delivered, a review of our figures revealed that a modest 5.5% profit remained after materials, overhead, labor and sales commission.

The chair project proved rewarding in several ways. We delighted in transforming large stacks of live-edged white cedar into symmetrical piles of parts. Learning new production methods introduced us to briskly paced teamwork, and the accurate record-keeping we devised advanced us into realistic business practices. The chair's success was all the more satisfying because we managed to improve a traditional design while producing a piece appropriate to our shop and its surroundings. □

*Bruce Beeken and Jeff Parsons are graduates of Boston University's Program in Artisanry. Their shop is in Shelburne, Vt.*

# Two Sleds

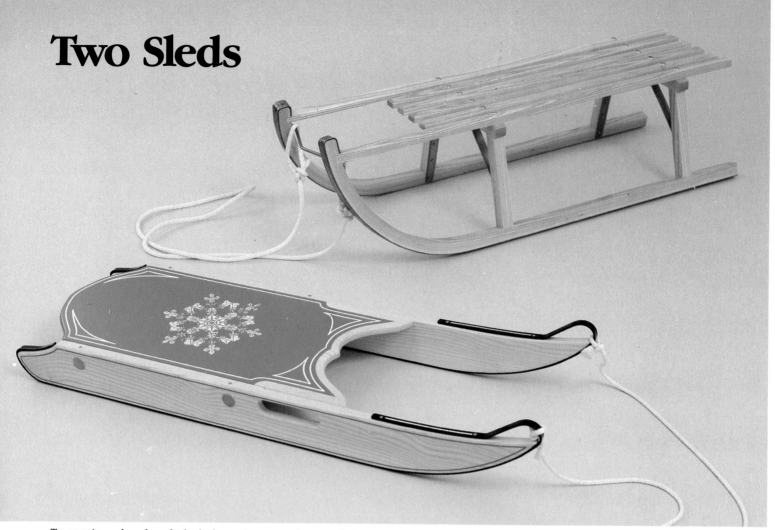

To survive a breakneck dash down a snowy slope, a sled's structure must be robust but relatively light, criteria met by both designs pictured here. Jonathan Shafer's Austrian sled, top, has laminated runners buttressed by steel underpinnings. John Sollinger's simpler hardwood clipper, below, was inspired by traditional 19th-century New England designs.

## *Shiny paint dresses up Vermont clipper*
by John Sollinger

I'd been employed as a full-time woodworker for most of my life and the work had always been satisfying. But ever since my wooden-model building days in grade school, I had always wanted my own shop. Yet I never knew quite what direction my design and building efforts should take. One day about six years ago, my wife suggested I stop talking about it and actually do it. She even had the product: wooden sleds.

Because I live in snowy Vermont, sleds have always been objects of wonder and beauty to me, natural enough, I suppose, from an object that earns its keep toting firewood and groceries yet can still carry passengers on a heart stopping joyride down a steep slope. The design inspiration for the sled shown here came from a couple of magazine articles describing styles of sleds produced in this country during the past century and a half. Substance was added to the style when a neighbor took me on a private tour of the nearby Shelburne Museum's collection of antique sleds and sleighs. The photographs, dimensions, and notes on construction details taken from the sleds at the museum led us to choose the hardwood clipper as our first sled project.

I began three sizes of clippers and finished the smallest in time for my daughter's first Christmas in 1980. An enthusiastic reception encouraged us to establish the Vermont Sled Co. We later added a rocking Holstein cow and some smaller items, but the sleds remain my favorite product. The clipper is handsome, simple and extremely rugged, all of which make it ideal for small-shop production. It's composed of five pieces of wood—a frame consisting of two stretchers tenoned into two runners and a seat or platform whose chief function is to keep the sledder from falling through to the snow, but which also strengthens the frame. The sled's real strength lies in the pinned tenons that join the stretchers to the runners. It's an attractive detail and capable of surviving the constant pounding sleds must endure. Since the runners are fixed, you steer by dragging a heel or toe (depending on riding position) on the side you want to turn toward.

The drawing on the facing page shows construction details. Dimensions can be scaled up or down for any desired size or function. Our sleds range from 32 in. long by 10½ in. wide to 45 in. long by 13 in. wide. Our largest sled, the Long Rider, has a slatted seat and the runners are pierced for lightness and looks. We use ash for the runners, sugar maple for the stretchers, white pine for the seat and hardwood dowels capped by mahogany plugs for pinning the tenons. The runners are shod with mild steel bar stock, available at hardware stores. The sleds are finished with a clear satin-finish polyurethane and

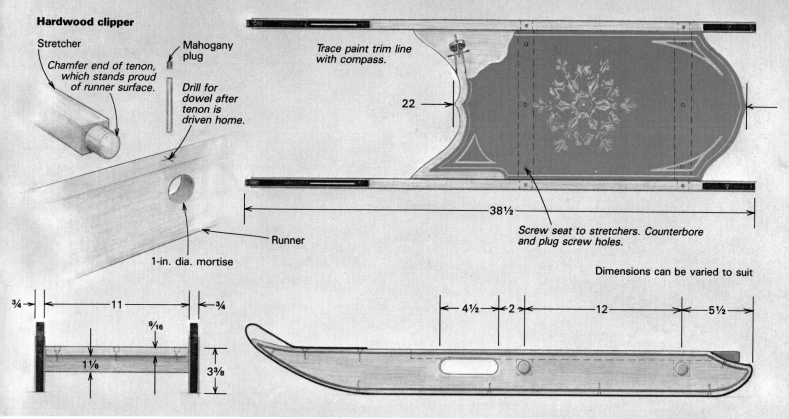

**Hardwood clipper**

Stretcher

Chamfer end of tenon, which stands proud of runner surface.

Mahogany plug

Drill for dowel after tenon is driven home.

1-in. dia. mortise

Runner

Trace paint trim line with compass.

22

38½

Screw seat to stretchers. Counterbore and plug screw holes.

Dimensions can be varied to suit

¾ — 11 — ¾

9/16

1⅛

3⅜

4½ — 2 — 12 — 5½

An extra runner, left, serves as a bending form for the sled's steel shoes. Bent cold, the steel is coaxed with a hammer where overbends are required. To paint the seat, Sollinger masks with tape to layout lines struck with a compass. Once the enamel has dried, he paints pinstripes with a striping wheel guided by hand or, where practical, a straightedge.

over that I spray a high-gloss exterior enamel for color.

Select a board for the runners wide enough to lay out both, top to top—that way color and figure will match. For obvious structural reasons, avoid checks or knots. We bandsaw the runners out of 4/4 stock before thickness planing and we use a pattern to guide final profiling on the shaper and overhead router. All sanding, except final touch-up, is done at this time using a pneumatic sander. Round mortises for the stretcher tenons are drilled after sanding, to keep the edge of the hole from rounding over, ensuring a crisp joint. We cut the stretcher tenons with a chucking tenoner that produces a 1-in.-dia. tenon with a square shoulder, however, you could just as easily turn the tenon on a lathe. Tenon length should be ⅛ in. longer than the thickness of the runner so it will stand proud of the runner's surface. Before assembly, we chamfer the end of the tenon on a disc sander to produce a nice decorative touch.

Pine for the seats is glued up then planed to 9/16 in. before being bandsawn to shape. We glue and screw these seats cross grain to the maple stretchers which is, strictly speaking, not good construction practice. However, we have had no problem with cracking because we avoid checked or figured wood and glue up only when the humidity is in the 40% to 60% range.

That way the seat will neither shrink nor swell enough to cause problems. If you are concerned about the seat cracking, you could skip the glue and fasten it with screws through slotted holes, but the sled will not be as strong. You could also make a slatted seat instead of a solid one.

Once the sled is assembled and sanded with 220-grit paper, you can finish as desired. We apply a coat of satin polyurethane (made by Zip-Guard), let it dry, sand with 220-grit, then spray a final coat. If you don't have a spray rig, brushing will give acceptable results. We use satin polyurethane because it's easy to apply and the enamel for the seat adheres well to it. For the seat's glossy finish, we use an oil-based enamel called Lustaquick made by Kyanize in Everett, Mass. 02149. Local paint stores can order this material and it is worth the wait. The paint has a high solids content and whether sprayed or brushed, it produces a beautiful, durable finish in one coat.

We mask the sled, spray the main color area and, when it has dried, paint the pin stripes with a striping wheel ($11.75 from Brookstone Co., 127 Vose Farm Road, Peterborough, N.H. 03458, catalog number 2812 or from auto-body supply stores). Practice with the wheel before tackling the sled. Good results can also be had with an appropriate-sized sword-striper brush, thinned paint

179

and a steady hand. The snowflake pattern on the seat is taken from a book by W.A. "Snowflake" Bentley, a Vermont farmer who photographed thousands of snowflakes as a hobby during the 1930s. We had a silk screen made to transfer the pattern. For just one sled, you could make a paper stencil and paint it by hand or hand letter a child's name as we are frequently asked to do.

To complete the sled, add steel shoes to the runners. The shoes are of ⅛-in.-thick by ½-in.-wide mild steel, cold bent around a form made from an extra runner screwed to an 8/4 pine base. I added hold downs and bumps where overbending is required to counteract the steel's natural springiness. Mild steel is flexible enough to take sharp bends without breaking and it drills easily. Before bending, we bore and countersink for the screw holes and grind off the flash. The steel is placed in the jig and pulled around, using a hammer and wood block to coax it into the tighter curves. Once bent, it's finished with a rustproof primer and a high-gloss enamel finish coat. Screw the shoes on, add a suitable length of rope and your sled is ready for use.

Our three original sleds have seen four Vermont winters. They're left outside from the first good ground cover (usually November) to the last possible day we feel they can still be used in late March. Off-season storage is in the rafters of our barn where the temperature and humidity reach rather unpleasant extremes. They get rained on, climbed on and generally abused. These sleds are tough and have far exceeded our expectations for usefulness and fun. We fully expect them to become valued possessions of our grandchildren.  □

*With his wife, Sharron, John Sollinger operates the Vermont Sled Co. in North Ferrisberg, Vt.*

# Austrian design has laminated runners                by Jonathan Shafer

One of my fondest childhood memories is of the Christmas I received a wooden wagon with removable sides. After many years of driving it with one leg out for propulsion, hauling people and things and using it as a saw horse in the yard, the wagon was retired to the garage while I finished growing up. I have since rescued the wagon, cleaned it up and built new removable sides. The project gave me the urge to create something unique for my own son, an object that would be worth rescuing from my garage someday. So, with my son's joy of the outdoors as apparent as my desire to graduate from straight-plane woodworking, I built an Austrian sled, based on a picture I saw in an L.L. Bean catalog.

As the drawing on the facing page shows, the sled has a slatted seat attached to a pair of frames that join the runners. The runners themselves are laminated using the form shown or, if you prefer, they can be steambent. In either case, you'll need to construct the bending form, as well as the jigs to cut the angled mortise and tenons that hold the frame together. The bending form should be made longer, both vertically and horizontally, than the runner so the laminae can be clamped to it. The excess runner length is cut off later.

I laminated the runners out of white ash but any species with good bending characteristics and straight grain will do, such as the oaks or hickories. I made my laminae ¼ in. thick so only four were required for each runner. Laminae this thick may have a tendency to spring back and if this becomes a problem, use thinner strips. If you soak the wood in hot water first, it will bend easier, but then you must clamp the strips in the form and let them dry overnight before gluing. I used epoxy glue for the runners, which, in addition to being waterproof, is good at filling any small gaps between the laminae.

The mortises in the runners that accept the uprights were cut on a shop-built horizontal router table, like that shown in *FWW* #42, pp. 50-51. So the sled will have good torsional strength, the uprights are splayed out 13°, requiring angled mortises where the uprights join the seat crosspieces. I devised the router mortising jig shown in the drawing to cut the angled mortises. I cut the tenons for the uprights on the tablesaw, using a dado blade and with the miter gauge set to 77°. To position the shoulder cuts precisely, I fastened a board to the miter gauge then clamped a stop block to it, referencing each shoulder cut against the stop block. If you don't have a dado blade, cut the tenons with repetitive passes over a regular blade, then clean up the cheeks with a sharp chisel.

After a dry run to check the fit of all the joints, glue the two uprights into each seat crosspiece using the fixture illustrated. Before applying clamp pressure, square the frames by measuring diagonally from the upright/crosspiece intersection to the inside of the crosspiece shoulder, adjusting the frame until the measurements are equal. When these joints have cured overnight, use the same fixture (move the cleats to accommodate the runner) to glue the uprights into the runners.

The seat, or deck, is composed of six slats. The two outermost ones are wedged-shaped in section and are let into an open mortise in the top inside edge of each runner. I found it easiest to mark the slat's cross section right on the runner then saw and chisel the mortise by hand. However, I didn't glue the exterior slats in place until after I'd fitted the steel runner caps so that I could butt the steel tightly against the wood. The four interior slats are rectangular in section but their edges are radiused with a ¼-in. roundover bit. All of the slats are attached to the crosspieces with flathead brass woodscrews and decorative washers.

Finish up by attaching frame braces, a tow bar and steel caps to the runners. The frame braces are of ⅛-in.-thick steel, ¾ in. wide and the runner caps are the same steel, 1 in. wide; the tow bar is a ¼-in.-dia. rod. Since I didn't have access to a forge, I cold bent the steel where possible. However, to bend the caps sharply around the tips of the runners, I heated the steel to a cherry-red glow in a barbeque grill then bent it around a wooden block identical to the runner's cross section. I also heated the ends of the tow bar and flattened them with a hammer to yield a better bearing surface where the bar contacts the runners. The metal parts are attached to the sled with countersunk wood screws. Three coats of Deft Exterior Clear Stain #2 polyurethane, applied over wood and metal parts, completed the project.  □

*Jonathan Shafer lives in Columbus, Ohio, where he works in the construction industry. The commercial version of the sled is made by Paris Manufacturing Co. in South Paris, Maine.*

## An Austrian sled

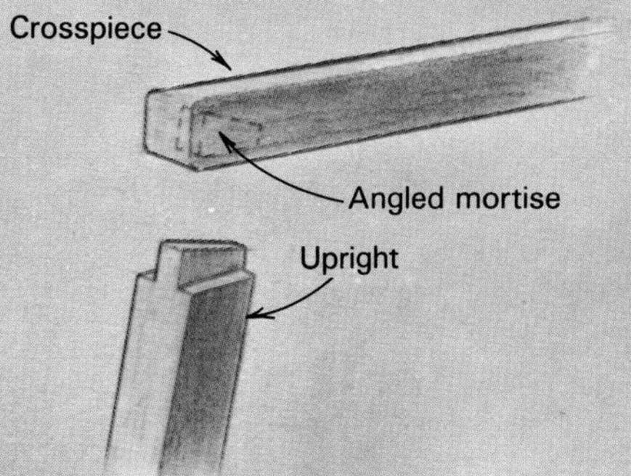

Crosspiece
Angled mortise
Upright


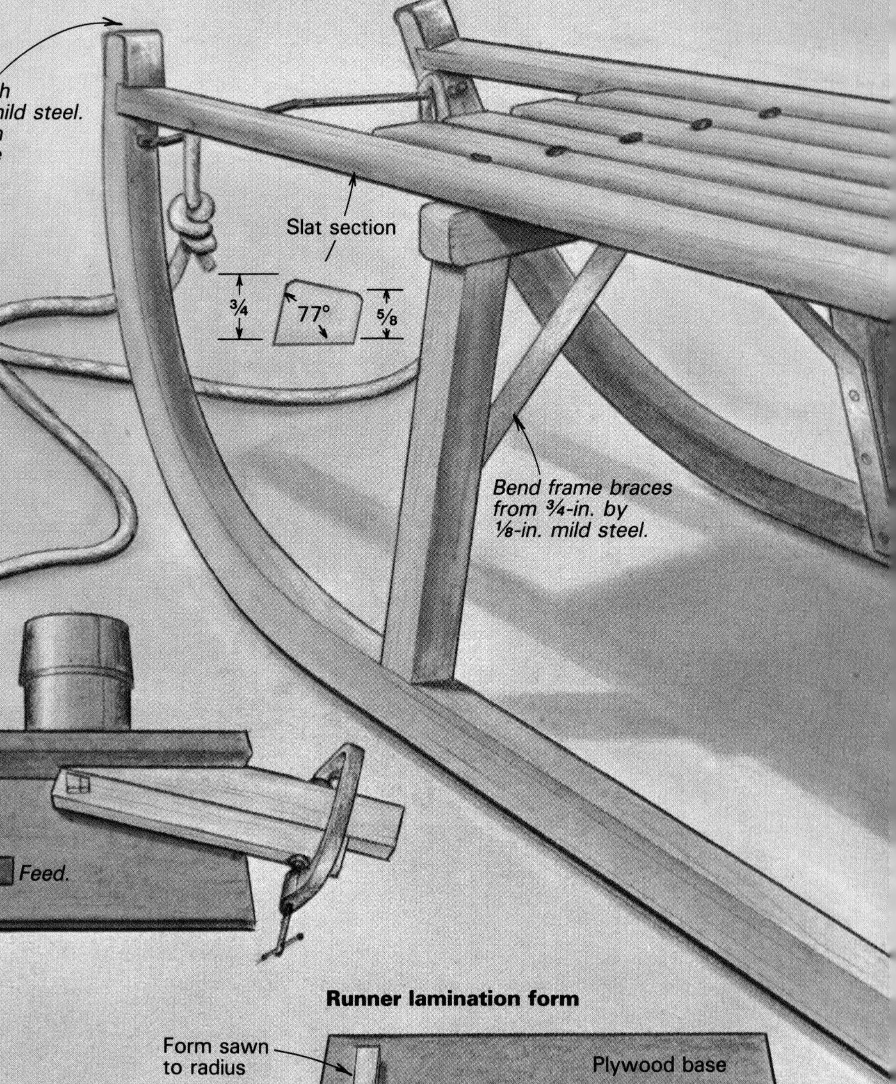

Cap runners with 1-in. by 1/8-in. mild steel. Bend and attach steel cap before gluing slat.
Slat section
3/4
77°
5/8
Bend frame braces from 3/4-in. by 1/8-in. mild steel.


**Angled-mortise router jig**

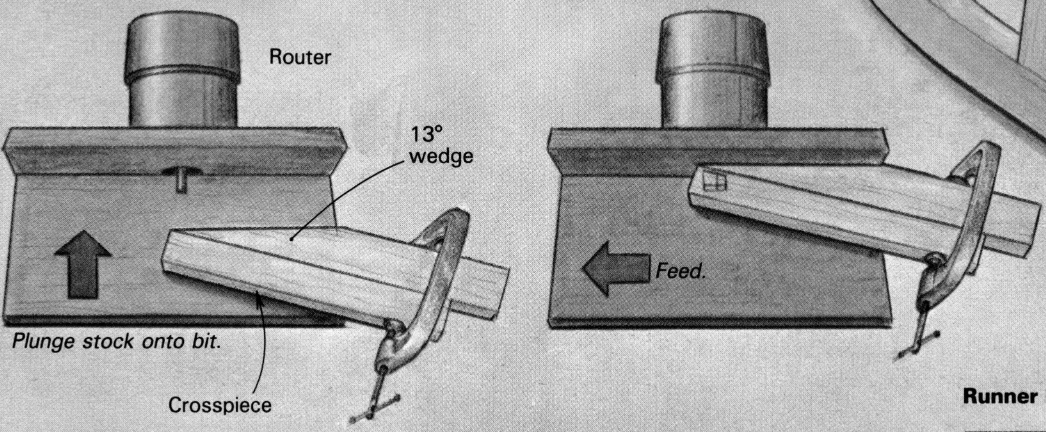

Router
13° wedge
Plunge stock onto bit.
Crosspiece
Feed.


**Runner lamination form**

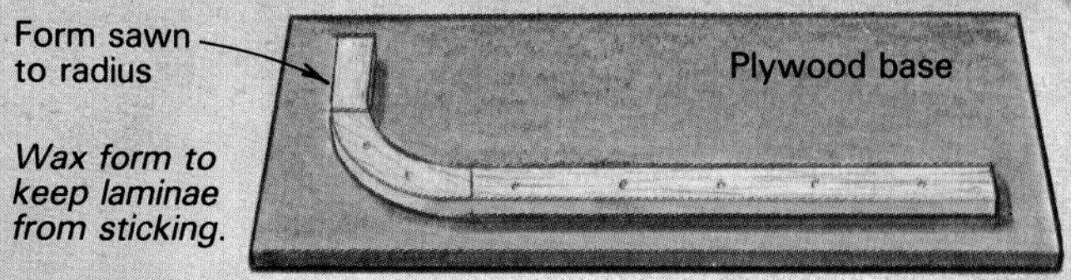

Form sawn to radius
Plywood base
Wax form to keep laminae from sticking.


**Upright and crosspiece glueup**

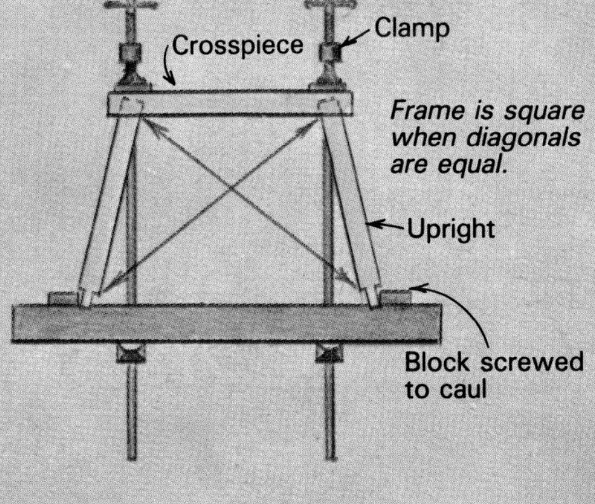

Crosspiece
Clamp
Frame is square when diagonals are equal.
Upright
Block screwed to caul


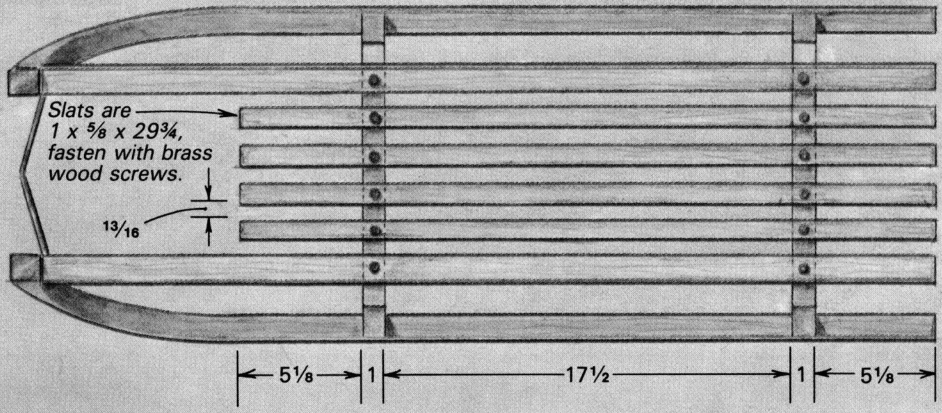

Slats are 1 x 5/8 x 29 3/4, fasten with brass wood screws.
13/16
5 1/8
1
17 1/2
1
5 1/8


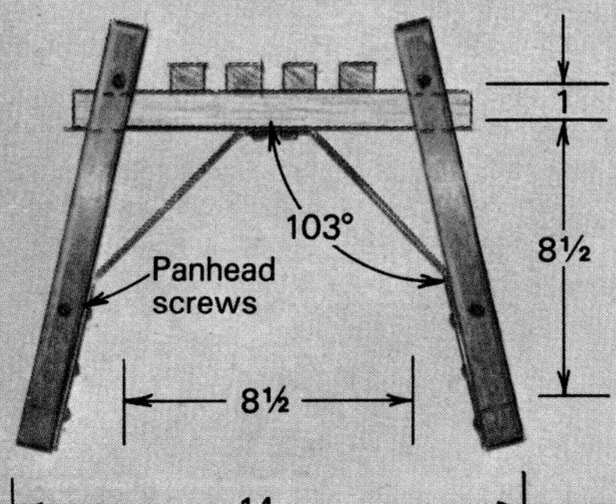

1
103°
8 1/2
Panhead screws
8 1/2
14


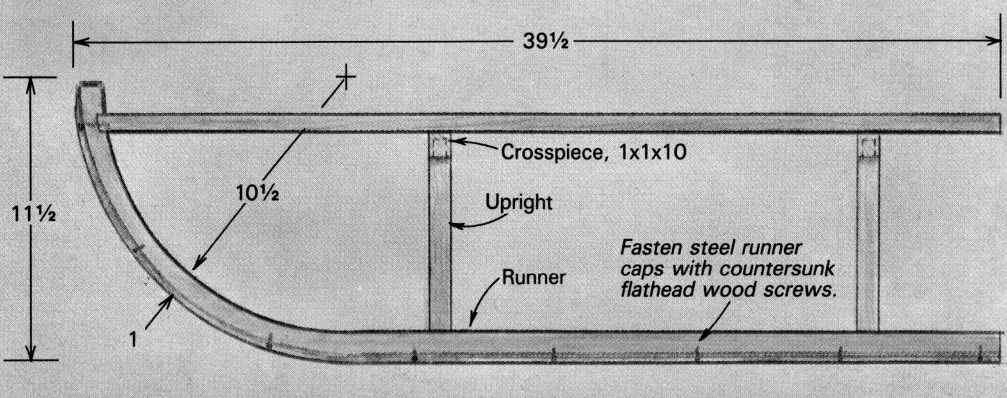

39 1/2
11 1/2
10 1/2
Crosspiece, 1x1x10
Upright
Runner
Fasten steel runner caps with countersunk flathead wood screws.
1

# Provincial Corner Cupboard
## No-frills country joinery

by Carlyle Lynch

Corner cupboards have long been popular for transforming useless room corners into efficient storage areas that seem to blend right into the walls. Even though these triangular pieces were designed to be purely functional, early craftsmen couldn't resist turning them into beautiful showcases of their own skill. Often they added distinctive touches like the arched panel doors on the cupboard shown above, which is now in the Great Hall of the Tuckahoe Plantation in Richmond, Va.

The simplicity of this one-piece walnut and riftsawn yellow pine cupboard suggests that it was made by a country craftsman at Tuckahoe shortly after the plantation was built in 1712. Tuckahoe, now a national historic landmark, is noted for its architecture and furnishings, so it's not surprising that a cabinetmaker working there would have tried to make the cupboard special. Later, as the cabinetmakers' art flourished in America, corner cupboards were embellished with more intricate moldings, bracket feet and delicately framed glass doors.

My measured drawing and bill of materials (pp. 183 and 184) show the lumber thicknesses of the original, but more conventional stock sizes will work all right. The carcase sides and doors can be ⅞ in. or ¹³⁄₁₆ in. thick. You could make the back panels from ½-in. boards and work the cornice from ¾-in. stock.

While it's impossible to know exactly how the original maker went about constructing the piece, I think that this practical worker might have made the shelves, bottom and top first, then simply nailed or pinned the two sides and back center piece to them. This formed a rigid skeleton to which the rails, molding and doors could be added. Even though the cabinetmaker used nails (you can feel them if you insert a thin knife between the shelves and sides), it's difficult to see any nail holes on the sides. I suspect that he filled the holes with tiny plugs, carefully matching the grain of the sides—pretty sophisticated work.

Since the hexagonal shelf units are 19 in. deep, you'll have to edge-glue several narrower boards to get the required width. Saw the pieces a little longer than needed in case individual boards shift slightly in the clamps. You can trim the shelves to size after the glue has cured. For additional strength, or perhaps because the cabinetmaker didn't bother to thickness-

plane parts that wouldn't show, the waist shelf, top and bottom on the original are thicker than the other shelves.

The sides and back center piece are made from single long boards. On each side, bevel the front edge 22½° so it can butt against the beveled door to form a 45° corner, and rabbet the back edge for the back panels. Bevel both edges of the back center piece to 45°. Now nail these pieces to the shelves—one way would be to prop up the hexagonal top on the floor and tack a side to it, then prop up the bottom and tack the side to it. All the shelves are permanent, so while the assembly is still on the floor, nail the remaining shelves to the side, then nail on the second side. The cupboard framing should now be rigid enough for you to flip it over and nail the back center piece to the shelves.

Next pin the top, waist and base rails to the cupboard. The rail ends are beveled 22½° and appear butted to the sides, forming a 45° angle between them. I suspect, however, that blind tenons or splines (figure 2) may have been used for extra strength. Once the rails are in place, nail the shiplapped boards to the back center piece, shelves and sides.

The basic cupboard is now ready for some decorative touches. Make and apply all moldings—the profiles used on the original are shown on the plan. Miter the waist molding to fit the 45° angles on the sides. For the cornice, make a coving cut on the tablesaw (FWW #35, pp. 65-67), then form the beads with a shaper or router. If you're really ambitious, you could also hand-carve or plane the molding. If you're less zealous, you may be able to find patterns close to the originals at a well-stocked mill shop.

Next make the doors. Make sure you work carefully—it's too late to change the carcase, should you make the doors undersize (which is why some cabinetmakers prefer to make the doors first, then build the carcase to fit). Through mortise-and-tenons are used on the original door frames, but figure 3 on p. 184 shows an easier way to build the frames with blind mortises. Cut all the door stiles and rails to size, then mold and plow the inside edges to accept the panels before you lay out and cut the mortises and tenons. On the original, the grooves are about ¼ in. to ⁵⁄₁₆ in. deep. To assemble the frames, you'll have to miter the molded edges of the stiles so they can be fitted to the rails. A 45° guide block and a sharp chisel will work well to miter the mold-

Photo: Taylor Dabney

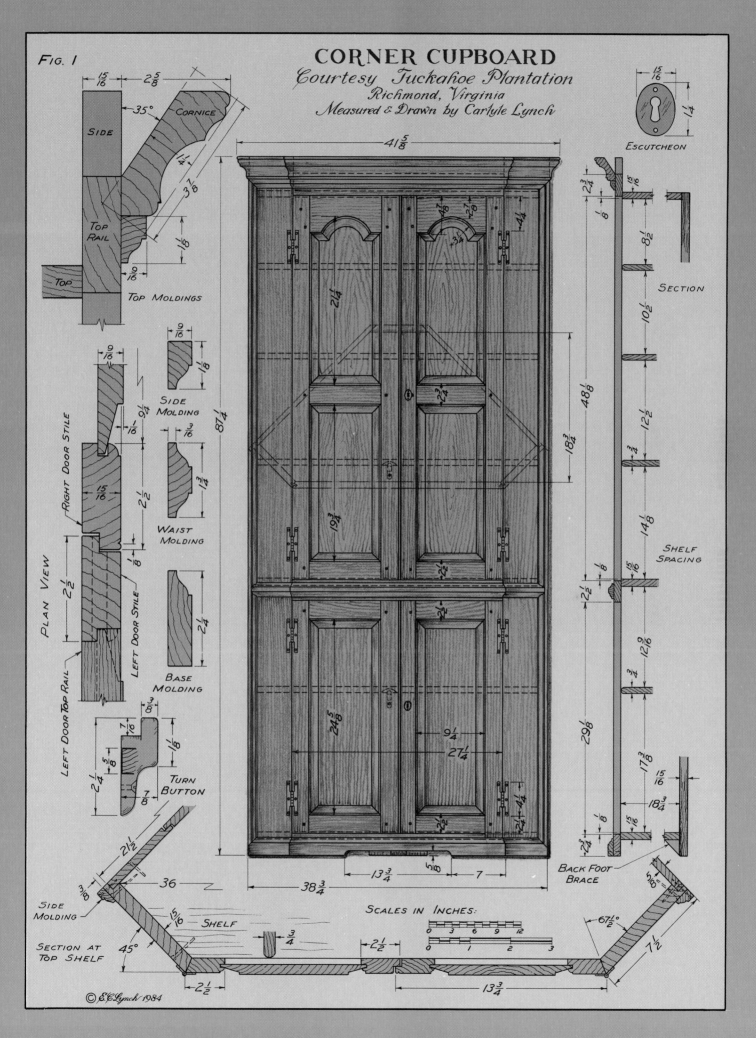

# CORNER CUPBOARD

*Courtesy Tuckahoe Plantation*
*Richmond, Virginia*
*Measured & Drawn by Carlyle Lynch*

FIG. 1

SIDE

CORNICE

TOP RAIL

TOP

TOP MOLDINGS

ESCUTCHEON

SECTION

SIDE MOLDING

WAIST MOLDING

BASE MOLDING

PLAN VIEW

RIGHT DOOR STILE

LEFT DOOR STILE

LEFT DOOR TOP RAIL

TURN BUTTON

SHELF SPACING

BACK FOOT BRACE

SIDE MOLDING

SHELF

SECTION AT TOP SHELF

SCALES IN INCHES:

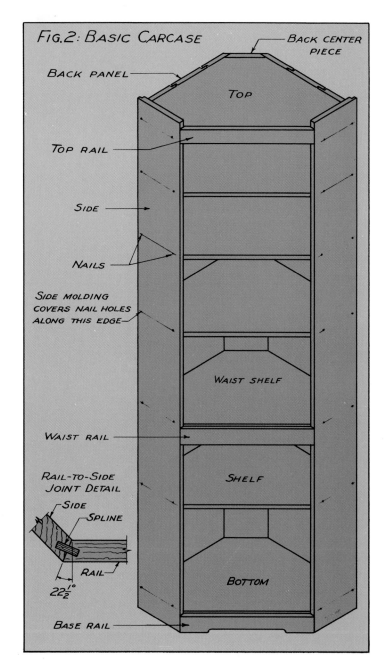

**FIG.2: BASIC CARCASE**

BACK CENTER PIECE

BACK PANEL

TOP

TOP RAIL

SIDE

NAILS

SIDE MOLDING COVERS NAIL HOLES ALONG THIS EDGE

WAIST SHELF

WAIST RAIL

RAIL-TO-SIDE JOINT DETAIL

SIDE

SPLINE

SHELF

RAIL

$22\frac{1}{2}°$

BOTTOM

BASE RAIL

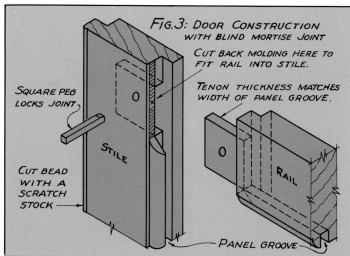

**FIG.3: DOOR CONSTRUCTION WITH BLIND MORTISE JOINT**

CUT BACK MOLDING HERE TO FIT RAIL INTO STILE.

SQUARE PEG LOCKS JOINT

TENON THICKNESS MATCHES WIDTH OF PANEL GROOVE.

STILE

CUT BEAD WITH A SCRATCH STOCK

RAIL

PANEL GROOVE

ing. (For more on scribed joints, see *FWW #33*, pp. 76-81.)

Once you know the size of the frames, you can make the panels. The straight ones can be cut with a shaper, with a table-saw and router, or by hand. The arched ones need handwork. Careful work with a chisel will raise the arch and give you a nice sense of accomplishment (see pp. 11-13 in this book).

Assemble the doors with glue and clamp them to dry, making sure they're flat and square. Fit the panels loosely (don't glue them) so they'll have room to swell when the weather turns damp. To ensure a tight fit, peg the frame joints with square pins.

Before you install the doors, rabbet one edge of each right-hand door to fit over the left-hand one. With a scratch stock, make a ⅛-in. bead on the right-hand doors. Bevel the hinge edges of the doors to 22½° to match the cupboard sides, and install the hinges with steel screws. After the doors are hung, remove the hardware, then sand and finish the cupboard. I recommend that you fill the grain with dark silica-base filler, then apply two coats of Minwax Antique Oil finish. When I rehang the doors, I usually substitute brass screws for the steel ones. □

*Carlyle Lynch, a designer, cabinetmaker and retired teacher, lives in Broadway, Va. Drawings by the author.*

| **BILL OF MATERIALS** | | | **Dimensions** | | | | | **Dimensions** |
|---|---|---|---|---|---|---|---|---|
| Amt. | Description | Wood | T x W x L | | Amt. | Description | Wood | T x W x L |
| 2 | Sides | walnut | $\frac{15}{16}$ x 7½ x 87¼ | | | Upper doors: | | |
| 2 | Top and base rails | walnut | $\frac{15}{16}$ x 2¾ x 27¼* | | 4 | stiles | walnut | $\frac{15}{16}$ x 2½ x 48 |
| 1 | Waist rail | walnut | $\frac{15}{16}$ x 2½ x 27¼* | | 2 | top rails | walnut | $\frac{15}{16}$ x 4⅞ x 9¼ s/s |
| 1 | Cornice | walnut | 1¼ x 3⅞ x 50** | | 2 | center rails | walnut | $\frac{15}{16}$ x 2¾ x 9¼ s/s |
| 1 | Waist molding | walnut | $\frac{9}{16}$ x 1¾ x 45** | | 2 | bottom rails | walnut | $\frac{15}{16}$ x 2½ x 9¼ s/s |
| 1 | Base molding | walnut | $\frac{9}{16}$ x 2¼ x 45** | | 2 | top panels | walnut | $\frac{9}{16}$ x 9¼ x 21¼ |
| 2 | Side moldings | walnut | $\frac{9}{16}$ x 1⅛ x 84 | | 2 | bottom panels | walnut | $\frac{9}{16}$ x 9¼ x 19¾ |
| 1 | Top molding | walnut | $\frac{9}{16}$ x 1⅛ x 45 | | | Lower doors: | | |
| 4 | Shelves | pine | ¾ x 19 x 36¼ | | 4 | stiles | walnut | $\frac{15}{16}$ x 2½ x 29 |
| 3 | Waist shelf, top, and bottom | pine | $\frac{15}{16}$ x 19 x 36¼ | | 4 | rails | walnut | $\frac{15}{16}$ x 2½ x 9¼ s/s |
| | | | | | 2 | panels | walnut | $\frac{9}{16}$ x 9¼ x 24⅝ |
| 1 | Back center piece | pine | $\frac{15}{16}$ x 7¾ x 83¼ | | 24 | Tenon pins | walnut | ¼ x ¼ x 1¼ |
| 2 | Back panels, shiplapped | pine | ⅝ x 21½ x 83¼ | | 1 | Back foot brace | pine | 2 x 2 x 2 |
| | | | | | 2 | Turn buttons | walnut | ⅝ x ⅞ x 2¼ |

Hardware: Eight polished-brass H-hinges, 1½ x 4¼; two wardrobe locks with barrel keys, 1¼-in. selvage to key pin; two polished-brass oval escutcheons.

* Long point to long point.
** Makes front and side moldings.
s/s = shoulder to shoulder. Allow 2¾ in. to 3 in. for through tenons.

# Klompen
## Shoes from trees

by Anne Siegel

Bob Siegel makes wooden shoes from green Aspen chunks with tools like this spoon auger used to hollow out each shoe. The shoes are wedged in a notch cut into his walnut-log workbench. The flat end of the bench is a cutting board for rough shaping the shoes with an ax. When not in use, the rest of his tools hang from pegs in the front of the bench.

About 15 years ago my father, obligingly following my mother into another Wisconsin antiques store, spotted something interesting and emerged with an armful of oddly shaped tools. A full-time insurance agent and weekend woodworker, he never dreamed that he was carrying the remnants of the dying European craft of wooden shoe making.

In 1912 there were about 4,000 carvers in the Netherlands who each year produced about six million pairs of inexpensive, durable shoes for the farmers, fishermen and other workers. Each carver made about five pairs per day—splitting each one out of a log with a froe, then shaping the exterior with an ax and long knife and hollowing the inside with a spoon-shaped auger. The Netherlands now produces about three million pairs per year, most of them for tourists, but today they're turned out by duplicating lathes and boring machines following models handcarved by the few remaining craftsmen.

The Dutch call their wooden shoes *klompen* after the "klomp, klomp" sound they make on cobblestone streets. In France they're called *sabots*. Workers protesting the 19th-century mechanical wonders that were putting them out of work, threw their *sabots* into the whirring machines at several factories. They didn't derail the Industrial Age but they created the word sabotage.

As his collection of old tools grew, my father, Bob Siegel Jr., (everyone calls him Sieg) became interested in the history and carving of these shoes. Sieg decided to learn how to use the tools so he could demonstrate the craft. He began in the early 70s by observing a master *klompenmaker* in Orange City, Iowa, and another in Holland, Mich. Later he spent three weeks in the Netherlands, where he studied with 12 *klompenmakers*.

Each man had his own methods of carving, and sometimes different tools, but the result was always the same—a shoe that fit the foot. The skill of the craft is not so much in using the tools or in the unique shape of the finished product, but in having the shape of the foot in mind and carving it by eye quickly and efficiently. The carvers found that the only way to master the art of carving a foot shape inside a block of wood was to carve a lot of shoes.

Aspen is the best shoe wood, although willow and beech can also be used. The wood should be lightweight, split and carve easily, resist checking and not discolor with age. Since the wood is always worked green, carvers would often move right out to the forest, cut down a tree and turn the whole thing into piles of shoes—a mature aspen yields about 75 pairs. Dry wood is harder to cut and tends to split when the shoe is hollowed out. The carved wet wood doesn't usually check when it dries, perhaps because the carving, from start to finish, takes less than two hours and the thin sides dry simultaneously inside and out.

Sieg works on a walnut-log workbench, trimmed underneath until it weighs about 70 pounds—light enough to carry, but still heavy enough to be stable. Instead of a vise, he's cut a deep, wide notch into one end of the bench top where he can wedge a pair of shoes while hollowing them. The top stands on three splayed legs secured from underneath with wedges. Removable pegs in the front and sides of the bench hold his tools—a mallet for securing wedges, a metric ruler, a rasp for enlarging the instep and a wooden bit brace to bore tiny holes in the sides to string the shoes together.

*Klompen* are carved in pairs, so the carver can concentrate on making the shoes the same size and give them the proper left-foot, right-foot contours. The carver needs three measurements—

the length of the person's foot; the length of the log section to be crosscut (20% longer than the foot gives you enough wood for a strong toe and heel) and the inside length of the shoe, which is generally a little greater than the footlength.

To carve a pair for a one-year-old child, for example, you need a 6-in. blank. Cross cut the log to length, then split it into quarters with a froe and maul. Sieg then uses a side ax, a one-hand version of the hewing ax, to smooth two adjacent surfaces at right angles to each other. These flat sides will be the side and the sole of the shoe. Then he chops the remaining sides until he has roughed out the shoe exterior to within a ¼-in. of its final contours. It takes about 10 minutes to chop out a pair.

Next, he refines the exterior shape with a block knife, a long blade with a handle at one end and a little curlicue at the other. The curlicue end fits loosely into a screw eye at one end of the bench, so the knife can be used like a paper cutter for straight cuts and rotated slightly in the screw eye to do a curved cut (photo 3, facing page). The long blade gives the knife powerful leverage and enough control to shave a pair of *klompen* to a nearly finished stage in about 20 minutes. It's important to accurately shape the exterior so that when the *klompen* are hollowed out to fit the foot, the top and side walls will be only about ⅜ in. thick.

The rough shoe is now wedged into the bench notch. With a spoon auger, Sieg bores a hole near the heel by pressing down hard on the shaft, while simultaneously twirling the handle. If you hold the auger handle with your right hand, you'd twist it clockwise; lefthanders go counterclockwise. You control the cut by holding the lower shaft with your other hand. The first wood section removed will look like a button. On large *klompen*, Sieg bores a second hole, just in front of the shoe's high crown (roughly equivalent to the top of the tongue on a leather shoe), then breaks out the wood between the holes. He spoons out the rest of the heel area, just as you would scoop ice cream from a bucket.

Working with his spoon auger, Sieg bores a hole from the heel to the toe, slightly longer than the person's foot, then enlarges the opening, scooping circular curls of wood from the lower half of the *klompen* until the walls are the right thickness and the arch is properly contoured. He can hollow out a pair of *klompen* in about 30 minutes.

Sieg releases the nearly completed shoes from the bench and trims them with the block knife. Finally, the inside front half of each shoe is smoothed with a long chisel that's hooked at the end and the outside is scraped smoooth with a metal scraper or a piece of glass. Sometimes the shoes are left unfinished, sometimes they are painted. In some European areas where the low-cost wooden shoes are considered poor people's fare, a Sunday pair might be painted black and outfitted with glued on laces and eyelets until they looked like real leather shoes. Sieg decorates many of his with carved tulips, hearts and windmills.

Sieg now demonstrates *klompen*-carving at trade shows, festivals and other events around the country and sells full-sized shoes for adults, who buy them for the same reasons that European workers do—*klompen* worn with thick socks are warm in winter; with thin socks they are cool in summer. They're good safety shoes and easy to slip on and off. They also keep your feet dry when working in the garden or another damp area, and, if you get tired of wearing them, they make unique mantle pieces. ☐

*Anne Siegel is editor of* Oregon Magazine *in Portland Ore. Bob Siegel lives in Mequon, Wisc.*

*A froe and mallet split the shoe blank out of the green log (1). A 10-in. diameter log yields four blanks. Sieg uses a side ax to square the sole and one side, then begins shaping the shoe (2). The ax is beveled only on the side away from the cut, making it an efficient planing and carving tool. After bracing the shoe with his bench and thigh (3), he refines the shoe shape with the lever-like block knife that pivots in a screw eye attached to the bench. The leverage of the long block knife makes it good for heavy crossgrain paring (4).*

*Sieg wedges the shoes to the bench, which he braces with his legs (5), then bores a hole in the heel with a T-handled spoon auger. After boring two holes, he uses the auger like a pry bar to break out large chunks of waste from between the two holes (6). After clearing the heel, Sieg uses the spoon auger like an ice cream scoop to enlarge the opening and shape it to fit the foot (7). Large curls of wood are removed from the top (8), until the wall reaches proper thickness and from the bottom until the arch is properly contoured for support and comfort.*

To hollow toe, Sieg turns the auger with his right hand while guiding the shaft with his left (9 and 10). The block knife creates a ready-to-wear finish (11).

# Queen Anne Handkerchief Table

*Building a three-cornered masterpiece*

by Eugene Landon

*Landon's reproduction of a rare 18th-century handkerchief table is a study in pure Queen Anne lines.*

In the middle of a very busy workday about four years ago, the phone rang. It was an elderly acquaintance who lived in a nearby town, calling to inquire whether I would be willing to repair a piece of furniture for her. "It's a handkerchief table," she said.

I couldn't leave what I was working on for a week or so, but agreed to go and look at the table when things slowed down a little. Secretly, I had my doubts about the piece—the handkerchief table is one of the rarest American furniture forms. Perhaps what she had was the larger version, usually called a breakfast table, or perhaps something else entirely. I mused about it for a moment, but almost as soon as I returned to what I had been doing, the table went completely from my mind.

Two years later, out of the blue, I heard the same voice over the phone again:

"Mr. Landon, aren't you interested in my table?" The earlier conversation came back to me instantly, along with a considerable flush of embarrassment. "I'll be right over," I said.

When I entered her home, I saw that she knew what she had all right.

The little table took my breath away. Even though it was missing the leaf, the hinged leg and all its knee blocks, it had a presence that epitomized pure Queen Anne, before cabinetmakers under the Chippendale influence began to add shells and gingerbread. I have nothing against Chippendale, but while such decoration may sometimes enhance a piece, it may also serve to disguise basic flaws in design. The little table was so stylistically pure that any such shortcomings would have stood out immediately. As I walked around the piece, I gradually realized that it had no flaws at all; it was perfect.

Much as I dislike extravagant claims, I believe that this handkerchief table is not only excellent Queen Anne, but that it is one of the finest pieces of furniture ever made in any time or place. You simply will not find a shaplier leg, nor one more perfectly proportioned to the rest of the table. The genius of the maker is evident everywhere: The four notched corners of the open top serve to restrain the eye's travel, yet when the leaf is down, the opened notches blend into a lovely curve. The back of the ankle is undercut just the right amount, the merest touch, to give the entire table poise and an irresistible uplifted energy. Even the chamfer on the front corner post strikes just the right balance—it defines the corner elegantly, yet is neither too sharp nor too weak.

It turned out that the table had been made in Boston, circa 1740, and that it had been in my client's family ever since the day it was made. The owner agreed to let me make a copy for myself, and I was so

convinced of the rarity and authenticity of the find that I took photos of it to Israel Sack, the antiques experts, in New York City. Robert Sack told me that the firm, in 32 years of business, had handled only one or two similar tables. My client's was truly as rare as I had thought.

I made my copy by following plans that I traced from the original. Figure 3 on p. 191, in fact, was adapted from a rubbing of the original table, which I made when I had the top off. The joinery has been added, and also the outline of the legs to show their orientation. I would advise you to redraw this top view full-size, and to add the joinery and wooden-hinge details as well. This step will immediately clarify the project and will also allow you to cut pieces to fit the sizes and angles on the drawing, rather than trying to measure them.

My table—my wife's table, as Jane would remind me—stands with its folded leaf against a wall in our living room. This shows the decorative apron on both sides. The table could also go in a corner, with the leaf folded down in front, or it could stand next to an armchair or a sofa, being just about the right height to hold a reading lamp. Because my table stands with its 90° corner facing forward, I'm calling that leg the front one; the folded leaf and the hinged leg are at the back of the table. The table also has a left leg and a right leg, both at the rear. The legs all end up different, so it is important to know which one is which.

The front leg is made like a regular Queen Anne leg, following the template shown in figure 1. Indeed, all the other legs *start* the same way, but then each must be modified. The rear legs, for example, are glued to the aprons, then their corner posts and the tops of their knees are reshaped to blend into the acute angle, as shown in the photo on p. 190. As also shown, the knee block of the left rear

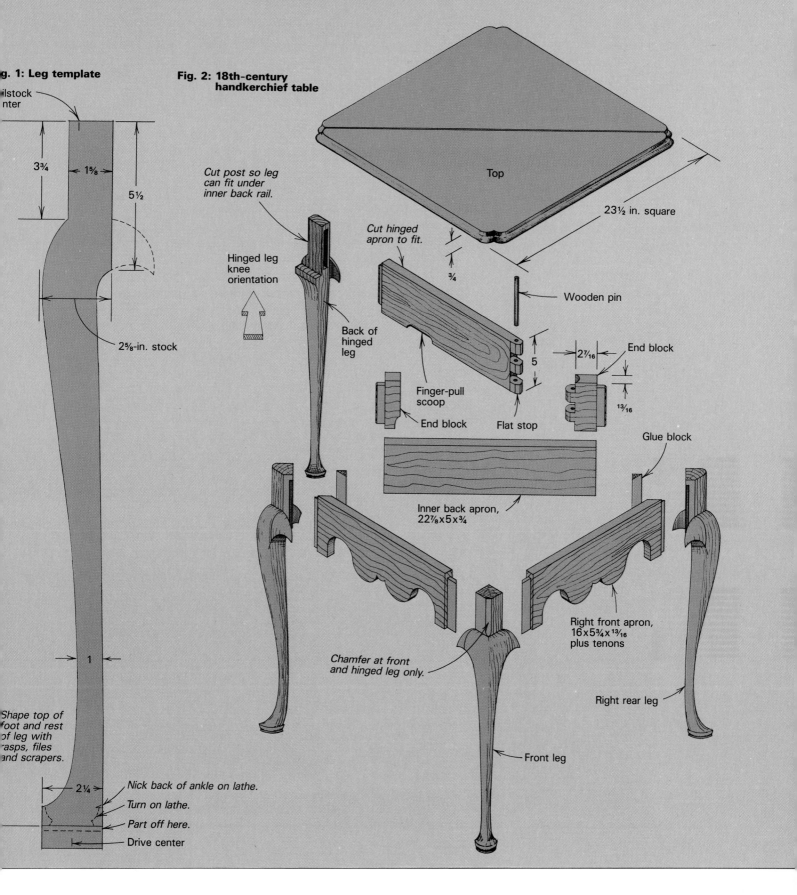

**Fig. 1: Leg template**

Tailstock center

$3\frac{3}{4}$

$1\frac{5}{8}$

$5\frac{1}{2}$

$2\frac{5}{8}$-in. stock

1

Shape top of foot and rest of leg with rasps, files and scrapers.

$2\frac{1}{4}$

Nick back of ankle on lathe.

Turn on lathe.

Part off here.

Drive center

**Fig. 2: 18th-century handkerchief table**

Cut post so leg can fit under inner back rail.

Hinged leg knee orientation

Cut hinged apron to fit.

Top

$23\frac{1}{2}$ in. square

$\frac{3}{4}$

Wooden pin

Back of hinged leg

5

Finger-pull scoop

End block

$2\frac{7}{16}$

End block

$\frac{13}{16}$

Flat stop

Inner back apron, $22\frac{7}{8} \times 5 \times \frac{3}{4}$

Glue block

Chamfer at front and hinged leg only.

Right front apron, $16 \times 5\frac{3}{4} \times \frac{13}{16}$ plus tenons

Right rear leg

Front leg

leg must be modified so that the knee of the hinged leg can nest behind it. These and other modifications will be considered as they arise.

The first step is to bandsaw all four legs to the curves shown on the template. Notice that the back of the foot is not undercut at this time—to do so is a common mistake that affects the visual balance of the leg and leaves the foot without suffi-

cient body for good looks. Center the bandsawn blanks on the lathe and turn the bottoms of the feet. Then just nick the back of the ankle to define the top of the foot. Do not remove too much wood—the nick at the back of the ankle should be no more than $\frac{1}{8}$ in. deep, and your chisel should barely graze the top of the foot at the front. These marks will be faired into a gentle curve as the leg is being shaped. I

use rasps, files and scrapers, repeating each step on all the legs with one tool before moving on to the next. When the legs are shaped and smoothed, set them aside. The knee blocks will be sawn and added after glue-up, then shaped on the table.

Cut the front aprons to length, but don't bandsaw the curves yet—that step comes just before glue-up. At the front end of both aprons, cut the tenons that will go

Drawings: Figures 2 and 4, Louis M. Bassler

into the front leg. Then cut the mortises in the front leg. There is a ½-in. shoulder at the top of the tenon—which leaves some wood at the top of the corner post for strength—but there is no shoulder at the bottom. I begin with an undersized bit in my drill press, being careful not to get too close to the lines, and not to go so deep that the brad-point will leave marks at the bottom of the finished mortise. (I don't like to leave any machine marks on my re-productions, even when they will be hid-den.) I complete the mortise with chisels prior to mitering the front tenons on the aprons, which I cut a little short so they don't touch inside the mortises. As a final touch, I undercut the shoulders a little so that the face of the apron will draw up snug to the post.

Now we come to the interesting part, the joinery at the back legs, which is shown both in figure 3 and in the ex-ploded drawing. The two front aprons are mortised to the back legs at 45°. There are two back aprons, one of which carries the hinged leg.

Cut the inner back apron to length (no-tice that this piece has no tenons). Then cut the hinged apron, leaving it about 8 in. overlong for the time being, and make the hinge. It is much like the card-table hinge I described in *FWW* #47, but there are a few noteworthy differences. It has a built-in stop at 64½°, and to make this work, the hinge pin must be offset more than half the board's thickness from the end. This leaves some extra wood to bear against the inner apron, as shown in the hinge de-tails in figure 3. Final fitting of the stop is done by trial and error before the hinge strip is glued to the inner back apron.

As also shown in figures 2 and 3, there is an end block at each end of the hinged apron. One of these blocks is the fixed part of the wooden hinge, and the other can be made from the excess length of the hinged apron. It is by means of the end blocks that the back-apron assembly is tenoned to the legs. There is some careful fitting to be done before gluing up this as-sembly. First mortise the back legs and cut the tenons on the end blocks, then fit the hinge together. Next bandsaw the left-hand end block so the hinged leg can nest

into it (see the photo below if this sounds confusing). You can use the leg template to determine the profile of the curve.

Now glue the end blocks to the inner back apron, but don't glue on any legs yet. As you can see in figure 2, the hinged leg's corner post must first be half cut away so the leg can swing under the inner back apron. Work on the mortise-and-tenon joint at the hinged leg until everything fits, paring back the shoulders on the hinged apron's tenon so that the leg ends up in exactly the right nesting position. Fi-nally, glue up the back-apron assembly, in-cluding the hinged leg but not the others.

Now on to the angled mortise-and-tenon, which is not nearly so difficult to make as it may look. First the tenon: I set a sliding bevel to the angle shown on the plans, then transfer it to the top and bot-tom edges of the apron blank—I always mark such lines with a knife, since pencil lines are too fat to be accurate. Then I sim-ply bandsaw close to the lines and pare down to them with a chisel, as shown in the photo below.

The mortise is a little trickier, but not

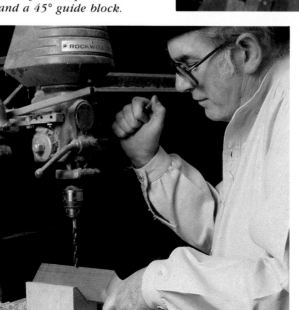

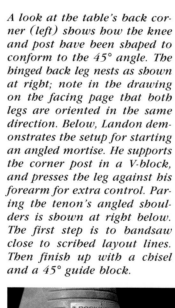

*A look at the table's back cor-ner (left) shows how the knee and post have been shaped to conform to the 45° angle. The hinged back leg nests as shown at right; note in the drawing on the facing page that both legs are oriented in the same direction. Below, Landon dem-onstrates the setup for starting an angled mortise. He supports the corner post in a V-block, and presses the leg against his forearm for extra control. Par-ing the tenon's angled shoul-ders is shown at right below. The first step is to bandsaw close to scribed layout lines. Then finish up with a chisel and a 45° guide block.*

really difficult. You can pre-drill most of the waste by supporting the corner post in a V-block as shown. Using the drilled holes as a guide, pare the mortise to full width with chisels. You can protect the very thin area at the inside corner from splitting off by using the 45° guide block, just as when cutting the tenons.

With the joinery cut, it is time to bandsaw the curves on the aprons. The pattern is centered on the apron and extends as far as the tips of the knee blocks, as shown in figure 4. After bandsawing the curves, remove the sawmarks with a rasp and chamfer the inner edges with a knife or chisel. The original table shows rasp marks clearly, and the ⅜-in. wide chamfering is a series of very bold cuts.

Glue the table together upside down on a flat surface, and when it is dry, rub on the interior glue blocks. The front angle on the original table was 88½° instead of 90°. I am not sure whether this was deliberate, so that the table would fit into a corner even if the room were slightly off-square, or whether it was just one of those things that happens. My table is also 88½°, and if you choose to follow the plans exactly, yours will be, too.

Now bandsaw the knee blocks and glue them on—but notice that the back knee block on the left rear leg must be relieved, as was done with the end block, so that the hinged leg can nest inside it. Bandsaw the relief cut before gluing on that knee block. Also notice that the forward-facing knee blocks at the back legs are larger than the others so they can meet the posts at a 45° angle. They must also be cut from slightly thicker stock, but these differences will be obvious when it comes time to make the blocks.

Reshape the tops of the knees on the back legs as well as the knee blocks to fair them back to the apron. Finish shaping the outsides of the back corner posts at the same time. Next chamfer the outside corners of the front leg and the hinged leg, then go ahead and make the top.

I cut the top's molded edge with an ogee plane and a hollow plane, but if you don't have these you can begin by cutting a shallow rabbet and then finish up with files. The notches are cut with bandsaw and chisels.

There is a curious joint where the leaf folds. It is not quite a rule joint, nor the tongue-and-groove that might have been found 50 years earlier, but rather a more delicate nesting rabbet-and-bead that does not conflict visually with the notched corners, whether the leaf is up or down. I

made mine with old planes, but any method will work. Pay particular attention to the location of the hinge pin, which determines how the leaf will align with the top in both the hanging and upright positions.

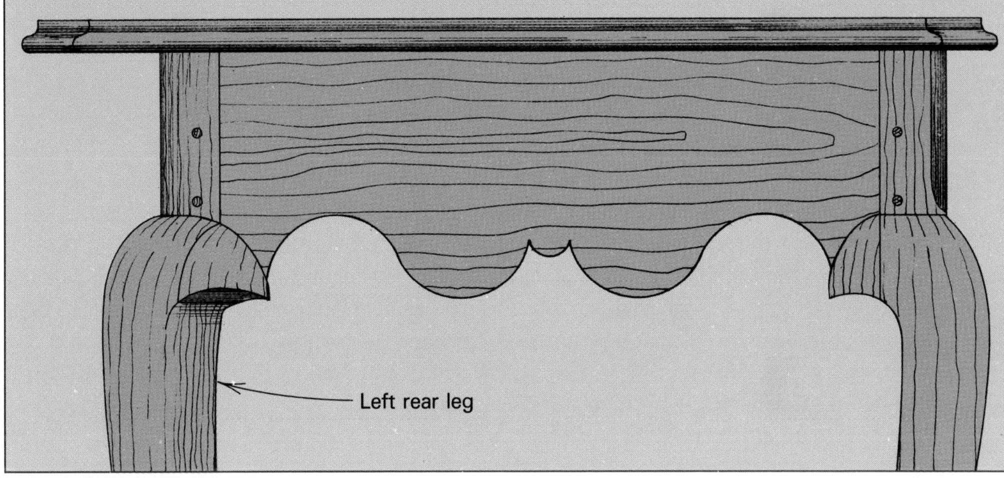

I attached the top with rubbed glue blocks and nails, the same method used on the original. This allows no provision for seasonal wood movement, and you could fasten your top differently if you'd like. Some old pieces eventually split, and some did not. My table, in fact, has a nice small split already, which I welcome as a sign of age. The original's top, ironically, is still fine after more than two hundred years.

I don't like to think of it as faking, but you could say that my table aged a little faster than the original. I added some wear marks where the original table had them, then eased the edges with a Scotch-

Brite pad. I smoothed the bottoms of the feet by rubbing them with a brick, duplicating the moving around that the original must have experienced in its lifetime. For the finish, I applied a home brew of green walnut husks steeped for a month or so in water. This helps darken Brazilian mahogany so that it looks more like the Cuban variety used by 18th-century cabinetmakers. I sealed this with a brushed coat of thin shellac. Five or six subsequent shellac coats were padded on, with some dry pigments mixed in to achieve a semitransparent patina. I took off the gloss with some 0000 steel wool, and everything came together at once. Suddenly there were two old tables side by side, a gathering of the rarest of the rare. □

*Gene Landon restores antiques and makes period reproductions in Montoursville, Pa.*

**Fig. 3: Posts, aprons and hinge**

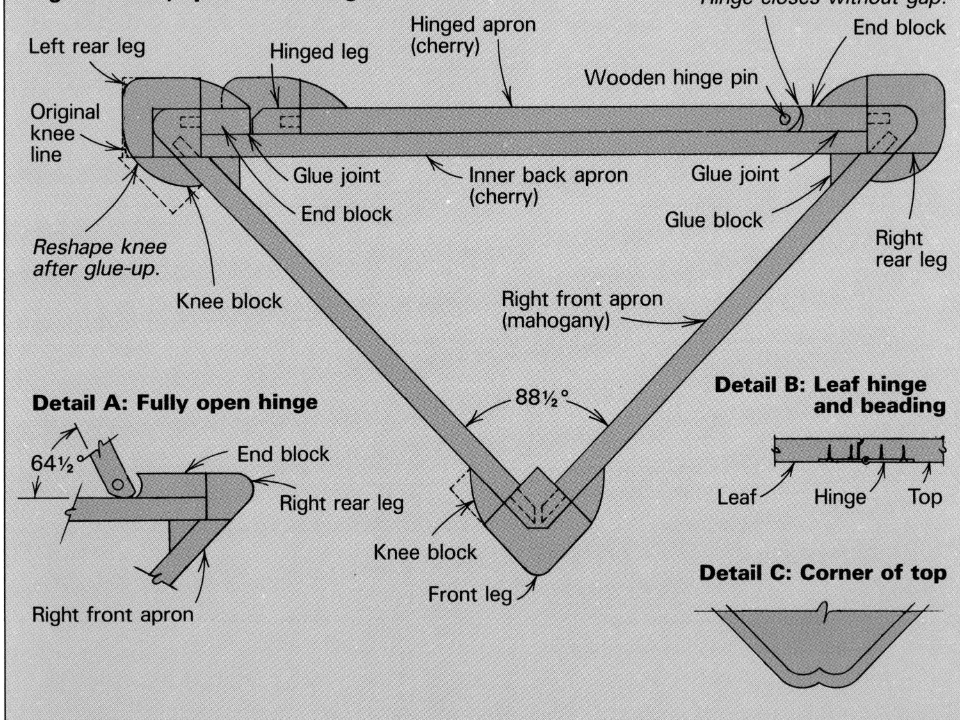

*Hinge closes without gap.*

Left rear leg · Hinged leg · Hinged apron (cherry) · End block · Wooden hinge pin · Original knee line · Glue joint · Inner back apron (cherry) · Glue joint · Glue block · Right rear leg · End block · *Reshape knee after glue-up.* · Knee block · Right front apron (mahogany) · 88½°

**Detail A: Fully open hinge**

64½° · End block · Right rear leg · Knee block · Front leg · Right front apron

**Detail B: Leaf hinge and beading**

Leaf · Hinge · Top

**Detail C: Corner of top**

**Fig. 4: Apron detail**

Left rear leg

# Perspective in Marquetry
## Renaissance work inspires contemporary maker

by Silas Kopf

As a marquetarian, I often used to feel that I was working far away in time and place from the roots of my craft, which began in Italy in the Renaissance and had its major flourishing in Europe before the 17th century. I had studied as much as I could of the old work in books, yet still yearned to see the real thing. So when the chance came to tour some of the old marquetry centers in Italy, I jumped at it.

Like anyone else working with veneers today, I take my power scroll saw for granted, and I enjoy a practically infinite variety of world timbers for my palette. It came as something of a shock to see how my craft was practiced in the old days. Although the tools were primitive, the workmanship was superb and the concepts went far beyond anything I had ever attempted. The trip changed my perceptions of what marquetry could be.

I traveled through Tuscany and Umbria with Judith and Alan Tormey, two scholars who know intarsia well and also know where the best work is to be found. We started in Siena, the intarsia center in the 14th century, from which master craftsmen were sent throughout northern Italy to ply their trade. There is also fine work in Perugia, Lucca, Bologna and Florence—a city that in 1480 had a population of 150,000, yet was able to sustain 84 workshops specializing in intarsia and wood decoration.

As practiced at that time, intarsia had aspects of both inlay and marquetry. In an inlay, a hole is routed into the background and plugged with a contrasting wood. The plug is then flushed off. Marquetry yields the same look but is, in fact, a veneered overlay—thin pieces of veneer are cut and assembled as a sheet, which is then glued to a thicker backing.

One method of intarsia was like a jigsaw puzzle glued one piece at a time to a panel of poplar or pine, about ¾ in. to 1 in. thick. In the second method, the major backgound pieces were glued to the panel, and then the smaller pieces were inlaid. The portrait shown at top left on the facing page is one of a set of panels done by Antonio Barili for the cathedral in Siena. Barili used a combination of the jigsaw-puzzle and inlay techniques. Another of his panels, shown top right on the facing page, portrays an open cupboard containing the tools of his trade—bowsaw, plane, dividers, layout tools, pliers, glue pot, and a long-handled knife.

The knife was Barili's main tool for cutting pieces to shape, because the fretsaw was not invented until about 1600. At the beginning of the 15th century, the picture parts were about ¼ in. thick. By the 1500s, the craftsmen were sawing the wood thinner, yet even so, after the wood was planed and ready for the picture, it was still about ⅛ in. thick. Barili would have been able to brace the knife's long handle against his shoulder for extra

leverage, but still, cutting and shaping such heavy veneer must have been a challenge, and very laborious.

The distinction between fine art and craft which many make today was unthought of in the 15th century. Intarsia was considered to be among the most important of the arts. According to Giorgio Vasari, a painter and chronicler, the intarsiatori Benedetto di Maiano achieved such renown that he was summoned to the court of the King of Hungary. "He made two chests with difficult and most splendid mastery of wood mosaic, to show to the King. So he packed his chests and sailed for Hungary." The King was anxious to see them but when he opened the parcels most of the veneers fell off, apparently because the glue had been softened by the dampness of the sea voyage. Benedetto repaired the damage, Vasari tells us, but "was disgusted with that kind of work, not being able to forget the vexation he had suffered, and gave it up, taking to carving instead."

Some of the panels have cracked and warped over the centuries, but on the whole the work I saw has held up remarkably well. I suspect that this is partly because the panels have been in churches, and therefore not subjected to the extremes of humidity found in a building with central heating. Neglect and insect damage have been much more damaging to the work than any problems with wood movement.

The intarsiatori chose their themes with care. The Renaissance interest in solid geometry paralleled the reborn interest in the Greek classics. Plato considered the five regular solids to be linked to the fundamental metaphysical elements. Writers in the Renaissance allied these forms (and mathematics as a whole) with concepts of perfection and order, representations of God. An influential book, *De Divina Proportione* (1498) by Luca Paciola, elaborated on these ideas.

Some panels were designed by famous Renaissance painters such as Botticelli and Piero della Francesca. They worked out the designs on paper and then turned them over to the intarsiatori to translate into wood. After assembling the panel, the craftsman  often added details of inlay, some pieces as small as a grain of rice and some lines as thin as 1mm. The finest intarsia pictures display a beautiful use of chiaroscuro by inserting small slivers of wood into larger shapes to create highlights or shadows through the way they are bunched together, much the same way modeling can be done in an etching by having many or few lines in a given area. The slivers will also sometimes curve to accentuate a rounded form, as shown in the drawing.

A story of one master, Fra Damiano da Bergamo, tells of an

*Inspired by Renaissance works such as this open-window panel by Barili (above left), Kopf responded with a whimsical cupboard with marquetry occupant.*

*Barili's intarsia tools seem stored away for another day's work in a panel in a church in Siena (top right). Kopf borrowed some* *of the master's techniques and concepts to give the illusion of a cabinet full of books, a violin and a pet chameleon.*

*The open 'doors' and the contents of Kopf's desk are actually two-dimensional marquetry, as is the drawer, even its pull.*

audience with Charles V of the Holy Roman Empire. The Emperor thought the wood in a particular picture must have been touched up with paint. Offended, Fra Damiano ran a plane over the picture, showing the Emperor that the colors and tones were not just applied to the surface. Some panels have been restored with wood fillers, but originally all the parts were wood, and they fit very tightly. Any hairline gaps were filled with earth pigments mixed with beeswax. The wood came mostly from northern Italy (tropical woods were not imported until the end of the 16th century). Nut woods and fruit woods were prevalent. These are all in the white to brown range, but the veneers could have been dyed for greater tonal variation.

There is some disagreement among scholars about how much dyeing was done. Although no one disputes that green was used (the evidence is still there to be seen), there is little remaining of other colors. There is good reason for this—most of the other colors would have faded over the centuries, or shifted in tone because of color changes in the woods they were applied to. I feel strongly that Renaissance intarsiatori took advantage of the large, varied palette available to them from the flourishing cloth-dyeing industry of the time. Wood could have been dyed much the same as cloth, using decoctions of cochineal insects for red, indigo for blue, and saffron or turmeric for bright yellow.

Marquetarians today prize veneers with bold figure and striking grain, but in the Renaissance straight-grained woods were the most common, probably because they were much easier to work with. It is only in the later intarsia that unusual grains are found. For example, Fra Damiano used burls to represent marble columns, and curly-figured wood for drapery in a door panel in

the choir of the church of San Pietro in Perugia. Visitors to such places often ask "how long did it take to make a panel?" We can make a guess. Barili contracted to make 19 panels for the cathedral in Siena. He had a nephew working with him at the time. The panels were to be completed in two years or Barili would forfeit a penalty. That works out to approximately one panel every eleven weeks per man. In fact, because of other commissions, the work was not finished for 20 years.

The strength of the classic intarsia was grounded in mathematics and the newly discovered principles of perspective geometry, whose basics are explained on the facing page. When the work did nothing more than mimic painting, it became stale. Vasari, presumably echoing (or leading) contemporary tastes, came to disdain the craft "as work requiring more patience than skill."

As for me, the challenge is still new. Before my trip, I had limited most of my marquetry to floral patterns. Now I am attempting three-dimensional illusions on furniture. Some subjects are humorous, some symbolic, but I hope that each design is harmonious with the piece of furniture and that the total concept proves provocative and interesting.

I picked up some good techniques in Italy, and I have gotten over my prior feeling that it is somehow cheating to use dyed wood—I'll use whatever I have to. In the cat cabinet shown at left, for example, the eyes and the pads of the feet are dyed. The cabinet, actually a fall-flap desk, is a mix of old and new techniques. I first made a full-size drawing in black and white, eye-balling the perspective instead of using geometry. A mathematically perfect drawing would have been accurate only from one viewing height and angle, so I tried instead to suggest the feeling of depth rather than attempt a strict portrayal of it.

Most important to the illusion are the tones of light and dark, the reason I made my working drawing in black and white rather than color. The lightness of the open door on the right thrusts it forward, as does the bright edge on the other door. Similarly, the cabinet's dark interior falls back visually from the surface plane.

With these bold areas established, I sketched the outline of the drawer and the cabinet's contents, then gave them depth by carefully plotting the contours of the shadow lines. Until I had seen the work of the old masters, I had never guessed how important shadows are to defining contours and shapes.

I had also not realized how important it was to overlap objects in the picture to help suggest depth. As I worked on the drawing, I took every chance to do so. One book overlaps the other, the cat's back leg overlaps both books, and the tip of the tail continues out over the drawerfront.

When the drawing was complete, I transferred it to various veneers with carbon paper, taking care to follow the lightness and darkness of the drawing so that the cabinet would look like one sort of wood exposed to various degrees of light intensity. I then cut the straight lines with a knife and the curved forms with the double-bevel technique. I taped the pieces together into a full-picture sheet and veneered it onto medium-density fiberboard, and then inlaid the fine details, such as the title of the book and the cat's whiskers. Studying the finished picture, I realized that the books did not stand out as well as they should, so I also inlaid a fine shadow line around their covers.

As a final touch, I inlaid the shadow of the left-hand door onto the solid-wood post of the leg. Barili, I hope, would have approved of his new apprentice's efforts. □

---

*Silas Kopf is a professional marquetarian in Northampton, Mass. He wrote about veneer-cutting techniques in* FWW #38.

# Basic rules of perspective

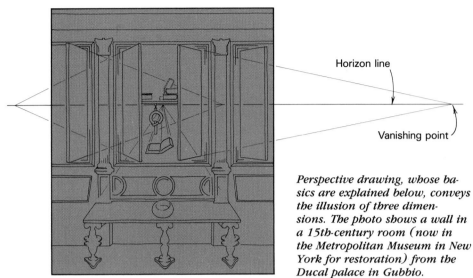

Perspective drawing, whose basics are explained below, conveys the illusion of three dimensions. The photo shows a wall in a 15th-century room (now in the Metropolitan Museum in New York for restoration) from the Ducal palace in Gubbio.

As shown in the drawing below, a picture contains a *horizon line,* always at "sea level" whether sea level is visible in the picture or not—in interior scenes, for example, it usually is not. The horizon line is always at the eye level of the observer. If the picture contains people the same height as the observer, the horizon line is at their eye level, too, provided that the land is flat. The farther away people and other objects are, the smaller they look.

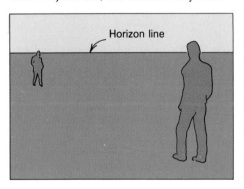

Parallel lines appear to get closer together with distance, until they meet at a *vanishing point,* as shown below. If the lines are also parallel to the earth's surface, they will converge on the horizon line or its extension outside the picture.

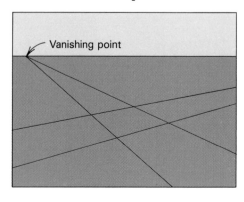

Planes, such as the sides of a box, converge to the same vanishing points as the box's top and bottom. In conventional drawing, planes perpendicular to the earth are drawn perpendicular, as in the drawing of the box, below. This assumes that the observer is looking straight ahead. Exceptions occur in unusual circumstances or for exaggeration, such as when looking up at a tall skyscraper—its sides would be drawn converging.

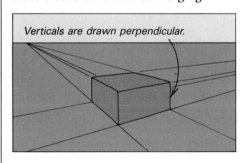

The plane of an open box lid is neither parallel to the earth nor perpendicular, hence its vanishing point is not on the horizon line. It may be above the line or below it, depending on the hinge location.

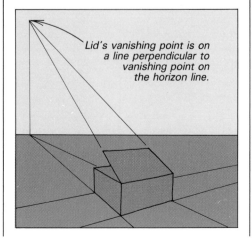

Circles in perspective are seen as ellipses. The more the circle is turned, the narrower the ellipse becomes.

The axis of a cylinder laid on its side is in a direct line with the minor axis of the ellipse representing its top. The cylinder's sides converge to a point along the axis.

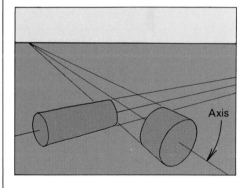

Many of the laws of geometry are still true in perspective drawings. For example, the center of a circle can be found at the intersection of the diagonals of a square drawn around it. The center of a circle in perspective can be found the same way: Draw a square in perspective around the ellipse and then connect the corners.

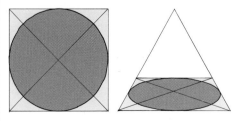

# Antebellum Shutters

## Movable louvers from simple jigs

by Ben Erickson

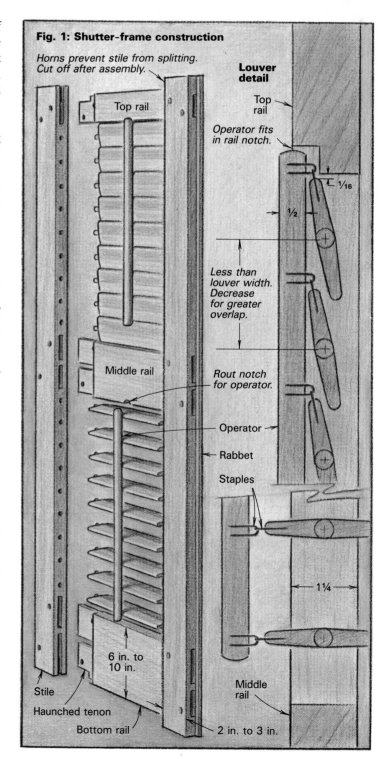

**Fig. 1: Shutter-frame construction**

Horns prevent stile from splitting. Cut off after assembly.

Top rail

Middle rail

6 in. to 10 in.

Stile

Haunched tenon

Bottom rail

**Louver detail**

Top rail

Operator fits in rail notch.

1/16

1/2

Less than louver width. Decrease for greater overlap.

Rout notch for operator.

Operator

Rabbet

Staples

1¼

Middle rail

2 in. to 3 in.

ntebellum frame houses are still common in my part of western Alabama. Some of these Greek-revival gems have decayed beyond repair, but many are being restored. Back then, all fine Southern houses sported exterior louvered shutters, many of which had movable louvers to control ventilation and light. After a century-and-a-half of sun and rain, it's a rare restoration indeed that doesn't need at least a couple of new ones. Reproducing these shutters is an important sideline of my woodworking business and I've developed some ways to speed the process.

Old shutters in my area are usually heart pine or cypress. These woods are scarce now so I use clear redwood. It's stable, holds paint well and is naturally resistant to decay. Windows in these old houses average 3 ft. by 6½ ft. and it takes about 50 b.f. of 2-in. lumber to make a pair of shutters for a window this size.

**The frame is** through mortised and tenoned, just like a frame-and-panel door frame. Pegs alone held the old ones together. I usually use a haunched tenon for the top and bottom rails. Figure 1 shows how a typical antebellum shutter goes together. If I'm making several shutters for the same house, I try to find an average one to copy because the dimensions can vary considerably from shutter to shutter. Old windows vary too, so it's best to measure each window. When laying out, add ¼ in. to the width of each shutter to allow for the rabbets where the shutters overlap in the center of the window.

After dimensioning the frame stock, lay out and chop the rail mortises in the stiles. I use a ⅜-in. hollow-chisel mortiser in the drill press. Next, I cut the rail tenons on the tablesaw. I mount two combination blades on the arbor, with washers and sheet-metal shims between them to get the right spacing. This setup cuts both tenon cheeks in one pass. Check the tablesaw setup with scrap stock exactly the same thickness as the frame stock and trial fit the test tenon in the stile mortise. The tenon should slide snugly into the mortise. Mark the face side of the rail stock and always keep this side against the fence of the tenoning jig as you cut the tenons to avoid alignment problems later. I cut the shoulders on the radial-arm saw and saw the haunch, if any, on the bandsaw. A stop block against the radial-arm-saw fence ensures that all the tenons are the same length.

Dry assemble the frame and check the outside dimensions against the window measurements. If you've made an error, it's best to find out now, before proceeding.

If you're copying an old shutter, measure the distance between the centers of the holes the louvers pivot in. These will probably vary, so measure several and average them. If you're working from scratch, here's one way to space the holes: On the

*With two blades on the tablesaw arbor Erickson cuts both rail tenon cheeks in one pass, above. Rather than risk fingers cutting free-hand, he's designed a tenoning push stick that rides the rip fence and holds the stock upright. A 1x2 table and fence support the stile while drilling the louver holes, right. The block system shown below ensures accurate hole spacing.*

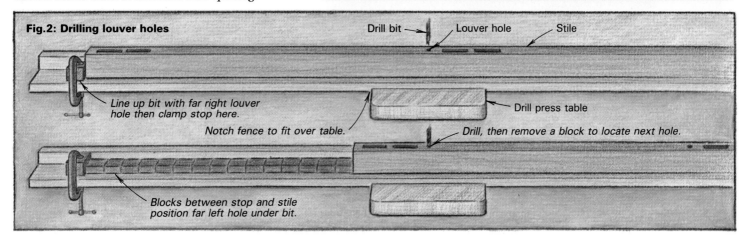

**Fig.2: Drilling louver holes**

Drill bit — Louver hole — Stile

Line up bit with far right louver hole then clamp stop here.

Notch fence to fit over table.

Drill press table

Drill, then remove a block to locate next hole.

Blocks between stop and stile position far left hole under bit.

stiles, mark the holes for the top and bottom louvers in each opening. These louvers should clear the rails by about ¹⁄₁₆ in. to allow the louvers to close completely. So, for a 2¼-in. wide louver, you'd mark the centers 1³⁄₁₆ in. from the rails. The louvers should overlap each other about ¼ in. Divide the distance between the two centers you just marked by the number of louvers you want. The result should be about ¼ in. less than louver width, or roughly 2 in. for 2¼-in. wide louvers. If larger, the louvers won't have enough overlap, so add another louver and divide again. If a lot smaller than ¼ in., try removing a louver. For example, to fit seventeen 2¼-in. wide louvers into a 35-in. space, divide 35 by 17 = 2¹⁄₁₇ in. Rules aren't graded in 17ths so set your dividers as close as you can and step off the distance (or measure in metrics and eliminate the fractions).

The method I use to drill the holes, shown in figure 2, ensures accurate spacing. I set a stop block on the radial-arm-saw fence and cut scrap blocks as long as the center-to-center distance between holes. A long combination fence/table extension on the drill press supports the stile. With the bit over the first hole on the right, I clamp a stop on the fence at the left end of the stile.

When I line up the blocks between that stop and the left end of the stile, the bit should be directly over the first hole on the left. You may have to make several sets of blocks with just slight variations in length before you get it right. Line up the blocks, drill a hole and remove a block to position the next hole. Both stiles may be drilled on the same setup.

**Antebellum louvers** are usually about ⅜ in. thick and 1¾ in. to 2¾ in. wide. Viewed from the end, the louver has an elongated diamond shape. I find it convenient to plane this shape on 4 ft. to 8 ft. lengths, then cut them to exact louver length.

After the stock is dimensioned rectangular (usually ⅜ in. x 2¼ in. or so), I taper the louvers on the thickness planer. As shown in figure 3, p. 198, my taper setup is simply a strip of wood as wide as the louvers and as long as my planer bed, ripped to a 3° angle. It's sandwiched tightly between two wooden guide strips which are clamped to the bed. I just feed the louver strip through on top of the angled wooden strip for the first two passes and double the angle for the third and fourth passes. Start with some sample pieces and run a marking gauge down the center. Scribble on the

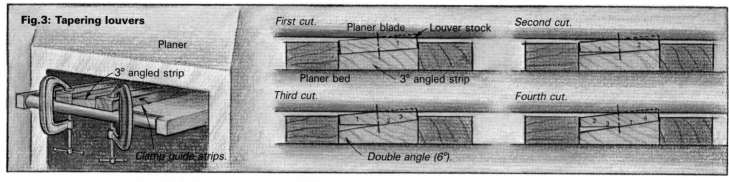

**Fig.3: Tapering louvers**

Planer

3° angled strip

Clamp guide strips.

*First cut.*
Planer blade — Louver stock

Planer bed — 3° angled strip

*Second cut.*

*Third cut.*

*Fourth cut.*

Double angle (6°).

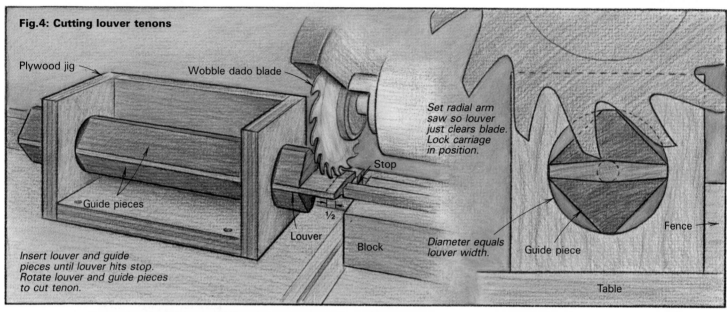

**Fig.4: Cutting louver tenons**

Plywood jig

Wobble dado blade

Set radial arm saw so louver just clears blade. Lock carriage in position.

Guide pieces

Stop

Louver

½

Block

Diameter equals louver width.

Guide piece

Fence

Table

Insert louver and guide pieces until louver hits stop. Rotate louver and guide pieces to cut tenon.

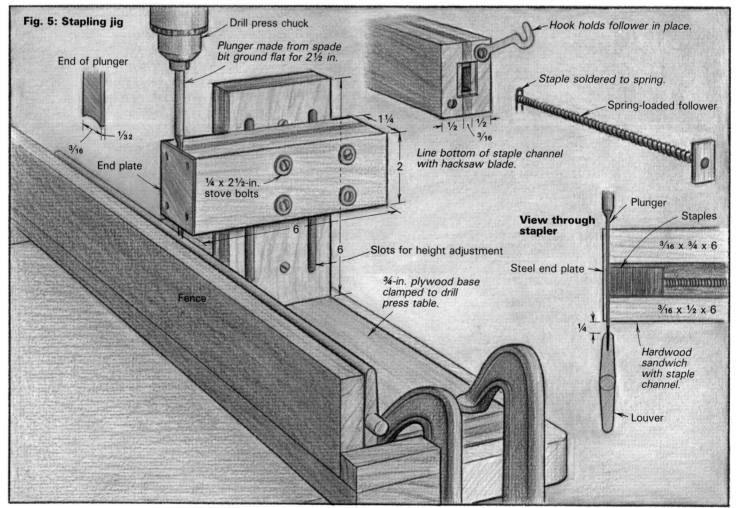

**Fig. 5: Stapling jig**

Drill press chuck

Plunger made from spade bit ground flat for 2½ in.

Hook holds follower in place.

End of plunger

1/32

3/16

End plate

¼ x 2½-in. stove bolts

1¼

2

6

6

½ | ½

3/16

Line bottom of staple channel with hacksaw blade.

Staple soldered to spring.

Spring-loaded follower

Slots for height adjustment

¾-in. plywood base clamped to drill press table.

Fence

**View through stapler**

Plunger

Staples

Steel end plate

3/16 x ¾ x 6

3/16 x ½ x 6

¼

Hardwood sandwich with staple channel.

Louver

sample with a pencil or crayon so you can see how close the planer cuts to the center line. The object is for the louver edges to end up about ¼ in. thick, while the center is a full ⅜ in. thick when viewed from the end. Adjust the planer height until it planes to the center line. Now, run all the louver stock through, flip the louvers over (without changing ends) and run the other side through. Double the angle either by adding another 3° angled strip on top of the first one, or replacing the first strip with a 6° strip. Using the samples again, readjust the planer height to cut to the middle of the louver. Reverse ends on all the pieces and run the remaining two sides through as you did the first two. It's easy to get confused and run the wrong side through, so work out a system of stacking to enable you remember which sides haven't been planed. After beveling, you can round the edges on the shaper or router table with a ¼-in. round-over bit.

Cut the louvers to length, usually ⅞ in. longer than the distance between the stiles. This allows for a ½-in. long round tenon at each end.

I cut the tenons on the radial-arm saw with the jig shown in figure 4. The louver fits snugly into the circular cutouts in the plywood uprights. So it doesn't wobble in the cutouts, I sandwich the louver between two triangular guides. I mount a wobble dado blade on the saw and adjust the blade height so that the louver, in a horizontal position, just slides under the blade. A stop that hits the end of the louver in its center (where the tenon will be) is clamped to the fence. This stop determines the length of the tenon. With the saw carriage locked in place and the saw running, insert the louver sandwich through the jig holes. Push it through horizontally under the blade until the end touches the stop block, then rotate it to cut the tenon.

**The operator is** a strip of round or half-round stock about ½-in. in diameter that moves the louvers in unison. Each louver is connected to it by two interlocking staples, one in the louver and one in the operator. I use U-shaped galvanized staples about ³⁄₁₆ in. wide and ⅝ in. long. Each shutter needs two operators, one for the louvers above the center rail, one for those below.

For small jobs in softwood, or for minor repair work, you can break up a row of staples with a knife or heat, then hammer them in with a tack hammer. However, if there are many to do, it can be very time consuming and if the wood is even moderately hard the staples tend to bend. To cope with these problems I designed a stapling jig that uses the drill press to press the staples into the louvers (see figure 5). It works just like a regular staple gun. It's basically a hardwood sandwich with a space in the center just wide enough and high enough for a row of staples to slide into. I lined the bottom of the staple channel with an old hacksaw blade to keep the staples from digging into the wood. I scavanged the spring-loaded follower from an old Arrow hand stapler. I ground the sides of the spring-loaded follower's rod down to fit through the row of staples, removed the clip at the end and reattached the spring with a lump of solder at the end of the rod to keep it from coming off. Unlike air staplers, my jig allows me to control the depth of penetration. By using the same blocks that I used to drill the louver holes, I can also space the interlocking operator staples perfectly. Accurate spacing here is essential for smooth operation.

To staple the louvers you'll need to make a fence to support the louver at 90° to the drill press table. Unplug the drill press, chuck up the jig's plunger (ground from a spade bit) and set up a stop on the fence that quickly centers the louvers under the stapler. Adjust the height of the stapler until it's about ¼ in. from the louver. Lower the quill to press in the staple. Adjust the drill-

Author photo

*After gluing the frame joints, Erickson inserts the louver tenons into their holes in one stile, then tightens the clamps enough to slip the other ends in the opposite stile. With both ends in place, he draws the clamps up tight. Louvered shutters were standard features on Southern antebellum houses. The shutters at left were made in the 1840s. Only the bottom louvers are movable.*

press depth stop so the staple protrudes about ³⁄₁₆ in. from the edge of the louver and staple all the louvers.

Replace the fence with one the same height as the thickness of the operator and center the operator's width under the stapler. Position the stapler above the operator so there's room enough to slip a louver under the stapler. Reset the depth stop on the press. On the long fence, line up the same set of blocks that you used to drill the louver holes and use a similar stop setup to locate the staples at the ends of the operator. Place the operator end against the stop block, and insert a louver under the stapler at right angles to the operator. Press in a staple that interlocks the louver staple. If you don't want to line up each louver by eye, set a stop and butt one end of the louver against it. If your operator is round, draw a pencil line down its length to keep the staples in a straight line.

Before assembling the frame, drill or rout a slot in the edges of the top and middle rails for the ends of the operators (see figure 1). I use Weldwood plastic resin glue for the frame joints because it's water resistant and sets up slowly. Spread the glue and pull the joints together with pipe or bar clamps until all of the joints are within an inch or so of being tight. Insert the louvers in one stile. Tighten the clamps until the opposite ends of the louvers almost touch the other stile, and insert these ends in the holes. Now pull the frame tight. Watch for any sign of binding that might indicate that a louver isn't in it's hole. When the glue is dry, drill and peg the tenons, cut off the horns and cut the rabbet where the shutters overlap. As a final touch, I run a decorative bead on the overlapping edge. □

*Ben Erickson is a professional woodworker in Eutaw, Ala.*

# Making Marionettes

## Carved figures bring life to wood

by Bruno Frascone

Wood has been important to us since the beginning of time. Even today when so many objects and gadgets employ man-made materials, wood is a precious gift that can play all sorts of roles—anything from a box to a home, and sometimes it can dance, talk and entertain.

I began to understand this miracle about 12 years ago while working with a marionette theater in France. I had fallen in love with the fascinating little people, jointed dolls that hang from the strings that control their movements, and I began making them, first with papier-mâché and wire, later from wood. My wooden marionettes worked best, but I knew they needed more sophisticated bodies if I was ever going to eliminate the false or "too-loose" movements that destroy their magical human-like behavior. Thus began my search for the perfect marionette.

By the time I moved to the United States in 1976, I had carved two all-wood marionettes that performed well, but I still was not happy with the way they moved. Then six months later, on my first Christmas in America, my quest ended when my wife gave me a book called *The Dwiggins Marionettes: A Complete Experimental Theater in Miniature* (by Dorothy Abbe, Harry N. Abrams Inc., New York, 1969). William A. Dwiggins, who worked his marionette magic from the '30s through the early '50s, was a remarkable artist who never received enough exposure to become well known (because the actors are seldom more than 20-in. tall and the stage is proportionally tiny, 30 to 40 persons is the maximum audience for a live marionette show). He was not only a good woodcarver, but he had learned how to balance each part of a marionette's body (figure 1) so that the control strings

*Father Time hobbles along in an endless march. His clothes conceal a variety of lever-like limbs and hinged joints custom-carved to duplicate the movements of the human body.*

working against the pull of gravity produced what he called "almost automatic human motions." I had found the system that would give life to my designs, like Father Time (photo at left). Even though Dwiggins showed me the secret of lifelike movement, he did not limit me to copying his work. I still could create my own individual world of marionettes: in terms of human anatomy, an old man doesn't have the same type of body as a ballerina or a juggler, so you could say their designs are not the same, even though the basic systems that give them life and movement are identical.

With the Dwiggins system, though, you don't have to create a perfect replica of the human body to make a good marionette. Since the body will be clothed, its appearance is not too important. Strings hook the body parts together (figure 2) and regulate posture, so you don't have to carve realistic knees or elbows, but these joints must be cut accurately for the marionette to move properly. Since the hands and head are painted, you can create many details with a brush instead of a carving knife.

**Sketching and shaping**—I first draw the front and side view of the figure I want to do, usually making it 14 in. to 20 in. tall. (Very small or very large marionettes behave erratically on the control strings.) Once you've got your basic sketch, try to visualize how the figure is broken down into its basic components according to the Dwiggins system, as shown in figure 3 on p. 202. Sketch these parts on both views of your figure, if you like. For a start, just use the Dwiggins pattern for a generic male (figure 4) to make cardboard patterns for both views of each piece. If the dimensions shown on the grid are respected, the marionette won't fail. With experience, you'll probably want to modify some of the

# The Dwiggins system

A marionette hangs from its head. So much of its natural action depends on accurately locating all points of support from the neck to the feet in a single plane perpendicular to the ground, as represented by the line through figure 1A. In this way, gravity does all the work—the strings simply control the motions that result from the pull of gravity.

The body parts themselves are simple levers that move in circular tracks about fixed points or fulcrums. The shapes of the parts, the mechanical design of the joints and the tension of the strings used to connect them limit the motion of the levers to certain planes and arcs of travel. The limits (what Dwiggins called stops) for these arcs and the slants of the planes are determined by watching a human being move, then carved into wood by a trial-and-fitting process. Dwiggins' goal was to make the action of every single articulation or joint as close as possible to its counterpart on the human body, although he used the same system for both males and females.

The torso is divided into three individually shaped cones representing the shoulders, waist and hips. The pieces are held together by a string that acts like a spinal cord from shoulders to hips. A loop called a side string, extending through the three pieces, in conjunction with the beveled center piece, controls how much the figure can bend from side to side and front to back. —B.F.

## Fig. 2: Stringing a marionette

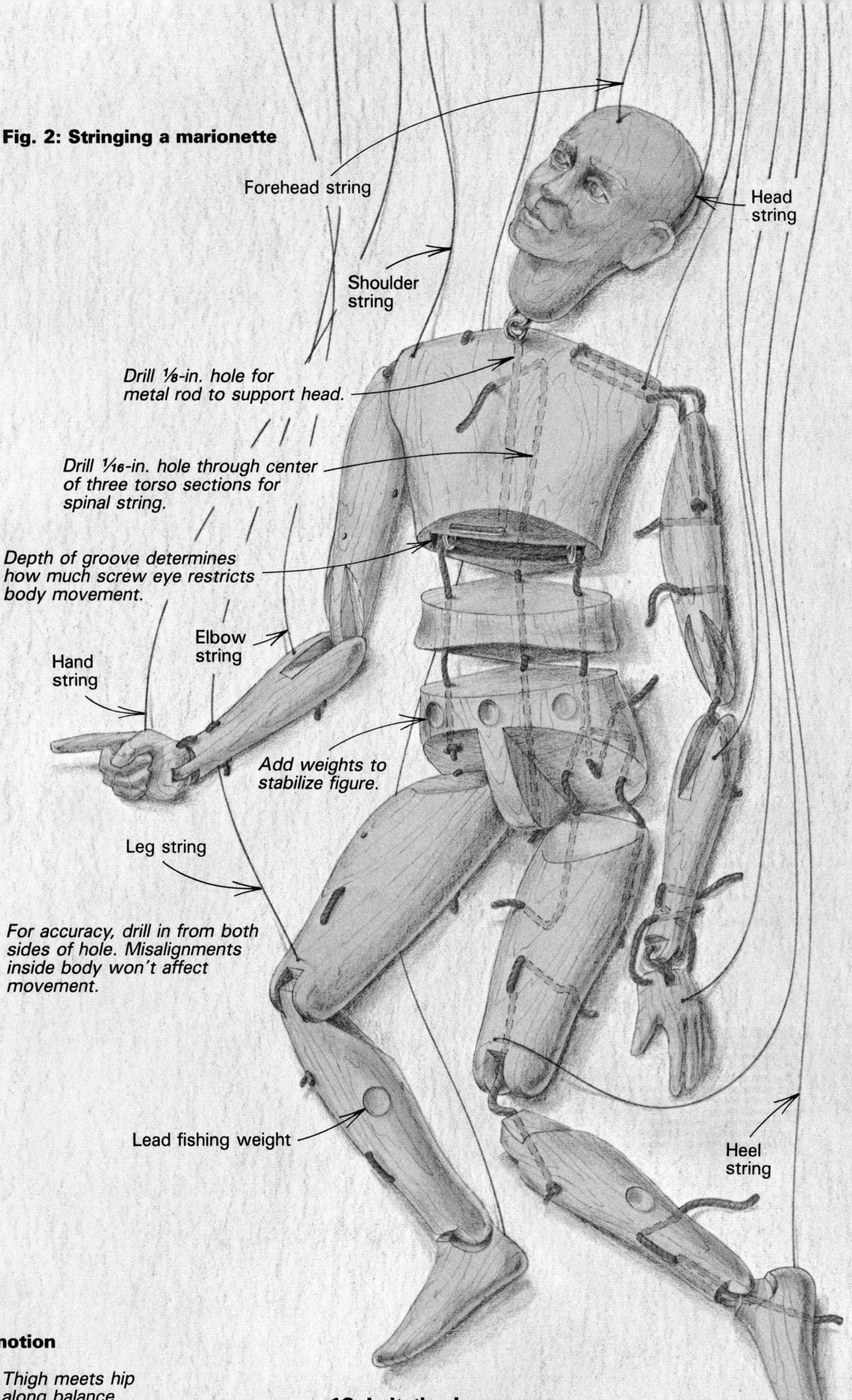

Forehead string

Head string

Shoulder string

Drill ⅛-in. hole for metal rod to support head.

Drill ¹⁄₁₆-in. hole through center of three torso sections for spinal string.

Depth of groove determines how much screw eye restricts body movement.

Hand string

Elbow string

Add weights to stabilize figure.

Leg string

For accuracy, drill in from both sides of hole. Misalignments inside body won't affect movement.

Lead fishing weight

Heel string

## Fig. 1: Marionette geometry

### 1A: Plane of balance

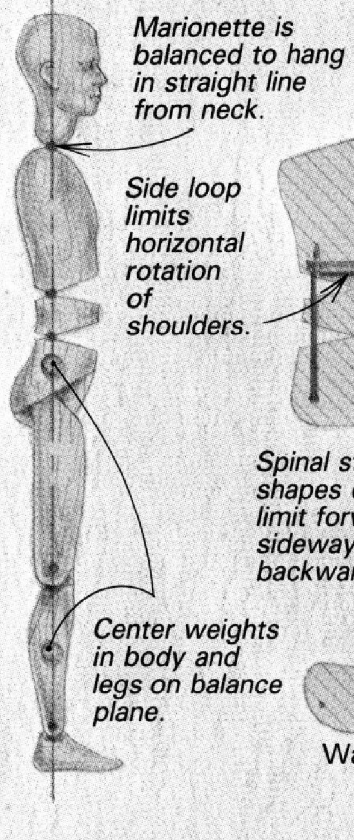

Marionette is balanced to hang in straight line from neck.

Side loop limits horizontal rotation of shoulders.

Center weights in body and legs on balance plane.

### 1B: Limiting motion

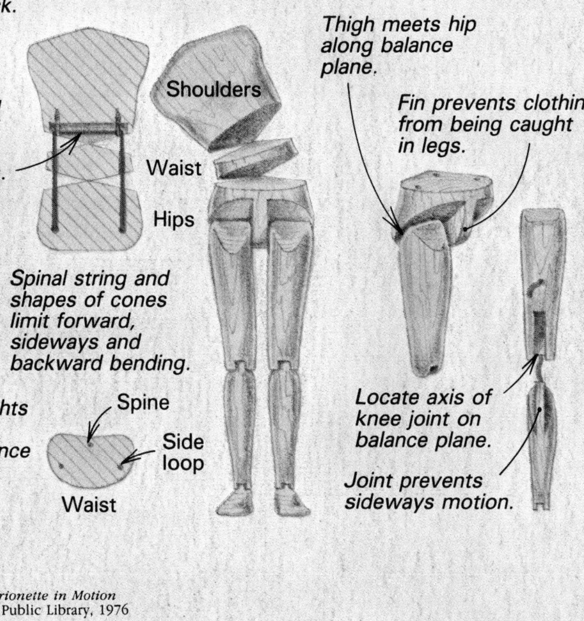

Shoulders

Waist

Hips

Spinal string and shapes of cones limit forward, sideways and backward bending.

Spine

Side loop

Waist

Thigh meets hip along balance plane.

Fin prevents clothing from being caught in legs.

Locate axis of knee joint on balance plane.

Joint prevents sideways motion.

### 1C: Imitating human arms

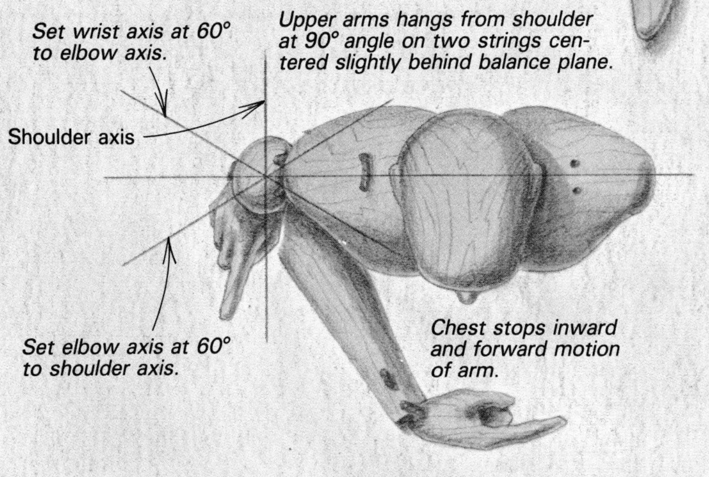

Set wrist axis at 60° to elbow axis.

Shoulder axis

Upper arms hangs from shoulder at 90° angle on two strings centered slightly behind balance plane.

Set elbow axis at 60° to shoulder axis.

Chest stops inward and forward motion of arm.

Drawing adapted from *Marionette in Motion* by W.A. Dwiggins, Boston Public Library, 1976

**Fig. 3: Father Time**

These are the author's working drawings for the marionette pictured on the previous page. The outline of the body parts used in the Dwiggins system can be seen under the clothes. A thin wire run like a control string from the figure to the control paddle lets the author turn the lantern on and off during performances.

*A pensive ballerina relaxes among the spring blossoms, her body parts delicately shaped to give her the flexibility and grace of a prima donna. Makeup paint conceals the joints in her limbs.*

parts, perhaps increase the angles of the cones forming the shoulders, waist and hips to create a limber ballerina (photo, above), or make the knee joints smaller and tighter to imitate the restricted gait of an elderly person.

For now, you'd be wise to limit your customizing to the proportions and characteristics of the feet, hands and head—details that are so important in conveying the personality of a marionette. The clown always wears big shoes, and the hands of the maestro are always large and delicate. A marionette head looks best if it equals one-quarter to one-fifth of the full height of the figure. Since marionettes are usually viewed from a distance, it's better to make the head too big than too small.

Once you've prepared all your patterns, trace them onto blocks of wood. Red cedar, white pine or some other soft wood is fine for the body parts, but hardwoods like mahogany, beech and birch are better for the more intricately carved head, hands and feet. So you'll be able to carve sym-

metrically, mark accurate centerlines on each face of every piece. If you have to cut off one of the centerlines in one operation, you can reestablish it using the remaining lines for reference. I carefully bandsaw one view of each piece, then tape the waste on so I'm working with a square block to cut the second view. Work by pairs—upper arm with upper arm, upper leg with upper leg, and so on—so you can remember to maintain the left and right mirror effect of each pair. Beginners should make two sets of pieces, just in case the first set isn't good enough or something breaks. Leave the edges of each piece square for now. You don't want to shape anything until after you've cut the tenons and notches that will form the joints. These joints, what Dwiggins called articulations, must be cut carefully because they determine how well the marionette will move.

Bandsaw the torso pieces to shape, but don't try to carve away any sharp ridges. Be very careful when cutting the hip joint, basically two notches flanking a center

ridge, into the lower torso. For the marionette to walk straight, the two notches must be identical—cuts on one side of the torso must be exactly parallel and in the same plane as cuts on the other side. I use a flexible plastic ruler to lay out the joint lines, then bandsaw the waste, cleaning up with a chisel or knife as needed. With a small gouge, cut a ¼-in. groove under the top part of the torso for the side string.

The mechanism of the leg works in a straight line, and each leg is parallel to the other. I notch the bottom of the knee joint by making two parallel bandsaw cuts, then clearing the waste with a ¼-in. chisel. You can bandsaw freehand, since the gently curved parts have not been shaped yet, but you might want to reattach the waste you previously cut from the back of the leg to help in cutting nice, parallel articulations. To cut the tenons for the knee notch, I angle the piece on end and make two cuts parallel to the length of the piece to establish the ¼-in. wide tongue, then I carve away the sides until the tenon fits into the notch and the upper and lower knee work nicely together. The farther back the tenon shoulders are, the more movement the joint will have, so be sure to leave enough of a shoulder to prevent excessive, unnatural movements. Cut the ankle joint the same way—bandsawing and chiseling a notch in the lower leg and carving the tenon on top of the foot to fit.

The mechanism of the arms is far more complex than that of the legs, and can be best understood by looking at your own body. If you let your arm hang naturally from your shoulder, you'll notice that the axis of the elbow joint points slightly inside of the straight-ahead mechanism of the knee. The wrist also works on another axis, pointing out this time, relative to the axis of the elbow. Dwiggins calculated that the difference between the axes of the shoulder and elbow and between those of the elbow and wrist was 60° in each case. You can use this 60° figure as a general guideline and work from your own body. Cut the elbow notch and tenon straight, just as you did for the knee joint. Establish the elbow angle by carving away the top of the arm where it hangs against the upper torso. Shape the upper arm until the marionette's arm hangs the same way yours does. Again work in pairs so the joints on the left side mirror those on the right side. After doing the elbow, use your body as a guide to approximate the wrist angle and carve out this articulation.

Now you're ready to shape all the body parts with a sharp knife. Use the centerline of each piece as a guideline and work the pieces in pairs to ensure symmetry. Your carving should accentuate the twist you've created in both the upper and lower arm. Proceed slowly, carving away the sharp corners left by the bandsaw. Remember, the pieces need not be perfectly shaped, since the body will most likely be clothed and viewed only from a distance.

Hands are the hardest part of the figure. Think how much you use your hands to express yourself—if you mess up the hands, you may kill the expressive effect of the marionette. One nice thing about creating little people, however, is that you always have a model with you. Use your own hands and other body features (keep a mirror handy) to answer any questions on shapes and gesture that might come up as you carve.

I begin by drawing the hands directly onto a small block of wood, arranging the block so the grain follows the fingers for maximum strength in these delicate areas. The fingers will also be stronger if you

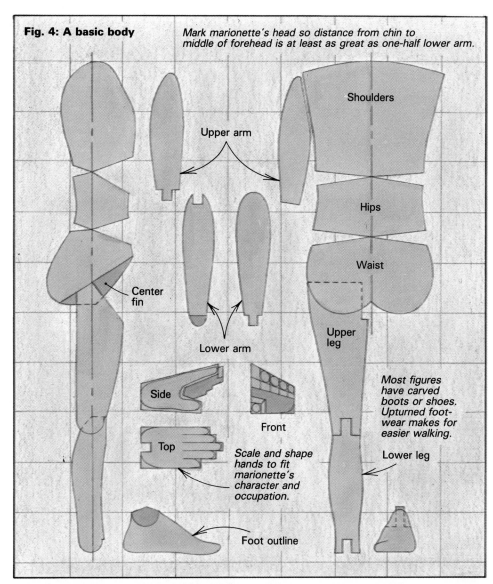

**Fig. 4: A basic body**

Mark marionette's head so distance from chin to middle of forehead is at least as great as one-half lower arm.

Upper arm

Shoulders

Hips

Waist

Center fin

Lower arm

Upper leg

Side

Front

Top

Scale and shape hands to fit marionette's character and occupation.

Most figures have carved boots or shoes. Upturned footwear makes for easier walking.

Lower leg

Foot outline

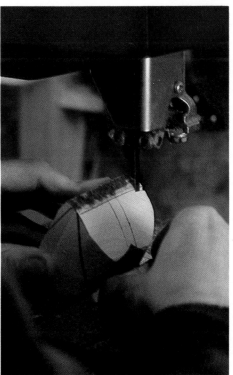 

*Steady the cone-shaped hip section with a scrap wedge while bandsawing the notches that accept the thighs, above left. Hold the leg piece on end and bandsaw parallel cuts to establish ¼-in. tenons, above right. Carve the shoulders with a knife.*

*Flexible wrist joints give the ballerina, left, such a repertoire of gestures that her wooden hands seem real. Study your own body to determine how each hand should be formed. Use a small file, below, to shape delicate areas of the palm and fingers where a knife might be too large or where there is danger of breakage.*

*During carving, Frascone frequently checks the marionette's emerging face from below. The change in perspective makes it easier to spot flaws and to visualize what the finished character really will look like.*

carve them joined together, rather than as five individual units. I clamp the block in a small vise and carve the fingers with a ¼-in. chisel, the chisel width setting the width of individual fingers. Small jewelers' files are very useful for fine details on hands, as well as on feet and heads.

Being aware of the centerline is especially important in carving the face and head. Take a block of wood large enough for the head, trace the outline of the head, and mark its centerline on front, back, top and bottom. I cut the main angles of the face with a bandsaw. If you make a cut on one side of the centerline, you must make a similar cut on the other side; if you curve one edge, curve the other. Never try to finish one side or a detail of one side before roughing out the other. I do most of my carving with ¼-in. and ½-in. shallow gouges, a small skew-shaped knife and a spade-foot knife, but the tools really don't matter as long as you never lose sight of the centerlines, or forget that you are working on two profiles—the front and the side. When you carve the eyes, make sure they are on the same level and square. As I carve, I look at the face from underneath, side and top, not just from the front. I also like to use a small mirror to view the emerging face—I always discover a totally different view there.

All pieces of the body are joined with and supported by string—30-lb. test braided nylon fishing line for controls and waxed string used in leathercraft for the joints. A ¹⁄₁₆-in. dia. metal pin supports the ankle, but string permits more supple movements in the other joints. Also, if you should accidentally drop the marionette, the string is likely to break or pull out, whereas metal pins tend to break the wood.

**Stringing the body**—To assemble the body, drill ¹⁄₁₆-in. holes at the locations shown in the plan. It's normal to have to do some final trimming as you string the pieces together. First, run the spine string through the three sections of the torso, leaving it loose, then add the side string. The side string runs from the lower front of one side, up the side hole of the center part, through the screw eye located in the groove of the upper part, over to the other screw eye, down through the other side hole of the center piece and to a lock hole in the lower section. You'll have to adjust both the side and spine strings to allow the right amount of motion, then secure the ends of each by driving sections of round toothpicks into the lock holes. Drill the holes for the knees and elbow and string these joints together. The shoulder

# Marionette motivation

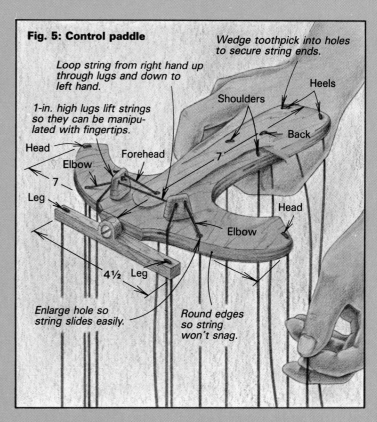

**Fig. 5: Control paddle**

Loop string from right hand up through lugs and down to left hand.

1-in. high lugs lift strings so they can be manipulated with fingertips.

Wedge toothpick into holes to secure string ends.

Head

Elbow

Forehead

Shoulders

Heels

Back

Leg

7

7

Head

Elbow

4½   Leg

Enlarge hole so string slides easily.

Round edges so string won't snag.

A balanced, well-made marionette comes to life with a series of strings using the control mechanisms Dwiggins developed. His controls are comfortable and fun to use, and comparable to a musical instrument that lets you discover chords, rhythm and melody.

The control is basically a smooth, paddle-shaped piece of ⅜-in. plywood, along with an auxiliary bar, that holds and separates the strings. The two lugs on top of the paddle make it easy to reach the strings most important to the marionette's expressions—they control the arms and hands, and move the head up and down. The strings should slide through the holes without resistance.

I suggest using about 4 ft. to 4½ ft. of string to connect the marionette to its control. Since the entire marionette hangs by strings in the head, these must be inserted first. Attach them just over and slightly forward of the ears. When you set these strings, the control must stand perfectly horizontal. As before, drill ¹⁄₁₆-in. holes for the strings, then wedge the ends in place with toothpicks.

You'll need at least 11 strings to control the figure. The hand-to-hand string loops from one hand through the holes of the two lugs, then down to the other hand. This string should be slightly taut and

support both hands naturally. The elbow strings are attached to the forearm right below the elbow articulation. They should be taut without carrying any weight. The knee strings, attached right above the knee articulation, are similarly taut and set on the pivoting bar in the very front of the control. The shoulder and back strings should be set so they support and control the body when the head is lowered.

Now you should be ready to experience the true magic of a marionette. With your thumb and middle finger, grasp the narrow part of the paddle handle from above, roughly parallel to an imaginary line connecting the head strings. Use your forefinger to manipulate the head string. Curl your remaining two fingers under the paddle to reach the shoulder and back strings. Use your other hand to manipulate strings to make the figure walk and move its hands and legs. You'll develop your own methods, but here are some guides to get you started.

**Head:** Tilting the control paddle down and forward will bow the head. Keeping the control in this down position as you alternately roll the paddle from right to left along its axis will produce a shaking-my-head "NO" movement. Holding the control horizontal while

lifting the forehead string with your index finger will lift the head. Pulling and releasing the forehead string with the control slightly bent down will give a "YES" nod. You can make the marionette bend or twist by using one of the fingers holding the control to manipulate the back and shoulder strings from below the control.

**Arms:** Use your second hand to manipulate the hands and arms. Pulling the hand string in combination with the elbow strings will give a variety of movements and expressions.

**Legs:** Make the legs walk by rhythmically moving the control forward and pivoting the bar carrying the

knee strings. When the control is tilted backward, allowing the back, shoulder and head strings to drop, the marionette will sit.

After you learn to control these basic strings, you may want to add others. Just remember—every additional string increases the chance of tangling. Despite that danger, you can create some interesting results by attaching strings to the bottom of the marionette's heels. The strings should hang very loosely so they don't interfere with normal walking, but when pulled they should lift the back of the feet, allowing the marionette to get on its knee, or fly like Superman, or dance on one leg. —B.F.

and the hip each hang by two strings which are adjusted to allow a natural looseness to the hips and shoulder. Drill the holes of the wrist and ankle and join them together.

Now that your marionette is all together, check its body mechanism. Hold the marionette by its head and lift the knee by the upper leg, watching the body and the lower legs—if they swing too much, add lead fishing weights to the lower legs until the movement seems natural. Check

all articulations to make sure they are not too tight or too loose. This takes practice, but you'll soon see how to work the strings and weights to balance the marionette.

I paint the marionette's hands, legs and face with two coats of gouache water paint (available at any art supply shop). I use fine wool or yarn for hair, drilling into the skull, inserting strands of fiber and pinching them in place with a toothpick. Now the marionette must be dressed. Generally, the clothes are simple designs, made of

lightweight fabrics or leather, and baggy enough to allow free movement. I'm not a tailor, so you're on your own. When the marionette has finally found something to wear, it is complete, although asleep, waiting only for control strings and your skills to give it full life. □

*Bruno Frascone is a professional marionette maker who teaches marionette making and produces miniature theater programs in Charlotte, N.C.*

# A Simple Banjo

## Make a wooden-top 5-string

by Richard Starr

I never would have thought to design a banjo if several kids in my school shop hadn't wanted to make one (nothing seems too complicated to a 12-year-old). Regular banjos have skin or plastic drum heads, but mine uses a wooden soundboard. It isn't as brilliant or quite as loud, but it has an appealing ker-chunky sound that is lovely for mountain-style clawhammer playing.

This banjo's structure couldn't be simpler. There is no fancy joinery or bolts and no bent wood. The soundboard is glued to the rim of the banjo, eliminating the need for complex and expensive tensioning hardware. To make the banjo, a bandsaw is indispensable and a power jointer speeds the work, but you can, as do my students, manage with hand planes.

Begin by drafting a full-size pattern for your instrument, both top and side view. My students used dimensions from the book *Foxfire 3,* edited by Eliot Wigginton (published by Anchor Press/Doubleday, 245 Park Ave., New York, N.Y. 10167), but you can use the dimensions shown in figure 1, or copy an existing instrument. If you have such a model, be sure to note the following dimensions: length of the neck; width of the neck at the nut, fifth fret and where it joins the rim; height of the strings above the last fret and at the nut. Measure the positions of the frets to the nearest millimeter, using the nut end of the fingerboard as zero. You may choose to make a fretless banjo—our design fits in well with the warm, primitive, fretless style of playing.

After drafting the basic shape of your instrument, mark out the extension of the neck through the rim by drawing lines parallel

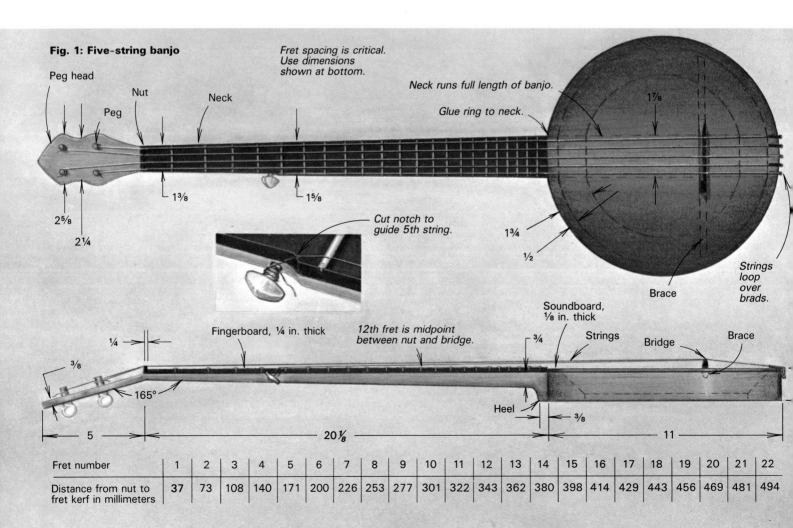

**Fig. 1: Five-string banjo**

Fret spacing is critical. Use dimensions shown at bottom.

Peg head

Nut

Peg

Neck

Neck runs full length of banjo.

Glue ring to neck.

1⅞

1⅜

1⅝

2⅝

2¼

Cut notch to guide 5th string.

1¾

½

Strings loop over brads.

Brace

Soundboard, ⅛ in. thick

Fingerboard, ¼ in. thick

12th fret is midpoint between nut and bridge.

¾

Strings

Bridge

Brace

¼

⅜

165°

Heel

⅜

5

20⅛

11

| Fret number | 1 | 2 | 3 | 4 | 5 | 6 | 7 | 8 | 9 | 10 | 11 | 12 | 13 | 14 | 15 | 16 | 17 | 18 | 19 | 20 | 21 | 22 |
|---|---|---|---|---|---|---|---|---|---|---|---|---|---|---|---|---|---|---|---|---|---|---|
| Distance from nut to fret kerf in millimeters | 37 | 73 | 108 | 140 | 171 | 200 | 226 | 253 | 277 | 301 | 322 | 343 | 362 | 380 | 398 | 414 | 429 | 443 | 456 | 469 | 481 | 494 |

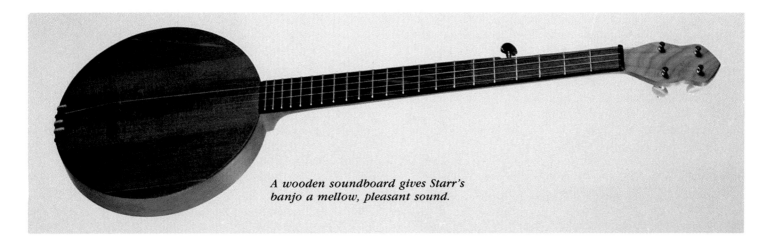

*A wooden soundboard gives Starr's banjo a mellow, pleasant sound.*

to the centerline, starting where the neck intersects the rim as shown in figure 1. This defines the width of the whole neck piece and the shape of the rim halves. Trace the neck and the rim halves onto another piece of paper and cut them out as patterns to trace on the wood.

**Frame**—Sturdy native hardwoods like maple, ash, cherry and hickory were used by mountain instrument makers. I made my banjo of 8/4 cherry. For the neck, choose stock a couple of inches longer than the entire banjo and a tad wider than the section of the neck that extends into the rim. If your peg head is to be wider than that dimension, add the length of a second peg head to the overall length of the neck blank. Joint one face and two edges of the stock. As you joint the second edge, bring the stock down to its finished width. If you're widening the peg head, cut the extra section off, rip it up the middle and glue the jointed edges of these two pieces to the sides of the neck.

The two C-shaped segments that form the rim are made from stock the same thickness as the neck. Joint a face and an edge, then trace the pattern with the ends of the C flush against the jointed edge. Bandsaw the C-shape and save the outer waste pieces to use later as gluing cauls.

Now bevel the inside edge of each rim segment. On the end of each segment, draw a line as shown in figure 2. This line establishes the 45° bevel. Use a compass to scribe a line around the inside of the rim as shown. Set the table of your bandsaw to 45° and carefully follow that line to guide your cut. Smooth the inner surfaces of the rim segments with a spokeshave and scrap-

er. This can also be done on a drum sander. The outside curve is best left rough until later.

Hold one of the rim segments in place against the neck and trace a line on the neck where the bevel meets the neck. Cut out the relief section of the neck as shown in figure 2.

Bandsaw the neck and peg head to shape. Glue the rim segments to the neck as shown in the photo below. When the glue is dry, check to see that the top edge of the rim is exactly even with the face of the neck. If it's not, true it up with a hand plane. Trim the tailpiece extension of the neck flush with the rim. Plane the back surface of the rim and neck so that they're smooth and flush with each other—I planed off about ¼ in.

**Soundboard**—Quartersawn spruce, cedar or redwood gives a rich, resonant sound. An easy way to get a decent soundboard is to pick through a pile of spruce or cedar clapboards at your local building-supply house. Look for annual rings that are perpendicular to the faces of the board. Cut two lengths of clapboard a couple of inches longer than the soundboard, joint the edges and glue them together to get the width you need. When the glue is dry, plane and sand the board a tad thicker than ⅛ in.

Trace the inside and outside edges of the rim on the bottom side of the soundboard. The soundboard is round, except for a flat section where it butts up against the fingerboard. Be sure that the grain of the soundboard runs parallel to the neck. Bandsaw the curved shape ⅛ in. outside the traced line, but cut right to the line on the flat section.

Cut a brace from spruce or pine as shown in figure 1 and glue

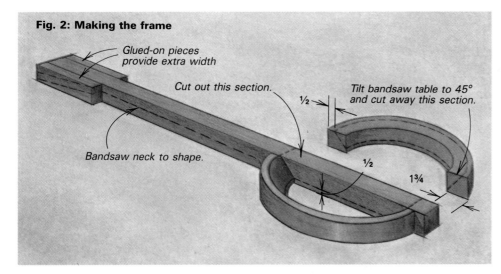

**Fig. 2: Making the frame**

Glued-on pieces provide extra width

Cut out this section.

Bandsaw neck to shape.

Tilt bandsaw table to 45° and cut away this section.

½

½

1¾

*In gluing the rim segments to the neck, the scrap pieces left from bandsawing the rim become the cauls. A few clamps and small cauls at the tail end keep the parts from slipping around while the pipe clamps are being tightened.*

it across the underside of the soundboard. This cross-grain brace helps resist the downward pressure of the bridge and reduces the chance of the soundboard splitting.

Now you're ready to glue the soundboard to the rim. Hold the banjo in a machine vise by the part of the neck that passes through the rim. Spread glue on the upper edge of the rim and set the soundboard in place. Be sure that the flat section of the disc is lined up where the neck joins the rim and that the sound-board overhangs the rim evenly all around.

For a good glue job, it's important to apply gentle clamping pressure at every point on the rim. When the glue is dry, use the bandsaw to trim the soundboard flush with the rim.

**Fingerboard**—A fingerboard that contrasts in color with the neck of the banjo is appealing. Mountain folk used native woods: walnut, cherry or maple would work well. No part of the instrument receives more wear and tear, so very dense woods are best—the finest banjos have ebony or rosewood fingerboards.

Cut a piece of stock slightly wider than the neck and a couple of inches longer than its length. Joint one face and one edge, then thickness the piece to about ¼ in. Pencil a line up the center of the stock and lay out the shape of the fingerboard centered on this line. If you want frets, mark the position of each fret along the jointed edge of the stock, then use a square to project each mark across the fingerboard.

Fretwire has a T-shaped cross section and the shank of the T is jammed into a slot in the fingerboard. You'll need about 5 ft. of fretwire and a fretsaw, or a dovetail saw whose kerf gives a snug fit to your particular fretwire. If the saw cuts too wide, you can narrow the kerf by sliding a file lightly along the sides of the saw, reducing the set of the saw's teeth. Don't make the kerf too tight or the neck will bow when you hammer all the frets in. Guide the saw against a block of wood clamped to the finger-board, as shown in the photo below. This block can also serve as a depth stop. Trim its height so that the back of the dovetail saw catches on its top edge when the cut is to depth—about ¹⁄₁₆ in. deeper than the shank of the fret. Practice cutting frets in scrap before trying it on your fingerboard.

After you've cut all the fret slots, saw the fingerboard to shape and glue it to the neck. Be sure that the centerline of the finger-board is true to the centerline of the neck and that the end butts up against the flat section of the soundboard. Use a scrap of

*To saw the fretwire slot, guide the saw against a block of wood clamped to the fingerboard. Trim the block height so that the back of the dovetail saw catches on its top edge when the cut is about ¹⁄₁₆ in. deeper than the shank of the fretwire.*

wood roughly the size of the fingerboard as a caul to distribute the clamping pressure. Now bandsaw the sides of the neck to match the shape of the fingerboard.

**Carving the neck**—Carving the back of the neck is probably the fussiest job in this project. The curve in cross section must be rounded almost to the top edge of the fingerboard, while the shape along the length is almost a straight line. At the same time, the neck gets slightly wider and thicker from the nut to the rim and is faired gently into the peg head and heel. Rough out the shape with a spokeshave and refine it with a scraper or file. Sand-paper on a hard block works best for truing the surface length-wise. A well-shaped neck is a musician's joy, so examine your work with your fingers, as well as your eyes. It's helpful to handle a completed banjo to get an idea of how a neck should feel.

**Fretting**—Inject a small amount of white or yellow glue in the fret's kerf and tap in a length of fretwire using a lightweight, deadblow hammer. Be sure to support the neck with a block of wood directly under the fret you're installing. Using a pair of nip-ping pliers, trim the overhanging ends of the fretwire. File the ends even with the fingerboard and round them slightly at the top, so no sharp edges protrude. If you file the wrong way, you'll lift the fretwire. To remove the file burrs, sand the edges of the fingerboard with 220-grit paper on a hard block. Run a long file lengthwise up and down the neck to level any high frets.

Now you can smooth the outer edge of the rim with a spoke-shave and sandpaper, and finish-sand the whole instrument.

**Set-up**—Install tuning pegs according to the manufacturer's instructions, or make your own tapered friction pegs. To guide the fifth string over the fifth fret, we cut a simple notch in the fingerboard. You could also insert a small round-head wood screw between the fourth and fifth frets so that the head of the screw holds the string down tight on the fifth fret. Instead of a tailpiece, we used five round-head brass brads driven into under-sized holes at the tail end of the instrument. These brads secure the ends of the strings. Be sure that the heads of the brads stand about ¹⁄₃₂ in. proud to catch the string's loop. Round the edge of the soundboard slightly where the strings bear on the corner. Fashion a nut and bridge from dense hardwood, and trim their height to give the proper action (the height of the strings at the nut and last fret). The nut glues against the peg head and the end of the fingerboard. File shallow notches for each string. String the banjo and position the bridge so that the 12th fret is midway between the nut and bridge. Adjust the bridge so that holding down each string at the 12th fret produces a tone one octave higher than the open string. Move the bridge slightly closer to the nut if the octave is flat, further away if it is sharp. Don't glue the bridge to the soundboard. The tension of the strings will hold it in place.

An oil finish, wet-sanded with 400-grit wet-or-dry paper, will give you a fine-looking and serviceable musical instrument. A good book for beginners is *How to Play the 5-String Banjo* by Pete Seeger (Oak Publications, Div. of Music Sales Corp., 799 Broadway, New York, N.Y. 10003). Good playing! □

*Richard Starr teaches woodworking at Richmond Middle School in Hanover, N.H., and is the author of the book* Woodworking with Kids *(The Taunton Press, 1982). Photos by the author. Banjo tuning pegs and strings are available from Stewart-MacDonald Mfg. Co., Box 900, Athens, Ohio 45701.*

# Designing With Veneers
## Illusion can be as strong as structure

by Ian J. Kirby

There's more to veneering than technique; in fact, the essence of veneering is design and actually using the material to create real furniture and pleasing visual effects. The series of buffet tables shown here are the result of class problems aimed at developing the design and craft skills of students at my school near Atlanta. A look at how these students handled the assignment shows you what is possible with veneers, and also gives you a glimpse at the whole process of designing.

The students already had learned to make torsion boxes and to handle basic veneering techniques, but some of them had never attempted a major piece of furniture. The buffet therefore seemed an ideal first project. It has a simple form and function—a food counter when a buffet meal is being served—but since it just stands idle in a room most of the time, it must also be an attractive piece of furniture. After discussing these requirements, I recommended that the students start with a basic table form and make it elegant by varying the proportions of the components. Then, if they could enhance their design with the visual

*Five different veneers—padauk, ebony, African walnut, makore and pecan—used in proportion to their visual intensity create an eye-catching highlight on the top of de Alth's buffet.*

*Carefully joined sections of veneer make George de Alth's buffet appear to be assembled from blocks of solid wood, rather than from sheets of medium-density fiberboard.*

Photos: Gary Bogue

details that can be created with veneers, they would be well on the way to successful pieces of furniture. Torsion boxes (*FWW #32*, pp. 96-102) were included in the assignment because they capitalize on modern, dimensionally stable substrates to create strong structural elements with smooth surfaces perfect for showcasing the visual drama and movement of veneers.

Don't be put off by the apparent complexity of these designs. You don't have to be a trained designer to experiment with veneer arrangements and proportions. Everyone, whether he or she realizes it, has an eye for visual relationships. You can increase your awareness of these relationships by looking carefully and by thinking about what details make a piece of furniture work in terms of appearance or function. That's mainly what it takes—there's nothing magical about visual design.

One word of caution. Even though you may develop many good ideas for using veneers, don't immediately run off on some grandiose project. If you have never done any veneering, my advice is to make up two or three 9-in. by 12-in. practice panels, using mahogany or some other easy-to-work veneer; avoid anything that's badly buckled. Following the methods I've discussed in the last two articles (see *FWW #46* and *#47*), prepare the substrate and apply the veneers. By the time you've finished the panels, you'll have learned enough to confidently use veneering technique on a real project.

As you study these pieces, you'll see two types of form: structural and visual. The torsion boxes establish the structural form of the buffets, and veneers create the illusion of form as they visually pull the components of the piece together. A good example of this type of visual unity is the buffet by George de Alth, shown on p. 209, in which he arranged the veneer grain patterns to flow from the top to the sides, linking the two surfaces into what appears to be one continous, solid structure.

No amount of playing around with surface decoration or structural detail, however, will compensate for any miscalcula-tion in the basic proportions. Although proportion may be discussed as a mathematical concept, complete with formulas to guide you, it's mainly something you learn to sense and feel through practice and a great deal of drawing. There is no substitute for drawing—it's the most effective way to explore proportions and the interaction of line, pattern, color and other visual effects until you've created relationships that please you. The product of this work at the drawing board—a graphic design—is later translated into a three-dimensional structure, first a model, then a full-size piece. The model can be anything from a small-scale replica to a full-size mock-up, complete with colors or shapes pasted or taped on, but it should be as accurate as possible. Otherwise, you won't have any real feel for what the completed piece of furniture will be like.

The buffet by de Alth shows how a graphic design can be converted into veneers. By far the jazziest of all the pieces shown here, its visual power is concentrated within one area of the top. Five different veneers were used, each in proportion to its visual strength and color. For instance, the smallest area of veneer—5 sq. in. of ebony—acts as the highlight. It draws the eye right to it and has great impact.

In the teak and ebony buffet shown in the photo at right below, John Sherman developed a strong visual relationship between the top and the elliptical legs, which appear to be coming through the top. In reality, what shows is a piece of ebony veneer cut to the exact section of the leg. The illusion is compounded by ebony strips running across the edges of the top and down the legs, seemingly connecting the two pieces. The legs are oval torsion boxes. The ebony was veneered to a piece of bendable 3mm plywood, which was then glued onto the oval leg. Sherman's buffet also features inlay—a technique which is almost as old as veneering itself. In this case a teak and ebony laminate is inlaid around the edge of the top to highlight its shape. To accentuate this configuration even more, the ebony

*A long strip of purpleheart ties the asymmetric form of Carter Sio's buffet table together visually (below left), while a veneer-deep illusion lets John Sherman's top grip his table's legs, which are oval torsion boxes.*

*The mitered chamfer on Joe Wilson's padauk buffet is accentuated by satinwood inlay, which joins the chamfer, leg and top. Satinwood is also the primary wood in the raised window-like grid.*

center panel mirrors the slightly bowed edges of the top.

Another example of how veneers can unify a piece is Carter Sio's buffet, shown at left on the facing page. Its form is asymmetric, but the components are held together by a long band of purpleheart veneer.

Joe Wilson similarly united his padauk and satinwood buffet (photo, above) with a detail: a chamfer highlighted by a satinwood inlay. This makes clear the relationship between the parts—chamfer, leg and raised top—and gives the piece much of its power. The legs are joined to the top very simply with a ledger and pocket on the leg, as shown in the drawing at right.

The grid on the top of Wilson's table is formed by solid padauk strips inlaid into satinwood veneer, which is raised above the mitered padauk border. This might somewhat limit the use of the buffet, but Wilson decided that the visual effect gained was worth what might be lost in function. The pattern looks good and seems right because of its proportions. The side of the square equals the width of the border, the number of squares makes sense, and the small squares emphasize the corners. The success of this piece is the result of careful thought at the drawing board and many developmental drawings.

Scott Jenson's buffet (top photo, p. 212) is a good example of the selection and clever mixing of superb materials. The heavier pillar appears to be 5-in. rosewood cubes stacked one on top of the other. The effect is in fact created by applying the veneer so that every 5 in. the direction of the grain is turned 90°. This understated detail is discovered only when you get near the object, and then it comes as a surprise and a joy.

Jim Allen's buffet (bottom photo, p. 212) is a torsion-box structure built with medium-density fiberboard (MDF) skins over an MDF core. The principal veneer is fiddleback teak; the secondary veneer is rosewood. The legs are slightly thicker than

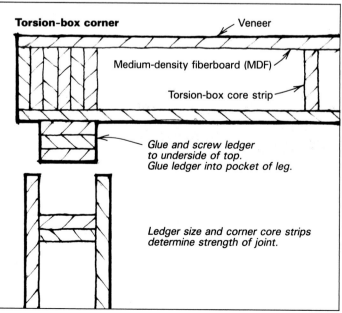

**Torsion-box corner**
Veneer
Medium-density fiberboard (MDF)
Torsion-box core strip

Glue and screw ledger
to underside of top.
Glue ledger into pocket of leg.

Ledger size and corner core strips
determine strength of joint.

*The larger pillar on Scott Jenson's glass-top table is veneered to look like a series of stacked 5-in. rosewood cubes.*

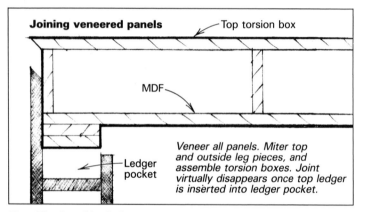

**Joining veneered panels** — Top torsion box

MDF

Ledger pocket

Veneer all panels. Miter top and outside leg pieces, and assemble torsion boxes. Joint virtually disappears once top ledger is inserted into ledger pocket.

the top, giving the piece a comfortable feel. (If the legs were the same thickness as the top, they would look spindly.) An interesting pattern is obtained by applying some of the fiddleback veneer at right angles to the grain direction of the main flow of veneer. On the top surface, the pattern is based on seven different-size rectangles, which create interest in the way that each juxtaposes to the next. The circle motif on the front edge is carried over the top, giving the illusion that the inlays are slices of a solid-wood cylinder. Circles also appear at the corners, where the rosewood veneer emphasizes the relationship of the legs to the top. There is a fairly important lesson to be learned here—the relationship of the parts, that is, the architecture of the piece, should be developed first. From these architectural lines come our first ideas about variations or decoration of the piece.

Allen worked within the architecture of the table to create illusions. How are the legs and top joined? Is the leg one piece, the top another piece, and the rosewood corner a third? What trickery holds the top to the leg, if the two pieces barely touch at the corners. Is there a tube of teak running through the center of the rosewood? To further suggest that the rosewood corner is a separate piece, Allen could have run a grooved line through the area where the rosewood contacts the teak. This would have created a shadow and a distinct gap on the surface.

Anybody can develop a sense of design. But keep in mind that complexity for complexity's sake is not good design. I find that new students tend to include their whole arsenal of techniques in each project, while more experienced workers generally refine a theme, then develop it fully. You should be aware of this difference as you start thinking about design. With attention to detail and practice, you can make your first major piece of veneered furniture something special. □

*Ian J. Kirby is a designer, cabinetmaker and educator in Cumming, Ga. He wrote about veneering in* FWW *#46 and #47. Drawings by the author.*

*Jim Allen's table, below, appears to be inlaid with slices of solid-wood cylinders.*

# Matchmaking

A good way to begin designing with veneers is to imagine that you are a graphic designer working with lines and color, pattern and rhythm, rather than a woodworker dealing with bits of wood. Veneer is so rich and varied that you can design in much the same way as an artist paints, with an entire palette of visual effects to accent, define or enrich a piece of furniture.

As you begin matching veneers, you'll find that the variations are almost endless—certainly there are more combinations than the conventional bookmatch, slipmatch and herringbone patterns you see diagramed in old veneering books. Such cataloging seems to indicate that there are rules or set patterns for veneering. Nothing could be further from the truth. When veneering, the only rules are visual, although you should realize that if you flip sheets of veneer you will have the tight side of one sheet next to the loose side of the next sheet (see *FWW #46*, p. 39). This will affect the looks of the panel when polished. There isn't a garish difference, but the two sheets will absorb finish differently and will reflect light differently. Other than that, don't be afraid to arrange veneer in any way you choose.

Figure 1 gives a glimpse of the kind of patterning that's possible. A single sheet of veneer is fairly uninspiring, unless it happens to be a particularly exotic species. Put it side by side with another sheet in a simple slipmatch (1A) and the effect is a little livelier. Arranging two consecutively cut veneer sheets to create a bookmatch (1B) is even more intriguing, but the four-sheet pattern in 1C just vibrates with life.

Finding good grain patterns for these more exotic matches takes a good eye and some careful searching. A simple but handy device is a homemade viewing window (figure 2A), which consists of stiff cardboard with a window cut to the shape and size of the sheet of veneer to be matched. It's quite extraordinary how grain and color come into focus when you isolate a section of a sheet through the window. Once you've found the section you like, you can find matching sections in the same position on successive sheets in the veneer stack and arrange them in a four-way match (2B).

To see what repeat-left, repeat-right or end-on-end matching will look like, hold a small mirror (an 8-in. by 5-in. mirror works well) at one end or edge of the window. If you want to see what a four-way match will look like, use two mirrors taped together to form a right angle (2C).

A pattern need not be complex to be eye-catching. A checkerboard, for instance, is a good example of the power of simplicity. The usual way to make a checkerboard is with alternating squares of light and dark veneers. An equally effective checkerboard can be made with only straight-grained ash squares assembled at right angles to each other. The result is dramatic, but somewhat more subtle than the usual black-and-white.

Another simple way to mix veneers is to use inlay and edgebanding. You'll find that a mix of approximately 90% major veneer with 10% inlay will generally create a pleasing effect. In these proportions, the alternate veneer acts as a highlight or color contrast to strengthen the shape or form of the object.

Veneer is available in a variety of thicknesses and species from local shops and mail-order houses. It's usually sold in bundles that have the sheets stored in the same order in which they were cut from the tree. Once you know the length and width of the veneer sheets you're buying, you can calculate the number of sheets required to give the pattern you want and the square footage you need. Since there are quite a number of variables here, including at least a 15% waste factor, it's usually impossible to get exactly the right amount, so it's best to buy extra. Otherwise, if you run out, you may be forced to use veneer from a different flitch, which could spoil the whole effect.

The best way to store veneer is to lay it on a larger board so there are no overhanging edges or ends that could get knocked and broken. Enclose the whole stack in an envelope of plastic sheeting to retain the moisture in the stack and to keep dirt out. Store the stack in a dark place—sunlight will rapidly fade veneer. Aging doesn't help veneer, but if the sheets are stored carefully, they can be saved for quite a few years. —*I.J.K.*

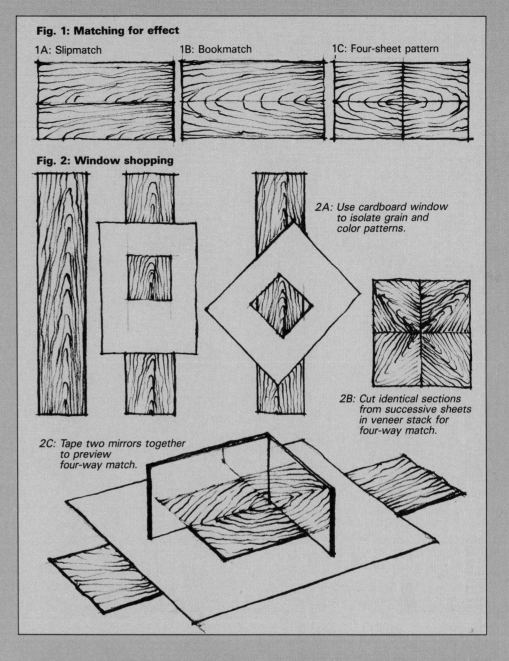

**Fig. 1: Matching for effect**

1A: Slipmatch   1B: Bookmatch   1C: Four-sheet pattern

**Fig. 2: Window shopping**

2A: Use cardboard window to isolate grain and color patterns.

2B: Cut identical sections from successive sheets in veneer stack for four-way match.

2C: Tape two mirrors together to preview four-way match.

# Making Room Screens

*A wooden hinge for every purpose*

by Steven Mackintosh

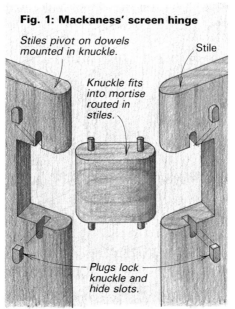

*Mackintosh's first screen, left, has a no-show back because slots routed into the frames for the knuckle hinge (drawing above) are visible from the rear.*

I don't really know why I got interested in making room screens, since they seem to be the antithesis of the kind of woodworking I'd been doing for several years. I had resolutely tried to design furniture that people would want to *use* every day, not just look at, and a screen is something you can't sit on, store things in or eat dinner at. But after I had made one screen, I found myself making another, and another, and another. Each was an attempt to solve a design problem whose dimensions kept growing with each apparent solution.

Before describing the design dilemmas

I found so irresistible, I'd better correct the impression that screens have no practical purpose. They do, although it's not always the reason people buy them nowadays. Before central heating, screens were used to minimize drafts. Today many screens—especially the more highly embellished variety—are purchased only for decoration. Yet they can have functional uses as well, such as shrinking large spaces to more intimate dimensions, providing privacy, hiding clutter, or keeping the cat out of the baby's room without having to close the door. The best use to which I've put my screens is in my booth

at craft fairs. A big screen is a real eye-catcher, and it doubles as a backdrop for some of my smaller pieces, such as a tea cart or a group of music stands.

The spark that ignited the screen-building boom in my shop was an article by Tim Mackaness in *FWW* #10 on making a wooden screen hinge. This hinge, shown in figure 1, answered the only design problem that had occurred to me at the time: what to do about ugly metal hinges. I had admired Chinese lacquered screens pictured in antiques magazines, but I was puzzled as to why someone would go to all the work of building one, only to limit its aesthetic impact and functional flexibility by installing obtrusive butt hinges. I designed and built my first screen around Mackaness' wooden hinge, using a frame-and-panel arrangement.

I was pretty pleased with that first screen. The overall effect was just what I had hoped for, and the wooden hinges enhanced the design rather than detracted from it, as metal hinges certainly would have done. But the solution to my first design problem instantly revealed three more. The first of these was the issue of "one front and one back side versus two front sides." I had mounted the panels with quarter-round molding, giving the screen a definite front and back. This effect was further emphasized by the hinges, whose pins were let into router-cut slots in the back of the frames. I had carefully filled the slots with matching pieces of wood, but a close look revealed their presence. How much more pleasing and functional, I thought, to have a screen with two presentable sides.

Next was the question of how many panels the ideal screen should have. A screen with two panels is nearly useless, and a three-panel screen is only a little less static. My five-panel original model could assume a couple of interesting shapes, but how about more panels to allow more variety? Finally, there was the matter of price, which I always consider as much a design problem as anything else. The frame-and-panel screen had been pretty expensive, and since hardly anybody *needs* a screen, a lower price figured to be more of an inducement to an impulse purchase.

So, to cut down on construction time, I decided to make the next screen out of solid wood. The result was a nine-panel structure of ¾-in. maple whose design dictated two changes in the hinges. First, I made them much thinner, about ¼ in. rather than 1 in. as on the previous screen. At the same time, I actually increased their strength by making them out of nine plies of veneer. Second, instead of using ¼-in. hardware-store dowels for the hinge pins, I used drill rod sized exactly to the width of the routed slot. To eliminate the screen's "back" side, I let the pins into slots in the edges of the panels, as shown in figure 2. It seemed faster to cut a groove the whole length of the panel's edge with the tablesaw rather than cut individual slots for each pin with the router. Also, the sawblade makes a very unobtrusive ⅛-in. groove in a place that's impossible to see when the screen is unfolded. I filled the grooves with splines, which had to be notched accurately to hold the pins snugly and to keep them from sliding out of their holes in the hinges.

Standing back from the finished product, I was pretty proud of the way I had resolved my first screen's shortcomings. The

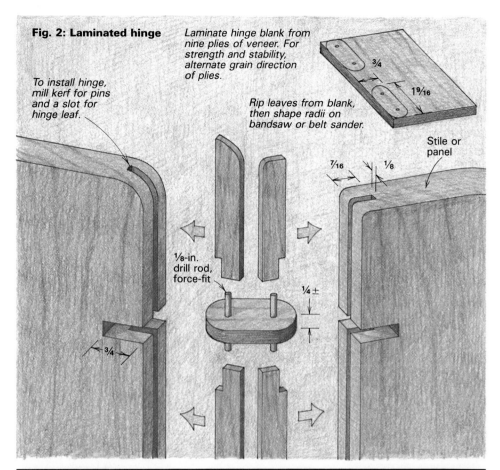

**Fig. 2: Laminated hinge**

Laminate hinge blank from nine plies of veneer. For strength and stability, alternate grain direction of plies.

To install hinge, mill kerf for pins and a slot for hinge leaf.

Rip leaves from blank, then shape radii on bandsaw or belt sander.

¾

1⁹⁄₁₆

Stile or panel

⁷⁄₁₆

⅛

⅛-in. drill rod, force-fit

¼ ±

¾

*Solid-wood panels and a thinner hinge made of built-up veneers let into slots in the panel edges produced a screen equally attractive from front or back.*

*A lighter screen with plywood panels called for a new hinge, so Mackintosh designed a knuckle hinge that pivots on dowels (drawing at right). Maple knuckles are let into mortises routed in the panels, then fastened with anodized aluminum interscrews.*

**Fig. 3: A wooden knuckle hinge**

**Construction sequence**

1. Mill groove in end grain. For safety, block should be at least 5 in. long.

2. Crosscut to final knuckle length.

3. Mount knuckle strip in vise, and radius edge with router. Cut off knuckles to final width.

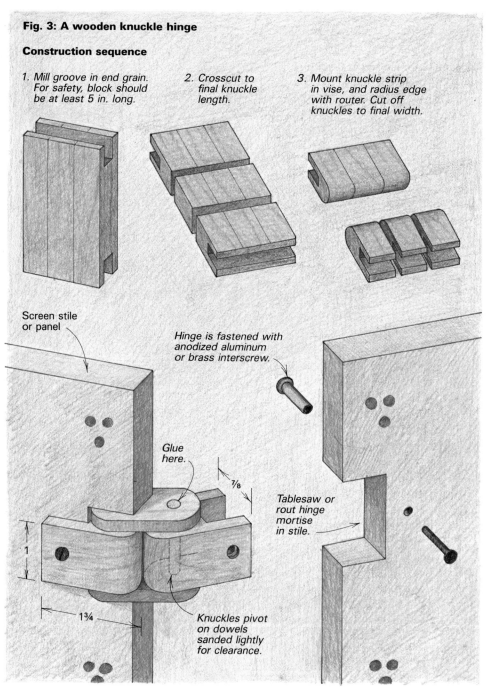

Screen stile or panel

Hinge is fastened with anodized aluminum or brass interscrew.

Glue here.

Tablesaw or rout hinge mortise in stile.

Knuckles pivot on dowels sanded lightly for clearance.

nine-panel screen allowed many interesting configurations, and it had no visually inferior back side. It had also taken a lot less time to make. As a bonus, it seemed much bigger than the first one, even though it was the same height and only about 10 in. wider. Its apparent size, I decided, had more to do with the somewhat monolithic nature of the design. At any rate, it was an imposing presence in my booth, able to catch the eye of even the most jaded craft-show regular.

Almost immediately, however, I began to have product-liability nightmares. Imagine the damage a falling 100-lb. maple wall could do to houseplants, furniture, pets and children, not to mention adults with ambitious lawyers. What I needed was a panel material lighter than solid wood that could hold its shape in 72-in. lengths. There may be some wonderful substance on the market out there somewhere, but the best I could come up with was premium-grade, ½-in. Philippine mahogany plywood, which weighs only half as much per square foot as maple does. The only problem was the untidy look of the edges, which I could solve by painting the screen.

These decisions led me to two more hinge-design variations. First, it wouldn't hurt if the hinges were visually interesting and rather prominent, since the panels were to be fairly plain-looking painted rectangles. Second, the hinges had to be removable so the panels could be repainted. The final version of the hinge, shown in figure 3, can be made quickly using the

tablesaw, router and drill press, and fit into notches cut into each panel's edge with a router, rub collar and template. I secured the hinges to the panels with aluminum interscrews—two-part fasteners consisting of a machine screw that fits into a threaded socket with a slot on its other end. They're sold by stationery suppliers as post-binding screws. To tone down the aluminum, I had the interscrews anodized black at a local plating shop.

As with the previous two screens, when I stepped back to assess what I had done, I had mixed feelings. This one passed several of my tests for screen success. It was nice and lightweight. The hinges, while more obvious than on either of the other screens I had done, still enhanced the

overall design. Best of all, the price was the lowest by far, as long as I didn't get carried away with the painting. But, as before, there was a major drawback I just couldn't get around—the ragged edges of the plywood. I'd thought that painting would hide them, but it didn't really work very well (and I'm not much of a painter anyway). I realized that what I was really after was a system that would allow many readily interchangeable panel treatments— paint, wallpaper, fabric, plain wood grain, wood with inlay.

This called for frames with easily removable panels, and hinges whose attachment method wouldn't interfere with panel removal. To achieve this, I devised the frame method shown in figure 4. I incor-

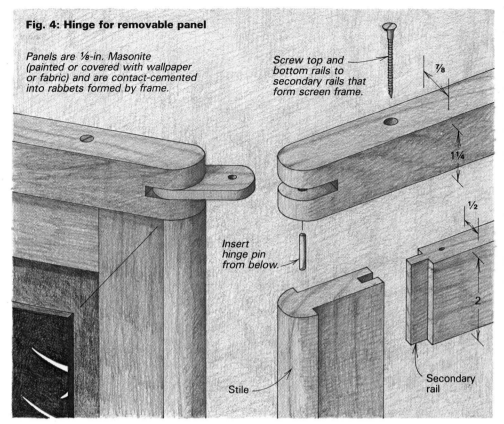

**Fig. 4: Hinge for removable panel**

Panels are ⅛-in. Masonite (painted or covered with wallpaper or fabric) and are contact-cemented into rabbets formed by frame.

Screw top and bottom rails to secondary rails that form screen frame.

⅞

1¼

½

2

Insert hinge pin from below.

Stile

Secondary rail

Author's lightest screen consists of wall-papered or fabric-covered panels contact-cemented into a cherry frame. The top and bottom rails (drawing at left) are permanently hinged but removable, so the panels can be pried out for re-covering.

## A wooden box hinge

by Eric Brostoff

For this pink ivorywood box, Brostoff sculpted the hinges out of ebony.

**Brostoff's box hinge**

⅛-in. brass pin

Round these edges for clearance.

Shape hinge after cutting fingers.

Two years ago I acquired a nearly perfect piece of pink ivorywood, a hard, dense material said to be one of the rarest woods. Native to South Africa, it was once the royal wood of the Zulus. As legend has it, the chief's son had to fashion a spear from ivorywood as part of a ritual signifying his manhood. With such a special piece of wood, I didn't want to make just any ordinary box, so I raided my stash of exotic woods and designed the ebony hinges shown here.

I made the hinges with a box-joint jig on a Shopsmith, cutting a series of fingers, then slicing off sections the width of each hinge. Before I shaped the hinge parts with belt and flap sanders, I assembled the two halves and drilled for the ⅛-in. brass hinge pin, which is held fast with a dab of superglue. You could sand or carve any shape you like, but if the hinge is to work smoothly, the sharp edges of the fingers have to be rounded over a little to provide clearance. The box carcase is African blackwood, which doesn't glue well, so I attached the hinges with epoxy. ☐

*Eric Brostoff operates Mountain Top Box Works in Lake Oswego, Ore. Photo by the author.*

porated the hinges into show rails that screw into the top and bottom of each panel frame. The frame's structural rails—which are ultimately hidden by the panel and top and bottom rails—are tenoned into the stiles, each of which has a ⅛-in. deep rabbet into which a Masonite panel fits. The Masonite can be covered with wallpaper or fabric, then glued into the frame with contact cement. If you want to change panels, you need only unscrew the hinge rails from one end and work a knife between the frame and the panel. Besides being light, this arrangement has one other important advantage: one side of the screen can have an entirely different treatment from the other.

After all my experimenting with fabric-covered, airbrushed and wallpapered panels, the final incarnation of this screen has ⅛-in. birch plywood panels decorated with colored epoxy inlays. We're using it to cover a door in our living room that we never use. It's doing such a fine job that I don't think I'll try to sell it. Almost a year has passed since I made it, and looking at it every day has made me think a lot about screens. I don't have to justify them to myself anymore, which is a good thing, since I have lots of new ideas I'm going to try. ☐

*Besides designing screens, Steven Mackintosh builds furniture in Deansboro, N.Y. Photos by the author.*

217

# Newport-Style Tall Clock

## Tackling the tricky details

by Robert Effinger

When I moved to Maine in 1970, I left behind a career as a tool-and-die maker. Working with wood instead of metal, I managed to eke out a living selling my turned bowls and wooden novelties to tourists who drove through town in the summer. One day a local gentleman stopped in to ask me if I could make a tall clock. I'd never attempted anything that ambitious before but I took the job. Since then, I've turned out quite a few. Along the way I've developed some methods that make short work of the details; I'll explain several of these in this article.

The clock shown is based on an 18th-century mahogany tall clock attributed to Newport, R.I., cabinetmaker John Goddard (1745-85). I scaled up the plan from a measured drawing in Wallace Nutting's book, *Furniture Treasury: Vol. III* (1933, MacMillan Publishing Co.).

I'm not a period purist so my clock isn't built exactly like the Goddard original. I'll improve on the old construction methods if I can. For example, unlike many old clocks, mine are built to allow for seasonal wood movement in places where the old clocks might have nails, glue blocks and, more often than not, cracks. The most radical change I've made is in the supports for the seat board—the horizontal board that supports the clockworks. On old clocks, the waist sides extended up into the hood and the seat board was nailed across them. My adjustable seat-board assembly slides up or down until the movement's at the correct height, then screws tight against the waist sides.

The ¼-in. plywood bottom of my clock is another break from tradition. Old clocks had a thick bottom that was often dovetailed to the base sides. This construction works fine until a weight cable breaks and the cast-iron weight wrecks the bottom, feet and sides of the clock. A falling weight will smash through my thin plywood bottom, without damaging the rest of the clock.

Buy the movement and make the dial before you start cutting anything. The depth of the movement determines the depth of the case and the dial must be made to fit the hood or vice versa. It's easier to make your own dial than it is to redesign the Goddard hood around a store-bought dial. Some of the fancy old engraved dials were made from brass, but I cut mine from 16-gauge sheet steel and sent it out to be hand painted. The sources of supply on p. 221 list a few of the many companies that sell movements. The movement I used in this particular clock is a cable-wound, nine nested-bell movement (No. 213) from the Concord Clock Co., 96 Main St., Plaistow, N.H. 03865.

Think of the clock case as three separate sections: the base,

*Built with the aid of 20th-century technology, Effinger's stately mahogany tall clock captures the graceful proportions and crisp carving of the 18th-century Rhode Island original. The dial face was hand painted by Judith W. Akey.*

Photo this page: Schopplein Studio

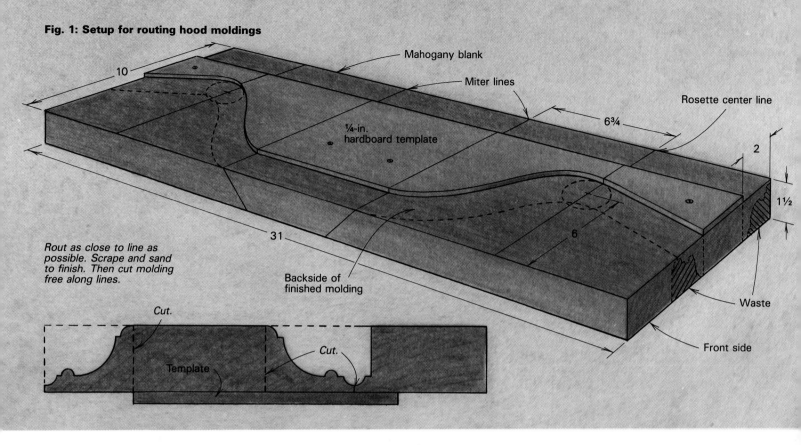

**Fig. 1: Setup for routing hood moldings**

10

Mahogany blank

Miter lines

¼-in. hardboard template

Rosette center line

6¾

2

1½

Rout as close to line as possible. Scrape and sand to finish. Then cut molding free along lines.

31

6

Backside of finished molding

Cut.

Cut.

Template

Waste

Front side

waist and hood. Figure 3 (p. 222) and figure 4 (fold-out section) show how these sections are built and how they fit together. The waist sides screw to the base while the hood just rests on the waist. The hood slides off the front to allow access to the works. The ¾-in. pine back ties all three parts together, as shown in figure 4. In general, the waist must be about ¾ in. wider inside than the swing of the pendulum. Most old clock waists measure 13⅞ in. across the outside and 7 in. to 8 in. from front to back. I increased the depth of my clock case because modern musical movements are larger than the old ones.

I made the special one-piece hinges for the hood door from ⅛-in.-thick sheet brass. These hinges screw to the top and bottom of the door and pivot on ⅜-in. #2 woodscrews in the scroll board and hood molding. The waist door also requires special hinges with an offset to match the ¼-in.-thick lip on the hinge stile as shown in the detail, figure 4. Ball and Ball is the only company I've found that makes these hinges.

**The curved goose-neck, or swan-neck moldings** at the top of the hood are often the most intimidating part of a tall clock case. In the old days they were shaped by carving and scraping, but I prefer to make them with a pin router. My method of pattern routing cuts both of the curved moldings and both of the return moldings that run along either side of the hood at the same time, from the same piece of mahogany.

To make the moldings, I've converted my drill press into a pin router (see *FWW* #37, pp. 26-27). My setup guarantees that the moldings will match up perfectly at the corner miters.

Start with a mahogany blank 1½ in. thick, 10 in. wide and 31 in. long. Make a template by drawing the molding curves on a 6-in.-wide piece of ¼-in. hardboard, as shown in figure 1 and bandsawing to shape. On this template, mark off the miter lines and the center lines for the rosettes.

Place the template on the bottom of the mahogany blank and transfer the miter lines and rosette center lines to the blank.

With a square, extend these lines across the width of the blank, extend the line of the curve over the end of the blank. Fasten the template to the mahogany with small screws making sure that the template marks line up with the lines drawn on the blank. Draw the molding profile on the ends of the blank as shown in the drawing. You'll set your router bit against this profile.

One-quarter-in.-thick wooden discs in increments of ¹⁄₁₆-in. in diameter fit over a pin in the auxiliary drill-press table directly underneath the bit. With the template side of the blank down on the table, I select a disc that positions the bit where I want it against the profile on the blank end, adjust the bit to the right height, then guide the template against the disc to make the cut, as shown in the photo, p. 220. One pass hogs the straight return moldings, another pass at the same setting cuts the curves. Next I switch to a smaller disc to move the stock closer to the bit or a larger disc to move the stock away. The idea is to rout as close as possible to the molding profile you've drawn on the end of the blank. I do as much hogging as I can with a ⅝-in. straight bit then I switch to smaller straight bits followed by whatever curved bit gets closest to the line. After routing, I scrape and sand out any imperfections in the molding.

After routing, trace around the template on the back side of the blank. This line will become the cutting line for the top edge of the molding. Remove the template, set the tablesaw blade to 45° and cut the blank along the miter lines.

To mark for the rosette, score about ⅛ in. deep with a 2½-in.-diameter hole saw on the back of the blank. This gives you a definite line to follow later on the bandsaw. Rip the return molding off the blank along the straight template line. Now, with the back side up, bandsaw along the curved template line that marks the top edge of each goose-neck molding, including the radius marked by the hole saw. Flip the molding over. The cutting line for the bottom edge of the molding lies at the lowest point of the radius, as shown in figure 1. If you run a pencil along the bottom of this groove, it's easier to follow with the bandsaw.

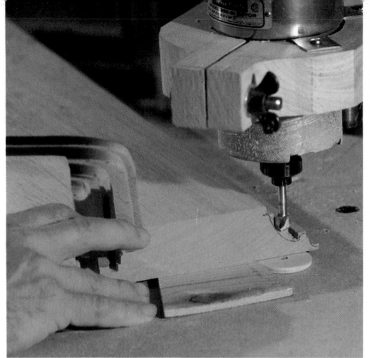

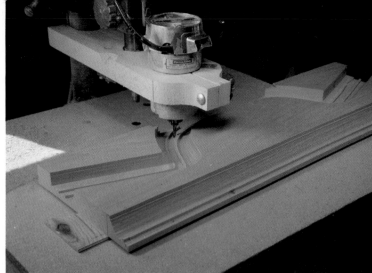

*With his drill press converted to a pin router, Effinger routs out the pediment moldings. The template rides against a wooden disc over a pin under the work. Bit height is adjusted against the molding profile drawn on the end of the blank (above). After a pass along the straight molding, the goose-neck molding gets a pass at the same setting (top right). After sawing the miter, the rosette location is scored with a hole saw (right), then the goose-neck is bandsawn from the blank. After sawing the top edge and the rosette, the blank is flipped over and the lower molding edge is bandsawn free (far right).*

The moldings are now ready to glue to the scroll board.

The smaller scroll-board arch moldings can be made using the same technique, but I find it easier to mount a router on a cobbled-up pivot to cut the semi-circular part and guide the hand-held router against a straight edge to cut the straight sections. You could also turn the semicircular molding on the lathe.

**The quarter columns** on the waist of old clocks were just that, ¼ of a circle. To my eye, these look sort of flat. I thought that the effect would be more dramatic if the columns were just slightly more than ¼ of a circle. Here's the method I developed to turn a "quarter" column that's really a 120° section of a circle.

Make a fixture from two pieces of ¾-in. scrap stock as long as the column. Rip one piece 2 in. wide and one 1¼ in. wide and butt glue them to make an L-shaped fixture, as shown in figure 2. Cut a 1¼-in.-square piece of mahogany for the column. Screw this square blank into the L-shaped piece as shown. Make sure that your screws are recessed enough that you don't turn into them later. Lay out the center on each end, remove the corners on the tablesaw, if you prefer, and turn the column and the jig to shape. A new L-shaped jig must be made for each quarter column.

If your lathe has an indexing head, you can rig up a router box and cut the flutes right on the lathe with a small veining bit in a router (see *FWW* #37, p. 34 and #38, p. 40), but I have a different method. I have an old indexing jig that holds the column between centers and allows me to slide it across the drill-press table against a cutter chucked up in the drill press. My cutter is a ⁵⁄₃₂-in. Woodruff key seat cutter that I've ground to a radius as shown (available unground from Manhattan Supply Co., Inc., 151 Sunnyside Blvd., Plainview, N.Y. 11803). A bronze sleeve over the shaft acts as a bushing and limits the depth of cut.

**There are lots of ways to make ogee bracket feet** but I think that my method is the easiest. I cut and glue up the joints while the stock is still square. By clamping the glued-up foot to a small

### Fig. 2: Turning "quarter" columns

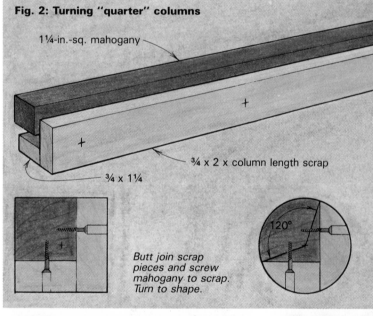

1¼-in.-sq. mahogany

¾ x 2 x column length scrap

¾ x 1¼

Butt join scrap pieces and screw mahogany to scrap. Turn to shape.

120°

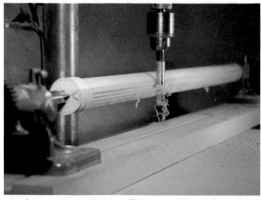

*Author cuts column flutes with a Woodruff key seat cutter ground to a radius and chucked up in the drill press. Indexing jig rests on drill-press table and slides by cutter. Sleeve on cutter limits depth of cut.*

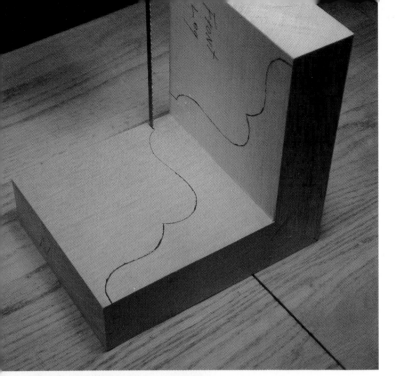

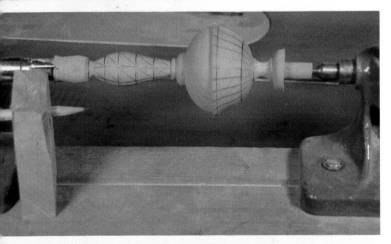

*Ogee bracket feet are glued up while square then cut to shape on the bandsaw. Supporting the foot over a wooden box allows the ogee profile to be cut on the bandsaw (left). Finial is lathe turned, then flutes are marked out in indexing jig and carved by hand. To lay out the flame, divide flame into six longitudinal sections and five latitudinal sections to form a grid (below). Connect points on the diagonal to form spiral lines. Pencil holder shown marks out axis lines.*

wooden box for support, as shown in the photo at left, I cut the ogee curve on the bandsaw.

The front feet are joined with a splined miter. I cut the spline slot on the tablesaw with the blade at 45°. The back feet are joined with half-blind dovetails. The rear section of the back feet is made from thinner stock and left flat to allow the clock to sit closer to a wall.

**The flame finials that crown the hood are turned** from 3-in.-square blocks about 8½ in. long. Turn the finial in the middle of the stock leaving about 1 in. of waste on each end, as shown in the photo. For now, just turn the flame section to shape—carving comes later. On the bottom of the urn, mark off 24 divisions for reeding and stop fluting. If your lathe has an indexing head, you can mark and carve the finial between centers. I carve the reeds with a V-tool working from larger diameter to smaller diameter. Tipping the tool to the left and right, I take off the sharp edges to round over the reed. About ⅛ in. down from the top of the reeding I mark a line around the circumference and another line about ¾ in. from the first. This designates the lengths of the shallow flutes within the reeds. I carve these with a small gouge.

On old clocks, the flames on the outside finials spiral in opposite directions. To lay out the flame spiral, I draw lines parallel to the finial axis that divide the circumference of the cylinder into six equal sections. Then I draw lines around the circumference, spaced ½ in. apart, to form a grid. I connect the intersections with diagonal lines to form the spirals. Carve between the spiral lines with a small gouge. After the flame has been carved, cut the waste off and finish to a point. I sand the completed finial with a 220-grit flap sander chucked up in the drill press.

One other detail worth specific mention is the shell carving on the waist door. Some of the old ones were glued onto the door panel after carving. I like to make the door panel and shell from one board as thick as the combined thickness of the shell and panel. I set the thickness planer to remove ⅛ in. and I stop the planer before the shell area goes through. The finished shell is about ⅛ in. higher than the panel and overhangs each edge by ⅛ in. I set the jointer for a ⅛-in. cut and joint the panel edge stopping when I get to the shell area. □

*Robert Effinger makes period furniture in Fryeburg, Me.*

## Sources of supply

These firms sell tall-clock movements, clock supplies and hardware, except as noted.

Selva-Borel, 347 13th St., P.O. Box 796, Oakland, Calif. 94604.

Mason & Sullivan Co., 586 Higgins Crowel Rd., West Yarmouth, Mass. 02673.

Turncraft Clock Imports Co., 7912 Olson Highway 55, Golden Valley, Minn. 55427.

Klockit, P.O. Box 629, Highway H, North, Lake Geneva, Wisc. 53147.

Craft Products Co., 2200 Dean St., St. Charles, Ill. 60174.

Ball and Ball, 463 West Lincoln Hwy., Exton, Pa. 19341 (authentic reproductions of hood-door hinges, offset waist-door hinges and clock hardware).

Judith W. Akey, 173 Harbourton Rd., Pennington, N.J. 08534 (hand paints clock dials).

The Dial House, Rt. 7, Box 532, Dallas, Ga. 30132 (custom dials and hand painting).

**Fig. 4: Newport-style tall clock**

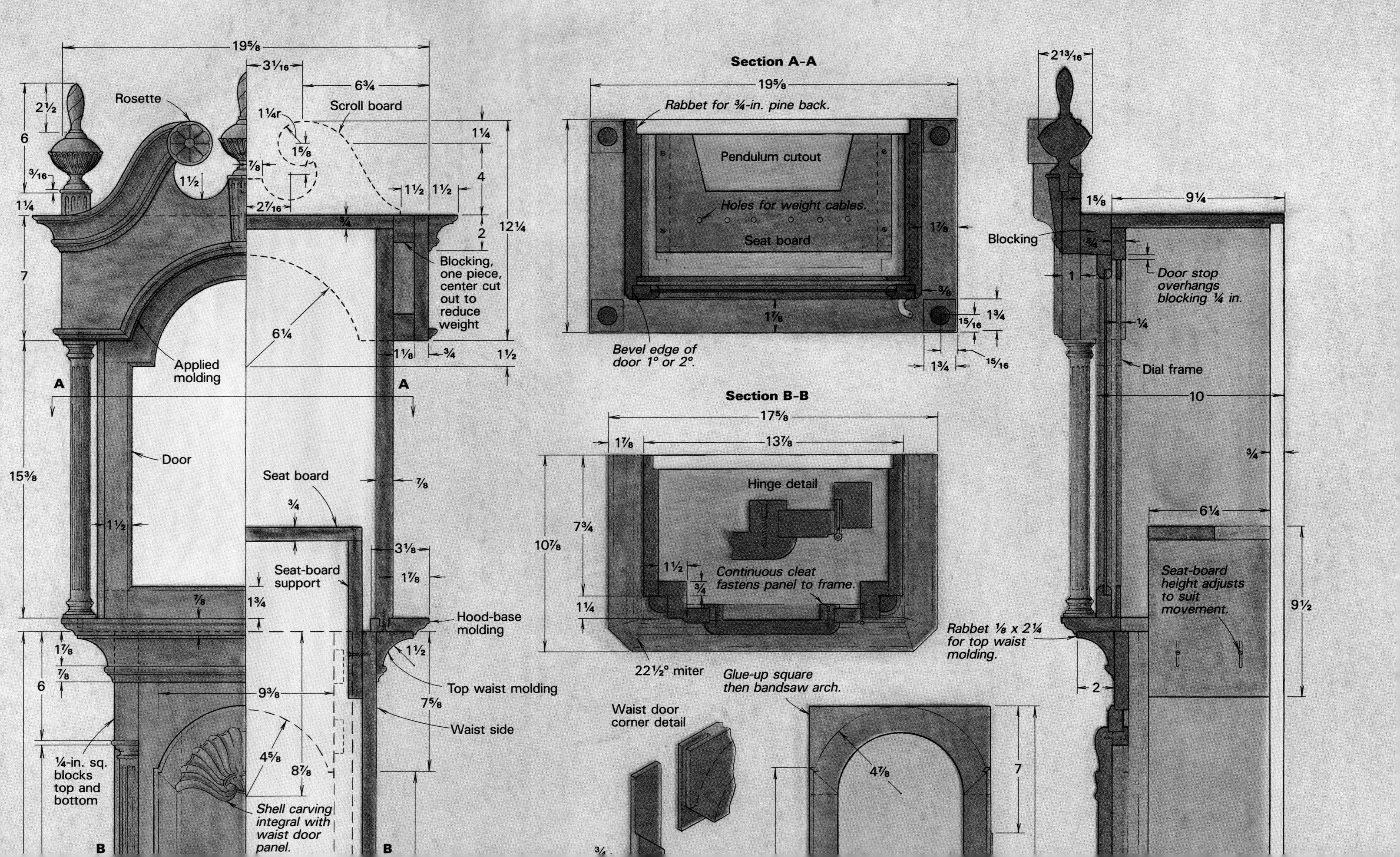

**Section A-A**

Rabbet for ¾-in. pine back.

Pendulum cutout

Holes for weight cables.

Seat board

Bevel edge of door 1° or 2°.

19⅝

1⅞    ⅜

1⅞

1¾

15/16    1¾

13/16    15/16

**Section B-B**

Hinge detail

Continuous cleat fastens panel to frame.

¾

1½

1⅛

22½° miter

Rabbet ⅛ x 2¼ for top waist molding.

Glue-up square then bandsaw arch.

Waist door corner detail

17⅝

13⅞

7¾

10⅞

1¼

7

4⅞

3/

**Door stop overhangs blocking ¼ in.**

Dial frame

Blocking

9¼

9¼

15/8

2 13/16

¾

1

¼

¾

9½

10

6¼

2

Seat-board height adjusts to suit movement.

**Blocking, one piece, center cut out to reduce weight**

Scroll board

Rosette

Applied molding

Door

Seat board

Seat-board support

Shell carving integral with waist door panel.

Hood-base molding

Top waist molding

Waist side

¼-in. sq. blocks top and bottom

19⅝

3 1/16

1¼r

1⅝

⅞

2 7/16

1½

1½

6¾

12¼

1¼

4

2

¾

1⅛

1½

A    A

1½

7

6

2½

3/16

1¼

15⅜

6¼

¾

1½

⅞

7/8

3⅛

1⅛

1½

7⅝

1½

1¾

9⅜

4⅝

8⅞

⅞

1⅛

⅞

6

B    B

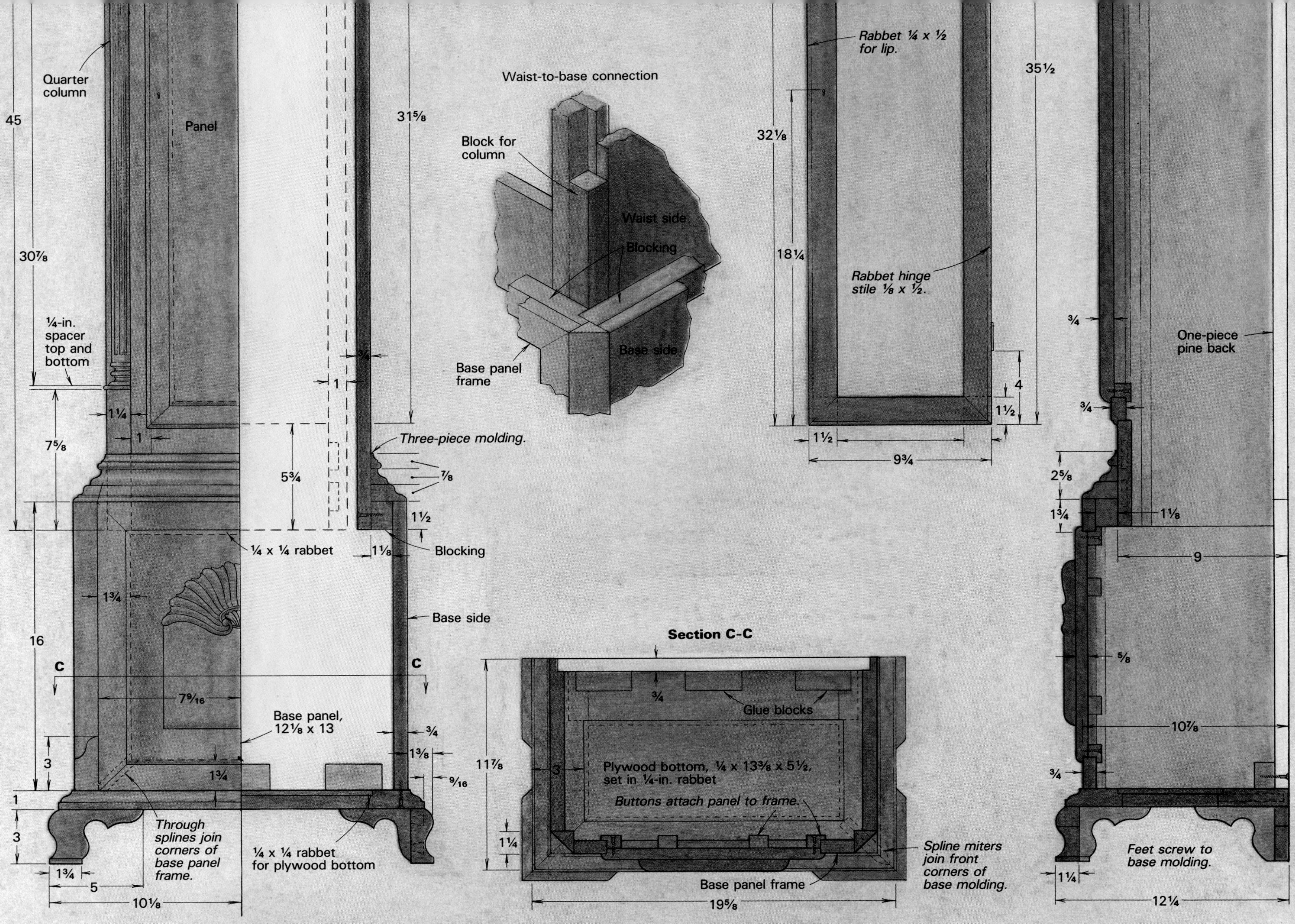
Quarter column
45
Panel
30⅞
¼-in. spacer top and bottom
1¼
1
7⅝
31⅝
¾
1
5¾
Three-piece molding.
⅞
1½
¼ x ¼ rabbet
1⅛
Blocking
1¾
Base side
16
C
C
7⁹⁄₁₆
Base panel, 12⅛ x 13
¾
1⅜
⁹⁄₁₆
3
1¾
1
3
Through splines join corners of base panel frame.
¼ x ¼ rabbet for plywood bottom
1¾
5
10⅛
Waist-to-base connection
Block for column
Waist side
Blocking
Base side
Base panel frame
Section C-C
¾
Glue blocks
11⅞
3
Plywood bottom, ¼ x 13⅜ x 5½, set in ¼-in. rabbet
Buttons attach panel to frame.
1¼
Spline miters join front corners of base molding.
Base panel frame
19⅝
Rabbet ¼ x ½ for lip.
32⅛
18¼
Rabbet hinge stile ⅛ x ½.
4
1½
1½
9¾
35½
¾
One-piece pine back
¾
2⅝
1¾
1⅛
9
⅝
10⅞
¾
Feet screw to base molding.
1¼
12¼

**Fig. 3: Hood construction**

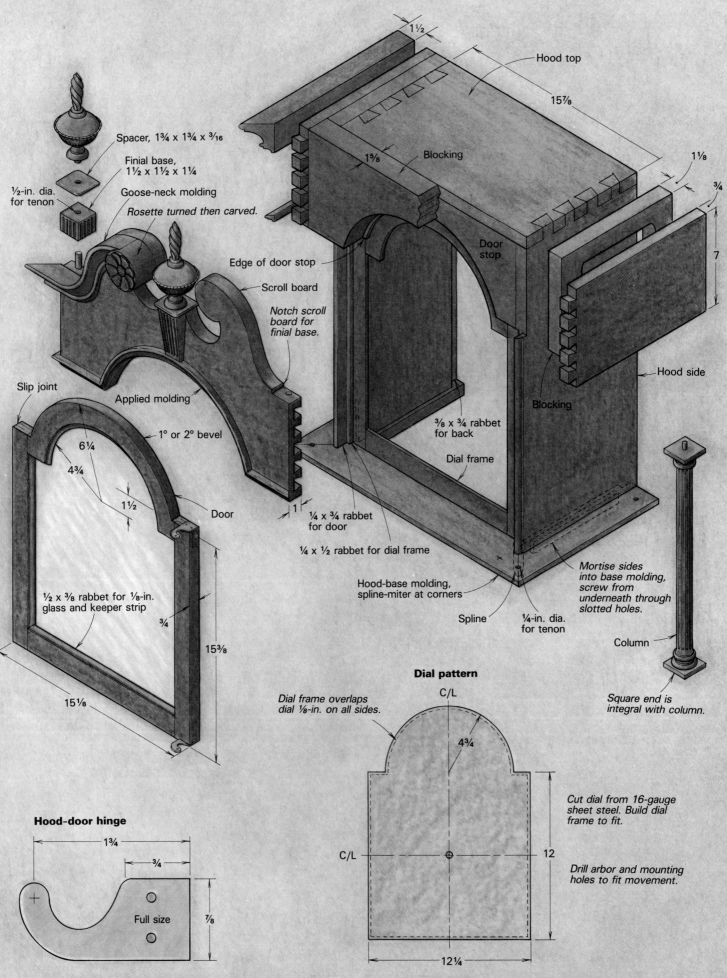

Spacer, 1¾ x 1¾ x ³⁄₁₆

Finial base,
1½ x 1½ x 1¼

½-in. dia.
for tenon

Goose-neck molding

*Rosette turned then carved.*

Edge of door stop

Scroll board

*Notch scroll board for finial base.*

Applied molding

1° or 2° bevel

Slip joint

6¼

4¾

1½

Door

½ x ³⁄₈ rabbet for ⅛-in. glass and keeper strip

¾

15³⁄₈

15⅛

1

¼ x ¾ rabbet for door

¼ x ½ rabbet for dial frame

Hood top

1½

15⅞

Blocking

1⅝

1⅛

¾

7

Door stop

Hood side

Blocking

³⁄₈ x ¾ rabbet for back

Dial frame

Hood-base molding, spline-miter at corners

Spline

¼-in. dia. for tenon

*Mortise sides into base molding, screw from underneath through slotted holes.*

Column

*Square end is integral with column.*

**Hood-door hinge**

1¾

¾

Full size

⅞

**Dial pattern**

*Dial frame overlaps dial ⅛-in. on all sides.*

C/L

4¾

C/L

12

12¼

*Cut dial from 16-gauge sheet steel. Build dial frame to fit.*

*Drill arbor and mounting holes to fit movement.*

224

## Veneering an ogee curve

*I'd like to reproduce an old clock that has a veneered ogee molding with the grain of the veneer running across the width of the molding—at right angles to the substrate grain. How was this done? Why hasn't the veneer cracked from movement of the substrate?*

*—Raymond R. Smith, Shippensburg, Pa.*

**Ian Kirby replies:** It's not surprising that the veneer hasn't cracked even though the veneer grain is at right angles to the substrate. Because the substrate is so narrow, the amount of movement is insignificant.

There are many techniques that could have been used to veneer the ogee. Chances are, the veneer was laid with hot hide glue and a hot iron—heat helps make veneer pliable. Another technique was to dampen the veneer and press it between matching male and female forms until dry.

Here's how I'd do it: Make an accurate female mold of the ogee from scrap pine. One way is to rough out the shape on the tablesaw and finish with hand tools and sandpaper. Soften and heat the veneer by dampening and ironing. Apply white glue to the substrate, and when the veneer is pliable, clamp it down with a piece of ½-in. thick high-density foam rubber between the female mold and the veneer. The foam will take up any inaccuracies in the female mold. [Ian Kirby is a designer, educator and furnituremaker in Cumming, Ga.]

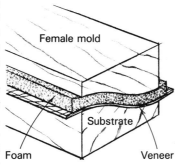

## The strength of Queen Anne legs

*I like Queen Anne legs, but I'm a little concerned about how strong those slender legs are. Would four of these cabriole legs support a 44-in.-wide, 6-ft.-long mahogany dining-room table, which will open out to 9 ft., that I am planning to build? Also, what mechanism would be best for extending the table?* *—John Turbeck, Lexington, Ky.*

**Norm Vandal replies:** Four Queen Anne legs can certainly support your table. The legs have long been used to support highboys, which weigh more than your table will. I'm more worried about design. The largest Queen Anne tables were swing-leg, drop-leaf types, which never approached the dimensions you've given. Your table would have to have table slides fixed to the underside of the two main sections, which, when pulled apart, could support a third, and perhaps a fourth leaf. These slides are commercially available from The Woodworkers Store, 21801 Industrial Blvd., Rogers, Minn. 55374, and work well. Opening the table this way, however, will separate the two halves of the apron, and this would negate the visual appeal of the scrollwork that is so fundamental to the designs of Queen Anne tables and to the bases of lowboys and highboys. The apron creates the illusion, both real and imaginary, of adding support to the table. Your opened-up skirt would appear weak and insufficient.

Instead of building one Queen Anne table, you might consider making two smaller ones that could be placed together for special occasions when you need a lot of room. Or, jump into the future a bit to the Federal period, when dining tables as large as yours were more common. These tables were made in two half-round "demi-lune" tables with leaves at the back that can be raised and supported by swing-out legs. A three-part table would have two "demi-lune" ends without leaves and a matching center drop-leaf-style table. The drop-leaf table, which would naturally be the same height as the demi-

lunes, could be used with both leaves open, with one leaf open, or with both side leaves down. When not in use, the demi-lunes are placed against the wall as side tables. These tables are a forest of legs, as many as 16, but they were obviously created to fill a void in table designs not filled by the Queen Anne or Chippendale forms. If you still want Queen Anne legs, I recommend you bandsaw them from 3-in. squares and keep the design of the leg somewhat straight for maximum strength. Make sure the square portion at the top of the legs is large enough to safely accommodate the mortises needed to house the apron tenon—I would think about 1⅞ in. [Norm Vandal makes period furniture in Roxbury, Vt.]

## Curved handrail

*I'm making a winding staircase and need help with the curved railing. What's the best way to bend 2½-in. thick stock? How do I profile the curved rail on the shaper?*

*—Hap Davis, Calgary, Alta.*

**Gary Boudreaux replies:** Forget about bending 2½-in. thick stock. Laminate your railing. I've had good luck laminating handrails as shown in the drawing. Make the outer layers as you would any molding and laminate them to flat inner pieces no thicker than ¼ in. These inner laminations should be wider than the finished railing and planed to shape after glue-up.

For bending and clamping, you need to make a negative caul of the molding out of a soft wood like pine. Cut this caul into short pieces to support the rail and to give it backing at its clamping stations. Depending on your staircase design, you may be able to bend the railing around the outside stringer. If not, you'll have to build a bending form from plywood and 2x4s as shown, the same diameter and height as the staircase. The railing will follow the same rise and run as the stair treads, so lay out the clamping stations accordingly. I find it helpful to do a dry run. When everything is laid out properly, apply a slow-setting glue like yellow glue to the laminations, then drive a finishing nail through the entire stack, right in the middle of its length. This will help keep the laminations from sliding out of alignment. With at least one other person to help, start clamping in the middle and work out toward each end, bending and clamping as you go.

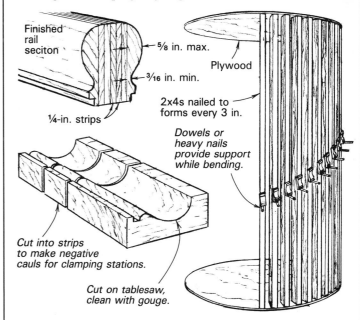

The only problem I've had with this system is the need for so many clamps (two every 3 in.). The thin lower edge of the railing wants to flare out, so use plenty of clamps to avoid gaps in the laminations.

[Gary Boudreaux builds staircases in Nevada City, Calif.]

# A Cabinetmaker's Baskets

*In the Nantucket tradition*

by Charles H. Carpenter, Jr.

*Some lightship basket variations: The large photo shows an oval purse basket (8¾ in. by 7¼ in., 6 in. high) of oak and mahogany, which Hilbert made in 1977. The caning in each half of the double lid is inlaid into a recess. The open-top basket at top left has ear handles of bent oak and a turned mahogany bottom. The lid of the other small basket is fully caned, and the mahogany rims were bricklaid of many small pieces for stability. The basket, with its ivory finial, is at the Museum of Fine Arts, Boston.*

Harry Hilbert is a former antique dealer from southern Connecticut with a great love of American decorative arts. He is also a woodworker of considerable skill. He has made his share of reproduction furniture over the past 45 years—tea tables, corner chairs, chests of drawers, children's furniture and so on. It is his baskets, however, that give Harry Hilbert a special place in the American craft scene.

In 1974, while visiting with my wife, Mary Grace, and me on Nantucket Island, Hilbert studied Mary Grace's collection of old Nantucket baskets and said: "I'm going to make one of those." In the years since, he has made dozens, no two exactly alike and none made for sale. Hilbert makes baskets solely for the joy of it.

In the 19th century, Nantucket baskets were made on board the lightships anchored in the dangerous shoals off Nantucket, hence the name lightship baskets. They are a distinctive type of American handicraft that came out of the maritime cooperage

tradition. The process entails as much woodworking as it does basketry—the staves are related to the staves of a Nantucket cooper's whale-oil barrel.

In the old Nantucket baskets, the bottom of the basket is usually solid pine, but sometimes a hardwood. A groove is cut into the edge of the bottom and then oak or hickory staves (water-soaked to make them supple) are fitted into the groove and shaped around a form. When the staves have dried they more or less retain the form's shape. The staves are then interwoven with fine cane in a plain or decorative pattern. Small ear handles like those in one of Hilbert's first baskets (photo above, top left) are a typical way to finish up. Other baskets had flat wooden lids attached by leather-thong hinges wrapped with cane. Although some of the early lightship baskets had bottoms with turned scratched lines for decoration, many bases were so plain that they didn't even have beveled bottom edges. The lightship-

basket tradition continued in the 20th century, mostly in the form of open-top baskets, round or oblong. The round baskets were sometimes made in nests of six or seven. After World War II, lidded baskets became popular as purses and a cottage-industry grew up to produce them.

Hilbert, with his high-style cabinetmaker's instincts, has continued to refine the basic designs, adding features such as shopmade brass hinges instead of leather and all sorts of inlaid and applied decoration on the lids and tops.

Not all of Hilbert's refinements are purely decorative, as the small basket with pagoda-like lid in the photo on the facing page illustrates. If the mahogany rims of this basket had been turned from solid wood, they would constantly "move" with changes in relative humidity, becoming slightly oval, then round, then oval again. To ensure that the top and basket rims would stay round regardless of the weather, Hilbert laminated them from numerous thin pieces of wood in a bricklaid fashion. This also eliminates short-grain from the rims, greatly strengthening them. Functional as this basket is, it may also be considered a work of art. In fact, it was recently acquired by the Museum of Fine Arts in Boston and a similar one is now in the Art Museum of Yale University in New Haven.

**Making a basket purse**—The accompanying step-by-step photographs and drawings show how Hilbert makes one of his basket purses. The top photo at right shows two partially finished baskets with materials in the foreground. Hilbert makes the 6½-in.-long oak staves by splitting a wedge of oak from his own land, then bandsawing it into thin radial slices that resemble ⅛-in.-thick veneer. He then bandsaws these into staves that taper in width from about ⅜ in. at the top down to ¼ in. at the bottom. He handplanes these smooth, to a final thickness of about 1/16 in.

The weaving cane is a grade called superfine chairseat cane, which can be bought from many hobby shops or mail-ordered from general suppliers such as Constantine. One bundle of cane is enough for about six baskets. The top photo also shows the oval base of cherry or other hardwood, and brass ears sawn from 1/16-in. stock. The brass ears will serve to attach the lid, and can be made in whatever size is appropriate.

The next photo shows an oval basket mold, 5¾ in. by 8½ in. by 5½ in. high (about 1 in. higher than the finished basket). Hilbert makes molds by bandsawing four layers of 1⅜-in.-thick fir. He saws the top oval first, tilting the bandsaw table about 3° so the sides of the oval will taper. Then he traces the next oval from the bottom of the first, and so on. After glue-up, Hilbert rasps and files the lower edge to a graceful curve and sands the mold smooth. The dowel at the top will serve as an axle, allowing Hilbert to rotate the work in a simple benchtop jig while weaving.

The staves will be glued into a 1/16-in.-wide sawkerf around the edge of the base. The bottom photo shows Hilbert cutting the groove with a 1¾-in.-dia. sawblade in his drill press. The kerf is one-third down from the top, and the shopmade fence is set so the kerf is about 3/16-in. deep. The kerf could also be cut with a handsaw, which is undoubtedly how they did it in the old days. The base is a 2⅞-in. by 4⅞-in. oval, ⅜-in. thick.

To shape the outside bottom rim of the base, Hilbert uses a router bit in the drill press. The top of the base is next shaped by hand to remove the sharp corner at its edge. Hilbert uses a spokeshave and file to gently round the top surface to blend down to the sawkerf, as shown in the drawing on p. 229. The base will be completely smoothed and sanded before weaving begins.

Hilbert next traces the base onto the bottom of the mold, and

*Top photo shows two partially finished baskets and the makings of another—hardwood oval base, oak staves, superfine chairseat cane and shopmade brass 'ears' as anchor points for the hinges. The middle photo shows the built-up wooden form that controls the shape. At bottom, Hilbert cuts a groove in the base for the staves, using a small circular sawblade in a drill press.*

routs a recess in the mold to accept the base. The recess brings the sawkerf in the rim of the base flush with the bottom of the mold. He then screws the base into position.

In the top photo on this page, weaving is under way. To get to this point, Hilbert first softens the staves by soaking them in water for three days, then inserts them into the slot one at a time, bending each to conform to the mold. A rubber band around the top of the mold keeps things in position as he proceeds. The staves were originally tapered on the bandsaw to allow space between them for the cane, and some of them must be tapered some more at this time, particularly where there are tight curves. The objective is to keep the gap between staves more or less uniform—it should be a little more than ⅛ in. at the top, and a little less than ⅛ in. at the bottom. After all the staves are inserted (as with any basket, always end up with an odd number), Hilbert wraps them tightly with cord and allows them to dry for 24 hours.

Hilbert advises gluing the staves in place after the shape has set. He pulls the bottom of each stave from its slot, applies a dab of glue, and reinserts it. He then starts the cane (which has been soaked in water) by drilling a small hole next to the center stave on one side, as shown in the drawing. From there, he weaves the cane around alternate staves, keeping it pulled taut to the mold and straightening and pushing each row down toward the base with the tip of a screwdriver, being careful to keep the rows of cane straight and even. In weaving, Hilbert suggests that instead of trying to push the cane under and over the staves in a straight line, as if sewing, it is much more efficient to slip the cane down from the top of the staves. Until the basket has been well started, this tends to spread the staves out from the form. Hilbert has devised a loose oval collar (of plywood and an inner tube) that fits around the top of the form. This prevents the staves from springing out too far, yet is loose enough for him to work the cane over and under the tops of the staves.

When Hilbert reaches the end of the first strand of cane, he interweaves a new piece (also shown in the drawing). Hilbert emphasizes that the staves should be kept vertical as weaving proceeds. He marks vertical reference lines at places around the sides of the mold as a guide.

When the weaving is within about 2½ in. from the top of the form, Hilbert marks a level line all the way around the top of the staves, gauging down about 1 in. from the top of the mold, and cuts the staves to the left and right of the center staves to final length with a sharp chisel (the rest of the staves will be trimmed when weaving is finished). He then makes a pair of brass ears to fit the basket and rivets these to the inside with No. 18 brass escutcheon pins (from Constantine). Hilbert removes the basket from the form while riveting the ears, then puts it back to continue weaving. The cane goes right over the brass, to within about ¼ in. of the gauged line.

A bentwood rim fits just above the last row of cane and binds the staves together. Hilbert planes, scrapes and sands two ⁵⁄₁₆-in. half-round oak strips (one for the inside, one for the outside), soaks them in water for three days, then boils them for 30 minutes before wrapping them into a pair of bending forms, as shown in the center photo. Drying takes three days. Then the inner rim is dry-fitted to the basket, stretching it as much as possible before marking it for cutting. Both ends of the strip are feathered to make a scarf joint, as shown in the drawing, overlapped and glued. Hilbert then does the same with the outer rim, but this time he makes the joint on the other side of the basket, diagonally opposite the first.

When the glue is dry, he positions both rims on the basket and

*Successive rows of cane that have been straightened and pushed toward the base with the tip of a screwdriver. To keep rows even, apply slightly more pressure on the sides than at the ends.*

*Half-round oak rims—one for the inside, one for the outside— are boiled, then wound into shopmade bending forms for drying.*

*Hilbert reinforces the wood at the hinge points by epoxying brass strips into saw kerfs. Lid is bandsawn oval after fitting.*

marks and trims the staves so they will be flush with the top of the rim. He then drills and rivets the rims clear through every third or fourth stave, making sure that a rivet goes through each glued scarf joint to secure it. The drill bit is simply a No. 18 steel brad with the head clipped off. Hilbert places the brass pins in the holes as he goes along, cutting off the head and any excess length on the inside with pliers. He smooths the nipped ends with a file, leaving enough for final riveting with a ball-peen hammer. He then files the riveted ends even with the oak, covers the upper edges of the stave-ends with a single strip of medium cane, and binds around the top with weaving cane, as shown in the drawing. If you don't have medium cane, Hilbert suggests that you can plane down the strip of heavier cane that suppliers routinely tie around the chairseat cane.

He next bends the oak handle around a horseshoe-shaped ply-

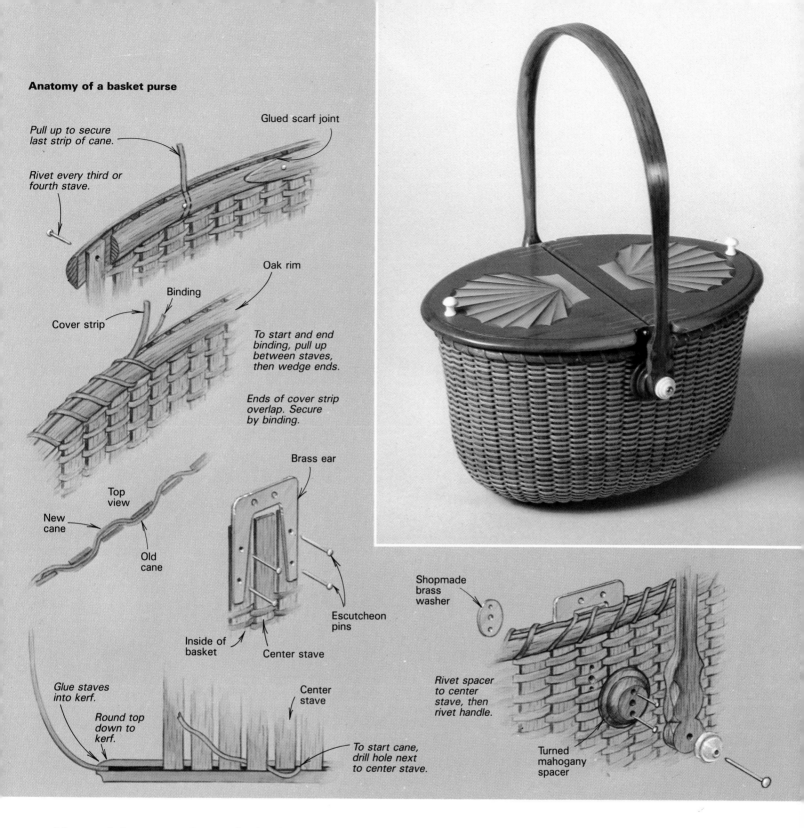

**Anatomy of a basket purse**

*Pull up to secure last strip of cane.*

*Rivet every third or fourth stave.*

Glued scarf joint

Oak rim

Binding

Cover strip

*To start and end binding, pull up between staves, then wedge ends.*

*Ends of cover strip overlap. Secure by binding.*

New cane

Top view

Old cane

Brass ear

Inside of basket

Center stave

Escutcheon pins

*Glue staves into kerf.*

*Round top down to kerf.*

Center stave

*To start cane, drill hole next to center stave.*

Shopmade brass washer

*Rivet spacer to center stave, then rivet handle.*

Turned mahogany spacer

wood form and clamps it in place to dry for three days. He has had his best success working with green oak, soaked in water for three days, then boiled for 30 minutes. After drying, the handle can be shaped with spokeshave, rasps and files. Hilbert suggests that it is much easier to shape the inside surface of the handle if the bent blank is clamped in a U-shaped plywood cradle held in a vise—if you try to do it freehand, it's like wrestling with a snake. Each craftsman tends to shape handles differently, something of a personal trademark.

Hilbert hinges the double lid by means of 1-in. No. 2 brass wood screws through the ears. He reinforces the wood by epoxying thin strips of brass into bandsawn kerfs (bottom photo, facing page). With the lid blanks hinged in place, he marks the profile by tracing the basket's rim, then removes the lid, bandsaws it to shape, and proceeds with edge treatment and decoration.

This particular basket has shell inlays made of 14 pieces of satinwood, charred on one edge in hot sand to create shading, and 13 pieces of crescent-shaped mahogany. Turned mahogany spacers keep the handle from contacting the lid. They are riveted to the center stave with No. 18 escutcheon pins, as shown in the drawing, then the handle and its decorative ivory knobs are riveted through with No. 12 escutcheon pins. Finishing touches include turned ivory knobs on the lids and a finish of one coat of thin shellac and two coats of satin varnish, applied to the cane as well as the wood. The basket is then waxed and buffed. □

*Charles Carpenter is an author and art historian who lives part of the year on Nantucket Island. For more on bending wood for baskets and other purposes, see* FWW on Bending Wood, *which is a collection of articles from back issues of* FWW.

Photos: Arthur d'Arazien; drawing: Mark Kara

# INDEX